Python Interview Preparation

Master the Python skills and ace your technical interviews through 100 coding challenges and solutions

Ashutosh Shashi

www.bpbonline.com

First Edition 2026

ISBN: 978-93-65897-937

To View Complete BPB Publications Catalogue Scan the QR Code:

www.bpbonline.com

Dedicated to

Every learner who turns curiosity into knowledge —
and my family, who stood quietly behind my journey

About the Author

Ashutosh Shashi is a software architect with over two decades (over 20 years) of experience in designing enterprise systems for global clients in retail, travel, hospitality, education, manufacturing, public sector, and finance. He is certified in AWS, GCP, Azure, PMP, and TOGAF 9.0. Over 48,000 students have learned from his Udemy courses, in addition to his published books. He additionally produces simple and practical tech content for his YouTube channel, IT in Focus, and publishes blog posts on Medium to assist learners and professionals in career development.

About the Reviewers

- **Priyanka Priyadarshini** is a highly proficient PCEP and PCAP certified Python developer who supports businesses globally, from Australia to the United States and India. She has worked extensively in Python programming, Django, and Flask. She has developed high-performance and low-latency REST APIs using Python, Django Rest Framework, PostgreSQL, and Redis database. In addition, she was involved in multiple projects with API integrations, object-oriented programming, data wrangling, serializing/deserializing data, Celery, JavaScript, and cloud services such as AWS EC2, Lambda, S3, etc. Priyanka engages herself in creating her own Python projects such as games, data analysis tools, and works in freelancing projects as well.

- **Harvendra Singh** is a distinguished technology leader specializing in cloud engineering, architecture, automation, and AI-powered solutions. He designs and implements scalable, secure systems utilizing Azure, .NET, C#, Python, GCP, Kubernetes, Databricks, and other cutting-edge technologies. With expertise in cloud-native applications, microservices, event-driven architectures, and distributed systems, Harvendra drives innovation in cloud and AI ecosystems, delivering high-impact solutions that drive business value and sustainable growth.

Acknowledgement

I would like to express my sincere gratitude to all those who contributed to the completion of this book. I am deeply thankful to the global community of learners, job seekers, and professionals who continuously strive to master their craft. Your dedication inspired every page of this book.

Foremost, I extend my heartfelt appreciation to my family and friends for their unwavering support and encouragement throughout this journey. Their love and encouragement have been a constant source of motivation.

I am immensely grateful to BPB Publications for their guidance and expertise in bringing this book to fruition. Their support and help were invaluable in navigating the complexities of the publishing process.

Special thanks to my reviewers, editors, and mentors who provided honest feedback and to the publishing team for their support and professionalism throughout this journey.

Finally, I would like to thank every reader of this book. Your commitment to learning and growth is the reason this book exists, and I hope it plays a meaningful role in your journey.

Preface

Passing coding interviews can be difficult, particularly when you have to solve problems on a whiteboard under pressure and meet high expectations. This book, *Python Interview Preparation*, eased that burden and guides aspiring developers, students, and professionals in mastering Python with the confidence that turns interviews into opportunities.

The inspiration behind this book stems from years of experience preparing candidates and participating in technical interviews. While many books focus on theory or syntactic details, this book takes a practical, challenge-based approach. Every problem is handpicked to reflect real-world scenarios and common interview questions, presented with multiple solutions and insights to help you think like an interviewer and perform like a top candidate.

The book has 8 detailed sections, each targeting a specific skill area.

Section 1: Python Basics and Syntax - This section lays the foundation. You will explore variables, loops, conditionals, and functions through hands-on challenges designed to solidify core Python syntax and logic.

Section 2: Object-Oriented Programming - This section will look into Python classes and OOP design. You will implement real-world models like a bank account, stack, queue, and shopping cart to build reusable, maintainable code.

Section 3: Data Structures Arrays and Strings - This section will help you tackle popular array and string problems seen in interviews. Learn optimized ways to manipulate sequences and handle tricky edge cases.

Section 4: Searching and Sorting Algorithms - This section will help you develop mastery over classic sorting algorithms like merge sort, quick sort, and counting sort, along with key searching techniques including binary search and heap-based solutions.

Section 5: Recursion and Backtracking - This module trains your problem-solving brain to think recursively. You will explore factorials, subset generation, the N-queens problem, and backtracking logic used in puzzles and constraint problems.

Section 6: Dynamic Programming - This module will help you decode dynamic programming with challenges like coin change, longest subsequences, and knapsack problems. Learn tabulation, and space optimization techniques.

Section 7: Graphs and Trees - This section will help you build fluency in BFS, DFS, and tree operations. You will solve graph traversal problems, detect cycles, find shortest paths, and master binary trees.

Section 8: Advanced Topics and System Design - This section will help you prepare for system design rounds with problems like building an LRU cache, designing Twitter clones, rate limiters, and implementing data structures like tree and message queues.

We crafted each problem in this book with clear explanations, multiple approaches, complexity analysis, and real-world analogies to help you not only solve problems but understand them deeply.

Code Bundle

Please follow the link to download the
Code Bundle of the book:

https://rebrand.ly/94caa7

The code bundle for the book is also hosted on GitHub at **https://github.com/bpbpublications/Python-Interview-Preparation.** In case there's an update to the code, it will be updated on the existing GitHub repository.

We have code bundles from our rich catalogue of books and videos available at **https://github.com/bpbpublications.** Check them out!

Errata

We take immense pride in our work at BPB Publications and follow best practices to ensure the accuracy of our content to provide an indulging reading experience to our subscribers. Our readers are our mirrors, and we use their inputs to reflect and improve upon human errors, if any, that may have occurred during the publishing processes involved. To let us maintain the quality and help us reach out to any readers who might be having difficulties due to any unforeseen errors, please write to us at: **errata@bpbonline.com**

Your support, suggestions and feedback are highly appreciated by the BPB Publications' Family.

Piracy

If you come across any illegal copies of our works in any form on the internet, we would be grateful if you would provide us with the location address or website name. Please contact us at business@bpbonline.com with a link to the material.

If you are interested in becoming an author

If there is a topic that you have expertise in, and you are interested in either writing or contributing to a book, please visit www.bpbonline.com. We have worked with thousands of developers and tech professionals, just like you, to help them share their insights with the global tech community. You can make a general application, apply for a specific hot topic that we are recruiting an author for, or submit your own idea.

Reviews

Please leave a review. Once you have read and used this book, why not leave a review on the site that you purchased it from? Potential readers can then see and use your unbiased opinion to make purchase decisions. We at BPB can understand what you think about our products, and our authors can see your feedback on their book. Thank you!

For more information about BPB, please visit www.bpbonline.com.

Join our Discord space

Join our Discord workspace for latest updates, offers, tech happenings around the world, new releases, and sessions with the authors:

https://discord.bpbonline.com

Table of Contents

SECTION 1

Python Basics and Syntax

Introduction

Welcome to the exciting world of Python programming! This section is where your journey begins. Whether you are just starting out are already familiar with Python, getting a solid foundation of the basics is essential. Think of this section as your first step into a much larger programming world, but do not worry, we will take it one step at a time together.

Imagine you are learning how to build a house. You must understand the foundation before working on the roof or painting the walls. The same is true for Python. To become proficient, you first need to grasp the fundamentals, the essential building blocks that form every program you will ever write. This section is about laying that solid foundation; by the end, you will be ready to tackle more complex challenges with confidence.

In Python, the basics are not just dull lessons you have to get through. They are powerful tools that will help you solve real-world problems. From creating small scripts that automate repetitive tasks to writing the code that powers websites, games, and apps, it all starts here.

Why basics matter: No matter how advanced, every great coder always returns to the basics. In interviews, you will often be asked about fundamental concepts like loops, variables, and strings because employers want to know how well you understand the foundation. It is like asking a musician to play basic scales. If you cannot do that well, you will not be able to tackle more complex pieces. This section helps you get those scales right.

Objectives

We will begin by mastering **variables** and **data types**. Think of variables as little boxes where you can store information. It is like labeling a jar on a shelf; you need to know what is inside before using it. We will teach you how to use these *boxes* to store numbers, words, and other information in your programs.

Next, we will look at **conditional statements**. Have you ever decided based on a condition, like, *If it is raining, I will bring an umbrella*? That is precisely what Python does with **if, else, and elif** statements. These allow your program to decide and take different actions depending on the situation. In Python, these decisions are crucial to building interactive, responsive programs.

We will also cover **loops**, which are used to repeat actions. Think about a washing machine spinning repeatedly until the clothes are clean. Loops do the same in programming, running a code block until a condition is met. You will learn to use loops to automate repetitive tasks and process large data sets.

And what is programming without **functions**? Functions allow you to bundle up code that does a specific task and reuse it whenever you need. Imagine writing instructions on how to bake a cake and sharing it with your friends; that is what functions do. You write the instructions once, and then you or anyone else can use them repeatedly without having to rewrite everything.

Challenges ahead: Throughout this section, you will solve problems challenging your understanding of these basic concepts. We will start with more straightforward tasks, like reversing a string, where you will take a word and flip it backward, just like reading in a mirror. Then, we will move on to slightly trickier problems like the famous **FizzBuzz** challenge, a coding test many companies use to see if you understand loops and conditionals.

Each challenge will come with step-by-step guidance, real-world examples, and tips to improve your solutions. As you complete each challenge, you will notice that coding is like learning a language. At first, it might feel slow and awkward, but soon, the syntax and logic will flow naturally.

Python's magic: One of the best things about Python is that it is easy to read and understand. Unlike some other programming languages, Python feels natural, almost like writing sentences in English. That is why it is so popular with beginners and professionals alike. However, do not be fooled by its simplicity! Companies like *Google*, *NASA*, and *Netflix* use Python to run some of the most complex systems in the world. And it all starts with understanding the basics.

You will have written multiple Python codes by the time you finish this section. Each will give you a taste of what you can do with Python, from manipulating text to controlling the flow of your programs. And most importantly, you will have built the confidence to tackle the more advanced coding challenges that lie ahead in this book.

Engagement through challenges: Remember, the challenges in this section engage your mind and sharpen your skills. Each problem is like a puzzle waiting to be solved, and as you progress, you will see how each concept builds on the last. The sense of accomplishment you will feel when you solve each challenge will motivate you to keep going, and by the end of this section, you will have mastered the foundation of Python.

Problem 1: Reverse a string

Problem statement: Given a string s, write a function that returns the string reversed. For example, if s = "hello", the output should be "olleh".

Understanding the problem: At first glance, this problem seems simple: you need to reverse the order of characters in a string. However, your ability to handle this challenge effectively and optimize the solution can make a big difference in a coding interview. The interviewer may also ask you about different approaches, edge cases, and the efficiency of your solution.

Let us break down this problem:

- **Input**: A string s (e.g., "hello").
- **Output**: A reversed string (e.g., "olleh").

Approach 1: The simple way, using Python's slicing

One of Python's strengths is its simplicity when handling strings. Using slicing, we can reverse a string in just one line of code.

The step-by-step explanation is as follows:

1. Python allows you to slice sequences (such as strings) with the following syntax: **`sequence[start:stop:step]`**
2. By using a step value of 1, we can reverse the string. This tells Python to start from the end of the string and move backward.

The code example is as follows:

```
def reverse_string(s):
    return s[::-1]
```

The explanation is as follows:

- **Explanation**: The [::-1] slice tells Python to take the string and step through it from the end (1 step) to the beginning, effectively reversing it.
- **Time complexity**: *O(n)* – Python has to traverse the entire string once.
- **Space complexity**: *O(n)* – The reversed string will take up the same space as the original string.

Approach 2: Using a loop

In some interviews, you may be asked to solve problems *without using Python-specific features* like slicing. The interviewer might want to test your understanding of loops and how strings are manipulated manually. Let us reverse the string using a loop.

The step-by-step explanation is as follows:

1. Create an empty string or list to hold the reversed characters.
2. Loop through the string from the last character to the first.
3. Append each character to the new string or list.

The code example is as follows:

```
def reverse_string(s):
    reversed_str = ""
    for char in range(len(s)-1, -1, -1):
        reversed_str += s[char]
    return reversed_str
```

The explanation is as follows:

- **Explanation**: We loop through the string starting from *len(s)-1* (the last index) and going backward to 0. Each character is appended to the new string.
- **Time complexity**: *O(n)* – The loop runs once for each character in the string.
- **Space complexity**: *O(n)* – We create a new string to hold the reversed version.

Potential follow-up question

Is this the best way to solve it?

The code above works, but string concatenation (+=) in Python is inefficient because strings are immutable, meaning each time we concatenate, a new string is created. This makes the code slower for larger strings.

Approach 3: Using a list for efficiency

To solve the issue of inefficiency in Approach 2, we can use a **list** instead of a string. Lists in Python are mutable, meaning you can append characters without creating a new object each time.

The step-by-step explanation is as follows:

1. Initialize an empty list to hold the characters.
2. Loop through the string from the last character to the first.
3. Append each character to the list.
4. Convert the list back into a string.

The code example is as follows:

```
def reverse_string(s):
    reversed_list = []
    for char in range(len(s)-1, -1, -1):
        reversed_list.append(s[char])
    return ''.join(reversed_list)
```

The explanation is as follows:

- **Explanation**: Instead of concatenating to a string, we append each character to a list, which is more efficient. Finally, we use ''.join() to combine the list into a string.
- **Time complexity**: *O(n)* – The loop runs once for each character in the string.
- **Space complexity**: *O(n)* – We use a list that grows to the same size as the input string.

Approach 4: Two-pointer technique

The **two-pointer** technique is commonly used for problems that involve reversing or manipulating sequences. In this approach, we use two pointers; one starting at the beginning of the string and one at the end. We swap characters at both pointers and move them toward the center.

The step-by-step explanation is as follows:

1. Convert the string into a list (because strings are immutable in Python).
2. Initialize two-pointers: left at index 0 and right at the last index (*len(s) - 1*).
3. Swap the characters at the left and right pointers.
4. Move both pointers inward: increment left and decrement right.
5. Repeat until the two pointers meet in the middle.
6. Convert the list back into a string.

The code example is as follows:

```
def reverse_string(s):
    s = list(s)  # Convert string to list
    left, right = 0, len(s) - 1

    while left < right:
        s[left], s[right] = s[right], s[left]  # Swap characters
        left += 1
        right -= 1

    return ''.join(s)  # Convert list back to string
```

The explanation is as follows:

- **Explanation**: We swap characters at the beginning and end of the list until the pointers meet. This reduces the number of operations and is efficient.
- **Time complexity**: $O(n)$ – The loop runs n/2 times, which simplifies to $O(n)$.
- **Space complexity**: $O(n)$ – We use a list to store the characters, which takes the same space as the original string.

Dig deeper

Interview insights: How to think about this problem:

- **Clarify the problem:** In an interview, the first thing you should do is clarify any uncertainties. For example, ask whether the input string can be empty or contain special characters. Clarify if you are allowed to use built-in methods like slicing.
- **Brute-force first, then optimize:** It is often helpful to start with a simple brute-force solution (e.g., using a loop or slicing), and then explain how you can optimize the code. For example, using a list for efficiency or a two-pointer approach to reduce the number of operations.
- **Time and space complexity:** Always discuss the time and space complexity of your solution. Interviewers want to see that you understand the trade-offs between different approaches. For example, while slicing is simple, it may not be the best in terms of understanding the mechanics of the problem.
- **Consider edge cases:** What happens if the string is empty (s = "")? What if it contains a single character (s = "a") or special characters like spaces or punctuation? Always think about these cases in interviews and address them in your solution.
- **Communicate clearly:** In an interview, it is not just about solving the problem; it is also about how you explain your thought process. Walk the interviewer through each step of your approach, explaining why you made certain choices. Avoid jumping directly into the code.

Edge cases to consider are as follows:

- **Empty string**: What should your function return if the input string is empty? The expected result should be an empty string:

  ```
  reverse_string("") → ""
  ```

- **Single character**: If the string contains only one character, it is already "reversed."

  ```
  reverse_string("a") → "a"
  ```

- **Strings with spaces**: Make sure the solution correctly handles spaces.

  ```
  reverse_string("hello world") → "dlrow olleh"
  ```

The key takeaways for the interviews are as follows:

- Always clarify the problem first.
- Start with a simple solution and discuss optimizations.
- Clearly explain the time and space complexity of your solution.
- Be prepared to handle edge cases and explain how your solution scales with larger inputs.

Problem 2: FizzBuzz

Problem statement: Write a program that prints the numbers from 1 to 100. However, for multiples of 3, print **`Fizz`** instead of the number, and for multiples of 5, print **`Buzz`**. For numbers that are multiples of both 3 and 5, print **`FizzBuzz`**.

Understanding the problem: FizzBuzz is one of the most famous coding interview questions, often used to test how well candidates can handle simple logic, loops, and conditionals. While the problem is simple, interviewers often use it to assess your understanding of basic coding principles and how clearly you can explain your approach.

Let us break down the problem:

- **Input**: A range of numbers from 1 to 100.
- **Output**: For each number:
    - Print **`Fizz`** if the number is divisible by 3.
    - Print **`Buzz`** if the number is divisible by 5.
    - Print **`FizzBuzz`** if the number is divisible by both 3 and 5.
    - Print the number itself if none of the above conditions apply.

Approach 1: Simple loop and conditional statements

The most straightforward approach involves using a for loop to iterate over the numbers from 1 to 100, and using if, elif, and else statements to handle the multiple conditions.

The step-by-step explanation is as follows:

1. **Loop through the range**: Use a for loop to go through each number from 1 to 100.
2. **Check conditions**:
    a. If the number is divisible by both 3 and 5 (using the modulo operator %), print **`FizzBuzz`**.
    b. If the number is divisible by 3, print **`Fizz`**.
    c. If the number is divisible by 5, print **`Buzz`**.
    d. Otherwise, print the number.

The code example is as follows:

```
def fizzbuzz():
    for i in range(1, 101):
        if i % 3 == 0 and i % 5 == 0:
            print("FizzBuzz")
        elif i % 3 == 0:
            print("Fizz")
        elif i % 5 == 0:
            print("Buzz")
        else:
            print(i)
```

The explanation is as follows:

- The modulo operator (%) checks the remainder when dividing by a number. If the remainder is 0, the number is divisible by that number.
- We first check if i is divisible by both 3 and 5, as this condition is more specific (we want **FizzBuzz** to appear instead of just **Fizz** or **Buzz**).
- Then we check for divisibility by 3 and 5 separately.
- If none of the conditions are met, we print the number.

Optimization and interview insights: In a coding interview, the basic solution may not be enough. Interviewers often ask follow-up questions to see how you can improve or optimize the solution.

Optimizing conditionals

You could also eliminate the need for elif by storing the output in a string and adding **Fizz** or **Buzz** based on the conditions.

The code example for optimized conditional is as follows:

```
def fizzbuzz():
    for i in range(1, 101):
        output = ""
        if i % 3 == 0:
            output += "Fizz"
        if i % 5 == 0:
            output += "Buzz"
        if output == "":
            output = str(i)
        print(output)
```

The explanation is as follows:

- Instead of checking all conditions in sequence using elif, we build the output by appending **Fizz** or **Buzz** when the conditions are met.
- This simplifies the structure and avoids having to repeatedly check conditions.
- If neither condition is met, we set the output to the number itself.

The time and space complexity includes:

- **Time complexity**: *O(n)* – The loop runs from 1 to 100, so the time complexity is linear in terms of n, where n is the number of iterations.
- **Space complexity**: *O(1)* – The space used is constant because we are only storing a small amount of information (the string output).

Dig deeper

Edge cases to consider: While this problem does not have many tricky edge cases, it is important to ask the interviewer if the range of numbers could be different (e.g., starting from a number other than 1 or extending beyond 100).

Possible edge cases are:

- **Empty range**: What if the range is from 1 to 0? (In this case, there would be no output.)
- **Negative numbers**: What if the range includes negative numbers? (In that case, modulo calculations will still work, but the output might look odd.)
- **Non-standard range**: What if the range is from 50 to 150 instead of 1 to 100? (This can test your flexibility in coding.)

In the standard form, FizzBuzz is well-defined, but clarifying the range or any potential edge cases shows good interview etiquette.

How to approach the problem in an interview:

- **Clarify the requirements:** In any coding interview, the first thing you should do is ask clarifying questions. For example, you might ask: *Should I print the results, or return them in a list?* or *Can the range of numbers change?*
- **Start with a simple solution:** Begin by explaining the simplest approach (like the basic for loop with conditionals). Walk the interviewer through your thought process clearly.
- **Optimize and discuss:** Once you have written the simple solution, explain how you could optimize it (like using string concatenation instead of multiple conditionals).
- **Talk About complexity:** Even though the complexity here is straightforward (*O(n)* time), mentioning it shows the interviewer that you are thinking critically about the efficiency of your code.

Common interview follow-up questions

Can you solve this without using conditionals?

In some cases, interviewers may ask you to avoid using if, elif, and else. While this is a rare edge case, you could use Python's **ternary conditional** or dictionary mapping to achieve the same result:

```
def fizzbuzz():
    for i in range(1, 101):
        output = "Fizz" * (i % 3 == 0) + "Buzz" * (i % 5 == 0)
        print(output or i)
```

Here, we are using Python's ability to multiply strings by a Boolean. If the condition *i % 3 == 0* is true, **`Fizz`** is printed. Otherwise, it is an empty string.

This approach avoids conditionals entirely by leveraging Python's string manipulation features.

What if the range of numbers is very large?

In an interview, they may ask what happens if the range is much larger, like from 1 to 10^6. In this case, you can discuss the memory and performance implications.

You can optimize by storing the result in a list and returning the list instead of printing each result immediately:

```
def fizzbuzz_large(n):
    result = []
    for i in range(1, n + 1):
        output = ""
        if i % 3 == 0:
            output += "Fizz"
        if i % 5 == 0:
            output += "Buzz"
        if output == "":
            output = str(i)
        result.append(output)
    return result
```

This would allow you to handle larger inputs more efficiently, as returning the result as a list avoids the overhead of multiple print calls.

The key takeaways for the interviews are as follows:

- **Clear problem-solving**: Always walk the interviewer through your thought process. Start with the simplest approach (brute-force), then discuss ways to optimize it.

- **Clarity in code**: Write clean, easy-to-read code. Avoid overcomplicating the solution, especially for simple problems like FizzBuzz.
- **Complexity**: Mention the time and space complexity of your solution. Even for a straightforward problem, discussing complexity shows that you understand performance implications.
- **Edge cases**: Always ask about edge cases. Even if the problem seems simple, consider cases where the input might be unusual or non-standard.
- **Communication**: How you explain your solution is just as important as solving the problem itself. Be sure to articulate your thought process clearly.

Problem 3: Find the maximum of three numbers

Problem statement: Write a function that takes three numbers as input and returns the largest of the three.

For example:

- Input: 3, 5, 1
- Output: **5**

Understanding the problem: At first glance, this is a simple problem: you're asked to find the largest of three numbers. It is a classic problem used in coding interviews to assess a candidate's ability to work with conditional statements and comparisons.

In this problem:

- **Input**: Three numbers (e.g., a = 3, b = 5, c = 1).
- **Output**: The largest of the three numbers (5 in this case).

While the problem is relatively straightforward, it offers an opportunity to explore different approaches, optimization, and handling edge cases such as negative numbers or identical numbers.

Approach 1: Simple conditional comparison

The simplest way to solve this problem is by using **conditional statements** (if, elif, else). We will compare the three numbers to find the largest one.

The step-by-step explanation is as follows:

1. Compare the first two numbers (a and b).
2. Then compare the result with the third number (c).
3. Return the largest number.

Code example:

```
def find_max_of_three(a, b, c):
    if a >= b and a >= c:
        return a
    elif b >= a and b >= c:
        return b
    else:
        return c
```

The explanation is as follows:

- We start by checking if a is greater than or equal to both b and c. If this condition is true, a is the largest.
- If not, we check if b is greater than or equal to both a and c. If this condition is true, b is the largest.
- If neither condition is true, c must be the largest.
- **Time complexity**: *O(1)* – We are simply comparing three numbers, so the time complexity is constant.
- **Space complexity**: *O(1)* – We are using a fixed amount of space regardless of the input.

Optimizing with Python's built-in max() function

Python provides a built-in function called `max()` that simplifies finding the maximum of multiple values. In an interview, you can mention this built-in solution, as it is a more **Pythonic** approach.

The step is as follows:

1. Use Python's `max()` function to compare the three numbers directly.

Code example:

```
def find_max_of_three(a, b, c):
    return max(a, b, c)
```

The details are as follows:

- **Explanation**: The `max()` function compares all the input values and returns the largest one.
- **Time complexity**: *O(1)* – Python's max() function internally performs comparisons in constant time.
- **Space complexity**: *O(1)* – We do not use any additional space.

Interview tip: While using built-in functions like `max()` can make your code cleaner and shorter, be sure to explain the logic behind the comparisons. This shows the interviewer that you understand how the function works internally.

Approach 2: Ternary conditional operator

Another approach to solving this problem involves using Python's **ternary conditional operator** to condense the conditional logic into a single line.

The step is as follows:

1. Use the ternary operator (a if condition else b) to compare a, b, and c.

Code example:

```
def find_max_of_three(a, b, c):
    return a if a >= b and a >= c else (b if b >= c else c)
```

The details are as follows:

- **Explanation**:
  - o We first check if a is greater than or equal to b and c. If true, a is the largest.
  - o Otherwise, we check if b is greater than or equal to c. If true, return b, otherwise return c.
- **Time complexity**: *O(1)* – We are still performing a constant number of comparisons.
- **Space complexity**: *O(1)* – No additional space is used.

This approach is concise, but readability can suffer in longer, more complex problems. In interviews, it is often better to write clear, easy-to-understand code than to prioritize conciseness.

Dig deeper

Edge cases to consider: As with any coding challenge, it is essential to consider and address edge cases:

- **All numbers are equal**: If a, b, and c are all the same, the function should still return that number.
  - o **Example: `find_max_of_three(7, 7, 7)` → 7.**
- **Negative numbers:** If the numbers are negative, the function should still correctly return the largest one.
  - o **Example: `find_max_of_three(-1, -5, -3)` → 1.**
- **Mixed positive and negative numbers**: The function should handle cases where some numbers are positive and others are negative.
  - o **Example: `find_max_of_three(3, -2, 5)` → 5.**
- **Zero**: Ensure that zero is correctly handled, as it is often considered a special case in some problems.
  - o **Example: `find_max_of_three(0, -5, 3)` → 3.**

By addressing these edge cases in your solution, you demonstrate to the interviewer that you can think critically about different inputs.

How to approach the problem in an interview:

- **Clarify the input:** Begin by asking the interviewer if there are any special conditions you should be aware of (e.g., are the inputs guaranteed to be integers? Could they be floats?).
- **Start with the simplest solution:** As always, start with a basic, readable solution like the conditional comparison approach. Walk the interviewer through your thought process, explaining why you are using if, elif, and else statements.
- **Optimize the solution:** Once you have explained the basic solution, mention Python's built-in `max()` function and how it can simplify the task. While using `max()` may seem trivial, it shows that you are familiar with Python's powerful features.
- **Discuss edge cases:** Bring up any potential edge cases and explain how your solution handles them. This is a crucial step in interviews, as it shows that you think about real-world applications of your code.
- **Explain time and space complexity:** Although the complexity in this case is *O(1),* mentioning it helps the interviewer understand that you are considering the efficiency of your solution.

Key takeaways for interviews:

- **Understand the problem**: This problem is simple but provides an opportunity to show that you understand how to handle comparisons, conditionals, and edge cases.
- **Use built-in functions**: In Python, using built-in functions like `max()` can make your solution more concise. However, always explain what the function does and how it works under the hood.
- **Consider edge cases**: Even in simple problems, thinking about edge cases (e.g., negative numbers, identical numbers) demonstrates attention to detail.
- **Communicate clearly**: Walk the interviewer through your approach step by step, explaining your reasoning behind each decision.

Possible follow-up questions

What if the input is extended to more than three numbers?

If the number of inputs grows to four, five, or more, we could modify the function to accept a list or an arbitrary number of arguments.

```
def find_max_of_numbers(*args):
    return max(args)
```

Here, we use Python's **`args`** to accept any number of inputs and return the largest one using **`max()`**.

What if we need to handle non-integer inputs like floats?

The solution remains the same, as Python's comparison operators work for floats as well. You could clarify this with the interviewer to ensure you're not missing any special requirements.

How can you modify the function to return both the maximum number and its index?

In some variations of this problem, you might be asked to return the maximum number and its index in the input list.

```
def find_max_and_index(a, b, c):
    numbers = [a, b, c]
    max_value = max(numbers)
    max_index = numbers.index(max_value)
    return max_value, max_index
```

This solution stores the numbers in a list, finds the maximum value, and then uses **`.index()`** to find its position.

Problem 4: Palindrome check

Problem statement: Write a function that checks whether a given string is a **palindrome**. A palindrome is a word, phrase, number, or other sequence of characters that reads the same forwards and backwards, ignoring spaces, punctuation, and capitalization.

For example:

- **Input**: "racecar"
- **Output**: True (since "racecar" reads the same forward and backward)
- **Input**: "hello"
- **Output**: False (since "hello" does not read the same forward and backward)

Understanding the problem: A **palindrome** is a word or sequence of characters that remains the same whether you read it forward or backward. The task here is to check whether the input string qualifies as a palindrome, ignoring non-alphabetical characters and case differences.

For example, *A man, a plan, a canal, Panama!* should return True because it is a palindrome when you ignore spaces and punctuation.

Approach 1: Two-pointer technique

The most efficient way to check if a string is a palindrome is by using the **two-pointer technique**. This technique involves placing two pointers:

- One at the start of the string.
- One at the end of the string.

You compare the characters at both pointers and move them towards the center, checking for matches along the way.

The step-by-step explanation is as follows:

1. **Ignore non-alphanumeric characters**: We need to strip spaces, punctuation, and convert the string to lowercase.
2. **Initialize two-pointers**: One at the beginning (left = 0) and one at the end (right = len(s) - 1).
3. **Move inward**: While the pointers have not crossed each other:
    a. If the characters at left and right are the same, move both pointers inward.
    b. If the characters differ, return False (the string is not a palindrome).
4. **Return True**: If all the characters match, return True (the string is a palindrome).

Code example:

```
def is_palindrome(s):
    # Remove non-alphanumeric characters and convert to lowercase
    s = ''.join(char.lower() for char in s if char.isalnum())

    left, right = 0, len(s) - 1

    while left < right:
        if s[left] != s[right]:
            return False
        left += 1
        right -= 1

    return True
```

The details are as follows:

- **Explanation:**
    - First, we use a generator expression **`char.isalnum()`** to remove all non-alphanumeric characters and convert the string to lowercase.
    - We then use two pointers; one starting from the beginning and one from the end, moving inward and comparing characters until we either find a mismatch or confirm the string is a palindrome.
- **Time complexity**: *O(n)* – We iterate over the string twice: once to clean it up and once for the palindrome check.
- **Space complexity**: *O(n)* – We store a new string without non-alphanumeric characters.

Approach 2: Reverse the string

Another approach involves reversing the cleaned-up version of the string and checking if it is equal to the original cleaned-up version.

The step-by-step explanation are as follows:

1. **Clean the string**: Remove non-alphanumeric characters and convert it to lowercase.
2. **Reverse the string**: Use Python's slicing ([::-1]) to reverse the cleaned string.
3. **Compare**: Check if the cleaned string is the same as its reverse.

Code example:

```
def is_palindrome(s):
    # Remove non-alphanumeric characters and convert to lowercase
    cleaned = ''.join(char.lower() for char in s if char.isalnum())
    # Check if the cleaned string is equal to its reverse
    return cleaned == cleaned[::-1]
```

The details are as follows:

- **Explanation**: After cleaning the string, we check if it is equal to its reversed version.
- **Time complexity**: $O(n)$ – We clean the string and then reverse it, both of which take $O(n)$ time.
- **Space complexity**: $O(n)$ – We store the cleaned string and its reversed version.

Dig deeper

Which approach is better?

Both approaches are valid and efficient. However, the two-pointer technique may be slightly more space-efficient since it does not require storing a reversed version of the string.

Optimizing for large inputs

While the problem is simple, you might be asked in an interview how the solution performs for large inputs. If the input string is extremely large (e.g., millions of characters), you should mention that the two-pointer technique is more space-efficient since it avoids creating a new string.

The edge cases are as follows:

- **Empty string**: The function should return `True` for an empty string because an empty string is trivially a palindrome.
    - o **Example: `is_palindrome("")` → `True`**

- **Single character**: Any single character is a palindrome since it reads the same forwards and backwards.
    - **Example**: `is_palindrome("a")` → `True`
- **Strings with punctuation and spaces**: The function should correctly handle strings with punctuation, spaces, and mixed case.
    - **Example**: `is_palindrome("A man, a plan, a canal, Panama!")` → `True`

Time and space complexity

Both the two-pointer and the reverse-string approaches have the same time and space complexity:

- **Time complexity**: $O(n)$ – We traverse the string at least once to clean it and then either compare it with its reverse or use two-pointers.
- **Space complexity**: $O(n)$ – We use extra space to store the cleaned-up version of the string.

How to approach this problem in an interview:

- **Clarify the problem:** Start by asking if you should ignore non-alphanumeric characters and whether the string is case-sensitive. These are typical interview clarifications for the palindrome problem.
- **Start with a simple solution:** Walk the interviewer through a simple approach first, like using Python's slicing to reverse the string. This demonstrates that you can write clean, Pythonic code.
- **Optimize and explain:** Once the basic solution is explained, discuss more efficient solutions, like the two-pointer technique. Mention the trade-offs in terms of time and space complexity.
- **Handle edge cases:** Always mention edge cases (empty strings, single characters, special characters) to show that you are thinking about the problem comprehensively.
- **Talk about complexity:** Even though this problem is simple, discussing the time and space complexity is important. The solution is linear ($O(n)$), but demonstrating awareness of complexity shows a deeper understanding.

Interview insights

How to think about this problem:

- **Clarify requirements**: Ask if spaces, punctuation, and case should be ignored. This shows that you are thinking about real-world inputs.

- **Start with a brute-force solution**: In this case, a brute-force solution might involve reversing the string and checking for equality. Even if it is not the most efficient solution, it is simple and works.
- **Optimize with two-pointers**: Once you have walked through the basic solution, talk about optimizing it with the two-pointer technique. This approach uses less memory and is efficient for large inputs.
- **Consider edge cases**: Always think about edge cases, like empty strings or strings with special characters. Handling these cases shows thoroughness.

The key takeaways for interviews are as follows:

- **Simplify first**: Start with a simple, readable solution using Python's slicing or **`reversed ()`**.
- **Optimize later**: Once the interviewer understands the basic solution, you can talk about optimizing it with the two-pointer technique.
- **Discuss complexity**: Even if the solution is straightforward, mentioning time and space complexity shows that you are thinking critically about performance.
- **Edge cases matter**: Mention how your solution handles edge cases like empty strings, single characters, or strings with punctuation.

Possible follow-up questions

What if the input is a very long string (e.g., millions of characters)?

If the input is extremely large, you can talk about the space efficiency of the two-pointer technique, which avoids creating a reversed string.

What if we need to handle Unicode characters (e.g., emojis or non-English alphabets)?

You could mention that Python's **`isalpha ()`** method handles Unicode characters, and the solution would work for most inputs, but certain cases (e.g., combining characters) might need additional handling.

Problem 5: Count the occurrences of a character in a string

Problem statement: Write a function with two inputs: a string s and a character char. The function should return the number of times the character char appears in the string **s**.

For example:

- **Input**: s = "hello world", char = "o"
- **Output: 2**

Understanding the problem: This problem requires you to count how many times a specific character appears in a string. The task is straightforward, but interviewers often use such problems to assess how well you can handle string manipulation, loops, and edge cases.

For instance:

- **Input**: "hello world" and "o".
- **Output**: **2** (since the character "o" appears twice in "hello world").

Approach 1: Simple loop and counter

The most basic way to solve this problem is to loop through the string, checking each character. If the character matches the target character, increment a counter.

The step-by-step explanation is as follows:

1. **Initialize a counter**: Start with a counter set to 0.
2. **Loop through the string**: For each character in the string, check if it matches the target character.
3. **Increment the counter**: If the characters match, increment the counter.
4. **Return the result**: Once the loop finishes, return the counter.

Code example:

```
def count_occurrences(s, char):
    count = 0
    for c in s:
        if c == char:
            count += 1
    return count
```

The details are as follows:

- **Explanation**:
    - We initialize a counter count to keep track of how many times the character appears.
    - The loop goes through each character in the string s. If the character matches char, we increment the counter.
    - After the loop completes, the counter contains the total number of occurrences.
- **Time complexity**: *O(n)* – We go through each character in the string once.
- **Space complexity**: *O(1)* – We only use a few variables, so the space complexity is constant.

Approach 2: Using Python's built-in count() method

Python provides a built-in string method **`count()`** that counts the occurrences of a substring (or character) in a string. This is the most *Pythonic* way to solve this problem.

The step is as follows:

1. **Use count()**: Call the string's **`count()`** method to count how many times the character appears in the string.

   Code example:

   ```
   def count_occurrences(s, char):
       return s.count(char)
   ```

The details are as follows:

- **Explanation**: The **`count()`** method handles all the logic internally and returns the number of occurrences of the character char in the string s.
- **Time complexity**: *O(n)* – The **`count()`** method still has to traverse the string to count the occurrences.
- **Space complexity**: *O(1)* – No additional space is used.

Interview tip: While this approach is clean and efficient, explain how the **`count()`** method works internally. It still traverses the string once and has the same time complexity as a loop.

Approach 3: Using a dictionary for multiple character counts

In some interviews, the interviewer may ask you to extend the problem to count occurrences of *all characters* in the string, not just a single character. This can be done using a *dictionary* to store the counts of each character.

The step-by-step explanation is as follows:

1. **Initialize a dictionary**: Use a dictionary to store the count of each character.
2. **Loop through the string**: For each character in the string, increment its count in the dictionary.
3. **Return the count**: After processing the entire string, return the count of the specified character.

Code example:

```
def count_occurrences(s, char):
    char_count = {}
    for c in s:
```

```
        if c in char_count:
            char_count[c] += 1
        else:
            char_count[c] = 1
    return char_count.get(char, 0)
```

The details are as follows:

- **Explanation**:
  - We initialize a dictionary **`char_count`** to store character counts.
  - As we loop through the string, we update the count for each character in the dictionary.
  - Finally, we return the count for the specified character using **`char_count.get(char, 0)`**.
- **Time Complexity**: *O(n)* – We still traverse the string once.
- **Space Complexity**: *O(k)* – We use space proportional to the number of distinct characters in the string (*k*).

Dig deeper

The edge cases to consider are as follows:

- **Empty string:** If the input string is empty, the function should return 0 regardless of the character.
  - Example: **`count_occurrences("", "a")`** → **`0`**
- **Character not in string:** If the target character does not appear in the string, the function should return 0.
  - Example: **`count_occurrences("hello", "z")`** → **`0`**
- **String contains special characters:** The function should handle strings with spaces, punctuation, or special characters. The method remains the same, as these are treated like regular characters.
  - Example: **`count_occurrences("hello, world!", "o")`** → **`2`**
- **Case sensitivity:** Consider whether the function should be case-sensitive. By default, it is. You may ask the interviewer if the function should ignore the case.
  - Example: **`count_occurrences("Hello", "h")`** → **`0`** (since it is case-sensitive).

Optimizing the solution

While counting occurrences in a string is not a performance-intensive problem, interviewers may ask you to consider how to handle very large strings efficiently. For example, what if the input string contains millions of characters? The time complexity is still *O(n)*, but you may want to store intermediate results if you're counting multiple characters in multiple passes.

The time and space complexity are explained as follows:

- **Time complexity**: *O(n)* – Whether using a loop, **`count()`**, or a dictionary, we always need to traverse the string once.
- **Space complexity**: *O(1)* if only counting one character; *O(k)* if counting all characters using a dictionary, where *k* is the number of distinct characters in the string.

How to approach this problem in an interview:

- **Clarify the problem:** Ask if the problem is case-sensitive or if you should ignore special characters. Also, clarify if you need to count only one character or multiple characters.
- **Start with a simple solution:** Begin with the loop approach, where you count the occurrences by iterating through the string. This shows that you can write basic, efficient code.
- **Mention Python's built-in methods:** Once you have explained the simple solution, mention Python's **`count()`** method, which makes the code more concise. This demonstrates that you know how to leverage Python's built-in functions.
- **Edge cases:** Talk about edge cases such as empty strings, case sensitivity, and characters that do not appear in the string.
- **Optimize if necessary:** If the interviewer asks you to handle counting multiple characters, suggest using a dictionary to store counts for all characters in a single pass through the string.

The key takeaways for interviews are as follows:

- **Understand the problem**: In interviews, simple problems like this are often meant to test your basic problem-solving skills, so focus on clarity and correctness.
- **Leverage Pythonic features**: When appropriate, use Python's built-in methods (**`count()`**) to make your solution cleaner.
- **Edge cases matter**: Always mention edge cases like empty strings and case sensitivity to show you have thought through the problem comprehensively.
- **Discuss time and space complexity**: For simple problems like this, discussing complexity shows that you are aware of how your solution scales with input size.

Possible follow-up questions

What if you need to count multiple characters at once?

If the interviewer asks how you would handle counting occurrences of multiple characters, you could suggest using a dictionary to store counts for all characters in the string.

Can you solve this problem recursively?

While recursion is not the most efficient solution here, it is possible to implement a recursive version of this problem.

```
def count_occurrences_recursive(s, char):
    if not s:
        return 0
    return (1 if s[0] == char else 0) + count_occurrences_recursive(s[1:],
char)
```

This solution checks the first character and recursively counts the occurrences in the rest of the string.

Problem 6: Find the first non-repeating character in a string

Problem statement: Write a function that takes a string **s** as input and returns the first character that does not repeat. If there is no such character, return None.

For example:

- **Input**: "leetcode"
- **Output**: `'l'` (since 'l' is the first character that does not repeat)
- **Input**: "aabbcc"
- **Output**: **`None`** (since all characters repeat)

Understanding the problem: In this problem, you are asked to find the *first* character in a string that appears only once. If all characters in the string repeat, the function should return None. This problem helps test your knowledge of strings, dictionaries (hash maps), and how to track occurrences of elements efficiently.

For instance:

- **Input**: "swiss"
- **Output**: `'w'` (since 'w' is the first character that does not repeat)

Approach 1: Using a dictionary to track frequency

One of the most efficient ways to solve this problem is to use a *dictionary* to track the frequency of each character in the string. By counting each character's occurrences and then checking for the first non-repeating character, we can solve this problem efficiently.

The step-by-step explanation is as follows:

1. **Count the frequency:** Create a dictionary where the key is a character, and the value is the number of times that character appears in the string.

2. **Find the first non-repeating character:** Loop through the string again, and for each character, check its count in the dictionary. Return the first character with a count of 1.

3. **Edge case**: If there is no non-repeating character, return None.

   Code example:

```
def first_non_repeating_char(s):
    # Step 1: Count the frequency of each character
    char_count = {}
    for char in s:
        char_count[char] = char_count.get(char, 0) + 1

    # Step 2: Find the first character with a count of 1
    for char in s:
        if char_count[char] == 1:
            return char

    return None
```

The details are as follows:

- **Explanation**:
  - The **`char_count`** dictionary stores the number of times each character appears in the string.
  - We iterate over the string again to find the first character with a count of 1.
  - If no such character is found, return None.
- **Time complexity**: *O(n)* – We traverse the string twice (once to count frequencies and once to find the non-repeating character).
- **Space complexity**: *O(k)* – We use space proportional to the number of distinct characters in the string (*k*).

Approach 2: Using collections.OrderedDict (preserving insertion order)

You could also solve this problem using Python's **`collections.OrderedDict`** (before Python 3.7, where dictionaries became insertion-ordered by default). The idea is to maintain both the frequency and the order of characters in the string.

The step-by-step explanation is as follows:

1. **Use an OrderedDict**: This ensures that the characters are tracked in the order they appear.
2. **Count the occurrences**: Track how many times each character appears.

3. **Find the first non-repeating character**: Iterate through the **OrderedDict** to find the first character with a count of 1.

   Code example:

```
from collections import OrderedDict

def first_non_repeating_char(s):
    # Step 1: Use OrderedDict to preserve the insertion order
    char_count = OrderedDict()

    for char in s:
        char_count[char] = char_count.get(char, 0) + 1

    # Step 2: Find the first character with a count of 1
    for char, count in char_count.items():
        if count == 1:
            return char

    return None
```

The details are as follows:

- **Explanation:**
  - The **OrderedDict** preserves the order in which characters are added while tracking their frequencies.
  - We use **items()** to iterate over the dictionary, returning the first character with a frequency of 1.
- **Time complexity**: *O(n)* – The same as in the first approach since we still traverse the string twice.
- **Space complexity**: *O(k)* – The space used depends on the number of distinct characters in the string.

Approach 3: Using an array for frequency count (limited character set)

If the input string is guaranteed to contain only lowercase letters (a-z), you can optimize the solution by using an array of size 26 to track the frequency of each character.

The step-by-step explanation is as follows:

1. **Initialize an array**: Create an array of size 26 to represent the frequencies of the characters 'a' to 'z'.
2. **Populate the array**: Loop through the string and increment the corresponding index for each character.

3. **Find the first non-repeating character**: Loop through the string again and check the frequency array.

   Code example:

```
def first_non_repeating_char(s):
    # Step 1: Create a frequency array for lowercase letters
    char_count = [0] * 26

    # Step 2: Count the frequency of each character
    for char in s:
        char_count[ord(char) - ord('a')] += 1

    # Step 3: Find the first non-repeating character
    for char in s:
        if char_count[ord(char) - ord('a')] == 1:
            return char

    return None
```

The details are as follows:

- **Explanation**:
  - o The **char_count** array stores the frequency of each character, where the index corresponds to the character's position in the alphabet (e.g., 'a' is at index 0, 'b' at index 1, etc.).
  - o This approach assumes that the input only contains lowercase letters (a-z).
- **Time complexity**: *O(n)* – The time complexity remains linear.
- **Space complexity**: *O(1)* – Since the array size is fixed (26), this approach uses constant space.

Dig deeper

The edge cases to consider are as follows:

- **Empty string:** If the input string is empty, return **None** because there is no character to check.
  - o **Example: first_non_repeating_char("") → None**
- **All repeating characters:** If all characters in the string repeat, return **None**.
  - o **Example: first_non_repeating_char("aabbcc") → None**
- **Single character string:** A string with only one character is trivially non-repeating.
  - o **Example: first_non_repeating_char("z") → 'z'**

- **Case sensitivity:** Ask whether the function should be case-sensitive. In the current approach, it is case-sensitive.
    - **Example**: `first_non_repeating_char("AaBb")` → 'A'
- **Special characters:** If the string contains special characters or spaces, the method should still work as long as you handle non-alphabetical characters appropriately.
    - **Example**: `first_non_repeating_char("!a!b!")` → 'a'

Optimizing the solution

While the approaches discussed have linear time complexity, you can discuss how to handle edge cases or large inputs. The dictionary-based approach is the most general and can handle different types of characters, while the array-based approach is more space-efficient but assumes a restricted character set.

The time and space complexity are as follows:

- **Time complexity**: $O(n)$ – All approaches involve traversing the string twice (once to count frequencies and once to find the first non-repeating character).
- **Space complexity**: $O(k)$ – The space complexity depends on how we store the counts, whether using a dictionary ($O(k)$, where k is the number of distinct characters) or an array ($O(1)$ for a fixed character set).

How to approach this problem in an interview:

- **Clarify the problem:** Ask if the input string is case-sensitive and whether you should consider spaces or special characters. Clarify if there are any specific constraints (e.g., lowercase letters only).
- **Start with the dictionary approach:** The dictionary-based approach is general and works for all types of characters. It is a good starting point for explaining your solution.
- **Optimize if necessary:** If the interviewer asks for a more space-efficient solution, suggest using an array for a fixed character set like lowercase letters (a-z).
- **Edge cases:** Mention edge cases like an empty string, all repeating characters, or special characters. Handling these cases demonstrates attention to detail.
- **Discuss complexity:** Even though the problem is simple, discussing time and space complexity helps the interviewer see that you're thinking critically about performance.

The key takeaways for interviews are as follows:

- **Understand the problem**: Be clear about what counts as a non-repeating character and how you will track character frequencies.
- **Leverage data structures**: Use dictionaries or arrays to store character counts, as these provide efficient lookups.

- **Edge cases matter**: Always mention edge cases like empty strings, special characters, or case sensitivity.
- **Discuss complexity**: Even for simple problems, discussing time and space complexity is crucial.

Possible follow-up questions

What if you need to find the first non-repeating word instead of the first non-repeating character?

In this variation, you could split the string into words and use a similar approach with a dictionary to count the occurrences of each word.

What if the input is very large?

The dictionary approach works well for large inputs, but you could discuss how memory usage might increase with very long strings or large character sets.

Problem 7: Sum of list elements

Problem statement: Write a function that takes a list of numbers and returns the sum of all elements in the list.

For example:

- **Input:** [1, 2, 3, 4, 5]
- **Output:** `15` (since 1 + 2 + 3 + 4 + 5 = 15)
- **Input:** [-1, 2, -3, 4, 5]
- **Output:** `7` (since -1 + 2 - 3 + 4 + 5 = 7)

Understanding the problem: The task is simple: calculate the sum of all the numbers in a list. In Python, lists can hold multiple elements, and your task is to iterate through these elements and add them together.

For example:

- **Input:** [10, 20, 30]
- **Output:** `60`

This problem tests your ability to manipulate lists and apply a basic mathematical operation (addition) to all elements.

Approach 1: Using a simple loop

The most basic approach is to use a loop to iterate through the list, adding each element to a running total.

The step-by-step explanation is as follows:

1. **Initialize a variable**: Start with a variable total set to 0.
2. **Loop through the list**: For each number in the list, add it to the total.
3. **Return the result**: After the loop finishes, total will contain the sum of the list elements.

   Code example:

```
def sum_of_list_elements(lst):
    total = 0
    for num in lst:
        total += num
    return total
```

The details are as follows:

- **Explanation**:
    - We initialize a total variable to 0.
    - As we loop through the list, we add each element (**`num`**) to **`total`**.
    - After processing all the elements, **`total`** will hold the sum.
- **Time complexity**: *O(n)* – We iterate through all n elements of the list.
- **Space complexity**: *O(1)* – The space usage is constant since we only use a few variables.

Approach 2: Using Python's built-in sum() function

Python provides a built-in function, **`sum()`**, that calculates the sum of elements in an iterable like a list. This is a more Pythonic approach.

The step is as follows:

1. **Use sum()**: Call the **`sum()`** function on the list, which automatically returns the sum of all elements.

   Code example:

```
def sum_of_list_elements(lst):
    return sum(lst)
```

The details are as follows:

- **Explanation**: The **`sum()`** function internally performs the same operation as the loop, but it is more concise and readable.
- **Time complexity**: *O(n)* – The **`sum()`** function still iterates over the entire list.
- **Space complexity**: *O(1)* – No additional space is used.

Interview tip: If you use built-in functions like **`sum()`**, make sure to explain how they work internally (i.e., they still iterate through the list), as this shows that you understand the mechanics behind Python's built-ins.

Approach 3: Using recursion

Recursion is not the most efficient way to solve this problem, but it is an excellent exercise to understand recursion, especially for smaller inputs. This approach involves breaking down the list into smaller sublists and adding the first element to the sum of the remaining list.

The step-by-step explanation is as follows:

1. **Base case**: If the list is empty, return 0.
2. **Recursive case**: Return the first element plus the sum of the remaining list.

   Code example:

```
def sum_of_list_elements(lst):
    if len(lst) == 0:
        return 0
    return lst[0] + sum_of_list_elements(lst[1:])
```

The details are as follows:

- **Explanation**:
  - o The base case checks if the list is empty. If it is, the sum is 0.
  - o In the recursive case, we add the first element (**`lst[0]`**) to the sum of the rest of the list (**`lst[1:]`**).
- **Time complexity**: *O(n)* – We still process each element once.
- **Space complexity**: *O(n)* – Each recursive call uses additional stack space, so the space complexity is linear in the list size.

Dig deeper

When to avoid recursion: While recursion works for this problem, it can be inefficient for very large lists. Python has a recursion depth limit, and for large inputs, a recursive solution could cause a *stack overflow*.

The edge cases to consider are as follows:

- **Empty list:** If the list is empty, the function should return 0.
  - o **Example: `sum_of_list_elements([])` → `0`**
- **List with one element:** If the list contains only one element, the function should return that element.
  - o **Example: `sum_of_list_elements([5])` → `5`**

- **Negative numbers:** The function should handle negative numbers correctly.
  - Example: `sum_of_list_elements([-1, -2, -3])` → `6`
- **Floating-point numbers:** The function should also work with floating-point numbers.
  - Example: `sum_of_list_elements([1.5, 2.5, 3.0])` → `7.0`

Optimizing the solution

The built-in `sum()` function is already optimized for most practical use cases. If the list is very large and you are working in a memory-constrained environment, make sure to use an iterative solution rather than recursion to avoid stack overflow issues.

The time and space complexity are explained as follows:

- **Time complexity**: *O(n)* – All approaches (loop, `sum()`, recursion) iterate over the entire list.
- **Space complexity**:
  - **Loop and sum() approach**: *O(1)*, constant space usage.
  - **Recursive approach**: *O(n)*, as each recursive call adds to the call stack.

How to approach this problem in an interview:

- **Clarify the problem:** Confirm that the input list will contain only numbers and whether you should handle edge cases like an empty list.
- **Start with a simple solution:** Begin by explaining the loop approach, where you iterate through the list and accumulate the sum. This shows that you can write clear, efficient code.
- **Mention Python's built-in methods:** Once you have explained the simple solution, mention Python's `sum()` function, which makes the code more concise. This demonstrates that you know how to leverage Python's built-in functions.
- **Edge cases:** Talk about edge cases like an empty list or a list with a single element. Handling these cases shows attention to detail.
- **Optimize if necessary:** While this problem is simple and does not require advanced optimization, you could discuss why using recursion may not be suitable for very large lists.

The key takeaways for interviews are as follows:

- **Understand the problem**: Be clear about what kind of list you're summing and handle edge cases like an empty list or a list of one element.
- **Leverage built-in functions**: Use Python's `sum()` function to make your code more concise.

- **Edge cases matter**: Always mention edge cases like empty lists, single-element lists, or negative numbers.
- **Discuss complexity**: Even though the problem is simple, discussing time and space complexity shows you are thinking about how your solution scales.

Possible follow-up questions

What if the list is very large?

For very large lists, you can mention that Python's `sum()` function is efficient but avoids using recursion because of the risk of stack overflow.

How would you handle mixed data types?

If the list contains non-numeric values (e.g., strings), you can modify the function to either skip those values or raise an error.

How would you sum elements in a nested list?

If the list contains nested lists, you could use a recursive approach to flatten the list and then sum all the elements.

Problem 8: Find the second largest number in a list

Problem statement: Write a function that takes a list of numbers as input and returns the second-largest number in the list. If there is no second-largest number (i.e., if the list contains fewer than two distinct elements), return `None`.

For example:

- **Input**: [10, 5, 20, 8]
- **Output**: `10` (since 20 is the largest, and 10 is the second largest)
- **Input**: [5, 5, 5]
- **Output**: `None` (since there are no distinct numbers)

Understanding the problem: The goal of this problem is to find the second-largest distinct number in a list. This problem helps assess your understanding of loops, comparisons, and handling edge cases.

For example:

- **Input**: [100, 50, 20, 80]
- **Output**: `80`

We can solve this problem using several different approaches, including one that tracks the two largest numbers during a single pass through the list.

Approach 1: Single pass with two variables

One of the most efficient ways to solve this problem is by using two variables to keep track of the largest and second-largest numbers as you iterate through the list.

The step-by-step explanation is as follows:

1. **Initialize two variables**: Start by initializing two variables, first and second, to None. First will store the largest number, and second will store the second largest.
2. **Loop through the list**: For each number in the list:
    a. If the number is greater than the first, update the second to be the current first, and then update the first to be the current number.
    b. If the number is smaller than the first but greater than the second, update the second to be the current number.
3. **Return second**: After processing the list, return the second largest number.

    Code example:

```
def find_second_largest(lst):
    if len(lst) < 2:
        return None

    first, second = None, None

    for num in lst:
        if first is None or num > first:
            second = first
            first = num
        elif num != first and (second is None or num > second):
            second = num

    return second
```

The details are as follows:

- **Explanation**:
    - We initialize first and second to None. These variables will store the largest and second-largest numbers, respectively.
    - As we loop through the list, we update the first and second based on the current number.

- Finally, we return the value of the second. If no second-largest number exists (e.g., if all elements are the same), second will remain None.

- **Time complexity**: *O(n)* – We make a single pass through the list, processing each element once.
- **Space complexity**: *O(1)* – The space used is constant because we only use a few variables.

Approach 2: Sort the list and find the second largest

Another approach is to *sort* the list and return the second-largest element. While this solution is easy to understand, it is not the most efficient since sorting takes *O(n log n)* time.

The step-by-step explanation is as follows:

1. **Sort the list**: First, sort the list in descending order.
2. **Find the second distinct number**: After sorting, the largest number will be at index 0. The second largest will be the first distinct number after that (if it exists).

   Code example:

```
def find_second_largest(lst):
    # Remove duplicates and sort the list in descending order
    lst = list(set(lst))
    lst.sort(reverse=True)

    # Return the second element if it exists
    if len(lst) >= 2:
        return lst[1]
    else:
        return None
```

The details are as follows:

- **Explanation**:
  - We first remove duplicates by converting the list to a set.
  - Then, we sort the list in descending order and return the second element (at index 1) if it exists.
  - If the list contains fewer than two distinct numbers, we return None.
- **Time complexity**: *O(n log n)* – Sorting the list is the most time-consuming part.
- **Space complexity**: *O(n)* – We use extra space for the sorted list and the set to remove duplicates.

Dig deeper

The edge cases to consider are as follows:

- **List with fewer than two elements:** If the list contains fewer than two elements, return None because there is no second-largest number.
  - **Example:** `find_second_largest([7])` → `None`
- **All elements are the same:** If the list contains only one distinct number, return `None` because there is no second-largest number.
  - **Example:** `find_second_largest([5, 5, 5])` → `None`
- **List with negative numbers:** The solution should handle negative numbers correctly.
  - **Example:** `find_second_largest([-1, -3, -2, -4])` → `2`
- **Empty list:** If the list is empty, return `None`.
  - **Example:** `find_second_largest([])` → `None`

Optimizing the solution

The first approach is already optimized, as it finds the second-largest number in a single pass through the list. This is the most efficient way to solve the problem in *O(n)* time.

If the list is very large, make sure to avoid sorting the list, as that adds unnecessary time complexity (*O(n log n)*).

The time and space complexity are as follows:

- **Time complexity:**
  - **First approach:** *O(n)* – We only need to traverse the list once.
  - **Second approach**: *O(n log n)* – Sorting the list dominates the time complexity.
- **Space complexity:**
  - **First approach:** *O(1)* – Constant space for the two variables, first and second.
  - **Second approach:** *O(n)* – Additional space is required for the sorted list and the set.

How to approach this problem in an interview:

- **Clarify the problem:** Ask if you should consider duplicate numbers and if negative numbers are allowed. Also, confirm what to return if there is no second-largest number.
- **Start with the most efficient approach:** Explain the single-pass approach, where you maintain two variables (first and second) and update them as you iterate through the list. This shows that you understand how to write efficient code.

- **Edge cases:** Always mention edge cases, such as lists with fewer than two elements, lists with all identical elements, or empty lists.
- **Optimize if necessary:** If the interviewer asks for a more space-efficient solution, discuss the *O(1)* space solution where you only use two variables.

The key takeaways for interviews are as follows:

- **Understand the problem**: Be clear about how to handle edge cases like lists with fewer than two elements or all identical elements.
- **Optimize with two variables**: The single-pass approach using two variables (first and second) is efficient and has a time complexity of *O(n)*.
- **Edge cases matter**: Always handle edge cases like empty lists, lists with identical elements, or lists with negative numbers.
- **Discuss complexity**: Mention the time and space complexity of both the efficient *O(n)* approach and the less efficient *O(n log n)* sorting approach.

Possible follow-up questions

What if the list contains non-numeric elements?

If the list contains non-numeric elements (like strings or mixed data types), you would need to validate the input and either skip non-numeric elements or raise an error.

What if the list is extremely large?

For very large lists, you could discuss how the *O(n)* solution is more efficient than the *O(n log n)* sorting solution, making it more suitable for handling large inputs.

How would you find the third largest number in a list?

You can extend the same approach to track the largest, second largest, and third largest numbers using three variables.

Problem 9: Check if two strings are anagrams

Problem statement: Write a function that takes two strings as input and returns True if the strings are anagrams of each other, and False otherwise.

For example:

- **Input**: "listen", "silent"
- **Output**: `True` (since both strings contain the same characters in a different order)
- **Input**: "hello", "world"
- **Output**: `False` (since the characters in the two strings do not match)

Understanding the problem: An *anagram* is a word or phrase that is formed by rearranging the letters of another word or phrase, typically using all the original letters exactly once. For instance, "listen" and "silent" are anagrams because they contain the same letters but in a different order.

For example:

- **Input**: "cinema", "iceman"
- **Output**: `True` (since both strings contain the same characters)

The task is to determine whether two input strings are anagrams of each other. This problem tests your ability to manipulate strings and apply sorting or counting techniques.

Approach 1: Sorting the strings

The simplest way to check if two strings are anagrams is to *sort* the characters in both strings and then compare the sorted strings. If the sorted strings are identical, the input strings are anagrams.

The step-by-step explanation is as follows:

1. **Sort both strings**: Convert the strings to lists of characters, sort them, and compare the results.
2. **Return the result**: If the sorted versions of both strings are the same, return True. Otherwise, return False.

   Code example:

```
def are_anagrams(str1, str2):
    # Sort both strings and compare
    return sorted(str1) == sorted(str2)
```

The details are as follows:

- **Explanation**:
  - The **`sorted()`** function converts each string into a list of characters and sorts them alphabetically.
  - If the sorted lists are identical, the strings are anagrams.
- **Time complexity**: *O(n log n)* – Sorting both strings takes *O(n log n)*, where n is the length of the string.
- **Space complexity**: *O(n)* – We use extra space to store the sorted versions of both strings.

Approach 2: Using a character frequency count (optimized)

Another approach is to count the frequency of each character in both strings. If the frequency of all characters in the first string matches the frequency of characters in the second string, the strings are anagrams.

The step-by-step explanation is as follows:

1. **Check the lengths of the strings**: If the strings have different lengths, they cannot be anagrams.
2. **Count the frequency of characters**: Use a dictionary to count the occurrences of each character in both strings.
3. **Compare the frequencies**: If the frequency counts are the same for both strings, return True. Otherwise, return False.

   Code example:

```
def are_anagrams(str1, str2):
    # If lengths of the strings are not equal, they can't be anagrams
    if len(str1) != len(str2):
        return False

    # Create a dictionary to count characters in both strings
    char_count = {}

    # Count the characters in the first string
    for char in str1:
        char_count[char] = char_count.get(char, 0) + 1

    # Subtract the character count based on the second string
    for char in str2:
        if char not in char_count:
            return False
        char_count[char] -= 1

    # Check if all counts are zero (meaning both strings have the same
characters)
    for count in char_count.values():
        if count != 0:
            return False

    return True
```

The details are as follows:

- **Explanation**:
  - First, we check if the lengths of the two strings are equal. If they are not, they cannot be anagrams.
  - We create a dictionary (**`char_count`**) to store the frequency of each character in the first string.
  - Then, we loop through the second string, subtracting the character counts. If any character is missing or the counts do not match, we return False.
  - Finally, we check if all the character counts are zero, meaning the two strings have the same characters with the same frequencies.
- **Time complexity**: *O(n)* – We only loop through each string once to count the characters.
- **Space complexity**: *O(k)* – We use a dictionary that stores the counts for each character, where k is the number of distinct characters.

Approach 3: Using a fixed-size array for character counting

If the input strings are guaranteed to only contain lowercase English letters (a-z), you can use an array of size 26 to count the characters instead of using a dictionary. This is more space-efficient when you know the character set is limited.

The step-by-step explanation is as follows:

1. **Check the lengths of the strings**: If the strings have different lengths, return False.
2. **Use an array to count character occurrences**: Create an array of size 26, where each index corresponds to a letter (a-z), and count the occurrences in both strings.
3. **Compare the character counts**: If the counts match, the strings are anagrams.

   Code example:

```
def are_anagrams(str1, str2):
    if len(str1) != len(str2):
        return False

    # Create an array of size 26 for lowercase English letters
    count = [0] * 26

    # Count characters in both strings
    for i in range(len(str1)):
        count[ord(str1[i]) - ord('a')] += 1
        count[ord(str2[i]) - ord('a')] -= 1
```

```
    # Check if all counts are zero
    for c in count:
        if c != 0:
            return False

    return True
```

The details are as follows:

- **Explanation**:
    - o We use a fixed-size array of length 26 to store the frequency of each character.
    - o As we iterate through both strings, we increment the count for each character in `str1` and decrement the count for each character in `str2`.
    - o If the strings are anagrams, the counts will all be zero at the end.
- **Time complexity**: *O(n)* – We make one pass through both strings.
- **Space complexity**: *O(1)* – The size of the array is constant (26), so space usage does not depend on the input size.

Dig deeper

The edge cases to consider are as follows:

- **Strings of different lengths:** If the two strings have different lengths, they cannot be anagrams.
    - o **Example: `are_anagrams("abc", "abcd")` → `False`**
- **Empty strings:** Two empty strings are considered anagrams of each other.
    - o **Example: `are_anagrams("", "")` → `True`**
- **Case sensitivity:** Depending on the problem requirements, you may need to consider case sensitivity. By default, the solutions above are case-sensitive.
    - o **Example: `are_anagrams("Listen", "silent")` → `False`** (case-sensitive)
- **Special characters:** If the strings contain spaces or special characters, you need to account for them as well.
    - o **Example: `are_anagrams("a gentleman", "elegant man")` → `True`** (if spaces are ignored)

Optimizing the solution

The character frequency counting approach is the most efficient in terms of time complexity, as it runs in *O(n)* time. If you know that the strings only contain lowercase letters, you can further optimize space usage by using a fixed-size array instead of a dictionary.

If the input strings are very large, you should avoid the sorting approach (which takes *O(n log n)* time) and stick with the *O(n)* character counting method.

The time and space complexity are explained as follows:

- **Time complexity:**
    - **Sorting approach**: *O(n log n)* – Sorting the strings is the most time-consuming step.
    - **Character frequency counting**: *O(n)* – We only need to traverse the strings once.
- **Space complexity:**
    - **Sorting approach**: *O(n)* – We need space to store the sorted versions of the strings.
    - **Character frequency counting**: *O(k)*—If the character set is limited, we use space proportional to the number of distinct characters (*k*) or *O(1)* for a fixed-size array.

How to approach this problem in an interview:

- **Clarify the problem:** Ask if the strings should be case-sensitive and whether special characters or spaces should be considered.
- **Start with the most efficient approach:** Explain the character frequency counting approach, as it is both time and space efficient (*O(n)* time and *O(1)* space if using a fixed-size array).
- **Mention edge cases:** Always handle edge cases like empty strings, strings of different lengths, or strings containing special characters.
- **Optimize if necessary:** If the problem specifies that the input strings contain only lowercase letters, use the fixed-size array approach for optimal space efficiency.

The key takeaways for interviews are as follows:

- **Understand the problem**: Clarify how to handle case sensitivity and special characters.
- **Optimize with frequency counting**: The character frequency counting approach is more efficient than sorting, especially for large inputs.
- **Edge cases matter**: Handle cases like empty strings, case sensitivity, and special characters.
- **Discuss complexity**: Be sure to mention time and space complexity, and explain why counting characters is faster than sorting.

Possible follow-up questions

How would you handle case-insensitive anagrams?

Convert both strings to lowercase (or uppercase) before performing the comparison to handle case-insensitive anagrams.

What if the strings contain special characters or spaces?

You can modify the function to ignore non-alphabetic characters and only compare letters.

Problem 10: Merge two sorted lists

Problem statement: You are given two sorted lists of integers. Write a function that merges these two lists into a single sorted list.

For example:

- **Input**: list1 = [1, 3, 5], list2 = [2, 4, 6]
- **Output**: **`[1, 2, 3, 4, 5, 6]`**
- **Input**: list1 = [1, 3], list2 = [2, 4, 6, 8]
- **Output**: **`[1, 2, 3, 4, 6, 8]`**

Understanding the problem: The goal is to merge two sorted lists into one sorted list while maintaining the order of the elements. Both input lists are already sorted, so the solution should take advantage of this property to avoid sorting the entire merged list.

For example:

- **Input**: list1 = [0, 10, 20], list2 = [5, 15, 25]
- **Output**: **`[0, 5, 10, 15, 20, 25]`**

This problem tests your ability to work with lists and understand how to merge them efficiently.

Approach 1: Two-pointers

The most efficient way to merge two sorted lists is to use a *two-pointer approach*. This technique leverages the fact that both input lists are already sorted, allowing us to compare elements from each list and append the smaller element to the merged list.

The step-by-step explanation is as follows:

1. **Initialize two pointers**: One pointer starts at the beginning of **`list1`**, and the other starts at the beginning of **`list2`**.
2. **Compare elements**: At each step, compare the current element in **`list1`** and the current element in **`list2`**.

   a. If the element in **list1** is smaller, append it to the result and move the pointer for **list1**.

   b. If the element in **list2** is smaller, append it to the result and move the pointer for **list2**.

3. **Append remaining elements**: Once one of the lists is exhausted, append the remaining elements of the other list to the result.

4. **Return the merged list**: After both lists are processed, return the merged list.

   Code example:

```
def merge_sorted_lists(list1, list2):
    merged_list = []
    i, j = 0, 0

    # Traverse both lists
    while i < len(list1) and j < len(list2):
        if list1[i] < list2[j]:
            merged_list.append(list1[i])
            i += 1
        else:
            merged_list.append(list2[j])
            j += 1

    # Append remaining elements from list1
    while i < len(list1):
        merged_list.append(list1[i])
        i += 1

    # Append remaining elements from list2
    while j < len(list2):
        merged_list.append(list2[j])
        j += 1

    return merged_list
```

The details are as follows:

- **Explanation**:
  - o We initialize two pointers, **i** and **j**, at the start of **list1** and **list2**.
  - o We compare elements from both lists and append the smaller one to **merged_list**.
  - o After one list is exhausted, we append the remaining elements from the other list.
- **Time complexity**: $O(n + m)$ – Where n is the length of list1 and m is the length of list2. We traverse both lists once.

- **Space complexity**: *O(n + m)* – We store the merged list, which contains all elements from both lists.

Approach 2: Using Python's heapq.merge() function

Python's **`heapq`** module provides a **`merge()`** function that merges multiple sorted iterables (such as lists) into a single sorted iterable. This function is highly efficient and takes care of the merging process internally.

The step-by-step explanation is as follows:

1. **Use heapq.merge()**: Call the **`heapq.merge()`** function with **`list1`** and **`list2`** as input. This function merges the lists while maintaining the sorted order.
2. **Convert to a list**: Since **`heapq.merge()`** returns an iterator; convert it to a list.

   Code example:

```
import heapq

def merge_sorted_lists(list1, list2):
    return list(heapq.merge(list1, list2))
```

The details are as follows:

- **Explanation**: The **`heapq.merge()`** function merges multiple sorted lists into one sorted iterator. We convert this iterator to a list using the **`list()`** function.
- **Time complexity**: *O(n + m)* – The function efficiently merges the lists by iterating through both.
- **Space complexity**: *O(n + m)* – We store the merged list, which contains all elements from both lists.

Approach 3: Recursive merge

You can also solve this problem recursively, although this approach could be more efficient in terms of space because of the recursion stack. The idea is to compare the first elements of both lists and recursively merge the remaining elements.

The step-by-step explanation is as follows:

1. **Base case**: If either list is empty, return the other list.
2. **Recursive case**: Compare the first elements of both lists and append the smaller one to the result. Recursively merge the remaining elements.

   Code example:

```
def merge_sorted_lists(list1, list2):
    if not list1:
        return list2
```

```
    if not list2:
        return list1

    if list1[0] < list2[0]:
        return [list1[0]] + merge_sorted_lists(list1[1:], list2)
    else:
        return [list2[0]] + merge_sorted_lists(list1, list2[1:])
```

The details are as follows:

- **Explanation**:
    - The base case returns the non-empty list if one of the lists is empty.
    - In the recursive case, we compare the first elements of both lists and merge the rest recursively.
- **Time complexity**: $O(n + m)$ – We traverse both lists once.
- **Space complexity**: $O(n + m)$ – Each recursive call adds to the call stack, which takes additional space.

Dig deeper

The edge cases to consider are as follows:

- **One or both lists are empty:** If one or both input lists are empty, return the non-empty list (or an empty list if both are empty).
    - **Example**: `merge_sorted_lists([], [1, 2, 3])` → `[1, 2, 3]`
- **Lists with one element:** If one or both lists have only one element, the function should still work correctly.
    - **Example**: `merge_sorted_lists([1], [2])` → `[1, 2]`
- **Lists with identical elements:** If the lists contain identical elements, the merged list should contain duplicates.
    - **Example**: `merge_sorted_lists([1, 1], [1, 1])` → `[1, 1, 1, 1]`
- **Negative numbers:** The function should handle negative numbers correctly, maintaining the sorted order.
    - **Example**: `merge_sorted_lists([-3, -1, 2], [-2, 0, 4])` → `[-3, -2, -1, 0, 2, 4]`

Optimizing the solution

The two-pointer approach is already optimal in terms of both time and space complexity. If you are looking for simplicity and readability, the **`heapq.merge()`** function is a great built-in tool, but it does not offer any additional performance benefits over the two-pointer approach.

The time and space complexity are explained as follows:

- **Time complexity**: *O(n + m)* – Where n is the length of list1 and m is the length of list2. We traverse both lists once.
- **Space complexity**: *O(n + m)* – We need space to store the merged list, which contains all elements from both input lists.

How to approach this problem in an interview:

- **Clarify the problem:** Confirm that the lists are sorted and that you need to merge them into a single sorted list. Also, ask how to handle cases like empty lists.
- **Start with the most efficient approach:** Explain the two-pointer approach, where you compare elements from both lists and merge them in linear time. This approach is efficient and easy to understand.
- **Edge cases**: Discuss edge cases like empty lists, lists with one element, or lists with identical elements.
- **Optimize if necessary:** Mention that using Python's `heapq.merge()` is a built-in solution that simplifies the code but does not improve performance.

The key takeaways for interviews are as follows:

- **Understand the problem**: Be clear about how the input lists are sorted and how to handle empty lists.
- **Use the two-pointer approach**: The two-pointer approach is efficient, runs in *O(n + m)* time, and is easy to explain.
- **Leverage built-in functions**: If you are familiar with Python's `heapq.merge()` function, mention it as an alternative solution.
- **Edge cases matter**: Always handle edge cases like empty lists, lists with one element, or lists with identical elements.

Possible follow-up questions

How would you merge more than two sorted lists?

You could use the `heapq.merge()` function, which can merge multiple sorted lists into one sorted list. Alternatively, you could extend the two-pointer approach to merge multiple lists iteratively.

How would you merge linked lists instead of arrays?

The approach would be similar if the input were linked lists instead of arrays, but you would need to manage the pointers of the linked lists instead of array indices.

Problem 11: Remove duplicates from a list

Problem statement: Write a function that takes a list of integers and returns a new list with all duplicates removed while preserving the original order of elements.

For example:

- **Input**: [1, 2, 2, 3, 4, 4, 5]
- **Output**: `[1, 2, 3, 4, 5]`
- **Input**: [5, 5, 5, 5, 5]
- **Output**: `[5]`

Understanding the problem: The task is to remove duplicate elements from a list while keeping the order of the remaining elements intact. For example:

- **Input**: [1, 1, 2, 3, 2]
- **Output**: `[1, 2, 3]`

This problem tests your ability to work with lists, sets, and to preserve order.

Approach 1: Using a set to track seen elements

The simplest and most common approach to remove duplicates is to use a **set** to keep track of the elements we have seen so far. Since sets do not allow duplicates, we can use them to filter out the duplicate elements while iterating through the list.

The step-by-step explanation is as follows:

1. **Initialize an empty set**: This will keep track of the elements we have already encountered.
2. **Loop through the list**: For each element in the list, check if it is already in the set:
   a. If it is not, add it to both the set and the result list.
   b. If it is already in the set, skip the element.
3. **Return the result**: The result will contain the list without duplicates, in the original order.

   Code example:

```
def remove_duplicates(lst):
    seen = set()
    result = []

    for num in lst:
        if num not in seen:
            seen.add(num)
```

```
            result.append(num)
    return result
```

The details are as follows:

- **Explanation**:
  - We create a set called seen to store the elements we have already encountered.
  - As we iterate through the list, we check if each element is in the set.
  - If it is not, we add the element to both seen and result. This ensures that only unique elements are added to the result.
- **Time complexity**: *O(n)* – We traverse the list once, and set lookups to take *O(1)* on average.
- **Space complexity**: *O(n)* – We use extra space to store the unique elements in the seen set and result list.

Approach 2: Using collections.OrderedDict

In Python, you can also use the **`collections.OrderedDict`** to maintain the insertion order while ensuring that duplicates are removed. Since **`OrderedDict`** does not allow duplicate keys and preserves the order of insertion, it can be a neat solution to this problem.

The step-by-step explanation is as follows:

1. **Create an OrderedDict**: Use the **`fromkeys()`** method to create an **`OrderedDict`** from the list, which automatically removes duplicates while preserving order.
2. **Return the keys**: The keys of the **`OrderedDict`** will be the elements of the list, without duplicates and in the original order.

   Code example:

   ```
   from collections import OrderedDict

   def remove_duplicates(lst):
       return list(OrderedDict.fromkeys(lst))
   ```

The details are as follows:

- **Explanation**:
  - The **`fromkeys()`** method of **`OrderedDict`** creates a dictionary where the keys are the elements of the list. Since dictionaries do not allow duplicate keys, this removes duplicates while keeping the original order.
  - We convert the keys of the **`OrderedDict`** back to a list.
- **Time complexity**: *O(n)* – We make a single pass through the list.
- **Space complexity**: *O(n)* – We store the elements in the **`OrderedDict`**.

Approach 3: Using a list comprehension with a set

A more Pythonic approach is to use a list comprehension with a set. This combines the power of sets to remove duplicates with the readability of list comprehensions.

The step-by-step explanation is as follows:

1. **Use a set to track seen elements**: Create a set and use a list comprehension to build the new list, only adding elements that are not already in the set.
2. **Return the result**: The resulting list will contain unique elements in their original order.

Code example:

```
def remove_duplicates(lst):
    seen = set()
    return [num for num in lst if num not in seen and not seen.add(num)]
```

The details are as follows:

- **Explanation**:
    - This list comprehension iterates over the list and adds an element to the result only if it is not in the seen set. The not **seen.add(num)** part adds the element to the set and returns False so that it is not added again.
    - This is a compact solution, but it can be harder to read for those unfamiliar with set operations inside a list comprehension.
- **Time complexity**: *O(n)* – We traverse the list once, and set lookups are *O(1)* on average.
- **Space complexity**: *O(n)* – We use space to store the unique elements in the seen set.

Dig deeper

The edge cases to consider are as follows:

- **Empty list:** If the input list is empty, return an empty list.
    - **Example**: **remove_duplicates([]) → []**
- **List with no duplicates:** If the list contains no duplicates, the function should return the list as is.
    - **Example**: **remove_duplicates([1, 2, 3]) → [1, 2, 3]**
- **List with all duplicates:** If the list contains only duplicate elements, the function should return a list with one occurrence of the element.
    - **Example**: **remove_duplicates([4, 4, 4]) → [4]**

- **Mixed types (if applicable):** If the list contains elements of different types, ensure that all duplicates are properly removed.
  - **Example:** `remove_duplicates([1, '1', 1])` → `[1, '1']` (if considering 1 and '1' as distinct.)

Optimizing the solution

The set-based solution is already optimal in terms of both time and space complexity. Suppose you are looking for a more readable solution. In that case, the **`OrderedDict`** approach is an excellent alternative, especially if you are working with older versions of Python where sets need to preserve order.

The time and space complexity are explained as follows:

- **Time complexity**: *O(n)* – All approaches traverse the list once, so the time complexity is linear with respect to the size of the list.
- **Space complexity**: *O(n)* – All approaches use additional space to store the unique elements (either in a set, **`OrderedDict`**, or list).

How to approach this problem in an interview:

- **Clarify the problem:** Confirm that the goal is to remove duplicates while maintaining the order of the original list. Ask if the input list can contain elements other than integers, such as strings or mixed types.
- **Start with the set-based approach:** Explain how you can use a set to keep track of the elements you have already seen. This approach is both efficient and easy to understand.
- **Mention alternative approaches:** Discuss how Python's **`OrderedDict`** can also be used to remove duplicates while preserving order, and mention how the list comprehension with a set can achieve the same result in a more compact form.
- **Edge cases:** Handle edge cases like empty lists, lists with no duplicates, and lists with all duplicates.
- **Optimize if necessary:** If asked about space optimization, explain that this problem cannot be solved without using extra space since you need to track the elements you have already seen.

The key takeaways for interviews are as follows:

- **Understand the problem**: Clarify how to handle duplicates and preserve the original order of elements.
- **Use a set to track seen elements**: The set-based approach is optimal for removing duplicates while maintaining order.

- **Leverage built-in functions**: Mention Python's **`OrderedDict`** or list comprehension for more concise solutions.
- **Edge cases matter**: Always handle edge cases like empty lists and lists with no duplicates or all duplicates.

Possible follow-up questions

How would you handle removing duplicates from a list of mixed types?

You could modify the function to handle lists containing different types, such as strings or mixed types, by checking equality across all types.

How would you remove duplicates from a linked list?

If the input were a linked list instead of an array, you would need to traverse the linked list while keeping track of the seen elements using a set. You would also need to adjust the pointers of the linked list to remove duplicate nodes.

Problem 12: Rotate a list by K places

Problem statement: Write a function that takes a list and an integer K, and rotates the list to the right by K places. In other words, each list element should be shifted to the right by K positions, and elements that fall off the end of the list should wrap around to the front.

For example:

- **Input**: lst = [1, 2, 3, 4, 5], K = 2
- **Output**: **`[4, 5, 1, 2, 3]`**
- **Input**: lst = [10, 20, 30, 40, 50], K = 3
- **Output**: **`[30, 40, 50, 10, 20]`**

Understanding the problem: To *rotate* a list means to shift the elements by a certain number of positions. For example:

- **Right rotation by 2 places**: For *lst = [1, 2, 3, 4, 5]* and *K* = 2, the output should be *[4, 5, 1, 2, 3]*. Elements 4 and 5 move to the front, and the rest shift to the right.

This problem tests your understanding of array manipulation and how to handle index wrap-around.

Approach 1: Slicing the list

One of the simplest ways to rotate a list is to use Python's *list slicing*. By slicing the list at the position *len(lst)* - K and then concatenating the two parts, you can achieve the desired rotation.

The step-by-step explanation is as follows:

1. **Handle K greater than the length of the list:** If K is greater than the length of the list, you need to use the modulo operator (*K % len(lst)*) to handle wrap-around. This ensures that K is within the valid range.
2. **Slice the list into two parts:** Slice the list at *len(lst) - K*. The right part of the list will be placed first, followed by the left part.
3. **Concatenate the slices:** Concatenate the two slices to get the rotated list.

   Code example:

```
def rotate_list(lst, k):
    # Handle cases where k is greater than the length of the list
    k = k % len(lst)

    # Rotate the list using slicing
    return lst[-k:] + lst[:-k]
```

The details are as follows:

- **Explanation**:
  - The modulo operation ensures that `K` is within the bounds of the list length.
  - The slice **`lst[-k:]`** gives the last `K` elements, and the slice **`lst[:-k]`** gives the first part of the list up to **`len(lst) - k`**.
  - Concatenating these two slices gives the rotated list.
- **Time complexity**: *O(n)* – Where `n` is the length of the list. We are slicing and concatenating the list, which takes linear time.
- **Space complexity**: *O(n)* – We create a new list for the result, which takes up additional space.

Approach 2: Rotating the list in-place

Instead of creating a new list, you can modify it by performing the rotation step by step. This is more space-efficient but requires careful manipulation of the list indices.

The step-by-step explanation is as follows:

1. **Reverse the entire list:** First, reverse the entire list. This brings the last `K` elements to the front in reverse order.
2. **Reverse the first K elements:** Reverse the first `K` elements to restore their original order.
3. **Reverse the remaining elements:** Finally, reverse the remaining elements from index `K` to the end to restore their order.

Code example:

```
def reverse(lst, start, end):
    while start < end:
        lst[start], lst[end] = lst[end], lst[start]
        start += 1
        end -= 1

def rotate_list(lst, k):
    n = len(lst)
    k = k % n  # Handle cases where k is greater than the length of the
list

    # Step 1: Reverse the entire list
    reverse(lst, 0, n - 1)

    # Step 2: Reverse the first K elements
    reverse(lst, 0, k - 1)

    # Step 3: Reverse the remaining elements
    reverse(lst, k, n - 1)
```

The details are as follows:

- **Explanation:**
    - The helper function **`reverse()`** reverses the elements of the list between the indices start and end.
    - We first reverse the entire list, then reverse the first **`K`** elements, and finally reverse the remaining elements.
    - This technique efficiently rotates the list in-place without using extra space.
- **Time complexity**: *O(n)* – We reverse the list in three steps, each of which takes linear time.
- **Space complexity**: *O(1)* – We only use constant extra space for the start and end pointers.

Approach 3: Using a deque

Another efficient way to rotate a list is by using Python's deque from the collections module. The deque has an in-built **`rotate()`** method that shifts elements to the right or left by a specified number of places.

The step-by-step explanation is as follows:

1. **Convert the list to a deque:** Use the **`deque()`** constructor to create a deque from the input list.

2. **Rotate the deque:** Call the **`rotate()`** method with **`K`** as the argument. This method rotates the deque to the right by **`K`** places.
3. **Convert the deque back to a list:** After rotating, convert the deque back to a list and return it.

   Code example: From collections import deque:

   ```
   from collections import deque
   def rotate_list(lst, k):
       d = deque(lst)
       d.rotate(k)
       return list(d)
   ```

The details are as follows:

- **Explanation**:
  - The **`deque.rotate(k)`** method shifts the elements of the deque by **`k`** places to the right. If k is negative, it shifts to the left.
  - After rotating, we convert the deque back to a list and return it.
- **Time complexity**: *O(n)* – Converting the list to a deque and rotating it both take linear time.
- **Space complexity**: *O(n)* – The deque requires additional space proportional to the size of the list.

Dig deeper

The edge cases to consider are as follows:

- **K is greater than the list length:** If k is greater than the length of the list, we can take *k % len(lst)* to ensure that we rotate only by the remainder. Rotating a list by its own length or a multiple of it results in no change.
  - **Example: `rotate_list([1, 2, 3, 4, 5], 7)` → `[4, 5, 1, 2, 3]`** (since 7 % 5 = 2)
- **K is zero:** If *K = 0*, the list remains unchanged.
  - **Example: `rotate_list([1, 2, 3, 4, 5], 0)` → `[1, 2, 3, 4, 5]`**
- **Empty list:** If the input list is empty, return an empty list.
  - **Example: `rotate_list([], 3)` → `[]`**
- **List with one element:** If the list contains only one element, rotating it by any number of places should return the same list.
  - **Example: `rotate_list([10], 5)` → `[10]`**

Optimizing the solution:

- The slicing approach is already optimal in terms of time complexity, but requires additional space for the new list.
- The in-place reversal method is the most space-efficient approach, using *O(1)* space while maintaining *O(n)* time complexity.
- The deque method is a quick and easy solution using built-in functionality, but requires extra space for the deque object.

The time and space complexity are explained as follows:

- **Time complexity**: *O(n)* – All approaches involve traversing the list at least once, so the time complexity is linear.
- **Space complexity**:
    - **Slicing**: *O(n)* – A new list is created.
    - **In-place reversal**: *O(1)* – No extra space is needed.
    - **Deque**: *O(n)* – A deque object is used.

How to approach this problem in an interview:

- **Clarify the problem:** Make sure the interviewer confirms that K is the number of positions to rotate the list to the right. Also, confirm how to handle edge cases like *K = 0 or k > len(lst).*
- **Start with the slicing approach:** The slicing approach is easy to understand and implement. You can mention that it is both time and space-efficient for most cases.
- **Mention the in-place reversal:** If space optimization is important, explain the in-place reversal approach, which rotates the list without using extra space.
- **Discuss the deque solution:** You can mention that using Python's deque provides an elegant, built-in solution for rotating lists efficiently.
- **Edge cases:** Always remember to handle cases like *k > len(lst), k = 0,* and empty lists.

The key takeaways for interviews are as follows:

- **Use modulo for large K**: Remember to reduce *k* using the modulo operator when *k* is larger than the length of the list.
- **Space vs. time trade-off**: The in-place reversal method is space-efficient but may be harder to implement than the slicing approach.
- **Edge cases matter**: Always handle cases like *k = 0* or *k* being greater than the length of the list.

Possible follow-up questions

How would you rotate a linked list instead of an array?

To rotate a linked list, you would need to modify the pointers of the linked list nodes. Find the Kth node from the end, make it the new head, and update the pointers accordingly.

What if the list contains characters or mixed types?

The solution remains the same for lists containing characters or mixed types. The algorithm does not depend on the data type of the elements.

Problem 13: Flatten a nested list

Problem statement: Write a function that takes a list, which may contain nested lists, and returns a single, flattened list with all the elements in it.

For example:

- **Input**: [1, [2, [3, 4], 5], 6]
- **Output**: `[1, 2, 3, 4, 5, 6]`
- **Input**: [[[1, 2]], 3, [4, 5]]
- **Output**: `[1, 2, 3, 4, 5]`

Understanding the problem: A nested list contains other lists as its elements. This problem aims to "flatten" the nested structure into a single list. This can involve several layers of nested lists, and our function should handle these layers recursively, retrieving every element regardless of how deeply nested it is.

For example:

- **Input**: [[1, 2], [3, [4, 5]], 6]
- **Output**: `[1, 2, 3, 4, 5, 6]`

Approach 1: Recursive flattening

The most intuitive solution to flatten a nested list is to use recursion. We iterate over the list elements, and if an element is a list, we recursively flatten it. We add it directly to the result if it is not a list.

The step-by-step explanation is as follows:

1. **Base case:** If the input list is empty, return an empty list.
2. **Recursion:** For each element in the list:
    a. If the element is a list, recursively flatten it.
    b. If it is not a list, append it directly to the result.

3. **Return the result:** After traversing all elements, return the flattened result.

   Code example:

```
def flatten_list(nested_list):
    result = []
    for element in nested_list:
        if isinstance(element, list):
            result.extend(flatten_list(element))  # Recursively flatten
        else:
            result.append(element)
    return result
```

The details are as follows:

- **Explanation**:
    - We use the **isinstance(element, list)** function to check whether an element is a list.
    - If it is, we recursively call **flatten_list** on that element and extend the result with the flattened sublist.
    - If it is not a list, we simply append it to the result.
- **Time complexity**: *O(n)* – Where n is the total number of elements in the nested list (including all sublists).
- **Space complexity**: *O(n)* – The space complexity is proportional to the number of elements, as we create a new list to store the result.

Approach 2: Iterative flattening with a stack

Another approach is to use an *explicit stack* to simulate the recursive calls. This approach avoids recursion, which can be beneficial if the list is very deeply nested (since Python has a limit on recursion depth).

The step-by-step explanation is as follows:

1. **Initialize a stack:** Start with a stack containing the entire input list.
2. **Process elements:** While the stack is not empty, pop elements from the stack:
    a. If the element is a list, push its elements onto the stack (in reverse order to maintain the original order).
    b. If the element is not a list, append it to the result.
3. **Return the result:** Once the stack is empty, return the flattened list.

   Code example:

```
def flatten_list(nested_list):
```

```
    result = []
    stack = [nested_list]

    while stack:
        current = stack.pop()
        if isinstance(current, list):
            stack.extend(current[::-1])  # Add sublists in reverse order
to maintain order
        else:
            result.append(current)

    return result[::-1]  # Reverse the result since we processed it backwards
```

The details are as follows:

- **Explanation**:
    - We use a stack to process the elements. If an element is a list, we push its elements onto the stack in reverse order.
    - Non-list elements are appended to the result.
    - Finally, we reverse the result to correct the order.
- **Time complexity**: *O(n)* – We traverse each element in the list once.
- **Space complexity**: *O(n)* – We use additional space for the stack and the result.

Approach 3: Using Python's built-in functions

Python provides some built-in functions, such as **`itertools.chain`**, which can flatten lists, but these only work for shallow lists. For deeply nested lists, you will still need a custom solution.

You can use **`itertools.chain`** for a one-level deep flattening:

Code example (for one-level deep lists):

```
import itertools

def flatten_list(nested_list):
    return list(itertools.chain(*nested_list))
```

The details are as follows:

Explanation: This method uses **`itertools.chain()`** to flatten a list of lists. However, it only works for lists that are one level deep and will not work for lists with deeper nesting.

- **Time complexity**: *O(n)* – Where n is the number of elements in the top-level list.
- **Space complexity**: *O(n)* – Space is used to store the flattened result.

Dig deeper

The edge cases to consider are as follows:

- **Empty list:** If the input list is empty, return an empty list.
    - o **Example**: flatten_list([]) → []
- **No nested lists:**If the list contains no nested lists, return the list as is.
    - o **Example**: flatten_list([1, 2, 3]) → [1, 2, 3]
- **All elements are nested lists:** If the entire list consists of nested lists, the function should still return all the individual elements in a flat list.
    - o **Example**: flatten_list([[1, 2], [3, 4]]) → [1, 2, 3, 4]
- **Deeply nested lists:** The function should handle lists with multiple levels of nesting.
    - o **Example**: flatten_list([1, [2, [3, [4]]]]) → [1, 2, 3, 4]

Optimizing the solution

The recursive approach is simple and efficient for most cases, but it may hit recursion limits if the list is deeply nested. In such cases, the iterative approach with a stack is more robust, as it avoids recursion and handles deeply nested lists without risk of hitting Python's recursion limit.

The time and space complexity are explained as follows:

- **Time complexity**: *O(n)* – All approaches traverse the list once and process each element exactly once.
- **Space complexity**:
    - o **Recursive approach:** *O(n)* – The recursion stack takes up additional space.
    - o **Iterative approach**: *O(n)* – The stack and result list both take space proportional to the number of elements.
    - o **itertools.chain**: *O(n)* – Only works for shallow lists, but the space complexity is *O(n)*.

How to approach this problem in an interview:

- **Clarify the problem:** Confirm with the interviewer that the input can contain deeply nested lists, and clarify how to handle edge cases like empty lists or lists without any nested elements.
- **Start with the recursive approach:** The recursive approach is easy to understand and implement. It shows a clear grasp of how to traverse nested data structures.

- **Mention the iterative approach:** If the interviewer asks about recursion depth or space optimization, explain how the iterative approach with a stack avoids recursion and handles deeply nested lists.
- **Discuss built-in functions:** Mention that `itertools.chain()` is useful for one-level deep lists, but will not work for deeply nested lists.
- **Edge cases:** Handle cases like empty lists, no nested lists, and lists with multiple levels of nesting.

The key takeaways for interviews are as follows:

- **Use recursion for simplicity**: The recursive approach is straightforward and works for deeply nested lists.
- **Mention the stack-based iterative approach**: The stack-based approach avoids recursion limits and is space-efficient.
- **Edge cases matter**: Always handle edge cases like empty lists and lists without nested elements.

Possible follow-up questions

How would you flatten a list of arbitrary depth using a generator?

You can implement the recursive approach as a generator function, which yields elements one at a time instead of creating a list in memory.

How would you modify the function to handle non-list iterables like tuples?

You can modify the `isinstance()` check to include both lists and tuples, or any other iterable, by checking against `collections.abc.Iterable`.

Problem 14: Find the missing number in an array

Problem statement: Given an array containing n-1 distinct integers in the range from 1 to n, find the missing number. There will be precisely one missing number from this range.

For example:

- **Input**: [1, 2, 4, 5, 6]
- **Output**: `3`
- **Input**: [3, 7, 1, 2, 8, 4, 5]
- **Output**: `6`

Understanding the problem: The array should contain numbers from 1 to n, but one number is missing. Our task is to find that missing number. This problem tests basic mathematical understanding and efficient array manipulation.

For example:

- **Input**: [1, 2, 4, 5, 6]
- **Output**: `3` Explanation: The array is supposed to have all numbers from 1 to 6, but 3 is missing.

Approach 1: Sum formula

One efficient way to find the missing number is by using the sum formula. The sum of the first n natural numbers is given by:

```
Sum of first n numbers = n(n+1)/2
```

We can calculate the sum of the first n numbers and subtract the sum of the array elements. The result will be the missing number.

The step-by-step explanation is as follows:

- **Calculate the sum of numbers from 1 to n:** Use the formula *\(\frac{n(n+1)}{2} \)* to calculate the total sum of the numbers from 1 to n.
- **Find the sum of the array elements:** Sum all the numbers in the given array using Python's built-in **`sum()`** function.
- **Subtract the array sum from the total sum:** The difference will give you the missing number.

  Code example:

  ```
  def find_missing_number(arr):
      n = len(arr) + 1  # The range is from 1 to n, where n is len(arr) + 1
      total_sum = n * (n + 1) // 2  # Sum of numbers from 1 to n
      array_sum = sum(arr)  # Sum of elements in the array
      return total_sum - array_sum  # The missing number is the difference
  ```

The details are as follows:

- **Explanation**:
  - We calculate the total sum using the formula *\(\frac{n(n+1)}{2} \)*.
  - We calculate the sum of the array using Python's **`sum()`** function.
  - Subtracting the array sum from the total sum gives the missing number.
- **Time complexity**: *O(n)* – We iterate through the array once to compute the sum.
- **Space complexity**: *O(1)* – Only a few variables are used, so no extra memory is required.

Approach 2: XOR method

The XOR operation provides another efficient way to solve this problem. The XOR operation has two key properties:

- a ^ a = 0
- a ^ 0 = a

By XORing all the numbers from 1 to n with all the elements of the array, the repeated numbers cancel each other out, and the result will be the missing number.

The step-by-step explanation is as follows:

- **XOR all the numbers from 1 to n:** Perform XOR on all numbers from 1 to n.
- **XOR all the elements of the array:** XOR all the elements of the array.
- **XOR the two results:** XORing the two results will leave the missing number, as all the other numbers cancel out.

  Code example:

```
def find_missing_number(arr):
    n = len(arr) + 1  # The range is from 1 to n
    xor_all = 0
    xor_array = 0

    # XOR all numbers from 1 to n
    for i in range(1, n + 1):
        xor_all ^= i

    # XOR all elements in the array
    for num in arr:
        xor_array ^= num

    # XOR the two results to get the missing number
    return xor_all ^ xor_array
```

The details are as follows:

- **Explanation**:
  - We first XOR all numbers from 1 to n and then XOR all the elements in the array.
  - XORing the results will cancel out the repeated numbers, leaving only the missing number.
- **Time complexity**: *O(n)* – We iterate through the array and the numbers from 1 to n.
- **Space complexity**: *O(1)* – Only a few variables are used, so no extra memory is required.

Approach 3: Using a set

Another approach is to use a **set** to track the numbers in the array. By creating a **set** with numbers from 1 to n, and then removing all the numbers in the array, the only element left in the **set** will be the missing number.

The step-by-step explanation is as follows:

1. **Create a set of numbers from 1 to n:** Initialize a **set** containing all numbers from 1 to n.

1. **Remove the elements of the array from the set:** Iterate through the array and remove each element from the **set**.

2. **Return the remaining element in the set:** The only element left in the **set** is the missing number.

   Code example:

```
def find_missing_number(arr):
    n = len(arr) + 1  # The range is from 1 to n
    full_set = set(range(1, n + 1))  # Create a set with numbers from 1 to n

    for num in arr:
        full_set.remove(num)  # Remove each number in the array from the set

    return full_set.pop()  # Return the remaining number in the set
```

The details are as follows:

- **Explanation**:
  - We create a set containing all numbers from 1 to n.
  - We remove each number in the array from the set.
  - The remaining element is the missing number.
- **Time complexity**: *O(n)* – We iterate through the array once and perform constant-time operations on the set.
- **Space complexity**: *O(n)* – The set uses extra space proportional to the size of the array.

Dig deeper

The edge cases to consider are as follows:

- **First or last number missing:** The missing number could be the first number (1) or the last number (n).
  - **Example:** `find_missing_number([2, 3, 4, 5])` → `1`
  - **Example:** `find_missing_number([1, 2, 3, 4])` → `5`

- **Empty array:** If the array is empty, meaning all numbers from 1 to n are missing, the function should return 1.
    - **Example:** `find_missing_number([])` → 1

Optimizing the solution

The sum formula and XOR approaches are optimal in terms of time and space complexity, both running in *O(n)* time with *O(1)* space. The set-based approach uses *O(n)* space, which may be inefficient for large inputs but is simple to understand.

The time and space complexity are explained as follows:

- **Time complexity**: *O(n)* – All approaches require iterating over the array once.
- **Space complexity**:
    - **Sum formula and XOR:** *O(1)* – No extra memory is used beyond a few variables.
    - **Set approach:** *O(n)* – Extra space is required to store the set.

How to approach this problem in an interview:

- **Clarify the problem:** Make sure you and the interviewer are clear on the range of numbers and that exactly one number is missing.
- **Start with the sum formula:** This is the simplest and most efficient approach, and it is easy to explain. You can show your understanding of mathematical optimization.
- **Mention XOR as an alternative:** If asked for an alternative approach, explain the XOR method, which is space-efficient and works well for bitwise operations.
- **Consider edge cases:** Discuss edge cases, such as when the first or last number is missing or the array is empty.

The key takeaways for interviews are as follows:

- **Understand the sum formula**: This approach is quick and easy to implement, and it is efficient in both time and space.
- **XOR is a clever alternative**: Mention the XOR approach to demonstrate a deeper understanding of bitwise operations.
- **Edge cases matter**: Always handle cases where the missing number is at the start or end, and account for empty arrays.

Possible follow-up questions

How would you find two missing numbers in an array?

If two numbers are missing, you must modify the approach to track two missing values instead of one. This could involve using both sum and product formulas.

What if the array contains duplicate values?

If the array can contain duplicates, the problem changes, and you might need to find both the missing and duplicate values.

Problem 15: Check if a number is prime

Problem statement: Write a function that takes an integer as input and returns True if the number is prime, and False otherwise.

A prime number is a number greater than 1 that has no divisors other than 1 and itself.

For example:

- **Input**: 11
- **Output**: `True`
- **Input**: 15
- **Output**: `False`

Understanding the problem: A prime number is a natural number greater than 1 that has no positive divisors other than 1 and itself. The smallest prime number is 2, which is also the only even prime number. Any other even number greater than 2 cannot be prime because it is divisible by 2.

To determine if a number n is prime, we must check if any number between 2 and $\sqrt{n}$ divides **n** without leaving a remainder.

Approach 1: Trial division

The most straightforward approach to check if a number is prime is by **trial division**:

- If n is divisible by any number from 2 to $\sqrt{n}$, then n is not prime.
- Otherwise, n is prime.

We only need to check up to $\sqrt{n}$ because if n can be factored into two factors a and b (i.e., $n = a * b$), one of these factors must be less than or equal to $\sqrt{n}$.

The step-by-step explanation is as follows:

1. **Handle special cases:** If n is less than 2, return False (since prime numbers are greater than 1).
2. **Check divisibility:** Loop from 2 to $\sqrt{n}$ and check if n is divisible by any number in this range. If n is divisible by any number, it is not prime.
3. **Return the result:** If no divisors are found, return True (indicating that the number is prime).

Code example:

```
import math

def is_prime(n):
    if n <= 1:
        return False
    # Check divisibility from 2 to sqrt(n)
    for i in range(2, int(math.sqrt(n)) + 1):
        if n % i == 0:
            return False
    return True
```

The details are as follows:

- **Explanation:**
    - If n is less than or equal to 1, it is not prime.
    - We check divisibility from 2 to $\sqrt{n}$. If we find any divisor, we return False.
    - If no divisors are found, we return True.
- **Time complexity**: $O(\sqrt{n})$ – The loop runs up to $\sqrt{n}$, which significantly reduces the number of checks compared to looping through all numbers up to n.
- **Space complexity**: *O(1)* – We only use a few variables for checking divisibility.

Approach 2: Optimized trial division

We can further optimize the trial division method by observing that:

- If a number n is divisible by 2 or 3, it is not prime (except for 2 and 3 themselves).
- After checking for divisibility by 2 and 3, we can skip multiples of 2 and 3 by incrementing the loop by 6 (i.e., check divisibility by numbers of the form $6k \pm 1$).

This reduces the number of checks even further, especially for larger numbers.

The step-by-step explanation is as follows:

1. **Handle special cases:** If n is less than or equal to 1, return False. Return True if n is 2 or 3.
2. **Skip multiples of 2 and 3:** If n is divisible by 2 or 3, return False.
3. **Check the numbers of the form $6k \pm 1$:** Loop through numbers of the form $6k \pm 1$ from 5 to $\sqrt{n}$, and check divisibility.

    Code example:

    ```
    import math

    def is_prime(n):
    ```

```
    if n <= 1:
        return False
    if n <= 3:
        return True  # 2 and 3 are prime
    if n % 2 == 0 or n % 3 == 0:
        return False  # Skip multiples of 2 and 3

    # Check divisibility by numbers of the form 6k ± 1
    i = 5
    while i * i <= n:
        if n % i == 0 or n % (i + 2) == 0:
            return False
        i += 6
    return True
```

The details are as follows:

- **Explanation:**
  - We first handle numbers less than 2, 2, and 3.
  - We skip multiples of 2 and 3 by checking only numbers of the form 6k ± 1.
  - If no divisors are found, the number is prime.
- **Time complexity**: *O(√n)* – This approach runs in the same time as the trial division method, but it skips unnecessary checks.
- **Space complexity**: *O(1)* – Constant space is used.

Dig deeper

The edge cases to consider are as follows:

- **Small numbers:** Prime numbers start from 2. Make sure to handle numbers less than or equal to 1 correctly.
  - **Example**: `is_prime(1)` → `False`
  - **Example**: `is_prime(0)` → `False`
  - **Example**: `is_prime(-5)` → `False`
- **Even numbers:** Even numbers greater than 2 are not prime.
  - **Example**: `is_prime(4)` → `False`
- **Prime numbers:** Ensure that small prime numbers like 2, 3, 5, and 7 are correctly identified.
  - **Example**: `is_prime(7)` → `True`
- **Large prime numbers:** Efficiently handle large prime numbers like 7919 or 104729.

Optimizing the solution

The optimized trial division approach is the most practical for checking primality in coding interviews. It skips unnecessary checks by focusing on the numbers of the form $6k \pm 1$. This reduces the number of iterations, especially for large inputs.

The time and space complexity are explained as follows:

- **Time complexity**: $O(\sqrt{n})$ – Both the standard and optimized trial division methods run in $O(\sqrt{n})$ time.
- **Space complexity**: $O(1)$ – Constant space is required.

How to approach this problem in an interview:

- **Start with the basic trial division:** Explain the basic idea of checking divisibility up to $\sqrt{n}$, as it is intuitive and shows your understanding of the problem.
- **Introduce the optimization:** If the interviewer is interested in more efficiency, explain the optimized method, which skips multiples of 2 and 3.
- **Discuss edge cases:** Mention how your solution handles small numbers, even numbers, and large prime numbers.
- **Talk about time complexity:** Explain why the time complexity is $O(\sqrt{n})$ and why this is efficient for primality testing.

The key takeaways for interviews are as follows:

- **Trial division is simple and efficient:** The trial division method is straightforward, and checking up to $\sqrt{n}$ is the key to making it efficient.

Optimized check for multiples of 2 and 3: Skipping multiples of 2 and 3 further reduces the number of checks, making the solution faster.

Edge case awareness: Handling edge cases like numbers less than 2, even numbers, and large prime numbers shows attention to detail.

Possible follow-up questions

How would you check if a number is prime for large values of n, such as in the range of millions?

You could use a probabilistic method like the Miller-Rabin primality test for large numbers, which is much faster but may give false positives.

How would you find all prime numbers up to n?

This can be done using the Sieve of Eratosthenes, which finds all primes up to n in $O(n \log \log n)$ time.

SECTION 2

Object-Oriented Programming

Introduction

Welcome to one of the most potent concepts in programming: **Object-oriented programming (OOP)**. If the basics of Python are like learning the grammar and vocabulary of a new language, OOP is like understanding how to construct entire stories. This section will take your Python knowledge to a new level, helping you think and code like a professional developer.

Imagine you are building a complex project, such as a video game or a banking system. Trying to manage everything with basic variables and functions would quickly become chaotic. This is where OOP comes in. With OOP, you can organize your code into neat, reusable "blueprints" called *classes* representing real-world objects. These classes allow you to bundle data and behavior into cohesive, logical units, making your programs easier to understand, maintain, and expand.

Why OOP matters: In the real world, we constantly interact with objects: our phones, cars, and even cups of coffee. Each of these objects has properties (like the color of your phone or the size of your coffee) and behaviors (like making a call or drinking coffee). OOP brings this same concept into programming. It allows you to model real-world objects and their interactions in your code.

OOP is the answer if you have ever wondered how large, professional-grade software is built. By learning OOP, you will understand how developers manage massive codebases, build reusable components, and create scalable systems. Whether developing web applications, games, or data-driven systems, OOP is an indispensable tool that will take your programming from basic scripts to professional-level software development.

OOP in the real world: Most professional Python developers use OOP in their daily work. OOP is the backbone of many modern Python projects, from web applications like Django and Flask to games and even artificial intelligence models. Learning OOP will give you the confidence to contribute to large-scale projects, collaborate with teams, and design software that can handle growth and complexity.

OOP is often a key topic in interviews, especially for more advanced or senior-level roles. Companies want to know that you can structure your code efficiently and think critically about object relationships. The challenges in this section are designed to help you develop those skills and feel like an architect of software systems, not just a coder.

Objectives

This section will introduce you to core OOP concepts like **classes**, **objects**, **inheritance**, and **polymorphism**. You will learn how to create blueprints for objects and instantiate them, just like how factories produce identical products from a single design. Let us take a closer look at some of the key concepts:

- **Classes and objects**: Think of a class as a blueprint for creating objects. For example, a "Car" class might define properties like color, model, and speed, and behaviors like driving or honking. Once you have the blueprint, you can create as many car objects as you want, each with unique attributes.
- **Attributes and methods**: Attributes are the data stored in an object, while methods define what that object can do. This section will show you how to build objects that interact with one another and behave based on their attributes.
- **Encapsulation**: Encapsulation is one of the critical principles of OOP. It is the idea that an object's internal details should be hidden from the outside world. Just like you do not need to know how your phone's internals work to make a call, encapsulation lets you use objects without worrying about how they're implemented behind the scenes.
- **Inheritance**: Inheritance allows you to create new classes based on existing ones. This is a powerful way to reuse code and extend the functionality of your programs. For example, you could create a **`Vehicle`** class and then extend it to make specific classes like **`Car`** and **`Bicycle`**, each inheriting shared properties and behaviors from **`Vehicle`**.
- **Polymorphism**: Polymorphism lets you define methods in a way that allows different classes to use them in their specific way. This makes your code flexible and dynamic, enabling you to write more general, reusable functions.
- **Abstraction**: Abstraction lets you define the essentials of a concept while hiding the implementation details. In practice, you create abstract classes (or interfaces)

that declare which attributes or methods must exist, but leave the concrete work to subclasses. For example, an abstract class Vehicle might declare a method **`move()`**. Concrete classes like **`Car`**, **`Bicycle`**, or **`Drone`** each inherit from **`Vehicle`** and provide their own implementation of **`move()`**—without callers needing to know how each vehicle moves. Abstraction reduces complexity, enforces a common contract, and makes it easier to swap or extend components later.

Challenges ahead: As you work through this section, you will solve coding challenges designed to test your understanding of OOP. These problems will mirror real-world situations, where you will model objects like a *banking system, inventory management*, or a *game character*. By applying OOP principles, you will see how Python lets you structure your programs to be clean, efficient, and scalable.

One of the early challenges will involve creating a simple class, like a **`Rectangle`**, with attributes like length and width, and methods to calculate the area and perimeter. As you progress, you will look further into OOP concepts, such as creating parent and child classes for more complex behaviors. You will even tackle challenges like building a *library management system* where books, members, and transactions interact through multiple classes.

What you will gain: By the end of this section, you will have built a solid understanding of OOP concepts and know how to apply them to real-world problems. You will see how OOP makes your code cleaner, more organized, and easier to maintain. Whether building small applications or working on a large software team, OOP will become one of the most valuable tools in your programming toolbox.

With this knowledge, you will be ready to tackle more advanced coding problems and feel confident in technical interviews that focus on OOP. This section will make you think about Python differently, not just as a series of instructions but as a system of interacting objects that model the real world.

Engagement through challenges: Like in the previous section, the challenges here are designed to be engaging and practical. You will create real-world objects, build relationships between them, and implement dynamic behavior. Each problem will test your understanding of OOP concepts, helping you develop skills that can be applied directly to professional development work.

Remember, each concept builds on the last, so do not rush through this section. Take the time to think about the structure of your code, and by the end, you will have mastered the art of OOP.

Problem 16: Implement a BankAccount class

Problem statement: You are tasked with creating a **`BankAccount`** class that represents a simple bank account. This class should support basic operations such as depositing money, withdrawing money, and checking the balance. Additionally, you should prevent overdrawing the account.

The class should have the following methods:

- **deposit(amount):** Adds the given amount to the account.
- **withdraw(amount):** Withdraws the given amount if sufficient funds are available; otherwise, returns an error message.
- **get_balance():** Returns the current balance of the account.

For example:

- **Input**:

```
account = BankAccount(100)  # Opening balance of 100
account.deposit(50)  # Deposit 50
account.withdraw(30)  # Withdraw 30
account.get_balance()  # Should return 120
```

- **Output**:`120`

Understanding the problem: In this problem, you need to model a bank account using a Python class. The class will represent a user's bank account, and it will allow the user to deposit and withdraw money while ensuring that the account balance never becomes negative. If a withdrawal is attempted that exceeds the available balance, an error message should be returned.

The key concepts you will apply are *attributes* to store the account balance and *methods* to manipulate it. The goal is to encapsulate the operations in a well-structured class.

The step-by-step solution is as follows:

1. **Define the BankAccount class:** We will define a **`BankAccount`** class with the following attributes and methods:
    a. **Attributes**:
        i. **balance**: A private attribute to store the current balance.
    b. **Methods**:
        i. **deposit():** Adds money to the account.
        ii. **withdraw():** Withdraws money if a sufficient balance exists.
        iii. **get_balance():** Returns the current balance.
2. **Initialize the BankAccount class:** The **`__init__`** method will initialize the account with a starting balance, which can be passed as an argument. If no starting balance is given, it will default to zero.
3. **Implement the deposit method**: The **`deposit()`** method will take an amount as input and add it to the current balance.

4. **Implement the withdraw method:** The **withdraw()** method will check if the requested amount is less than or equal to the current balance. If so, it will deduct the amount from the balance; otherwise, it will return an error message.
5. **Implement the get_balance method:** The **get_balance()** method will simply return the current balance.

   Code implementation:

```
class BankAccount:
    def __init__(self, balance=0):
        # Initialize the bank account with an optional starting balance
        self._balance = balance

    @property
        def balance(self):
            return self.__balance

    def deposit(self, amount):
        # Adds the deposit amount to the balance
        if amount > 0:
            self._balance += amount
            return f"Successfully deposited {amount}."
        else:
            return "Deposit amount must be positive."

    def withdraw(self, amount):
        # Withdraws the amount if balance is sufficient, otherwise
returns an error
        if amount > self._balance:
            return "Insufficient funds for this withdrawal."
        elif amount <= 0:
            return "Withdrawal amount must be positive."
        else:
            self._balance -= amount
            return f"Successfully withdrew {amount}."

    def get_balance(self):
        # Returns the current balance of the account
        return self._balance
```

The step-by-step explanation is as follows:

1. **Initialization:** The **__init__** method initializes the balance when the object is created. If no balance is provided, it defaults to 0.

```
account = BankAccount(100)  # Creates an account with a balance of 100
```

2. **Deposit method:** The **`deposit()`** method checks if the deposit amount is positive. If so, it adds the amount to the balance.

   ```
   account.deposit(50)  # Deposits 50 into the account
   ```

3. **Withdraw method:** The **`withdraw()`** method checks if the requested amount is greater than the current balance. If it is, an error message is returned. If the withdrawal amount is valid, it is deducted from the balance.

   ```
   account.withdraw(30)  # Withdraws 30 from the account
   ```

4. **Get balance method:** The **`get_balance()`** method returns the current balance of the account.

   ```
   balance = account.get_balance()  # Retrieves the balance, should be 120
   ```

Dig deeper

The edge cases to consider are as follows:

- **Negative or zero deposits:** The **`deposit()`** method should not accept negative or zero amounts.
- **Insufficient funds:** The **`withdraw()`** method should return an error message if the requested withdrawal exceeds the available balance.
- **Negative or zero withdrawals:** The **`withdraw()`** method should not accept negative or zero amounts.
- **Initial balance:** Ensure that the **`__init__`** method properly handles an initial balance of zero or any positive value.

The time and space complexity are explained as follows:

- **Time complexity**: *O(1)* – All operations (deposit, withdraw, get_balance) are constant-time operations since they involve only simple arithmetic and comparisons.
- **Space complexity**: *O(1)* – The class only stores a single balance variable, so space usage is constant regardless of the number of operations.

How to approach this problem in an interview:

- **Explain the problem clearly:** Describe what a **`BankAccount`** class should do – deposit, withdraw, and return the balance.
- **Start with the class structure:** Lay out the class attributes and methods clearly, showing your understanding of OOP principles such as encapsulation and method definitions.
- **Mention edge cases:** Discuss how you handle invalid inputs like negative deposits or withdrawals, and how you prevent overdrawing the account.

- **Discuss efficiency:** Emphasize that all operations (deposit, withdraw, get_balance) are *O(1)* operations, making the class efficient.

The key takeaways from the interviews are as follows

- **Class structure**: Make sure to define a clear class structure with attributes and methods that match real-world behaviors.
- **Encapsulation**: The balance is encapsulated within the class and can only be modified through the provided methods.
- **Edge case handling**: Prevent invalid operations like negative deposits and withdrawals, and ensure the class handles insufficient funds gracefully.

Possible follow-up questions

How would you implement multiple accounts in a bank system?

You could create a `Bank` class that manages multiple `BankAccount` instances and allows for account creation, deletion, and transfers between accounts.

How would you add interest to the account?

You could add an `apply_interest()` method to the class, which calculates interest based on the current balance and adds it to the account.

Problem 17: Design a stack using classes

Problem statement: A stack is a **Last In, First Out** (**LIFO**) data structure where the last element added is the first one to be removed. You are tasked with designing a `Stack` class in Python that implements the following operations:

- **push(item):** Adds an item to the top of the stack.
- **pop():** Removes and returns the top item from the stack. If the stack is empty, return an error message.
- **peek():** Returns the top item of the stack without removing it. If the stack is empty, return an error message.
- **is_empty():** Returns True if the stack is empty; otherwise, returns False.
- **size():** Returns the number of elements in the stack.

For example:

- **Input**:

```
stack = Stack()
stack.push(10)
```

```
stack.push(20)
print(stack.pop())  # Should return 20
print(stack.peek())  # Should return 10
print(stack.is_empty())  # Should return False
print(stack.size())  # Should return 1
```

- **Output**:2010False1

Understanding the problem: A **stack** is a simple data structure used in many applications, such as undo mechanisms in text editors, parsing expressions, and more. The defining feature of a stack is that it follows the LIFO principle, meaning that the most recent element added is the first to be removed.

The key methods that define a stack include:

- **push**: Adding an element to the top of the stack.
- **pop**: Removing the top element.
- **peek**: Viewing the top element without removing it.
- **is_empty**: Checking whether the stack contains any elements.
- **size**: Knowing how many elements are currently stored.

The step-by-step solution is as follows:

1. **Define the stack class:** We will create a **Stack** class using Python. The class will store the elements of the stack in a **list** (since lists provide easy append and pop operations, ideal for simulating a stack).

2. **Implement the push method:** The **push()** method will add a new element to the top of the stack by appending it to the list.

3. **Implement the pop method:** The **pop()** method will remove and return the last element (the top element) from the list. If the stack is empty, it will return an error message instead.

4. **Implement the peek method:** The **peek()** method will return the last element (the top element) without removing it. If the stack is empty, it will return an error message.

5. **Implement the is_empty and size methods:** The **is_empty()** method will check if the stack has any elements, while the **size()** method will return the number of elements in the stack.

Code implementation:

```
class Stack:
    def __init__(self):
        # Initialize an empty stack using a list
        self.stack = []
```

```
    def push(self, item):
        # Add an item to the top of the stack
        self.stack.append(item)

    def pop(self):
        # Remove and return the top item from the stack
        if not self.is_empty():
            return self.stack.pop()
        else:
            return "Stack is empty, cannot pop."

    def peek(self):
        # Return the top item without removing it
        if not self.is_empty():
            return self.stack[-1]
        else:
            return "Stack is empty, nothing to peek."

    def is_empty(self):
        # Check if the stack is empty
        return len(self.stack) == 0

    def size(self):
        # Return the number of items in the stack
        return len(self.stack)
```

The step-by-step explanation is as follows:

1. **Initialization:** The **__init__** method initializes an empty list **self.stack**, which will represent our stack.
2. **Push method:** The **push()** method appends the given item to the list, adding it to the top of the stack.
   `stack.push(10)  # Adds 10 to the stack`
3. **Pop method:** The **pop()** method removes the last element (top of the stack) from the list using the **pop()** list method. If the stack is empty, it returns an error message.
   `stack.pop()  # Removes and returns the top element`
4. **Peek method:** The **peek()** method returns the last element in the list (top of the stack) without removing it. If the stack is empty, it returns an error message.
   `stack.peek()  # Returns the top element without removing it`
5. **Is empty method:** The **is_empty()** method checks whether the list has any elements. If the list is empty, it returns True; otherwise, it returns False.
   `stack.is_empty()  # Returns True if the stack is empty`

6. **Size method**: The **`size()`** method returns the length of the list, which corresponds to the number of elements in the stack.

```
stack.size()  # Returns the number of elements in the stack
```

Dig deeper

The edge cases to consider are as follows:

- **Empty stack:** The **`pop()`** and **`peek()`** methods should return error messages if called on an empty stack. Always check if the stack is empty before attempting to access or remove elements.
  - **Example**: **`stack.pop()`** when the stack is empty → "Stack is empty, cannot pop."
  - **Example**: **`stack.peek()`** when the stack is empty → "Stack is empty, nothing to peek."
- **Large stack:** Python's list can dynamically resize, but consider how your stack will behave with very large numbers of elements.
- **Multiple data types:** Ensure that the stack works with various data types, including integers, strings, and even objects.

The time and space complexity is explained as follows:

- **Time complexity:**
  - **push() – O(1):** Appending to a list takes constant time.
  - **pop() – O(1):** Removing the last item from a list takes constant time.
  - **peek() – O(1):** Accessing the last item of a list is constant time.
  - **is_empty() – O(1):** Checking the length of the list takes constant time.
  - **size() – O(1):** Returning the length of a list is a constant time operation.
- **Space complexity:**
  - **O(n)**: The space complexity grows linearly with the number of elements in the stack.

How to approach this problem in an interview:

- **Explain the LIFO principle:** Begin by explaining how a stack follows the Last In, First Out principle and how this data structure is used in various applications, like undo operations or call stacks.
- **Start with class structure:** Clearly define your class with the methods required for stack operations (push, pop, peek, etc.). Explain how you will use a Python list to implement these operations.

- **Mention edge cases:** Discuss how you will handle edge cases, such as popping from an empty stack or peeking when there are no elements.
- **Talk about time complexity:** Emphasize that all operations (push, pop, peek, etc.) are constant-time operations, making the stack very efficient.

The key takeaways for interviews are as follows:

- **LIFO structure**: A stack follows the Last In, First Out principle, which is essential for many applications, like managing function calls and undo operations.
- **Efficient operations**: All stack operations are *O(1)*, making the stack a very efficient data structure for adding, removing, and accessing elements.
- **Edge case handling**: Properly handle operations on an empty stack, ensuring the class behaves predictably even under unusual circumstances.

Possible follow-up questions

How would you implement a stack using a linked list instead of a Python list?

You would implement a **Node** class and use it to build the stack as a linked list, where the push operation adds a new node to the top of the stack.

Can you implement a stack using Python's collections.deque?

Yes, the **deque** class in Python provides an efficient way to implement stacks and queues.

Problem 18: Create a queue class with enqueue and dequeue methods

Problem statement: A queue is a **First In, First Out** (**FIFO**) data structure where the first element added is the first one to be removed. You are tasked with creating a **Queue** class in Python that implements the following operations:

- **enqueue(item):** Adds an item to the end of the queue.
- **dequeue():** Removes and returns the first item from the queue. If the queue is empty, return an error message.
- **peek():** Returns the first item of the queue without removing it. If the queue is empty, return an error message.
- **is_empty():** Returns True if the queue is empty; otherwise, returns False.
- **size():** Returns the number of elements in the queue.

For example:

- **Input**:
```
queue = Queue()
queue.enqueue(10)
queue.enqueue(20)
print(queue.dequeue())  # Should return 10
print(queue.peek())  # Should return 20
print(queue.is_empty())  # Should return False
print(queue.size())  # Should return 1
```
- **Output**: **`1020False1`**

Understanding the problem: A **queue** is a data structure that follows the FIFO principle. This means that the first element added to the queue will be the first one to be removed. Think of it like a line at a store: the first person in line is served first, and the last person in line is served last.

The key methods that define a queue include:

- **enqueue**: Adding an element to the back of the queue.
- **dequeue**: Removing the element at the front of the queue.
- **peek**: Viewing the element at the front without removing it.
- **is_empty**: Checking whether the queue contains any elements.
- **size**: Knowing how many elements are currently stored in the queue.

The step-by-step solution is as follows:

1. **Define the Queue class:** We will create a **`Queue`** class using Python. The class will store the elements of the queue in a *list*, but we will use it in a way that mimics a queue structure.

2. **Implement the enqueue method:** The **`enqueue()`** method will add a new element to the back of the queue by appending it to the list.

3. **Implement the** dequeue **method:** The **`dequeue()`** method will remove and return the first element from the list (the front of the queue). If the queue is empty, it will return an error message.

4. **Implement the peek method:** The **`peek()`** method will return the first element of the list (the front of the queue) without removing it. If the queue is empty, it will return an error message.

5. **Implement the is_empty and size methods:** The **`is_empty()`** method will check if the queue has any elements, while the **`size()`** method will return the number of elements in the queue.

Code implementation:

```
class Queue:
    def __init__(self):
        # Initialize an empty queue using a list
        self.queue = []

    def enqueue(self, item):
        # Add an item to the end of the queue
        self.queue.append(item)

    def dequeue(self):
        # Remove and return the first item from the queue
        if not self.is_empty():
            return self.queue.pop(0)
        else:
            return "Queue is empty, cannot dequeue."

    def peek(self):
        # Return the first item without removing it
        if not self.is_empty():
            return self.queue[0]
        else:
            return "Queue is empty, nothing to peek."

    def is_empty(self):
        # Check if the queue is empty
        return len(self.queue) == 0

    def size(self):
        # Return the number of items in the queue
        return len(self.queue)
```

The step-by-step explanation is as follows:

1. **Initialization:** The **`__init__`** method initializes an empty list **`self.queue`**, which will represent our queue.
2. **Enqueue method:** The **`enqueue()`** method appends the given item to the list, adding it to the back of the queue.

   ```
   queue.enqueue(10)  # Adds 10 to the queue
   ```

3. **Dequeue method:** The **`dequeue()`** method removes the first element (front of the queue) from the list using **`pop(0)`**. If the queue is empty, it returns an error message.

   ```
   queue.dequeue()  # Removes and returns the first element
   ```

4. **Peek method:** The **`peek()`** method returns the first element in the list (front of the queue) without removing it. If the queue is empty, it returns an error message.

   ```
   queue.peek()  # Returns the first element without removing it
   ```

5. **Is empty method:** The **`is_empty()`** method checks whether the list has any elements. If the list is empty, it returns **`True`**; otherwise, it returns **`False`**.

   ```
   queue.is_empty()  # Returns True if the queue is empty
   ```

6. **Size method:** The **`size()`** method returns the length of the list, which corresponds to the number of elements in the queue.

   ```
   queue.size()  # Returns the number of elements in the queue
   ```

Dig deeper

The edge cases to consider are as follows:

- **Empty queue:** The **`dequeue()`** and **`peek()`** methods should return error messages if called on an empty queue. Always check if the queue is empty before attempting to access or remove elements.
  - **Example**: **`queue.dequeue()`** when the queue is empty → "Queue is empty, cannot dequeue."
  - **Example**: **`queue.peek()`** when the queue is empty → "Queue is empty, nothing to peek."
- **Large queue:** Python's list can dynamically resize, but consider how your queue will behave with very large numbers of elements.
- **Multiple data types:** Ensure that the queue works with various data types, including integers, strings, and even objects.

The time and space complexity are explained as follows:

- **Time complexity:**
  - **enqueue() – O(1):** Appending to a list takes constant time.
  - **dequeue() – O(n):** Removing the first item from a list takes *O(n)* time because the remaining elements need to be shifted.
  - **peek() – O(1):** Accessing the first item of a list is constant time.
  - **is_empty() – O(1):** Checking the length of the list takes constant time.
  - **size() – O(1):** Returning the length of a list is a constant-time operation.
- **Space complexity:**
  - **O(n)**: The space complexity grows linearly with the number of elements in the queue.

How to approach this problem in an interview:

- **Explain the FIFO principle:** Begin by explaining how a queue follows the FIFO principle and how this data structure is used in various applications, like managing printer tasks or customer service lines.
- **Start with class structure:** Clearly define your class with the methods required for queue operations (enqueue, dequeue, peek, etc.). Explain how you will use a Python list to implement these operations.
- **Mention edge cases:** Discuss how you will handle edge cases, such as dequeuing from an empty queue or peeking when there are no elements.
- **Talk about time complexity:** Mention that while most operations (enqueue, peek, etc.) are *O(1)*, the `dequeue()` operation takes *O(n)* time due to list shifting.

The key takeaways for interviews are as follows:

- **FIFO structure**: A queue follows the FIFO principle, which is essential for many applications like task scheduling and buffering.
- **Efficient operations**: Most operations are *O(1)*, except for dequeueing, which is *O(n)* in a Python list implementation.
- **Edge case handling**: Properly handle operations on an empty queue, ensuring the class behaves predictably even under unusual circumstances.

Possible follow-up questions

How would you implement a queue using a linked list instead of a Python list?

You would implement a `Node` class and use it to build the queue as a linked list, where the enqueue operation adds a new node to the back, and the dequeue removes from the front.

Can you optimize the queue for O(1) dequeue using Python's collections.deque?

Yes, Python's deque provides an efficient way to implement queues with *O(1)* time complexity for both enqueue and dequeue operations.

Problem 19: Implement a linked list class

Problem statement: A **linked list** is a data structure where each element (node) contains two parts: the data and a reference (or pointer) to the next node in the sequence. You are tasked with creating a `LinkedList` class in Python that implements the following operations:

- **append(data):** Adds a new node with the given data to the end of the linked list.
- **prepend(data):** Adds a new node with the given data to the beginning of the linked list.

- **delete(data):** Removes the first occurrence of the node with the specified data from the linked list.
- **find(data):** Searches for the first node with the specified data and returns it.
- **print_list():** Prints all the elements of the linked list.

For example:

- **Input**:

```
linked_list = LinkedList()
linked_list.append(10)
linked_list.append(20)
linked_list.prepend(5)
linked_list.delete(10)
linked_list.print_list()  # Should print 5 -> 20
```

- **Output**:`5 -> 20`

Understanding the problem: A linked list is a linear data structure where each element (node) is stored in a container, and pointers connect the containers (nodes). Unlike arrays, linked lists do not require contiguous memory locations, making them efficient for dynamic memory allocation.

In this chapter, we will implement a **singly linked list**, where each node points to the next node in the sequence.

The key methods that define a linked list include:

- **append**: Adds a node at the end.
- **prepend**: Adds a node at the beginning.
- **delete**: Removes a node containing a specific value.
- **find**: Searches for a node with a specific value.
- **print_list**: Displays the data in all nodes in the list.

The step-by-step solution is as follows:

1. **Define the node class:** Each node in the linked list will consist of two parts:
   a. **Data**: The actual value stored in the node.
   b. **Next**: A reference to the next node in the list.

   We will define a **`Node`** class to represent each node in the linked list.

2. **Define the LinkedList class:** The **`LinkedList`** class will manage the nodes and provide methods to add, remove, and traverse the list. We will use a pointer (head) that will always point to the first node in the list.

3. **Implement the append method:** The **append()** method will add a new node to the end of the list. If the list is empty, it will set the new node as the head. Otherwise, it will traverse to the last node and add the new node.
4. **Implement the prepend method:** The **prepend()** method will add a new node to the beginning of the list. It will set the current head as the next node of the new node, and then update the head to point to the new node.
5. **Implement the delete method:** The **delete()** method will traverse the list, looking for the first node that matches the given data. Once found, it will remove the node by adjusting the pointers.
6. **Implement the find method:** The **find()** method will traverse the list and return the first node that contains the given data. If the node is not found, it will return None.
7. **Implement the print_list method:** The **print_list()** method will traverse the entire list, printing the data in each node, separated by arrows (->).

Code implementation:

```
class Node:
    def __init__(self, data):
        # Each node has data and a reference to the next node
        self.data = data
        self.next = None

class LinkedList:
    def __init__(self):
        # Initialize the linked list with an empty head
        self.head = None

    def append(self, data):
        # Add a new node with the given data to the end of the list
        new_node = Node(data)
        if not self.head:
            self.head = new_node
            return
        current = self.head
        while current.next:
            current = current.next
        current.next = new_node

    def prepend(self, data):
        # Add a new node with the given data to the beginning of the
list
        new_node = Node(data)
```

```
            new_node.next = self.head
            self.head = new_node

    def delete(self, data):
        # Remove the first occurrence of the node with the given data
        if not self.head:
            return "List is empty, nothing to delete."
        if self.head.data == data:
            self.head = self.head.next
            return
        current = self.head
        while current.next and current.next.data != data:
            current = current.next
        if current.next:
            current.next = current.next.next
        else:
            return f"Node with data {data} not found."

    def find(self, data):
        # Find and return the node with the given data
        current = self.head
        while current:
            if current.data == data:
                return current
            current = current.next
        return None

    def print_list(self):
        # Print all the elements of the linked list
        current = self.head
        if not current:
            print("List is empty.")
            return
        while current:
            print(current.data, end=" -> " if current.next else "\\n")
            current = current.next
```

The step-by-step explanation is as follows:

1. **Node class:** The **Node** class represents each node in the linked list. Each node stores data and a reference to the next node in the list.
2. **Initialization of LinkedList:** The **LinkedList** class manages the nodes. The **__init__** method initializes the list with an empty head, indicating that the list is initially empty.

3. **Append method:** The **append()** method adds a new node at the end of the list. If the list is empty (i.e., self.head is None), it sets the new node as the head. Otherwise, it traverses to the last node and adds the new node after it.

```
linked_list.append(10)  # Adds 10 to the end of the list
```

4. **Prepend method:** The **prepend()** method adds a new node at the beginning of the list by pointing the new node to the current head and then updating the head to the new node.

```
linked_list.prepend(5)  # Adds 5 to the beginning of the list
```

5. **Delete method:** The **delete()** method removes the first node with the given data. It handles the case where the node to be deleted is the head, as well as traversing the list to find and remove a non-head node.

```
linked_list.delete(10)  # Removes the node with the value 10
```

6. **Find method:** The **find()** method traverses the list, looking for a node with the given data, and returns it if found. If not, it returns None.

```
node = linked_list.find(20)  # Finds and returns the node with value 20
```

7. **Print list method:** The **print_list()** method prints all the nodes in the list, separated by arrows (>).

```
linked_list.print_list()  # Prints all elements in the list
```

Dig deeper

The edge cases to consider are as follows:

- **Empty list:** The **print_list()** and **delete()** methods should handle cases where the linked list is empty.
    - **Example: linked_list.print_list()** when the list is empty → "List is empty."
- **Head deletion:** If the node to be deleted is the head, the **delete()** method should correctly update the head to the next node.
- **Node not found:** If the node to be deleted or found does not exist in the list, the methods should handle it gracefully (e.g., returning None or an appropriate message).
- **Multiple data types:** Ensure that the linked list works with various data types, including integers, strings, and even objects.

The time and space complexity are explained as follows:

- **Time complexity:**
    - **append() – O(n):** You need to traverse the entire list to find the last node and append the new node.
    - **prepend() – O(1):** You directly add the new node at the head of the list.

- **delete() – O(n):** You may need to traverse the entire list to find the node to be deleted.
- **find() – O(n):** You may need to traverse the entire list to find the node.
- **print_list() – O(n):** You traverse the entire list to print the elements.

- **Space complexity:**
  - **O(n):** The space complexity grows linearly with the number of nodes in the list.

How to approach this problem in an interview:

- **Explain linked lists:** Describe what a linked list is and why it is useful, particularly in dynamic memory allocation scenarios where the list size changes frequently.
- **Start with the node class:** Begin by defining a simple `Node` class that stores data and a reference to the next node.
- **Explain LinkedList operations:** Walk through the methods like `append()`, `prepend()`, `delete()`, and `find()`, explaining how you would traverse the list and manipulate the nodes.
- **Handle edge cases:** Mention how you will handle edge cases, like deleting the head, handling an empty list, or searching for a node that does not exist.
- **Discuss time complexity:** Mention that while the prepend operation is *O(1)*, appending and deleting are *O(n)* operations due to the need to traverse the list.

The key takeaways for interviews are as follows:

- **Dynamic size**: Linked lists are useful for applications where the list's size changes frequently and you do not need random access to elements.
- **Efficient insertion/deletion**: Linked lists allow for efficient insertion and deletion, particularly at the beginning of the list.
- **Traversal cost**: Operations like appending, deleting, and finding take *O(n)* time because they require traversing the list.

Possible follow-up questions

How would you implement a doubly linked list?

In a doubly linked list, each node has two pointers: one to the next node and one to the previous node, allowing for traversal in both directions.

How would you reverse a linked list?

You can reverse a linked list by iterating through the list and adjusting the pointers so that each node points to the previous node instead of the next one.

Problem 20: Design a circular linked list

Problem statement: A **circular linked list** is a variation of a linked list where the last node points back to the head of the list, creating a circle. You are tasked with creating a **`CircularLinkedList`** class in Python that implements the following operations:

- **append(data):** Adds a new node with the given data to the end of the circular linked list.
- **prepend(data):** Adds a new node with the given data to the beginning of the circular linked list.
- **delete(data):** Removes the first occurrence of the node with the specified data from the circular linked list.
- **find(data):** Searches for the first node with the specified data and returns it.
- **print_list():** Prints all the elements of the circular linked list.

For example:

- **Input**:

```
cll = CircularLinkedList()
cll.append(10)
cll.append(20)
cll.prepend(5)
cll.delete(10)
cll.print_list()  # Should print 5 -> 20 (and back to the head)
```

- **Output:`5 -> 20 -> (back to head)`**

Understanding the problem: A **circular linked list** is similar to a singly linked list, but with a significant difference: the last node points back to the first node, forming a circle. This type of list is useful for tasks that require continuous traversal, such as buffering systems, round-robin scheduling, or games with a cyclic nature.

In this chapter, we will implement a **singly circular linked list** where each node has a reference to the next node, and the last node points back to the head.

The key methods that define a circular linked list include:

- **append**: Adds a node at the end of the list (before the head).
- **prepend**: Adds a node at the beginning of the list.
- **delete**: Removes a node containing a specific value.
- **find**: Searches for a node with a specific value.
- **print_list**: Displays the data in all nodes in the list, with an indication that the list is circular.

The step-by-step solution is as follows:

1. **Define the node class:** Each node in the circular linked list will consist of two parts:
    a. **Data**: The actual value stored in the node.
    b. **Next**: A reference (or pointer) to the next node in the list.

    We will define a **Node** class to represent each node.

2. **Define the CircularLinkedList class:** The **CircularLinkedList** class will manage the nodes and provide methods to add, remove, and traverse the list. We will use a pointer (head) that always points to the first node in the list. The last node's next pointer will point back to the head.

3. **Implement the append method:** The **append()** method will add a new node to the end of the list. If the list is empty, the new node will be set as the head, and its next pointer will point to itself. Otherwise, we will traverse to the last node and add the new node, updating the last node's next pointer to point to the head.

4. **Implement the prepend method:** The **prepend()** method will add a new node to the beginning of the list. If the list is empty, the new node will be the head and will point to itself. If the list is not empty, the new node will become the head, and the last node's next pointer will be updated to point to the new head.

5. **Implement the delete method:** The **delete()** method will traverse the list, looking for the first node with the given data. Once found, it will remove the node by adjusting the pointers.

6. **Implement the print_list method:** The **print_list()** method will traverse the list and print the data in each node, with an indication that the list is circular.

    Code implementation:

```
class Node:
    def __init__(self, data):
        # Each node has data and a reference to the next node
        self.data = data
        self.next = None

class CircularLinkedList:
    def __init__(self):
        # Initialize the circular linked list with an empty head
        self.head = None

    def append(self, data):
        # Add a new node with the given data to the end of the list
        new_node = Node(data)
        if not self.head:
```

```
            self.head = new_node
            self.head.next = self.head
        else:
            current = self.head
            while current.next != self.head:
                current = current.next
            current.next = new_node
            new_node.next = self.head

    def prepend(self, data):
        # Add a new node with the given data to the beginning of the list
        new_node = Node(data)
        if not self.head:
            self.head = new_node
            self.head.next = self.head
        else:
            current = self.head
            while current.next != self.head:
                current = current.next
            current.next = new_node
            new_node.next = self.head
            self.head = new_node
    def delete(self, data):
        # Remove the first occurrence of the node with the given data
        if self.head:
            if self.head.data == data:
                if self.head.next == self.head:
                    self.head = None
                else:
                    current = self.head
                    while current.next != self.head:
                        current = current.next
                    current.next = self.head.next
                    self.head = self.head.next
            else:
                current = self.head
                prev = None
                while current.next != self.head:
                    prev = current
                    current = current.next
                    if current.data == data:
                        prev.next = current.next
```

```
                break

    def print_list(self):
        # Print all the elements of the circular linked list
        current = self.head
        if not current:
            print("List is empty.")
            return
        while True:
            print(current.data, end=" -> ")
            current = current.next
            if current == self.head:
                break
        print("(back to head)")
```

The step-by-step explanation is as follows:

1. **Node class:** The **Node** class represents each node in the circular linked list. Each node stores data and a reference to the next node.
2. **Initialization of CircularLinkedList:** The **CircularLinkedList** class manages the nodes. The **__init__** method initializes the list with an empty head, indicating that the list is initially empty.
3. **Append method:** The **append()** method adds a new node at the end of the list. If the list is empty, the new node becomes the head and points to itself. Otherwise, the new node is added at the end, and the last node's next pointer is updated to point back to the head.

   ```
   cll.append(10)  # Adds 10 to the end of the list
   ```
4. **Prepend method:** The **prepend()** method adds a new node at the beginning of the list. If the list is empty, the new node becomes the head and points to itself. If the list is not empty, the new node becomes the head, and the last node's next pointer is updated to point to the new head.

   ```
   cll.prepend(5)  # Adds 5 to the beginning of the list
   ```
5. **Delete method:** The **delete()** method removes the first node with the given data. If the node to be deleted is the head, the head is updated accordingly, and the last node's next pointer is updated to point to the new head.

   ```
   cll.delete(10)  # Removes the node with the value 10
   ```
6. **Print list method:** The **print_list()** method traverses and prints all the nodes in the list. Since the list is circular, it prints each node's data followed by an arrow (>), and after printing all nodes, it shows "(back to head)" to indicate the circular nature.

   ```
   cll.print_list()  # Prints all elements in the list
   ```

Dig deeper

The edge cases to consider are as follows:

- **Empty list:** The `print_list()` and `delete()` methods should handle cases where the circular linked list is empty.
  - **Example**: `cll.print_list()` when the list is empty → "List is empty."
- **Single element list:** Special care must be taken when dealing with a list that contains only one node. For example, deleting the head of a single-node list should set `self.head` to `None`.
- **Multiple data types:** Ensure that the circular linked list works with various data types, including integers, strings, and even objects.
- **Circular nature:** Ensure that all operations respect the circular nature of the list by maintaining the connection from the last node back to the head.

The time and space complexity are explained as follows:

- **Time complexity:**
  - **append() – O(n):** You need to traverse the entire list to find the last node and append the new node.
  - **prepend() – O(n):** You may need to traverse the list to find the last node, then update the head and the last node's pointer.
  - **delete() – O(n):** You may need to traverse the entire list to find and delete the node.
  - **print_list() – O(n):** You traverse the entire list to print the elements.
- **Space complexity:**
  - **O(n):** The space complexity grows linearly with the number of nodes in the list.

How to approach this problem in an interview:

- **Explain circular linked lists:** Start by explaining the circular nature of the list, where the last node points back to the first node.
- **Start with class structure:** Define your `Node` and `CircularLinkedList` classes and explain how the nodes are connected in a circular manner.
- **Discuss edge cases:** Talk about how you handle cases like an empty list or deleting the only node in a list.
- **Explain time complexity:** Mention that most operations take *O(n)* time since you may need to traverse the entire list to find the last node.

The key takeaways for interviews are as follows:

- **Circular structure**: A circular linked list connects the last node back to the first node, allowing for continuous traversal.
- **Efficient for certain tasks**: Circular linked lists are particularly useful in scenarios like buffering systems or cyclic task scheduling.
- **Time complexity**: Most operations (append, prepend, delete) take *O(n)* time because you need to traverse the list.

Possible follow-up questions

How would you handle circular doubly linked lists?

In a circular doubly linked list, each node would have two pointers: one to the next node and one to the previous node, with the last node pointing to the head.

What are the use cases for circular linked lists?

Circular linked lists are often used in buffering systems (e.g., a round-robin buffer), games, or any system requiring continuous cyclic traversal.

Problem 21: Design a simple shopping cart system

Problem statement: A *shopping cart* is a critical component of any e-commerce platform. You are tasked with designing a simple shopping cart system using Python's OOP principles. The system should include the following functionality:

- **Cart class:**
  - **add_item(item, quantity):** Adds a specified quantity of an item to the cart.
  - **remove_item(item):** Removes the item from the cart.
  - **view_cart():** Displays the items in the cart, their quantities, and the total price.
  - **total_cost():** Returns the total price of all the items in the cart.
- **Item class:** Each item should have the following attributes: name, price, and quantity.

For example:

- **Input**:

```
item1 = Item("Laptop", 1000)
item2 = Item("Headphones", 100)
cart = Cart()
cart.add_item(item1, 2)
```

```
cart.add_item(item2, 1)
cart.view_cart()
cart.total_cost()
```

- **Output**:

```
Cart:
- Laptop: 2 @ $1000 each
- Headphones: 1 @ $100 each
Total cost: $2100
```

Understanding the problem: A *shopping cart system* is essential for e-commerce platforms, where customers can add, remove, and view items before purchasing. Each item in the cart has a name, price, and quantity, and the cart should be able to calculate the total cost based on the quantity of each item.

In this chapter, we will implement two classes: **`Item`** and **`Cart`**. The Item class will represent individual products, while the Cart class will manage the collection of items and provide the necessary functionality.

The step-by-step solution is as follows:

1. **Define the Item class:** The **`Item`** class will represent individual items in the shopping cart. Each item will have three attributes:
   a. **name**: The name of the item (e.g., "Laptop").
   b. **price**: The price of the item (e.g., 1000).
   c. **quantity**: The quantity of the item added to the cart.
2. **Define the Cart class:** The **`Cart`** class will manage the collection of items and provide methods to:
   a. **add_item**: Add an item to the cart with a specified quantity.
   b. **remove_item**: Remove an item from the cart.
   c. **view_cart**: View the contents of the cart, along with the total price of all items.
   d. **total_cost**: Calculate and return the total cost of all items in the cart.
3. **Implement the add_item method:** The **`add_item()`** method will add an item to the cart or update its quantity if it already exists in the cart.
4. **Implement the remove_item method:** The **`remove_item()`** method will remove the specified item from the cart.
5. **Implement the view_cart method:** The **`view_cart()`** method will display all the items in the cart, their quantities, and their prices. It will also display the total cost.
6. **Implement the total_cost method:** The **`total_cost()`** method will calculate and return the total cost of all the items in the cart.

Code implementation:

```
class Item:
    def __init__(self, name, price):
        # Each item has a name, price, and initial quantity
        self.name = name
        self.price = price
        self.quantity = 1

class Cart:
    def __init__(self):
        # Initialize the cart with an empty dictionary of items
        self.items = {}

    def add_item(self, item, quantity=1):
        if not hasattr(item, "name"):
            raise TypeError("item must have a 'name' attribute")
        # Add an item to the cart, or update the quantity if it already
exists
        if item.name in self.items:
            self.items[item.name].quantity += quantity
        else:
            item.quantity = quantity
            self.items[item.name] = item

    def remove_item(self, item_name):
        # Remove an item from the cart by its name
        if item_name in self.items:
            del self.items[item_name]
        else:
            print(f"Item {item_name} not found in cart.")

    def view_cart(self):
        # Display all items in the cart, their quantities, and total
price
        if not self.items:
            print("The cart is empty.")
            return
        print("Cart:")
        for item in self.items.values():
            print(f"- {item.name}: {item.quantity} @ ${item.price}
each")
        print(f"Total cost: ${self.total_cost()}")

    def total_cost(self):
        # Calculate and return the total cost of all items in the cart
```

```
        total = 0
        for item in self.items.values():
            total += item.price * item.quantity
        return total
```

The step-by-step explanation is as follows:

1. **Item class:** The **`Item`** class represents each product in the cart. It stores the name, price, and quantity of the product.

   ```
   item1 = Item("Laptop", 1000)  # Creates a laptop item with price 1000
   item2 = Item("Headphones", 100)  # Creates headphones item with price 100
   ```

2. **Cart class:** The **`Cart`** class manages the items. It uses a dictionary (**`self.items`**) to store the items, where the keys are the item names, and the values are the item objects.

3. **Add item:** The **`add_item()`** method adds the item to the cart or updates the quantity if the item already exists.

   ```
   cart.add_item(item1, 2)  # Adds 2 laptops to the cart
   cart.add_item(item2, 1)  # Adds 1 pair of headphones to the cart
   ```

4. **Remove item**: The **`remove_item()`** method removes the item from the cart by its name. If the item does not exist in the cart, it prints an error message.

   ```
   cart.remove_item("Laptop")  # Removes the laptop from the cart
   ```

5. **View cart:** The **`view_cart()`** method displays all the items in the cart, their quantities, prices, and the total cost.

   ```
   cart.view_cart()  # Displays the cart contents and the total cost
   ```

6. **Total cost:** The **`total_cost()`** method calculates and returns the total cost of all the items in the cart.

   ```
   total = cart.total_cost()  # Returns the total cost of items in the cart
   ```

Dig deeper

The edge cases to consider are as follows:

- **Empty cart:** The **`view_cart()`** and **`total_cost()`** methods should handle cases where the cart is empty. Ensure the cart displays a message like *The cart is empty* when no items are added.

- **Multiple items of the same type:** If a user adds the same item multiple times (e.g., two laptops), the cart should correctly update the quantity instead of adding duplicate entries.

- **Removing non-existent items:** If a user tries to remove an item that is not in the cart, the system should handle this gracefully and print an appropriate message.

The time and space complexity are explained as follows:

- **Time complexity:**
  - **add_item() – O(1):** Adding or updating an item in the cart is a constant-time operation due to the use of a dictionary.
  - **remove_item() – O(1):** Removing an item from the cart is a constant-time operation.
  - **view_cart() – O(n):** The time complexity is proportional to the number of items in the cart.
  - **total_cost() – O(n):** The time complexity is proportional to the number of items in the cart.
- **Space complexity:**
  - **O(n):** The space complexity grows linearly with the number of items in the cart.

How to approach this problem in an interview:

- **Explain the structure:** Start by describing the **`Item`** and **`Cart`** classes. Explain how the cart uses a dictionary to store items, making it easy to add, remove, and update items.
- **Walk through each method:** Walk the interviewer through the **`add_item()`**, **`remove_item()`**, and **`view_cart()`** methods. Show how they allow users to manage the cart's contents.
- **Handle edge cases:** Be sure to mention how you handle cases like an empty cart or removing an item that is not in the cart.
- **Discuss time complexity:** Explain that because of the dictionary, adding, removing, and updating items is *O(1)*, making the system efficient even with many items in the cart.

The key takeaways for interviews are as follows:

- **Efficiency with dictionaries**: Using a dictionary ensures that adding, removing, and updating items is done in constant time.
- **Real-world use case**: Shopping cart systems are critical in real-world applications like e-commerce platforms, making this problem relevant to many industries.
- **Handling quantities**: Be sure to handle scenarios where multiple quantities of the same item are added to the cart.

Possible follow-up questions

How would you handle discounts or promotions?

You could modify the **`total_cost()`** method to check for discount codes or apply promotions based on the items in the cart.

How would you store the cart in a database?

You could serialize the cart data (items, quantities, etc.) into a format like JSON and store it in a database, retrieving it when the user returns.

Problem 22: Implement a binary tree with traversal methods

Problem statement: In this problem, you need to design a **binary tree** and implement the three primary tree traversal methods:

- **In-order traversal**: Traverse the left subtree, visit the root, and then traverse the right subtree.
- **Pre-order traversal**: Visit the root first, then traverse the left and right subtrees.
- **Post-order traversal**: Traverse the left and right subtrees first, and then visit the root.

Your task is to create a `BinaryTree` class that can:

1. Insert nodes into the binary tree.
2. Perform in-order traversal.
3. Perform pre-order traversal.
4. Perform post-order traversal.

For example:

- **Input**:
```
tree = BinaryTree(1)
tree.insert(2)
tree.insert(3)
tree.insert(4)
tree.insert(5)
```
- **Traversals**:
    - **In-order**: 4 -> 2 -> 5 -> 1 -> 3
    - **Pre-order**: 1 -> 2 -> 4 -> 5 -> 3
    - **Post-order**: 4 -> 5 -> 2 -> 3 -> 1

Understanding the problem: A **binary tree** is a hierarchical data structure where each node has at most two children: a left child and a right child. Traversing a binary tree means visiting all its nodes in a specific order. In this problem, we will focus on three common traversal methods: **in-order**, **pre-order**, and **post-order**.

The step-by-step solution is as follows:

1. **Define the node class**: Each node in the binary tree will contain:
   a. **Data**: The actual value of the node.
   b. **Left**: A pointer to the left child.
   c. **Right**: A pointer to the right child.
2. **Define the BinaryTree class:** The `BinaryTree` class will manage the nodes and traversal methods. It will provide the following:
   a. **Insertion**: Add new nodes to the tree.
   b. **In-order traversal**: Traverse the left subtree, visit the root, and then traverse the right subtree.
   c. **Pre-order traversal**: Visit the root first, then traverse the left and right subtrees.
   d. **Post-order traversal**: Traverse the left and right subtrees, and then visit the root.
3. **Implement the insert method:** The `insert()` method will add nodes to the binary tree in a level-order fashion (like filling out a tree row by row).
4. **Implement the traversal methods:** We will implement the three traversal methods:
   a. **In-order traversal**: Left -> Root -> Right.
   b. **Pre-order traversal**: Root -> Left -> Right.
   c. **Post-order traversal**: Left -> Right -> Root.

Code implementation:

```
class Node:
    def __init__(self, data):
        # Each node has data and pointers to its left and right children
        self.data = data
        self.left = None
        self.right = None

class BinaryTree:
    def __init__(self, root):
        # Initialize the binary tree with a root node
        self.root = Node(root)

    def insert(self, data):
        # Insert data into the binary tree (level-order insertion)
        queue = [self.root]
        while queue:
            current = queue.pop(0)
```

```
            if not current.left:
                current.left = Node(data)
                return
            else:
                queue.append(current.left)
            if not current.right:
                current.right = Node(data)
                return
            else:
                queue.append(current.right)

    def inorder_traversal(self, node, result):
        # Perform in-order traversal (Left, Root, Right)
        if node:
            self.inorder_traversal(node.left, result)
            result.append(node.data)
            self.inorder_traversal(node.right, result)

    def preorder_traversal(self, node, result):
        # Perform pre-order traversal (Root, Left, Right)
        if node:
            result.append(node.data)
            self.preorder_traversal(node.left, result)
            self.preorder_traversal(node.right, result)

    def postorder_traversal(self, node, result):
        # Perform post-order traversal (Left, Right, Root)
        if node:
            self.postorder_traversal(node.left, result)
            self.postorder_traversal(node.right, result)
            result.append(node.data)

    def print_traversal(self):
        # Print the results of all three traversals
        inorder_result = []
        preorder_result = []
        postorder_result = []

        self.inorder_traversal(self.root, inorder_result)
        self.preorder_traversal(self.root, preorder_result)
        self.postorder_traversal(self.root, postorder_result)

        print(f"In-order Traversal: {' -> '.join(map(str, inorder_
result))}")
```

```
        print(f"Pre-order Traversal: {' -> '.join(map(str, preorder_
result))}")
        print(f"Post-order Traversal: {' -> '.join(map(str, postorder_
result))}")
```

The step-by-step explanation is as follows:

1. **Node class:** The **`Node`** class represents each node in the binary tree. Each node stores data and references to its left and right children.

2. **BinaryTree class:** The **`BinaryTree`** class manages the nodes and provides methods to insert nodes and perform different tree traversals.

3. **Insert method:** The **`insert()`** method adds new nodes in a **level-order** manner (i.e., filling each level of the tree from left to right). This is accomplished using a queue, which ensures that we always process nodes level by level.

4. **Traversal methods:**

    a. **In-order traversal**: The **`inorder_traversal()`** method visits the left subtree first, then the root, and finally the right subtree.

    b. **Pre-order traversal**: The **`preorder_traversal()`** method visits the root first, then the left subtree, and finally the right subtree.

    c. **Post-order traversal**: The **`postorder_traversal()`** method visits the left subtree first, then the right subtree, and finally the root.

5. **Print traversal:** The **`print_traversal()`** method performs all three types of traversal and prints the results.

Example execution:

```
# Create a binary tree with root value 1
tree = BinaryTree(1)

# Insert values into the tree
tree.insert(2)
tree.insert(3)
tree.insert(4)
tree.insert(5)

# Print the results of all three traversals
tree.print_traversal()
```

Output:

```
In-order Traversal: 4 -> 2 -> 5 -> 1 -> 3
Pre-order Traversal: 1 -> 2 -> 4 -> 5 -> 3
Post-order Traversal: 4 -> 5 -> 2 -> 3 -> 1
```

Dig deeper

The edge cases to consider are as follows:

- **Empty tree:** All traversal methods should return an empty list if the tree is empty (i.e., the root is None).
- **Single node tree:** If the tree consists of only one node (the root), all traversal methods should return the root's value.
- **Unbalanced trees:** The traversal methods should work efficiently even for unbalanced trees where one subtree is significantly larger than the other.

The time and space complexity are explained as follows:

- **Time complexity**: The time complexity of all traversal methods (in-order, pre-order, post-order) is *O(n)*, where n is the number of nodes in the binary tree. Each node is visited once.
- **Space complexity:** The space complexity is *O(h)*, where h is the height of the tree. This is the maximum depth of the recursion stack for tree traversal. In the worst case (for an unbalanced tree), this could be *O(n)*.

How to approach this problem in an interview:

- **Start by explaining the binary tree structure:** Begin by describing what a binary tree is and how it is structured. Explain the significance of left and right children for each node.
- **Discuss the traversal methods:** Explain the difference between in-order, pre-order, and post-order traversal. Illustrate how each method processes the tree differently.
- **Talk about efficiency:** Mention that each traversal method has a time complexity of O(n) because each node is visited exactly once. Also, discuss the space complexity, emphasizing the depth of recursion.
- **Consider edge cases:** Talk about edge cases such as empty trees or trees with a single node. Explain how your solution handles these cases.

The key takeaways for interviews are as follows:

- **Binary tree traversals**: Understanding how to traverse a binary tree is crucial for many tree-related problems. In-order, pre-order, and post-order are the most common traversal methods.
- **Recursion in trees**: Tree traversal is often implemented recursively, and understanding the recursive nature of trees is essential for interview questions on data structures.
- **Efficiency**: Be sure to explain the time and space complexity of the traversal methods and how they are affected by the tree's structure.

Possible follow-up questions

What is the difference between depth-first search (DFS) and breadth-first search (BFS) in trees?

DFS explores as far as possible along a branch before backtracking (which is what in-order, pre-order, and post-order do), while BFS explores all the nodes at the present depth before moving on to nodes at the next depth level.

How would you implement a binary tree using an iterative approach rather than recursion?

To implement tree traversals iteratively, you would use a stack (for DFS) or a queue (for BFS).

Problem 23: Design a class for a tic-tac-toe game

Problem statement: You are tasked with designing a *Tic-Tac-Toe* game where two players can play on a 3x3 grid. Implement a Python class that allows:

- Two players to take turns placing their marks ('X' or 'O') on the grid.
- Checking for a winner after each move.
- Detecting when the game ends in a draw.

The game should include the following functionality:

1. **TicTacToe class:**
    a. **make_move(row, col, player):** Allows a player to make a move on the board.
    b. **check_winner():** Checks if there is a winner after each move.
    c. **is_draw():** Checks if the game ends in a draw.
    d. **print_board():** Displays the current game board.

For example:

- **Input**:

```
game = TicTacToe()
game.make_move(0, 0, 'X')
game.make_move(1, 1, 'O')
game.make_move(0, 1, 'X')
game.make_move(2, 1, 'O')
game.make_move(0, 2, 'X')  # 'X' wins
game.print_board()
```

- **Output:**
```
X | X | X
---------
  | O |
---------
  | O |

X wins!
```

Understanding the problem: Tic-Tac-Toe is a two-player game where players take turns placing their mark (either 'X' or 'O') on a 3x3 grid. The first player to get three of their marks in a row (horizontally, vertically, or diagonally) wins. If all the squares are filled and no one has three in a row, the game ends in a draw.

We will design a TicTacToe class that handles:

- **Making moves**: Players can make a move by specifying a row and column on the grid.
- **Checking for a winner**: After each move, we will check whether the current player has won.
- **Detecting a draw**: If all squares are filled and no one has won, the game ends in a draw.

The step-by-step solution is as follows:

1. **Define the TicTacToe class**: The `TicTacToe` class will manage the game board, handle player moves, and check for a winner or draw after each move.
2. **Define the board:** The board will be represented as a 3x3 grid, where each cell can be empty, marked with 'X', or marked with 'O'. We will use a 2D list to store the board's state.
3. **Implement the make_move() method:** The `make_move()` method will allow a player to place their mark on the board. It will also check if the move is valid (i.e., the square is not already taken).
4. **Implement the check_winner() method:** The `check_winner()` method will check if the current player has won the game by examining the rows, columns, and diagonals.
5. **Implement the is_draw() method:** The `is_draw()` method will check if all squares are filled and no player has won.
6. **Implement the print_board() method:** The `print_board()` method will display the current state of the board in a readable format.

   Code implementation:
```
class TicTacToe:
    def __init__(self):
```

```
        # Initialize an empty 3x3 board
        self.board = [[' ' for _ in range(3)] for _ in range(3)]
        self.current_winner = None

    def print_board(self):
        # Print the current game board
        for row in self.board:
            print(' | '.join(row))
            print('-' * 9)

    def make_move(self, row, col, player):
        # Make a move if the chosen cell is empty
        if self.board[row][col] == ' ':
            self.board[row][col] = player
            # Check if this move wins the game
            if self.check_winner(row, col, player):
                self.current_winner = player
            return True
        else:
            print("This move is not valid. Try again.")
            return False

    def check_winner(self, row, col, player):
        # Check the row
        if all([self.board[row][i] == player for i in range(3)]):
            return True
        # Check the column
        if all([self.board[i][col] == player for i in range(3)]):
            return True
        # Check the diagonals
        if row == col and all([self.board[i][i] == player for i in 
range(3)]):
            return True
        if row + col == 2 and all([self.board[i][2 - i] == player for i 
in range(3)]):
            return True
        return False

    def is_draw(self):
        # Check if the game is a draw (all cells are filled and no 
winner)
        return all([self.board[row][col] != ' ' for row in range(3) for 
col in range(3)]) and self.current_winner is None
```

The step-by-step explanation is as follows:

1. **TicTacToe class:** The **`TicTacToe`** class manages the game board, tracks the winner, and provides methods for making moves, checking for a winner, and checking for a draw.
2. **Print board:** The **`print_board()`** method displays the current state of the board. It prints the board in a grid format, showing 'X', 'O', or empty spaces.
3. **Make move:** The **`make_move()`** method allows a player to place their mark ('X' or 'O') on the board. If the move is valid (i.e., the square is empty), the mark is placed, and the method checks whether the move results in a win.
4. **Check winner:** The **`check_winner()`** method checks whether the current move completes a winning row, column, or diagonal. If the player has three marks in a row, column, or diagonal, the player wins.
5. **Check for draw:** The **`is_draw()`** method checks if the board is full and no player has won, indicating a draw.

Example execution:

```
game = TicTacToe()
# Player 'X' makes the first move at (0, 0)
game.make_move(0, 0, 'X')

# Player 'O' makes a move at (1, 1)
game.make_move(1, 1, 'O')

# Player 'X' makes a move at (0, 1)
game.make_move(0, 1, 'X')

# Player 'O' makes a move at (2, 1)
game.make_move(2, 1, 'O')

# Player 'X' makes a move at (0, 2), completing a row and winning the game
game.make_move(0, 2, 'X')

# Print the final board and announce the winner
game.print_board()
if game.current_winner:
    print(f"Player {game.current_winner} wins!")
elif game.is_draw():
    print("The game is a draw!")
```

Output:

```
X | X | X
---------
  | O |
```

```
---------
  | O |
Player X wins!
```

Dig deeper

The edge cases to consider are as follows:

- **Invalid move:** The `make_move()` method should handle cases where a player tries to place a mark on a cell that is already occupied. In such cases, the move should be rejected.
- **Draw condition:** The `is_draw()` method should ensure that the game correctly detects a draw when all cells are filled and there is no winner.

The time and space complexity are explained as follows:

- **Time complexity:**
  - **make_move()**: *O(1)*, since we are updating a specific cell on the board.
  - **check_winner()**: *O(1)*, since we only check one row, one column, and at most two diagonals.
  - **is_draw()**: *O(n^2)*, where n is the size of the board (in this case, 3), as we need to check all cells to see if the game is a draw.
- **Space complexity:** *O(n^2)*, where n is the size of the board. The board occupies space proportional to its size.

How to approach this problem in an interview:

- **Start by explaining the game:** Begin by describing the basic rules of Tic-Tac-Toe. Talk about how players take turns and what constitutes a win or a draw.
- **Walk through the class design:** Explain how the TicTacToe class works. Focus on how the board is represented and how moves are made and checked.
- **Check for edge cases:** Mention how you handle cases like invalid moves (attempting to place a mark on an occupied cell) and detecting a draw.
- **Discuss time complexity:** Explain that most operations (making moves and checking for a winner) are *O(1)*, making the game highly efficient.

The key takeaways for interviews are as follows:

- **Class design**: This problem is a great example of object-oriented design, where you encapsulate game logic in a class with clear methods.
- **Efficient checking**: The `check_winner()` method is highly efficient, only checking the relevant row, column, and diagonals for each move.

- **Handling game states**: It is essential to handle all possible game states: ongoing, won, or drawn.

Possible follow-up questions

How would you extend this to a larger grid (e.g., 5x5 or 10x10)?

You can modify the class to accept the board size as a parameter and check for the required number of consecutive marks to win.

How would you implement a multiplayer version of Tic-Tac-Toe where more than two players can play?

You could modify the `make_move()` method to cycle through multiple players (e.g., 'X', 'O', 'Y') and adjust the winner-checking logic accordingly.

Problem 24: Implement a simple cash register class

Problem statement: In this problem, you need to design a *cash register* system that will allow customers to make purchases, apply discounts, and calculate the total bill. You will implement a class `CashRegister` with the following features:

- **Add items to the cart**: Allow customers to add items to the cart with their price.
- **Apply discounts**: Optionally apply a discount to the total bill.
- **Calculate the total bill**: Calculate the total amount to be paid after discounts.
- **Display all items in the cart**: Show a summary of items purchased and the final total.

For example:

- **Input**

```
register = CashRegister()
register.add_item("apple", 1.50)
register.add_item("banana", 2.00)
register.add_item("milk", 3.50)
register.apply_discount(10)
register.display_items()
```

- **Output**:

```
Items in cart:
apple: $1.50
banana: $2.00
milk: $3.50
Discount applied: 10%
Total: $6.30
```

Understanding the problem: A *cash register* system simulates the process of ringing up items in a store, calculating the total bill, and applying discounts. We will create a **`CashRegister`** class that handles the following:

- **Adding items**: The customer can add multiple items with their prices to the cart.
- **Applying discounts**: If applicable, a discount (in percentage) will be applied to the total bill.
- **Calculating the total bill**: The system will calculate the total amount to be paid after discounts.
- **Displaying items**: The system will provide a summary of items in the cart, their prices, and the final amount to be paid.

The step-by-step solution is as follows:

1. **Define the CashRegister class:** The **`CashRegister`** class will manage the list of items, prices, and any applicable discounts.
2. **Define the add_item() method:** The **`add_item()`** method will allow a customer to add items to the cart by specifying the item name and its price. These items will be stored in a dictionary where the key is the item name and the value is the price.
3. **Define the apply_discount() method:** The **`apply_discount()`** method will apply a percentage discount to the total bill.
4. **Define the calculate_total() method:** The **`calculate_total()`** method will calculate the total bill after applying the discount.
5. **Define the display_items() method:** The **`display_items()`** method will display all the items in the cart, their prices, the applied discount (if any), and the total amount to be paid.

   Code implementation:

```
class CashRegister:
    def __init__(self):
        # Initialize an empty dictionary to store items and prices
        self.items = {}
        self.discount = 0

    def add_item(self, item_name, price):
        # Add an item to the cart
        self.items[item_name] = price

    def apply_discount(self, discount):
        # Apply a discount percentage to the total bill
        self.discount = discount
```

```
    def calculate_total(self):
        # Calculate the total amount with the discount applied
        total = sum(self.items.values())
        if self.discount > 0:
            total = total - (total * self.discount / 100)
        return total

    def display_items(self):
        # Display all items, their prices, and the total with discount
        print("Items in cart:")
        for item_name, price in self.items.items():
            print(f"{item_name}: ${price:.2f}")
        if self.discount > 0:
            print(f"Discount applied: {self.discount}%")
        total = self.calculate_total()
        print(f"Total: ${total:.2f}")
```

The step-by-step explanation is as follows:

1. **CashRegister class:** The **`CashRegister`** class is responsible for managing the items in the cart and handling discounts.
2. **add_item() method:** The **`add_item()`** method allows the user to add items to the cart. Items are stored in a dictionary, where the key is the item name and the value is the price.
3. **apply_discount() method:** The **`apply_discount()`** method applies a discount (in percentage) to the total bill. The discount is stored in an instance variable.
4. **calculate_total() method:** The **`calculate_total()`** method calculates the total amount after applying the discount. It first sums up all the item prices and then reduces the total by the discount percentage (if any).
5. **display_items() method:** The **`display_items()`** method prints the list of items in the cart, their prices, and the final total after the discount.

Example execution:

```
# Create a Cash Register instance
register = CashRegister()

# Add items to the cart
register.add_item("apple", 1.50)
register.add_item("banana", 2.00)
register.add_item("milk", 3.50)

# Apply a 10% discount
register.apply_discount(10)
```

```
# Display the items and total
register.display_items()
```

Output:

```
Items in cart:
apple: $1.50
banana: $2.00
milk: $3.50
Discount applied: 10%
Total: $6.30
```

Dig deeper

The edge cases to consider are as follows:

- **Empty cart:** If the cart is empty and **display_items()** is called, the method should handle this gracefully and print a message like "No items in cart."
- **Discount of 0%:** If no discount is applied (0%), the total should remain unchanged, and no discount message should be printed.
- **Multiple items with the same name:** If the same item is added twice with different prices, the latest price should overwrite the previous one (based on the dictionary implementation). If you want to handle multiple quantities, you can extend the class to store both quantity and price.

The time and space complexity

- **Time complexity:**
  - **add_item()**: *O(1)*, as adding an item to the dictionary takes constant time.
  - **apply_discount()**: *O(1)*, since it only updates a variable.
  - **calculate_total()**: *O(n)*, where n is the number of items in the cart, as we need to sum all the prices.
  - **display_items()**: *O(n)*, as it iterates through all the items in the cart.
- **Space complexity:** *O(n)*, where n is the number of items in the cart, since we store each item and its price in the dictionary.

How to approach this problem in an interview:

- **Start by explaining the problem:** Begin by describing the basic functionality of a cash register. Talk about how items are added to the cart, discounts are applied, and the total is calculated.

- **Walk through the class design:** Explain how the **CashRegister** class is structured. Mention the importance of methods like **add_item()**, **apply_discount()**, and **calculate_total()**.
- **Discuss edge cases:** Talk about how you handle edge cases such as an empty cart or a discount of 0%.
- **Mention time complexity:** Be sure to discuss the time complexity of adding items, applying discounts, and calculating the total bill.

The key takeaways for interviews are as follows:

- **Object-oriented design**: This problem demonstrates your ability to design a class with clear functionality, including adding items, applying discounts, and calculating totals.
- **Handling edge cases**: It is important to discuss how your code handles cases like an empty cart or a 0% discount.
- **Efficient calculation**: You should explain that calculating the total bill and applying discounts is done efficiently, even as the number of items in the cart grows.

Possible follow-up questions

How would you extend this to handle item quantities?

You could modify the **add_item()** method to accept a quantity parameter and store both the item price and quantity in the dictionary.

How would you handle different types of discounts (e.g., fixed amount discounts or buy-one-get-one-free promotions)?

You could extend the class to support different types of discount methods. For example, you could have a **apply_fixed_discount()** method or handle promotions through conditional logic in the **calculate_total()** method.

Join our Discord space

Join our Discord workspace for latest updates, offers, tech happenings around the world, new releases, and sessions with the authors:

https://discord.bpbonline.com

SECTION 3

Data Structures Arrays and Strings

Introduction

Welcome to the world of **data structures**, where arrays and strings reign supreme! This section will look into how we store, manipulate, and analyze data collections, focusing on two of the most common structures in programming: **arrays** and **strings**. These two data structures form the foundation of countless algorithms and play a vital role in solving complex coding problems, especially in technical interviews at top companies like *Google*, *Amazon*, and *Facebook*.

Think of arrays as collections of items, similar to rows of neatly arranged books on a shelf. Each book (or item) has a specific place, and you can quickly find any book if you know its position. Similarly, strings are arrays of characters, like beads on a string, where each bead (or character) has a fixed order. Manipulating these structures efficiently is crucial in solving many real-world problems, from optimizing search algorithms to analyzing large datasets.

However, what makes this section truly exciting is the *challenges* you will face. These are not just about mastering syntax but about honing your problem-solving skills. The problems you will encounter in this section are designed to stretch your mind, encouraging you to think creatively about breaking down complex issues and building efficient solutions.

Why arrays and strings matter in interviews: When preparing for technical interviews, it is essential to understand why arrays and strings are so frequently used in interview questions. These data structures are incredibly versatile and can represent various real-world scenarios, from tracking users on a website to managing data in a database.

Top tech companies use array and string challenges to test how well candidates can:

- **Think logically**: Arrays and strings often require breaking problems into smaller steps.
- **Manipulate data**: Many software applications require efficient data sorting, searching, and transformation.
- **Handle edge cases**: Many problems with arrays and strings involve considering unusual or extreme cases, such as empty arrays, very large inputs, or cases where the data is not as expected.

By mastering arrays and strings, you will develop a keen understanding of the underlying principles that power much of programming.

Objectives

In this section, you will tackle *16 real-world coding challenges* frequently asked in technical interviews. Each challenge will build upon the last, gradually increasing complexity as you explore how arrays and strings can be manipulated to solve complex problems.

- **Array manipulation**: You will begin by learning how to find specific elements in arrays, like in the famous *Two Sum problem*. From there, you will explore more advanced operations like rotating arrays, removing duplicates, and handling edge cases with missing or duplicate elements.
- **String operations**: Strings are more than just sequences of characters. You will learn how to manipulate them to find the *longest palindromic substring*, reverse words, and search for common prefixes among a group of strings. These operations are foundational for text processing, web development, and search algorithms.
- **Efficiency**: Beyond solving problems, this section will teach you how *to optimize your solutions*. Many of the problems you will face can be solved in more than one way, and you will learn how to choose the most efficient solution by analyzing time and space complexity.

The challenges ahead are:

- **Two sum problem**: Start by solving this classic array problem, where you will need to find two numbers in an array that add up to a target sum. This challenge tests your ability to quickly find a solution using simple data structures like arrays and hash maps.
- **Longest palindromic substring**: In this problem, you will work with strings to find the longest sequence of characters that reads the same forward and backward. It is a great exercise in thinking about manipulating and searching within a string.
- **Kadane's algorithm**: This famous algorithm helps you find the *maximum subarray* in a given array. It is a perfect example of how a seemingly complex problem can be broken down into a simple, efficient solution using dynamic programming principles.

- **Product of array except self**: This problem asks you to find the product of all elements in an array except the current element without using division. It tests how well you can manipulate arrays and handle edge cases, like zeros in the input array.
- **Trapping rainwater problem**: One of the more advanced challenges in this section is that this problem asks you to calculate how much rainwater can be trapped between buildings of varying heights. It requires you to think creatively about using arrays and pointers to solve the problem efficiently.

How to approach this section: This section is designed to help you *build your problem-solving muscles*. Each challenge will push you to think critically about the data structures you are using and how best to manipulate them. As you progress through the challenges, keep these tips in mind:

- **Break the problem down**: Before jumping into the code, take the time to understand the problem entirely. What is the input? What is the desired output? Are there any edge cases you need to consider?
- **Think about efficiency**: Once you have solved the problem, ask yourself if there is a faster or more efficient way. Can you reduce the time complexity from $O(n^2)$ to $O(n)$? Can you minimize the space complexity?
- **Practice, practice, practice**: The more problems you solve, the better you will recognize patterns and choose the right tools. The problems in this section are not just about learning arrays and strings; they are about becoming a more confident, efficient problem-solver.

Key takeaways for interviews: In interviews, you will often encounter array and string problems that are deceptively simple at first glance. These problems test how well you can think critically, solve efficiently, and handle unexpected inputs. By the end of this section, you will have a solid understanding of how to tackle these problems head-on, giving you a significant advantage in your technical interviews.

Are you ready to level up your data structure skills? Let us look at the first challenge, the *Two Sum* problem, and see how to master arrays and strings in Python.

Problem 25: Two sum

Problem statement: Given an array of integers **`nums`** and an integer **`target`**, return the *indices* of the two numbers such that they add up to the target. You may assume that each input would have *exactly one solution*, and you may not use the same element twice.

For example:

- **Input**:

```
nums = [2, 7, 11, 15]
target = 9
```

- **Output**:

  `[0, 1]`

- **Explanation**: The numbers at indices 0 and 1 (2 + 7) add up to the target of 9.

Understanding the problem: The *Two Sum problem* is a classic coding challenge that tests your ability to work with arrays and hash maps. The goal is to identify two numbers in an array that sum up to a given target value and return their indices. The problem might seem straightforward at first, but achieving an efficient solution requires careful thought.

The step-by-step solution is as follows:

1. **Brute-force approach:** The most basic solution would be to use *two nested loops* to check each pair of numbers and see if they add up to the target. While this approach works, it has a time complexity of $O(n^2)$, which can be inefficient for large arrays.

   a. **Brute-force code example:**

   ```
   def two_sum(nums, target):
       # Check each pair of numbers
       for i in range(len(nums)):
           for j in range(i + 1, len(nums)):
               if nums[i] + nums[j] == target:
                   return [i, j]
   ```

   b. **Time complexity**: $O(n^2)$, since you have to check every possible pair.

   c. **Space complexity**: $O(1)$, since you are not using any additional data structures.

   While the brute-force approach is easy to implement, it is not the most efficient solution. In an interview, it is important to demonstrate that you can come up with better solutions.

2. **Optimized approach using a hash map:** A more efficient way to solve the problem is to use a **hash map**. The hash map allows us to store the numbers we have already seen as we iterate through the array. For each number, we check if the *complement* (the number needed to reach the target) is in the hash map. If it is, we return the indices.

   a. **Optimized code example:**

   ```
   def two_sum(nums, target):
       # Dictionary to store number and its index
       seen = {}

       for i, num in enumerate(nums):
           # Calculate complement
           complement = target - num

           # Check if complement exists in the dictionary
   ```

```
        if complement in seen:
            return [seen[complement], i]

        # Store the number and its index in the dictionary
        seen[num] = i
```

   b. **Time complexity**: *O(n)*, as we only iterate through the array once.

   c. **Space complexity**: *O(n)*, since we store elements in the hash map.

This solution is much more efficient, reducing the time complexity to *O(n)*. It also demonstrates a deeper understanding of algorithm design, which is crucial in coding interviews.

The step-by-step explanation is as follows:

1. **Create a hash map (dictionary):** We use a dictionary called seen to store the numbers we have already encountered, with the number as the key and its index as the value.

2. **Iterate through the array:** For each number in the array, we calculate its complement (the value that would add up to the target). We check if the complement is already in the dictionary.

3. **Check for the complement:** If the complement is found in the dictionary, we have found the two numbers that add up to the target, so we return their indices.

4. **Store the number and its index:** If the complement is not in the dictionary, we store the current number and its index in the dictionary for future reference.

Example execution: Let us walk through an example:

```
nums = [2, 7, 11, 15]
target = 9
```

The steps are:

1. **(i = 0, num = 2):**
   a. Complement = 9 - 2 = 7.
   b. Is 7 in seen? No.
   c. Add 2 to seen → seen = {2: 0}.
2. **(i = 1, num = 7):**
   a. Complement = 9 - 7 = 2.
   b. Is 2 in seen? Yes!
   c. Return [0, 1].

The solution finds that **`nums[0] + nums[1]`** equals the target (2 + 7 = 9), so it returns [0, 1].

Dig deeper

The edge cases to consider are as follows:

- **Negative numbers:** The solution works for negative numbers as well. For example, if the array contains negative integers, the hash map approach will still find the two numbers that sum up to the target.

- **Repeated elements:** If the array contains repeated elements, the hash map approach will still work because we only store the index of the first occurrence of each number. If the complement is found, we return the indices.

- **Single element or empty array:** If the input array is too short to contain a valid pair, the function should handle it gracefully (for example, by returning None or an error message).

The time and space complexity are explained as follows:

- **Time complexity**: $O(n)$, where n is the number of elements in the array. We only need to iterate through the array once, and hash map lookups take constant time.
- **Space complexity**: $O(n)$, since we store up to n elements in the hash map.

How to approach this problem in an interview:

- **Explain the problem:** Start by clearly explaining the problem and your understanding of the task. Mention that you need to return the indices of two numbers that sum up to a given target.

- **Discuss the brute-force approach:** Briefly describe the brute-force solution using two nested loops. Acknowledge that while it works, it is inefficient, with a time complexity of $O(n^2)$.

- **Introduce the hash map approach:** Next, introduce the more efficient solution using a hash map. Explain how the hash map allows you to store numbers and look up their complements in constant time.

- **Edge cases:** Discuss how the solution handles different edge cases, such as negative numbers, repeated elements, and arrays with only one or zero elements.

- **Mention time and space complexity:** Conclude by analyzing the time and space complexity of the solution.

The key takeaways for interviews are as follows:

- **Efficient use of hash maps**: This problem demonstrates your ability to use hash maps to solve problems efficiently.

- **Time and space optimization**: You can solve this problem in $O(n)$ time by carefully using a dictionary to store and look up values.

- **Handling edge cases:** This solution handles different input scenarios, including arrays with negative numbers and repeated elements.

Possible follow-up questions

What if the input array is sorted? How would you optimize the solution in that case?

If the array is sorted, you could use the *two-pointer technique* to solve the problem in $O(n)$ time without needing extra space. This involves starting with two pointers, one at the beginning and one at the end, and moving them inward based on the sum.

What if there are multiple pairs that sum up to the target?

You could modify the solution to return all pairs that sum up to the target, not just the first one found.

Problem 26: Find the longest palindromic substring

Problem statement: Given a string **s**, find the longest palindromic substring in **s**. A palindrome is a string that reads the same forward and backward.

For example:

- **Input:**
  `s = "babad"`
- **Output:**
  `"bab"`

Note: **"aba" is also a valid answer.**

Another example:

- **Input:**
  `s = "cbbd"`
- **Output:**
  `"bb"`

Understanding the problem: A **palindrome** is a string that reads the same forward and backward. For example, "racecar" is a palindrome, while "hello" is not. In this problem, you need to find the *longest palindromic substring* within a given string.

This is an interesting problem because it requires you to look for specific patterns within a string. It is frequently asked in interviews to test your understanding of string manipulation and dynamic programming concepts.

The step-by-step solution is as follows:

1. **Brute-force approach:** The simplest solution is to check every possible substring and determine if it is a palindrome. This involves generating all possible substrings and checking if each is a palindrome.

   a. **Brute-force code example:**

```
def longest_palindrome(s):
    def is_palindrome(substring):
        return substring == substring[::-1]

    n = len(s)
    longest = ""

    for i in range(n):
        for j in range(i, n):
            if is_palindrome(s[i:j + 1]) and len(s[i:j + 1]) >
len(longest):
                longest = s[i:j + 1]

    return longest
```

   b. **Time complexity**: $O(n^3)$, where n is the length of the string. We check every substring, and each check takes $O(n)$ time.

   c. **Space complexity**: $O(1)$, since we only store the longest palindrome.

   While the brute-force solution works, it is too slow for large strings.

2. **Optimized approach, expand around center:** A more efficient way to solve this problem is to *expand around the center* of potential palindromes. The idea is that a palindrome mirrors around its center. For each character in the string, we can consider it as the center and expand outward to check for palindromes.

   There are two types of palindromes:

   a. **Odd-length palindromes**, where the center is a single character.

   b. **Even-length palindromes**, where the center is between two characters.

   c. **Optimized code example**:

```
def longest_palindrome(s):
    def expand_around_center(left, right):
        while left >= 0 and right < len(s) and s[left] ==
s[right]:
            left -= 1
            right += 1
        return s[left + 1:right]
```

```
    if len(s) == 0:
        return ""

    longest = ""

    for i in range(len(s)):
        # Check for odd-length palindromes
        palindrome_odd = expand_around_center(i, i)
        if len(palindrome_odd) > len(longest):
            longest = palindrome_odd

        # Check for even-length palindromes
        palindrome_even = expand_around_center(i, i + 1)
        if len(palindrome_even) > len(longest):
            longest = palindrome_even

    return longest
```

d. **Time complexity**: $O(n^2)$, where n is the length of the string. We expand around each character, which takes linear time.

e. **Space complexity**: $O(1)$, since we only store the current longest palindrome.

This approach improves the time complexity to $O(n^2)$, which is much better than the brute-force $O(n^3)$ solution.

The step-by-step explanation is as follows:

1. **Expand around the center:** The key idea here is that every palindrome mirrors around its center. For each character (and every pair of adjacent characters for even-length palindromes), you expand outward as long as the characters on both sides are equal. The moment they differ, you stop and check the length of the palindrome found.

2. **Odd vs. even palindromes:** You need to handle both *odd-length* and *even-length* palindromes. For example, in the string "babad", "aba" is an odd-length palindrome, while in the string "cbbd", "bb" is an even-length palindrome.

3. **Edge case (empty string):** If the input string is empty, simply return an empty string.

   a. **Example execution**: Let us walk through an example:

   ```
   s = "babad"
   ```

   b. The code steps are as follows:

      i. **(i = 0, center = "b"):**

         - **Odd-length palindrome**: Expand around center at index 0. The palindrome is "b".
         - **Even-length palindrome**: No even-length palindrome at this center.

ii. **(i = 1, center = "a"):**

- **Odd-length palindrome**: Expand around center at index 1. The palindrome is "aba".
- **Even-length palindrome**: No even-length palindrome at this center.

iii. **(i = 2, center = "b"):**

- **Odd-length palindrome**: Expand around the center at index 2. The palindrome is "bab".
- **Even-length palindrome**: No even-length palindrome at this center.

iv. **(i = 3, center = "a"):**

- **Odd-length palindrome**: Expand around center at index 3. The palindrome is "a".
- **Even-length palindrome**: No even-length palindrome at this center.

v. **(i = 4, center = "d"):**

- **Odd-length palindrome**: Expand around center at index 4. The palindrome is "d".
- **Even-length palindrome**: No even-length palindrome at this center.

The longest palindrome found is "bab", but "aba" is also valid.

Dig deeper

The edge cases to consider are as follows:

- **Single character:** If the input string contains only one character, it is already a palindrome. The function should return that character.
- **All characters are the same:** If the input string contains repeated characters like "aaaa", the entire string is a palindrome, and the function should return it.
- **No palindrome longer than 1:** If there is no palindrome longer than one character (e.g., "abc"), the function should return any one of the single characters.

The time and space complexity are explained as follows:

- **Time complexity**: $O(n^2)$, where n is the length of the string. We perform an $O(n)$ operation (expanding around the center) for each character in the string, leading to $O(n^2)$ total operations.
- **Space complexity**: $O(1)$, since we are only storing the longest palindrome and the pointers for expansion.

How to approach this problem in an interview:

- **Explain the problem:** Start by explaining what a palindrome is and your goal of finding the longest palindromic substring in a given string.
- **Discuss the brute-force approach:** Briefly describe the brute-force approach of checking every possible substring, and mention that it has a time complexity of $O(n^3)$, which is inefficient for large inputs.
- **Introduce the expand around center approach:** Explain how this method improves the time complexity to $O(n^2)$ by expanding around potential palindrome centers.
- **Edge cases:** Talk about how your solution handles edge cases, such as single-character strings, all identical characters, and cases where there is no palindrome longer than one character.
- **Time and space complexity:** Conclude by discussing the time and space complexity of your solution.

The key takeaways for interviews are as follows:

- **Efficiency**: This problem demonstrates your ability to optimize a brute-force solution using the expand-around-center approach.
- **Understanding strings**: You will showcase your understanding of string manipulation, which is a crucial skill for coding interviews.
- **Edge case handling**: You will be able to discuss how to handle common edge cases like single characters or repeated characters.

Possible follow-up questions

Can you find the longest palindromic substring using dynamic programming?

Yes, a dynamic programming approach can also solve this problem in $O(n^2)$ time, but it uses $O(n^2)$ space. You can use a table to store whether each substring is a palindrome and expand the table iteratively.

How would you modify the solution if you needed to find all palindromic substrings, not just the longest one?

You could expand around every center and store all the palindromes' substrings in a list.

Problem 27: Find the maximum subarray

Problem statement: Given an integer array `nums`, find the contiguous subarray (containing at least one number) that has the largest sum and return its sum.

For example:

- **Input**:

  `nums = [-2,1,-3,4,-1,2,1,-5,4]`
- **Output**:

  `6`
- **Explanation**: The subarray [4,-1,2,1] has the largest sum = 6.

Another example:

- **Input**:

  `nums = [1]`
- **Output**:

  `1`

Understanding the problem: This problem is known as the **Maximum Subarray** problem. The goal is to find the subarray (a contiguous portion of an array) with the largest sum. This problem can be solved efficiently using **Kadane's** algorithm, which is one of the most famous dynamic programming algorithms for array manipulation.

The brute-force approach would involve checking every possible subarray and calculating its sum, but that is inefficient. Kadane's algorithm, on the other hand, offers an elegant solution in $O(n)$ time, which makes it an essential technique to know, especially for coding interviews.

The step-by-step solution is as follows:

1. **Brute-force approach:** In the brute-force solution, we iterate over all possible subarrays, calculate their sum, and keep track of the largest sum encountered. While this method works, it has a time complexity of $O(n^2)$, making it impractical for large arrays.

   a. **Brute-force code example:**

   ```
   def max_subarray(nums):
    if not nums:
           return 0
       max_sum = float('-inf')

       for i in range(len(nums)):
           current_sum = 0
           for j in range(i, len(nums)):
               current_sum += nums[j]
               max_sum = max(max_sum, current_sum)

       return max_sum
   ```

   b. **Time complexity**: $O(n^2)$, as you need to evaluate all possible subarrays.

   c. **Space complexity**: $O(1)$, since no additional data structures are used.

2. **Optimized approach, Kadane's algorithm:** Kadane's algorithm improves upon the brute-force approach by maintaining a running sum of the current subarray and updating the maximum sum as you traverse the array. The key idea is to decide at each element whether to *continue* with the current subarray or *start a new subarray* from that element.

   a. **Kadane's algorithm code example:**

```
def max_subarray(nums):
if not nums:
        return 0
    # Initialize max_sum as the first element
    max_sum = current_sum = nums[0]

    for num in nums[1:]:
        # Either continue the subarray or start a new one
        current_sum = max(num, current_sum + num)

        # Update the max_sum if current_sum is larger
        max_sum = max(max_sum, current_sum)

    return max_sum
```

   b. **Time complexity**: *O(n)*, where n is the number of elements in the array.

   c. **Space complexity**: *O(1)*, since we are only using variables to track the maximum and current sum.

   This solution is highly efficient and runs in linear time, making it suitable for even large arrays.

The step-by-step explanation is as follows:

1. **Initialize variables:**

   a. `max_sum` is initialized to the first element in the array. This keeps track of the highest sum found so far.

   b. `current_sum` is also initialized to the first element and will store the sum of the current subarray.

2. **Iterate through the array:** For each element in the array, decide whether to:

   a. Continue the current subarray by adding the element to `current_sum`.

   b. Start a new subarray beginning with the current element if it is larger than the sum of the current subarray plus the element.

3. **Update max_sum:** After updating `current_sum`, compare it to `max_sum` and update `max_sum` if `current_sum` is larger. This ensures that the largest subarray sum found so far is tracked.

4. **Return the result:** Once all elements have been processed, return **`max_sum`**, which contains the largest subarray sum.

   a. **Example execution:** Let us walk through an example:

      `nums = [-2, 1, -3, 4, -1, 2, 1, -5, 4]`

   b. The steps of the code are as follows:

      i. **(Initialization):**

         - `max_sum = -2`
         - `current_sum = -2`

      ii. **(i = 1, num = 1):**

         - `current_sum = max(1, -2 + 1)` = 1
         - `max_sum = max(-2, 1)` = 1

      iii. **(i = 2, num = -3):**

         - `current_sum = max(-3, 1 - 3)` = -2
         - `max_sum = max(1, -2)` = 1

      iv. **(i = 3, num = 4):**

         - `current_sum = max(4, -2 + 4)` = 4
         - `max_sum = max(1, 4)` = 4

      v. **(i = 4, num = -1):**

         - `current_sum = max(-1, 4 - 1)` = 3
         - `max_sum = max(4, 3)` = 4

      vi. **(i = 5, num = 2):**

         - `current_sum = max(2, 3 + 2)` = 5
         - `max_sum = max(4, 5)` = 5

      vii. **(i = 6, num = 1):**

         - `current_sum = max(1, 5 + 1)` = 6
         - `max_sum = max(5, 6)` = 6

      viii. **(i = 7, num = -5):**

         - `current_sum = max(-5, 6 - 5)` = 1
         - `max_sum = max(6, 1)` = 6

      ix. **(i = 8, num = 4):**

         - `current_sum = max(4, 1 + 4)` = 5
         - `max_sum = max(6, 5)` = 6

The largest subarray sum is 6, which corresponds to the subarray [4, -1, 2, 1].

How the subarray is identified (conceptually):

Each time **`current_sum`** would be better by starting fresh at **`nums[i]`** than by extending, so we restart the candidate window at i. When **`current_sum`** exceeds **`max_sum`**, we record the current window as the best. For this input, the best window starts at index 3 (value 4) and last updates at index 6 (value 1), giving [4, -1, 2, 1].

Dig deeper

The edge cases to consider are as follows:

- **All negative numbers:** If the array contains only negative numbers, Kadane's algorithm will return the largest single negative number since adding more negative numbers would only decrease the sum.
- **Single-element array:** If the array has only one element, the algorithm will return that element as the maximum subarray sum.
- **Empty array:** If the input array is empty, you should handle this case by returning 0 or an error message, depending on the problem constraints.

The time and space complexity are explained as follows:

- **Time complexity**: *O(n)*, where n is the number of elements in the array. We only iterate through the array once.
- **Space complexity**: *O(1)*, since we are only using a few variables to store intermediate results (no extra data structures are used).

How to approach this problem in an interview:

- **Explain the problem:** Start by clearly explaining the goal: to find the contiguous subarray with the largest sum. Mention that the array may contain both positive and negative numbers.
- **Discuss the brute-force approach:** Briefly describe the brute-force solution, where you check every possible subarray, and mention that its time complexity is $O(n^2)$, making it inefficient for large arrays.
- **Introduce Kadane's algorithm:** Explain how Kadane's algorithm efficiently solves the problem in linear time by maintaining a running sum and updating the maximum sum encountered.
- **Edge cases:** Discuss how the solution handles edge cases, such as arrays with all negative numbers, single-element arrays, or empty arrays.
- **Time and space complexity:** Conclude by mentioning the time complexity of *O(n)* and the space complexity of *O(1)*, showing that this solution is optimal in both time and space.

The key takeaways for interviews are as follows:

- **Efficiency**: Kadane's algorithm is a must-know technique for optimizing problems involving subarrays and maximum sums. It demonstrates your ability to recognize and apply dynamic programming principles.
- **Real-world applications**: This algorithm can be applied to various problems, such as stock price analysis (finding the best time to buy and sell stocks) and maximum profit calculation.
- **Edge case handling**: This problem helps you think through and handle various edge cases, such as arrays of negative numbers or single-element arrays.

Possible follow-up questions

Can you modify Kadane's algorithm to return the actual subarray, not just the sum?

Yes, you can modify the algorithm to return the subarray itself by maintaining its start and end indices.

What if you need to find the maximum product subarray instead of the sum?

A variation of this problem involves finding the subarray with the largest product. You can solve it using a similar approach, but with adjustments to handle the product of positive and negative numbers.

Problem 28: Product of array except for self

Problem statement: Given an integer array **`nums`**, return an array answer such that **`answer[i]`** is equal to the product of all the elements of **`nums`** except **`nums[i]`**. The solution must be written without using division and should run in *O(n)* time.

For example:

- **Input**:

  `nums = [1, 2, 3, 4]`

- **Output:**

  `[24, 12, 8, 6]`

Another example:

`nums = [-1, 1, 0, -3, 3]`

Output:

`[0, 0, 9, 0, 0]`

Understanding the problem: The challenge is to create a new array where each element is the product of all elements in the input array except for the one at the current index. Importantly, we cannot use division, which would make the problem trivial. Instead, we need to find a way to compute the result using only multiplication and without affecting the time complexity.

The step-by-step solution is as follows:

1. **Brute-force approach:** The most straightforward solution is to use two loops. For each element in the array, multiply all the other elements to compute the result. This approach has a time complexity of *O(n²)*, which is inefficient for large arrays.

    a. **Brute-force code example:**

    ```
    def product_except_self(nums):
        n = len(nums)
        answer = []

        for i in range(n):
            product = 1
            for j in range(n):
                if i != j:
                    product *= nums[j]
            answer.append(product)
        return answer
    ```

    b. **Time complexity**: *O(n²)*, as you are using two nested loops to compute the product for each element.

    c. **Space complexity**: *O(n)*, since we are storing the result in the answer array.

    This solution works but is inefficient for large arrays due to its quadratic time complexity.

2. **Optimized approach without division:** To solve this problem in *O(n)* time, we can take a two-pass approach, where we compute the product of elements *to the left* and *to the right* of each element in two separate loops. We will build the answer array using this strategy.

    The key insight is that the product of all elements except **`nums[i]`** can be expressed as:
    `product_except_self[i] = product_of_elements_to_left[i] * product_of_elements_to_right[i]`

3. **Two-pass solution**:

    - **Left pass:** Create an array that stores the product of all elements to the left of the current index.

    - **Right pass:** Create another array (or update the result array) to store the product of all elements to the right.

    - Optimized code example:

    ```
    def product_except_self(nums):
    ```

```
    n = len(nums)
    answer = [1] * n

    # Step 1: Fill in the left products
    left_product = 1
    for i in range(n):
        answer[i] = left_product
        left_product *= nums[i]

    # Step 2: Multiply by the right products
    right_product = 1
    for i in range(n - 1, -1, -1):
        answer[i] *= right_product
        right_product *= nums[i]

    return answer
```

- **Time complexity**: *O(n)*, since we pass through the array twice (once from left to right and once from right to left).
- **Space complexity**: *O(1)*, not counting the output array (which is required), as we only use two variables (**`left_product`** and **`right_product`**).

The step-by-step explanation is as follows:

- **Left pass:** As we traverse the array from left to right, we keep a running product of all elements to the left of each index. For example, if **`nums = [1, 2, 3, 4]`**, the left products array would be [1, 1, 2, 6] (because there is nothing to the left of index 0, and for index 2, the product of elements to the left is *1* * 2 = 2).
- **Right pass:** After the left pass, we perform another pass from right to left, multiplying the current value in the result array by the product of elements to the right. For example, for **`nums = [1, 2, 3, 4]`**, the right products array would be [24, 12, 4, 1]. As you go through this pass, you combine the left and right products to get the final result.
- **Example execution:** Let us walk through an example:

  `nums = [1, 2, 3, 4]`
- The code steps are:
  1. **(Left Pass):**
     a. answer = [1, 1, 2, 6] (product of all elements to the left of each index).
  2. **(Right Pass):**
     a. Multiply the values in the answer by the products of all elements to the right of each index.
     b. answer = [24, 12, 8, 6].

  Thus, the final result is [24, 12, 8, 6].

Dig deeper

The edge cases to consider are as follows:

- **Array with zeros:** If the array contains zeros, the product for those elements should be 0 (except for the special case where there is exactly one zero, in which case the result for that index is the product of all other elements).
- **Single-element array:** If the input array has only one element, the output should be [1] because there are no other elements.
- **All ones or all negative numbers:** The solution should handle arrays of all identical numbers or all negative numbers.

The time and space complexity are explained as follows:

- **Time complexity**: *O(n)*, where n is the number of elements in the array. We pass through the array twice.
- **Space complexity**: *O(1)*, not counting the output array, since we only use a few extra variables.

How to approach this problem in an interview:

- **Explain the problem:** Start by clarifying that the goal is to return an array where each element is the product of all the other elements except for the current one, and you cannot use division.
- **Discuss the brute-force approach:** Briefly mention the brute-force solution that uses two nested loops and has $O(n^2)$ time complexity, but note that it is inefficient.
- **Introduce the two-pass approach:** Explain the two-pass solution, where you calculate the left and right products separately and combine them to get the final result.
- **Edge cases:** Discuss how the solution handles arrays with zeros and single-element arrays.
- **Time and space complexity:** Conclude by mentioning that the solution has *O(n)* time complexity and *O(1)* space complexity (excluding the output array).

The key takeaways for interviews are as follows:

- **Efficient array manipulation**: This problem showcases your ability to solve array manipulation problems efficiently using linear-time algorithms.
- **Avoiding division**: Many interviewers test your ability to come up with creative solutions when division is not allowed. This solution demonstrates how to solve the problem without relying on division.
- **Handling edge cases**: The problem also tests your ability to think about edge cases, such as arrays with zeros or single-element arrays.

Possible follow-up questions

What if you were allowed to use division? How would that change the solution?

If division were allowed, you could compute the product of all elements and then divide that by the current element for each index. This would be an *O(n)* solution, but would not handle cases with zeros.

Can you solve this problem with additional space for the left and right product arrays?

Yes, you could maintain two separate arrays to store the left and right products and then multiply them together, but this would increase the space complexity to *O(n)*.

Problem 29: Find the intersection of two arrays

Problem statement: Given two arrays, **`nums1`**, and **`nums2`**, return an array that contains their intersection. Each element in the result must be unique, and you may return the result in any order.

For example:

- **Input**:
  ```
  nums1 = [1, 2, 2, 1]
  nums2 = [2, 2]
  ```
- **Output**:
  ```
  [2]
  ```

Another example:

- Input:
  ```
  nums1 = [4, 9, 5]
  nums2 = [9, 4, 9, 8, 4]
  ```
- Output:
  ```
  [9, 4]
  ```

Understanding the problem: The *intersection* of two arrays consists of all elements that appear in both arrays, without any duplicates. This is a common interview problem as it tests your ability to manipulate arrays and work with sets.

There are several ways to approach this problem, including brute-force solutions, hash sets, and sorting-based methods.

The step-by-step solution is as follows:

1. **Brute-force approach:** The brute-force approach would be to iterate over each element in the first array and check if it exists in the second array. To ensure uniqueness, we could store the result in a set to avoid duplicates.

a. Brute-force code example:

```
def intersection(nums1, nums2):
    result = set()

    for num in nums1:
        if num in nums2:
            result.add(num)

    return list(result)
```

b. **Time complexity**: *O(n * m)*, where n and m are the lengths of **nums1** and **nums2**. For each element in **nums1**, we check if it exists in **nums2**.

c. **Space complexity**: *O(n + m)*, due to the space used by the result set and for storing the result.

While the brute-force method works, it is inefficient for larger arrays.

2. **Optimized approach using sets:** A more efficient solution leverages Python's set data structure. Sets allow for fast lookups (*O(1)* on average) and automatically handle duplicates. Here is how the optimized solution works:

   a. Convert one of the arrays (say, **nums1**) into a set.

   b. Iterate through **nums2** and check if each element exists in the set.

   c. Add any element found in both arrays to the result set.

   d. Optimized code using sets:

```
def intersection(nums1, nums2):
    set1 = set(nums1)
    result = set()

    for num in nums2:
        if num in set1:
            result.add(num)

    return list(result)
```

   e. **Time complexity**: *O(n + m)*, where *n* is the length of **nums1** and *m* is the length of **nums2**. Inserting into a set and checking for membership both take *O(1)* on average.

   f. **Space complexity**: *O(n + m)*, for the set storage.

3. **Sorting-based approach:** Another approach involves sorting both arrays first and then using two pointers to find the intersection. This method is more efficient than brute-force; it requires sorting the arrays first, which takes *O(n log n)* time.

a. **Sorting and two pointers code example:**

```
def intersection(nums1, nums2):
    nums1.sort()
    nums2.sort()

    i, j = 0, 0
    result = set()

    while i < len(nums1) and j < len(nums2):
        if nums1[i] == nums2[j]:
            result.add(nums1[i])
            i += 1
            j += 1
        elif nums1[i] < nums2[j]:
            i += 1
        else:
            j += 1

    return list(result)
```

b. **Time complexity**: *O(n log n + m log m)*, due to sorting both arrays.

c. **Space complexity**: *O(n + m)*, for storing the result.

The step-by-step explanation is as follows:

- **Brute-force method:** The brute-force solution iterates through each element of the first array and checks if it exists in the second array. This approach is straightforward but inefficient, with a time complexity of *O(n * m)*.
- **Optimized approach using sets:** The set-based solution is much faster and more efficient. By converting **nums1** into a set, we reduce the membership check to *O(1)* on average. We then iterate through **nums2** and check if each element exists in the set. This results in a time complexity of *O(n + m)*.
- **Sorting-based approach:** The sorting method involves sorting both arrays and then using two pointers to find common elements. While it is efficient in terms of memory, sorting takes *O(n log n)* time, which makes this approach slightly slower than the set-based approach for large arrays.

Example execution: Let us walk through an example:

```
nums1 = [4, 9, 5]
nums2 = [9, 4, 9, 8, 4]
```

The code's explanation is as follows:

- Convert **nums1** to a set: {4, 9, 5}.
- Iterate through **nums2**:

    - 9 is in the set, so add it to the result.
    - 4 is in the set, so add it to the result.
    - Ignore duplicates (e.g., the second occurrence of 9).
- Final result: [9, 4].

Dig deeper

The edge cases to consider are as follows:

- **Empty arrays:** If one or both arrays are empty, the intersection should be an empty array.
- **No intersection:** If there are no common elements between the two arrays, return an empty array.
- **Duplicate elements:** Since the result should contain only unique elements, you need to ensure that duplicates are handled correctly.
- **Arrays of different sizes:** The solution should handle arrays of different sizes efficiently.

The time and space complexity are explained as follows:

- **Time complexity**: *O(n + m)*, where n and m are the lengths of `nums1` and `nums2`. We convert nums1 to a set in *O(n)* time and then check each element in `nums2` in *O(m)* time.
- **Space complexity**: *O(n + m)*, due to the space used by the sets to store the unique elements.

How to approach this problem in an interview:

- **Explain the problem:** Start by explaining that you need to find the intersection of two arrays and that the result should contain unique elements.
- **Discuss the brute-force approach:** Briefly mention the brute-force method, which has *O(n * m)* time complexity, and explain why it is inefficient.
- **Introduce the set-based approach:** Explain how converting one array to a set allows you to check for membership in *O(1)* time, leading to an *O(n + m)* solution.
- **Edge cases:** Discuss how the solution handles edge cases, such as empty arrays, no intersection, and duplicate elements.
- **Time and space complexity:** Conclude by mentioning that the solution has *O(n + m)* time complexity and *O(n + m)* space complexity, making it efficient for large arrays.

The key takeaways for interviews are as follows:

- **Efficient array operations**: This problem demonstrates your ability to manipulate arrays using data structures like sets efficiently.

- **Handling duplicates**: The problem also tests your understanding of handling duplicates and ensuring the result contains only unique elements.
- **Edge case handling**: You will need to think about various edge cases, such as empty arrays or arrays with no common elements.

Possible follow-up questions

How would you modify the solution to return the intersection with duplicates (i.e., all occurrences of common elements)?

You could use a counter from the collections module to count the occurrences of each element and return the minimum count for each common element.

What if the arrays are extremely large and cannot fit into memory?

If the arrays are too large to fit into memory, you could use external sorting or process them in chunks.

Problem 30: Remove element from an array

Problem statement: Given an array **`nums`** and a value **`val`**, remove all instances of that value in-place and return the new length of the array. You must do this without allocating extra space for another array and modify the input array in place with *O(1)* extra memory.

For example:

- **Input**:

  `nums = [3, 2, 2, 3], val = 3`
- **Output**:

  `2, nums = [2, 2]`

Another example:

- **Input**:

  `nums = [0, 1, 2, 2, 3, 0, 4, 2], val = 2`
- **Output**:

  `5, nums = [0, 1, 3, 0, 4]`

Understanding the problem: The task is to remove all occurrences of a given value from the array in place, meaning that you are not allowed to use additional arrays to store the results. Instead, the input array itself should be modified, and the function should return the length of the modified array.

The challenge here is to do this in *O(1)* extra space while maintaining *O(n)* time complexity, where n is the number of elements in the array.

The step-by-step solution is explained as follows:

1. **Brute-force approach:** A brute-force approach would involve iterating over the array and moving all non-val elements to a new array. However, this requires extra space, which violates the problem's constraints. Let us skip this approach and directly move to an efficient solution.

2. **Two-pointer approach:** To solve this problem efficiently, we can use a *two-pointer technique*. One pointer (**i**) traverses the entire array, and another pointer (**k**) keeps track of where to place the non-val elements. As you traverse the array, you skip over the elements equal to **val**, and for all other elements, you move them to the correct position in the array using the **k** pointer.

   a. Code example (two-pointer approach):

   ```
   def remove_element(nums, val):
       k = 0

       for i in range(len(nums)):
           if nums[i] != val:
               nums[k] = nums[i]
               k += 1

       return k
   ```

   b. **Time complexity**: *O(n)*, where n is the number of elements in the array.

   c. **Space complexity**: *O(1)*, since we are only using the array and a couple of extra variables.

The step-by-step explanation is as follows:

1. **Initialize the k pointer:** Start with a pointer **k** set to 0. This pointer will be used to keep track of where the next non-val element should be placed in the array.

2. **Traverse the array:** Loop through each element in the array with a pointer **i**. For every element that is *not* equal to **val**, copy the value to the position indicated by the **k** pointer and increment **k**.

3. **Ignore the val elements:** Whenever the current element is equal to **val**, simply skip it and move to the next element.

4. **Return the new length:** After completing the traversal, return **k**, which represents the new length of the modified array.

Example execution: Let us walk through an example:

```
nums = [3, 2, 2, 3], val = 3
```

The code is as follows:

- **Initial state:**

  `nums = [3, 2, 2, 3], val = 3, k = 0`

  - **(i = 0):**
    - **nums[0] = 3** (which is equal to **val**), so skip this element.
    - **k** remains 0.
  - **(i = 1):**
    - **nums[1] = 2 (**which is not equal to **val**), so move it to position **k = 0**.
    - Now, **nums = [2, 2, 2, 3]**, and increment **k** to 1.
  - **(i = 2):**
    - **nums[2] = 2** (which is not equal to **val**), so move it to position k = 1.
    - Now, **nums = [2, 2, 2, 3]**, and increment **k** to 2.
  - **(i = 3):**
    - **nums[3] = 3** (which is equal to **val**), so skip this element.
    - **k** remains 2.
- **Final state: k = 2**. The first **k** elements are [2, 2]. The array may look like [2, 2, 2, 3] overall, but only **nums[:k]** is considered.

Dig deeper

The edge cases to consider are as follows:

- **Empty array:** If the array is empty, the result should be 0, as there are no elements to remove.
- **All elements equal to val:** If all elements in the array are equal to **val**, the result should be 0, and the modified array will be empty.
- **No elements equal to val:** If no elements in the array are equal to **val**, the array should remain unchanged, and the length of the array will be the same as the original.
- **Single element array:** Handle cases where the array contains just one element, whether it is equal to **val** or not.

The time and space complexity are explained as follows:

- **Time complexity**: *O(n)*, where n is the number of elements in the array. We traverse the array once to perform the modifications.
- **Space complexity**: *O(1)*, since we are only using a few extra variables (**k** and **i**).

How to approach this problem in an interview:

- **Explain the problem:** Start by explaining that the task is to remove all occurrences of a given value from the array in place and return the new length.
- **Discuss the brute-force approach:** Mention that a brute-force approach would involve creating a new array to store the result, but this violates the space constraint.
- **Introduce the two-pointer approach:** Explain the two-pointer technique, where one pointer (`k`) keeps track of where to place non-val elements, and the other pointer (`i`) traverses the array.
- **Edge cases:** Discuss how the solution handles edge cases, such as an empty array, all elements equal to `val`, or no elements equal to `val`.
- **Time and space complexity:** Conclude by mentioning that the solution runs in $O(n)$ time and uses $O(1)$ extra space, making it optimal for large arrays.

The key takeaways for interviews are as follows:

- **In-place modifications**: This problem tests your ability to modify an array in place without using extra memory, which is a common constraint in coding interviews.
- **Efficient array traversal**: The two-pointer technique is a valuable tool for efficiently traversing and modifying arrays in linear time.
- **Handling edge cases**: This problem encourages you to think about various edge cases, such as empty arrays and arrays with no matching elements.

Possible follow-up questions

What if the array were sorted? Could you use that information to optimize the solution?

If the array is sorted, you could potentially break out of the loop early once you encounter an element greater than `val`, but the time complexity would remain $O(n)$.

What if you needed to remove multiple different values from the array?

You could modify the function to accept a list of values to remove and check if each element is in that list before deciding whether to skip it.

Problem 31: Find the majority element

Problem statement: Given an array `nums`, find the majority element. The majority element is the element that appears more than n // 2 times, where n is the length of the array. You may assume that the array always contains a majority element.

For example:

- **Input**:

  ```
  nums = [3, 2, 3]
  ```

- **Output**:

  ```
  3
  ```

Another example:

- **Input**:

  ```
  nums = [2, 2, 1, 1, 1, 2, 2]
  ```

- **Output**:

  ```
  2
  ```

Understanding the problem: The majority element is defined as an element that appears more than n // 2 times in an array. The task is to find this element in the array, and by the problem's constraints, you are guaranteed that a majority element exists.

The simplest approach might involve counting the occurrences of each element and returning the one with the highest count. However, a more efficient approach is the *Boyer-Moore voting algorithm*, which works in linear time and constant space.

The step-by-step solution is as follows:

1. **Using a hash map (brute-force):** One straightforward solution is to count the occurrences of each element in the array using a hash map. We iterate through the array once, counting the occurrences of each element. Then, we check which element has a count greater than n // 2.

   a. **Code example (brute-force approach):**

   ```
   from collections import Counter

   def majority_element(nums):
       counts = Counter(nums)
       for num, count in counts.items():
           if count > len(nums) // 2:
               return num
   ```

   b. **Time complexity**: *O(n)*, where n is the length of the array.

   c. **Space complexity**: *O(n)*, due to the extra space used by the hash map.

2. **Boyer-Moore voting algorithm (optimal):** The *Boyer-Moore voting algorithm* is a much more efficient approach that solves the problem in *O(n)* time and *O(1)* space. The algorithm maintains a **`candidate`** element and a **`count`** of how many times the candidate has been seen. If the count reaches zero, the algorithm picks a new candidate. The majority element will emerge as the final candidate because it appears more than half the time.

   a. **Code example (Boyer-Moore voting algorithm):**

   ```
   def majority_element(nums):
   ```

```
candidate = None
count = 0

for num in nums:
    if count == 0:
        candidate = num
    count += (1 if num == candidate else -1)

return candidate
```

b. **Time complexity**: *O(n)*, since we pass through the array once.

c. **Space complexity**: *O(1)*, as we only use a couple of variables (candidate and count).

The step-by-step explanation is as follows:

1. **Initialize variables:** Start with candidate = None and count = 0. The candidate will store the potential majority element, and the count will track how many times it has been encountered.

2. **Traverse the array:** For each element in the array, check if the count is zero. If it is, set the current element as the new candidate. If the current element matches the candidate, increase the count; if it does not, decrease the count.

3. **Return the candidate:** After completing the traversal, the remaining candidate will be the majority element.

   a. **Example execution:** Let us walk through an example:
      `nums = [2, 2, 1, 1, 1, 2, 2]`

   b. The breakdown of the code is as follows:

      - **Initial state: `candidate = None, count = 0`**
         - **Step 1 (i = 0):**
            - **`nums[0] = 2`**
            - **`count == 0`**, so set **`candidate = 2`**.
            - Increment count to 1.
         - **Step 2 (i = 1):**
            - **`nums[1] = 2`** (same as candidate).
            - Increment count to 2.
         - **Step 3 (i = 2):**
            - **`nums[2] = 1`** (different from candidate).
            - Decrement count to 1.

- **Step 4 (i = 3):**
  - `nums[3] = 1` (different from candidate).
  - Decrement count to 0.
- **Step 5 (i = 4):**
  - `count == 0`, so set candidate = 1.
  - Increment count to 1.
- **Step 6 (i = 5):**
  - `nums[5] = 2` (different from candidate).
  - Decrement count to 0.
- **Step 7 (i = 6):**
  - `count == 0`, so set **`candidate = 2`**.
  - Increment count to 1.

- **Final state:** The majority element is 2.

Dig deeper

The edge cases to consider are as follows:

- **Single-element array:** If the array has only one element, that element is the majority element.
- **All elements are the same:** If all elements in the array are the same, the algorithm will correctly return that element as the majority.
- **Edge case with just enough majority:** If the majority element just crosses the threshold of appearing more than n // 2 times, the algorithm will still identify it correctly.

The time and space complexity are explained as follows:

- **Time complexity**: *O(n)*, where n is the number of elements in the array. We traverse the array exactly once, making the algorithm efficient.
- **Space complexity**: *O(1)*, since we only use a couple of variables to keep track of the candidate and count.

How to approach this problem in an interview:

- **Explain the problem:** Start by explaining that the task is to find the majority element, which is defined as the element that appears more than n // 2 times.
- **Introduce the brute-force approach:** Mention that you could use a hash map to count occurrences of each element, but this approach takes *O(n)* space.

- **Introduce the Boyer-Moore voting algorithm:** Explain how the algorithm works by maintaining a candidate and a count to track the majority element efficiently in *O(n)* time and *O(1)* space.
- **Edge cases:** Discuss how the solution handles edge cases like a single-element array or arrays where all elements are the same.
- **Time and space complexity:** Conclude by mentioning that the Boyer-Moore voting algorithm is optimal with *O(n)* time and *O(1)* space.

The key takeaways for interviews are as follows:

- **Efficient majority element search**: This problem tests your ability to find the majority element efficiently, which is a common coding interview problem.
- **Understanding of *O(1)* space solutions**: Using the Boyer-Moore voting algorithm demonstrates an understanding of space-efficient algorithms, which is valuable in interviews.
- **Handling edge cases**: Be prepared to discuss edge cases like arrays with a single element, arrays where the majority element only marginally crosses the threshold, and arrays with all identical elements.

Problem 32: Rotate image (matrix rotation)

Problem statement: You are given an n x n 2D matrix representing an image. Rotate the image by 90 degrees (clockwise).

For example:

- **Input**:

```
matrix = [
    [1, 2, 3],
    [4, 5, 6],
    [7, 8, 9]
]
```

- **Output**:

```
[
    [7, 4, 1],
    [8, 5, 2],
    [9, 6, 3]
]
```

Another example:

- **Input**:

```
matrix = [
```

```
        [5, 1, 9, 11],
        [2, 4, 8, 10],
        [13, 3, 6, 7],
        [15, 14, 12, 16]
    ]
```

- **Output**:

```
    [
        [15, 13, 2, 5],
        [14, 3, 4, 1],
        [12, 6, 8, 9],
        [16, 7, 10, 11]
    ]
```

Understanding the problem: You are tasked with rotating an n x n 2D matrix (square matrix) by 90 degrees clockwise. The rotation involves transforming the rows of the matrix into columns. Importantly, you must achieve this transformation **in place**, meaning that you cannot use additional memory for another matrix.

The transformation can be broken down into two main operations:

- **Transpose the matrix**: Convert rows into columns.
- **Reverse each row**: Reverse the elements in each row to get the desired 90-degree rotation.

To rotate a matrix by 90 degrees clockwise, the process involves the following two steps:

1. **Transpose the matrix:** Transposing the matrix involves converting the rows into columns. In this step, the element at **`position [i][j]`** is swapped with the element at **`position [j][i]`**.

    a. Example of a transpose operation:

        i. **Original matrix:**

```
    [
        [1, 2, 3],
        [4, 5, 6],
        [7, 8, 9]
    ]
```

        ii. **Transposed matrix:**

```
    [
        [1, 4, 7],
        [2, 5, 8],
        [3, 6, 9]
    ]
```

2. **Reverse each row:** Once the matrix is transposed, the next step is to reverse each row to achieve the final rotated matrix.

   a. For the transposed matrix:

   ```
   [
       [1, 4, 7],
       [2, 5, 8],
       [3, 6, 9]
   ]
   ```

   b. After reversing each row:

   ```
   [
       [7, 4, 1],
       [8, 5, 2],
       [9, 6, 3]
   ]
   ```

   This gives the desired 90-degree clockwise rotation.

   c **Code implementation:** Rotate image:

   ```
   def rotate(matrix):
       n = len(matrix)

       # Step 1: Transpose the matrix
       for i in range(n):
           for j in range(i, n):
               matrix[i][j], matrix[j][i] = matrix[j][i], matrix[i][j]

       # Step 2: Reverse each row
       for i in range(n):
           matrix[i].reverse()
   ```

   d. **Time complexity**: *O(n^2)* because we traverse every element in the matrix once during the transposition and once during the row reversal.

   e. **Space complexity**: *O(1)* because we are performing all operations in place, without using additional memory.

The step-by-step explanation is as follows:

1. **Transpose the matrix:** The first step is to transpose the matrix. This involves swapping elements across the diagonal. The element at **`position [i][j]`** is swapped with the element at **`position [j][i]`**. After this step, the matrix will be transposed, but not yet rotated.

2. **Reverse each row:** Once the matrix is transposed, the next step is to reverse the elements in each row. This final step completes the 90-degree clockwise rotation.

Example walkthrough: Let us go through an example step by step:

a. **Given input:**

```
matrix = [
    [1, 2, 3],
    [4, 5, 6],
    [7, 8, 9]
]
```

b. **Transpose the matrix:** Transpose the matrix by swapping elements across the diagonal:

```
[
    [1, 4, 7],
    [2, 5, 8],
    [3, 6, 9]
]
```

c. **Reverse each row:** After reversing each row, the final matrix is:

```
[
    [7, 4, 1],
    [8, 5, 2],
    [9, 6, 3]
]
```

This matrix is the result of rotating the original matrix by 90 degrees clockwise.

Dig deeper

The edge cases are as follows:

- **Single-element matrix:** A matrix with only one element remains unchanged after rotation. For example:

```
matrix = [[1]]
```

- **2x2 matrix:** A simple 2x2 matrix should also be handled correctly:

```
matrix = [
    [1, 2],
    [3, 4]
]
```

- After rotation, it becomes:

```
[
    [3, 1],
    [4, 2]
]
```

The time and space complexity are explained as follows:

- **Time complexity**: *O(n^2)*, where n is the number of rows (or columns) in the matrix. This is because both the transpose and row-reversal steps involve iterating through each element of the matrix.
- **Space complexity**: *O(1)*, as the rotation is done in place without using any additional memory.

How to approach this problem in an interview:

- **Clarify the problem:** Ensure you understand that the task is to rotate an n x n matrix in place by 90 degrees clockwise. Clarify any assumptions, such as matrix size and whether it will always be square.
- **Brute-force solution:** You could mention the brute-force solution that uses an additional matrix to store the result, but note that this would require *O(n^2)* space.
- **Introduce the optimal solution:** Explain the two-step process: transpose the matrix and reverse each row. This is an efficient in-place solution with *O(n^2)* time complexity and *O(1)* space complexity.
- **Walk through an example:** Show how the matrix is transformed step by step, from transposing the elements to reversing each row.
- **Edge cases:** Discuss how the solution handles small matrices (1x1, 2x2) and ensure that the code does not break for these cases.
- **Time and space complexity:** Be sure to emphasize the solution's efficiency in terms of both time and space.

The key takeaways for interviews are as follows:

- **In-place rotation**: This problem is a classic test of your ability to manipulate arrays in place, an essential skill for data structure problems.
- **Matrix operations**: Understanding matrix transposition and row reversal is crucial in solving various 2D array problems.
- **Optimization**: Knowing how to solve problems with *O(1)* space complexity demonstrates strong coding optimization skills, which interviewers highly value.

Problem 33: Trapping rainwater

Problem statement: Given n non-negative integers representing an elevation map where the width of each bar is 1, compute how much water it can trap after raining.

For example:

- **Input**:

  ```
  height = [0,1,0,2,1,0,1,3,2,1,2,1]
  ```

- **Output:**

  6

Understanding the problem: In this problem, you are given a list of non-negative integers representing an elevation map. The height of each element in the list represents the elevation of the terrain at that point. The task is to calculate how much water can be trapped between the bars after it rains.

Water can only be trapped between two higher bars. The amount of water trapped above a bar depends on the minimum height of the tallest bars to the left and right of the bar.

Approach

We will solve the problem using two methods:

- **Brute-force (Naive) solution:** This approach computes the amount of water trapped at each bar by looking at the highest bar on the left and the highest bar on the right. The water trapped at that position is determined by the smaller of these two heights minus the height of the current bar.
- **Two pointers (optimal) solution:** This is an optimized solution that uses two pointers (one starting from the left and the other from the right) to calculate the water trapped in a single pass.

The step-by-step solution is as follows:

1. **Brute-force approach:** In the brute-force approach, for every index **i**, we calculate the maximum height to the left and the maximum height to the right of that index. The amount of water trapped above index **i** is the difference between the minimum of these two heights and the height of the current bar.

   a. **Code example (brute-force solution):**

   ```
   def trap(height):
       n = len(height)
       water_trapped = 0

       for i in range(n):
           left_max = max(height[:i+1])  # Maximum height to the left
   of the current bar
           right_max = max(height[i:])   # Maximum height to the
   right of the current bar
           water_trapped += min(left_max, right_max) - height[i]

       return water_trapped
   ```

   b. **Time complexity**: *O(n^2)*, as we calculate the left and right maximum heights for each bar in the array.

c. **Space complexity**: *O(1)*, as we are not using any additional space beyond the input.

2. **Two pointers (optimal) approach:** The two-pointer approach significantly reduces time complexity to *O(n)* while keeping the space complexity at *O(1)*.

3. **Initialize two pointers:** One pointer starts from the leftmost bar (left = 0), and the other starts from the rightmost bar (right = n-1).

4. **Move the pointers towards the center:** As we traverse the elevation map, we maintain two variables, **`left_max`** and **`right_max`**, which store the maximum height encountered so far from the left and right, respectively.

5. **Trap water based on the smaller height:** At each step, the water trapped above the current bar depends on the minimum of **`left_max`** and **`right_max`**. Move the pointer that has the smaller height (either left or right), and calculate how much water can be trapped above that bar.

   a. **Code example (two pointers solution):**

```
def trap(height):
    if not height:
        return 0

    left, right = 0, len(height) - 1
    left_max, right_max = height[left], height[right]
    water_trapped = 0

    while left < right:
        if left_max < right_max:
            left += 1
            left_max = max(left_max, height[left])
            water_trapped += left_max - height[left]
        else:
            right -= 1
            right_max = max(right_max, height[right])
            water_trapped += right_max - height[right]

    return water_trapped
```

   b. **Time complexity**: *O(n)*, as we only traverse the elevation map once.

   c. **Space complexity**: *O(1)*, as we are using constant extra space for the pointers and **`left_max`**, **`right_max`**.

The step-by-step explanation is as follows:

1. **Initialize variables:** Set up two pointers: left starts at the beginning of the array, and right starts at the end. We also initialize `left_max` to the height at left and `right_max` to the height at right.
2. **Traverse the array:** As long as left is less than right, we move the pointer with the smaller maximum height. If `left_max` is smaller, we move the left pointer to the right; otherwise, we move the right pointer to the left.
3. **Calculate water trapped:** For each step, calculate the difference between the current height and the maximum height encountered so far (`left_max` or `right_max`). This difference gives the amount of water trapped at that bar.
4. **Update maximum heights:** As we move the pointers, update `left_max` or `right_max` to reflect the maximum height encountered so far.
    a. **Example walkthrough:** Let us walk through the example:

       `height = [0,1,0,2,1,0,1,3,2,1,2,1]`

    b. The breakdown of steps is as follows:
        i. **Initial setup:**
            - `left = 0`, `right = 11`
            - `left_max = 0`, `right_max = 1`
            - `water_trapped = 0`

        ii. **First step:** Since `left_max < right_max`, move the left pointer to 1:
            - `left_max = max(0, 1) = 1`
            - No water trapped at index 1 because `height[1] = 1`.

        iii. **Second step:** Move the left pointer to 2:
            - `left_max = 1`
            - Water trapped at index 2: `left_max - height[2] = 1 - 0 = 1`.
            - `water_trapped = 1`.

    c. **Continue**: Follow this process, moving the pointer with the smaller maximum height, until the entire array is traversed.

       By the end of the traversal, the total amount of water trapped is 6.

Dig deeper

The edge cases are as follows:

- **Empty array:** If the input array is empty, return 0 because there are no bars to trap water.

- **All bars are of equal height:** If all bars have the same height, no water can be trapped, and the output should be 0.
- **Array with less than 3 bars:** If the array has fewer than 3 bars, no water can be trapped because there is no space between the bars.

The time and space complexity

- **Time complexity**: *O(n)*, where n is the number of elements in the array. We traverse the array once using the two-pointer technique.
- **Space complexity**: *O(1)*, as we use only a few extra variables.

How to approach this problem in an interview:

- **Clarify the problem:** Ensure you understand that the task is to calculate the amount of water that can be trapped between the bars, and that the bars' heights are given as an array.
- **Introduce the brute-force approach:** Mention that you can solve the problem by checking the maximum heights to the left and right of each bar, but this would take *O(n^2)* time.
- **Introduce the optimal two-pointer approach:** Explain how using two pointers allows you to solve the problem in *O(n)* time while using constant space.
- **Edge cases:** Discuss how your solution handles edge cases such as an empty array or arrays where all bars are of equal height.
- **Time and space complexity:** Emphasize the efficiency of the two-pointer solution, with *O(n)* time and *O(1)* space complexity.

The key takeaways for interviews are as follows:

- **Two-pointer technique**: This problem is an excellent test of your ability to implement the two-pointer technique, a common optimization in array problems.
- **Optimization**: Being able to transition from a brute-force solution to an optimized *O(n)* solution demonstrates strong problem-solving skills in coding interviews.
- **Handling edge cases**: Make sure to discuss edge cases and demonstrate how your solution accounts for them.

Problem 34: Find the minimum in a rotated sorted array

Problem statement: Suppose an array of length n is sorted in ascending order but rotated at some pivot unknown to you beforehand (i.e., [0,1,2,4,5,6,7] might become [4,5,6,7,0,1,2]). You are tasked with finding the minimum element of this array. The array does not contain any duplicates.

For example:

- **Input**:
  `nums = [3, 4, 5, 1, 2]`
- **Output**:
  `1`

Another example:

- **Input**:
  `nums = [4, 5, 6, 7, 0, 1, 2]`
- **Output**:
  `0`

Understanding the problem: In a rotated sorted array, the minimum element is the "pivot" where the rotation occurred. Our goal is to efficiently find this minimum element in an array that was originally sorted but has been rotated.

The naive solution is to search the array linearly, but since the array is partially sorted, we can use a more efficient binary search approach. The idea is to divide and conquer by checking the middle of the array and comparing it to the boundaries.

The most efficient way to solve this problem is using **binary search**, which allows us to find the minimum element in *O(log n)* time. The step-by-step solution is as follows:

1. **Binary search approach:**
   a. **Key observations:**
      i. In a rotated sorted array, one of the two subarrays (either left or right) will always be sorted.
      ii. The minimum element is always in the unsorted part of the array.
   b. **Midpoint and comparisons:**
      i. At each step, check the middle element of the current range.
      ii. If the middle element is greater than the rightmost element, the minimum must be in the right half.
      iii. If the middle element is less than or equal to the rightmost element, the minimum must be in the left half.
   c. **Code implementation**: Binary search:

```
def find_min(nums):
    left, right = 0, len(nums) - 1

    # If the array is not rotated (sorted in ascending order)
```

```
    if nums[left] <= nums[right]:
        return nums[left]

    while left < right:
        mid = (left + right) // 2

        # Check if the minimum is in the right half
        if nums[mid] > nums[right]:
            left = mid + 1
        else:
            right = mid

    return nums[left]
```

d. **Time complexity**: *O(log n)* since we halve the search space with each iteration.

e. **Space complexity**: *O(1)*, as we are not using any additional space beyond a few variables.

The step-by-step explanation is as follows:

1. **Initial setup:** Set left to 0 and right to **`len(nums) - 1`**. Check if the array is already sorted by comparing **`nums[left]`** and **`nums[right]`**. If the array is sorted, return **`nums[left]`** as the minimum element.

2. **Binary search:** While left is less than right, calculate the middle index using **`(left + right) // 2`**. Compare the middle element with the rightmost element:

   a. If **`nums[mid] > nums[right]`**, it means the minimum is in the right half, so move left to **`mid + 1`**.

   b. Otherwise, the minimum is in the left half, so move right to mid.

3. **Return the minimum:** After the loop finishes, left will point to the minimum element in the rotated array.

   a. **Example walkthrough:** Let us walk through an example step by step:

   Given input:

   `nums = [4, 5, 6, 7, 0, 1, 2]`

   i. **Initial setup:**

      - **`left = 0`**, **`right = 6`**
      - **`nums[left] = 4`**, **`nums[right] = 2`**
      - Since **`nums[left] > nums[right]`**, the array is rotated, so we continue with the binary search.

   ii. **First iteration:**

      - **`mid = (0 + 6) // 2 = 3`**

- `nums[mid] = 7, nums[right] = 2`
- Since `nums[mid] > nums[right]`, the minimum must be in the right half.
- Update `left = mid + 1 = 4`.

iii. **Second iteration:**

- `mid = (4 + 6) // 2 = 5`
- `nums[mid] = 1, nums[right] = 2`
- Since `nums[mid] < nums[right]`, the minimum must be in the left half.
- Update `right = mid = 5`.

iv. **Third iteration:**

- `mid = (4 + 5) // 2 = 4`
- `nums[mid] = 0, nums[right] = 1`
- Since `nums[mid] < nums[right]`, the minimum is in the left half.
- Update `right = mid = 4`.

Now, `left == right`, so return `nums[left]`, which is 0.

Dig deeper

The edge cases are as follows:

- **Array with one element:** If the array has only one element, that element is the minimum:

  ```
  nums = [1]  # Output: 1
  ```

- **Array with no rotation:** If the array is already sorted in ascending order, the first element is the minimum:

  ```
  nums = [1, 2, 3, 4, 5]  # Output: 1
  ```

- **All elements are the same:** If all elements are identical, the array can be treated as already sorted:

  ```
  nums = [2, 2, 2, 2]  # Output: 2
  ```

The time and space complexity are as follows:

- **Time complexity**: *O(log n)*, where n is the number of elements in the array. This is because we use binary search to reduce the search space by half in each iteration.
- **Space complexity**: *O(1)*, as we only use constant extra space for the left, right, and mid pointers.

How to approach this problem in an interview:

- **Clarify the problem:** Ensure you understand that the problem is about finding the minimum element in a rotated sorted array, and there are no duplicate elements.
- **Brute-force approach:** Mention that a brute-force solution could involve a linear search through the array to find the minimum, but this would take *O(n)* time.
- **Introduce the binary search approach:** Explain how binary search can be applied to solve the problem in *O(log n)* time by comparing the middle element with the rightmost element to determine which half contains the minimum.
- **Edge cases:** Discuss how the solution handles edge cases like arrays with one element, arrays with no rotation, and arrays where all elements are the same.
- **Time and space complexity:** Highlight that the binary search solution is optimal with O(log n) time and *O(1)* space complexity.

The key takeaways for interviews are as follows:

- **Binary search in rotated arrays**: This problem is an excellent test of your ability to apply binary search in non-standard cases, such as rotated arrays.
- **Optimized search**: Being able to reduce the time complexity from *O(n)* to *O(log n)* shows strong problem-solving and optimization skills.
- **Edge case handling**: Make sure to discuss edge cases like arrays with one element or no rotation during the interview to show thoroughness.

Problem 35: Longest consecutive sequence

Problem statement: Given an unsorted array of integers, find the length of the longest consecutive element sequence.

The algorithm must run in *O(n)* time complexity.

For example:

- **Input**:

  ```
  nums = [100, 4, 200, 1, 3, 2]
  ```

- **Output**:

  ```
  4
  ```

- **Explanation**: The longest consecutive sequence is [1, 2, 3, 4]. Its length is 4.

Another example:

- **Input**:

  ```
  nums = [0, 3, 7, 2, 5, 8, 4, 6, 0, 1]
  ```

- **Output**:

  ```
  9
  ```

- **Explanation**: The longest consecutive sequence is [0, 1, 2, 3, 4, 5, 6, 7, 8]. Its length is 9.

Understanding the problem: In this problem, we need to find the longest sequence of consecutive integers in an unsorted array. For example, in the array [100, 4, 200, 1, 3, 2], the sequence [1, 2, 3, 4] is consecutive, and its length is 4.

Our goal is to find such consecutive sequences and return the length of the longest one. A naive solution would sort the array and look for consecutive numbers, but sorting would take *O(n log n)* time, which is not efficient enough. Instead, we can solve this problem using a *hash set* to achieve *O(n)* time complexity.

The step-by-step solution is as follows:

1. **Optimal approach using a hash set:** We will use a hash set to store all the elements of the array. Then, we will iterate over each element in the array and, for each element, try to find the beginning of a consecutive sequence. Once we find the beginning of a sequence, we will keep checking for consecutive elements and count their length.
2. **Add all elements to a hash set:** This allows us to check in constant time whether a number exists in the array.
3. **Check for the start of a sequence:** For each element, check if it is the start of a sequence by ensuring that `num - 1` is not in the hash set. If `num - 1` is not present, it means `num` is the smallest number in the sequence.
4. **Count the length of the sequence:** Once we identify the start of a sequence, we check if `num + 1`, `num + 2`, etc., are in the hash set and count how long the sequence is.

   a. **Code implementation:** Longest consecutive sequence:

```
def longest_consecutive(nums):
    if not nums:
        return 0

    num_set = set(nums)  # Store all numbers in a hash set
    longest_sequence = 0

    for num in num_set:
        # Only check for the start of a sequence
        if num - 1 not in num_set:
            current_num = num
            current_sequence = 1

            # Check for the next consecutive numbers
            while current_num + 1 in num_set:
```

```
                current_num += 1
                current_sequence += 1

            # Update the longest sequence
            longest_sequence = max(longest_sequence, current_sequence)

    return longest_sequence
```

b. **Time complexity**: *O(n)* because we visit each element of the array once.

c. **Space complexity**: *O(n)* because we store the elements of the array in a hash set.

The step-by-step explanation is as follows:

1. **Hash set creation:** Convert the array into a set to allow for *O(1)* lookups. This enables us to check whether a number exists in the array in constant time.
2. **Iterate over each number:** Loop through each element in the set. For each element, check if it is the start of a sequence by checking if **`num - 1`** is present in the set. If **`num - 1`** is not present, then **`num`** is the beginning of a sequence.
3. **Count the sequence length:** Once the beginning of a sequence is found, keep checking for consecutive elements (**`num + 1`**, **`num + 2`**, etc.) and count the length of the sequence.
4. **Update the longest sequence:** After counting the length of the current sequence, update the **`longest_sequence`** variable if this sequence is longer than the previously found sequences.

    a. **Example walkthrough:** Let us walk through an example step by step.

    - **Given input:**
      `nums = [100, 4, 200, 1, 3, 2]`
    - The steps in the code are as follows:

        i. **Add all elements to a set:**

        `num_set = {1, 2, 3, 100, 4, 200}`

        ii. **Iterate over each number**: We start with 1. Since 0 is not in the set, 1 is the start of a sequence. We check for consecutive elements and find 2, 3, and 4. The sequence [1, 2, 3, 4] has a length of 4.

        iii. **Check other numbers:** We continue with other elements in the set, but none of them are the start of a longer sequence. For example, 100 and 200 are isolated and do not have any consecutive elements following them.

    - **Final result:** The longest consecutive sequence is [1, 2, 3, 4] with a length of 4. The function returns 4.

Dig deeper

The edge cases are as follows:

- **Empty array:** If the array is empty, return 0 because there are no elements to form a sequence.

  ```
  nums = []  # Output: 0
  ```

- **Array with one element:** If the array contains only one element, the longest consecutive sequence is just that element, with a length of 1.

  ```
  nums = [5]  # Output: 1
  ```

- **All elements are the same:** If the array contains the same number repeated multiple times, the longest consecutive sequence has a length of 1.

  ```
  nums = [7, 7, 7, 7]  # Output: 1
  ```

The time and space complexity are explained as follows:

- **Time complexity**: *O(n)*, where n is the number of elements in the array. Each element is visited once when we add it to the set, and we only process each number once when checking for sequences.
- **Space complexity**: *O(n)*, as we store the array elements in a hash set.

How to approach this problem in an interview:

- **Clarify the problem:** Ensure you understand the task is to find the length of the longest consecutive sequence of integers in an unsorted array, and the algorithm must run in *O(n)* time.
- **Brute-force approach:** Mention that sorting the array and finding the consecutive sequence is a simple solution, but it has a time complexity of *O(n log n)*, which is not efficient enough for this problem.
- **Introduce the hash set approach:** Explain how using a hash set allows us to check for consecutive elements in *O(1)* time and how the algorithm achieves *O(n)* time complexity overall.
- **Edge cases:** Discuss how the solution handles edge cases like an empty array, an array with one element, or an array with all elements being the same.
- **Time and space complexity:** Emphasize that this approach runs in *O(n)* time and *O(n)* space, which is the most efficient solution for this problem.

The key takeaways for interviews are as follows:

- **Optimal time complexity**: This problem is a great test of your ability to find an optimal solution using *O(n)* time, which is required in interviews for efficiency.
- **Hash set for fast lookups**: Using a hash set to solve this problem demonstrates your knowledge of how to use data structures to optimize time complexity.

- **Edge case consideration**: Be sure to explain how your solution handles edge cases and avoids unnecessary complexity.

Problem 36: Find the missing element in a sorted array

Problem statement: You are given a sorted array of distinct integers, which is missing exactly one number from a range of consecutive integers. The task is to find the missing number.

For example:

- **Input**:

  `nums = [1, 2, 3, 5]`

- **Output**:

  `4`

Another example:

- **Input**:

  `nums = [10, 11, 12, 13, 14, 16, 17]`

- **Output**:

  `15`

Understanding the problem: You are provided with a sorted array of distinct integers, but one number is missing from the consecutive sequence. In a normal sequence of consecutive numbers, the difference between two adjacent numbers is 1. When one number is missing, the difference will be greater than 1 between the two numbers. Your task is to identify that missing number efficiently.

We will solve this problem using two different approaches:

- **Brute-force approach:** In this approach, you can iterate through the sorted array and check if the difference between two consecutive numbers is greater than 1. If it is, the missing number is between those two numbers.

- **Binary search approach:** Since the array is sorted, we can use binary search to find the missing number in *O(log n)* time.

Approach 1: Brute-force solution

The brute-force solution iterates through the array, checking the difference between consecutive elements. If the difference is greater than 1, the missing number is between those two elements.

Code example (brute-force solution):

```
def find_missing(nums):
    if not nums:
      return None
    for i in range(len(nums) - 1):
        if nums[i + 1] - nums[i] > 1:
            return nums[i] + 1
```

Time complexity: *O(n)*, where n is the number of elements in the array.

Space complexity: *O(1)*, as we are not using any extra space.

Approach 2: Binary search solution

Since the array is sorted, we can use **binary search** to solve the problem more efficiently in *O(log n)* time. The idea is to compare the element at the middle index to its expected value based on the index. If the element is less than its expected value, the missing number is in the left half of the array; otherwise, it is in the right half.

Code example (binary search solution):

```
def find_missing(nums):
    left, right = 0, len(nums) - 1
    while left <= right:
        mid = (left + right) // 2
        # Check if the current element matches the expected value
        if nums[mid] != nums[0] + mid:
            right = mid - 1
        else:
            left = mid + 1
    return nums[0] + left
```

Time complexity: *O(log n)*, where n is the number of elements in the array.

Space complexity: *O(1)*, as no additional space is used.

The step-by-step explanation is as follows:

1. **Brute-force approach:**
    a. Iterate through the array, and for each pair of adjacent elements, check if the difference between them is greater than 1.
    b. If the difference is greater than 1, return the missing number, which is the number between them.

2. **Binary search approach:**
    a. The idea is to leverage the fact that the array is sorted. In a perfectly sorted array of consecutive numbers, the element at index **`i`** would be equal to **`nums[0] + i`**.
    b. Compare the middle element (**`nums[mid]`**) to its expected value. If **`nums[mid]`** is less than the expected value, the missing number is in the left half. Otherwise, it is in the right half.
    c. Continue narrowing down the search space until you find the missing number.

Example walkthrough: Let us walk through an example step by step:

Given input:

```
nums = [1, 2, 3, 5]
```

The steps of the code are as follows:

1. **Binary search setup:**
    a. **`left = 0, right = 3`** (the length of the array minus 1).
    b. The array starts at 1, so the expected value of each element is **`nums[0] + index`**.
2. **First iteration:**
    a. Calculate **`mid = (0 + 3) // 2 = 1`**.
    b. The expected value of **`nums[1] is 1 + 1 = 2`**, which matches **`nums[1] = 2`**. So, the missing number must be in the right half.
    c. Update **`left = mid + 1 = 2`**.
3. **Second iteration:**
    a. Calculate **`mid = (2 + 3) // 2 = 2`**.
    b. The expected value of **`nums[2] is 1 + 2 = 3`**, which matches **`nums[2] = 3`**. So, the missing number must be in the right half.
    c. Update **`left = mid + 1 = 3`**.
4. **Third iteration:** Now, **`left = 3`** and **`right = 3`**, and **`nums[3] = 5`**. The expected value is 1 + 3 = 4, but **`nums[3]`** is 5, meaning the missing number is 4.

    Thus, the missing number is 4.

Dig deeper

The edge cases are as follows:

- **Array with no missing number:** If the array is perfectly consecutive with no missing number, you should return a message or handle the case as needed. However, the problem assumes exactly one number is missing.

- **Array with one element missing:** If the array has only two elements, this solution works as expected. For example:

  ```
  nums = [1, 3]  # Output: 2
  ```

- **Array at the lower or upper bound of the range:** If the missing number is the smallest or largest possible value, the solution still handles it correctly.

The time and space complexity are explained as follows:

- **Time complexity**: *O(log n)*, because we use binary search to find the missing element.
- **Space complexity**: *O(1)*, since the binary search is done in place without additional data structures.

How to approach this problem in an interview:

- **Clarify the problem:** Ensure that you understand the array is sorted, contains distinct integers, and is missing exactly one number. The goal is to find the missing number efficiently.
- **Brute-force solution:** Mention that the brute-force solution would iterate through the array and check the difference between adjacent numbers, which takes *O(n)* time.
- **Introduce binary search:** Explain how binary search allows you to find the missing number in *O(log n)* time by leveraging the sorted property of the array and comparing elements to their expected values.
- **Edge cases:** Discuss how the solution handles edge cases, such as arrays with no missing number or arrays where the missing number is the first or last element.
- **Time and space complexity:** Emphasize that the binary search solution is optimal with *O(log n)* time and *O(1)* space.

The key takeaways for interviews are as follows:

- **Binary search in a sorted array**: This problem is an excellent test of your ability to apply binary search to find elements in a sorted array.
- **Efficiency**: Using binary search instead of brute-force demonstrates your ability to think of more efficient solutions.
- **Edge case handling**: Be sure to mention how your solution handles different edge cases and how it scales with larger arrays.

Problem 37: Reverse words in a string

Problem statement: Given an input string s, reverse the order of the words. A word is defined as a sequence of non-space characters. The words in s will be separated by at least one space. Your task is to reverse the order of the words while keeping the characters in each word unchanged. You should also remove any extra spaces.

For example:

- **Input**:

  `s = "  the sky is   blue  "`

- **Output**:

  `"blue is sky the"`

Another example:

- **Input**:

  `s = "hello world"`

- **Output**:

  `"world hello"`

Understanding the problem: The problem asks us to reverse the order of words in a string. We are given a sentence where words may be separated by multiple spaces. We need to ensure the output has words in reverse order and remove any extra spaces.

For example, in the string " the sky is blue ", the words "the", "sky", "is", and "blue" must be reversed, and the result should be "blue is sky the" with no extra spaces.

The step-by-step solution is as follows:

- **Split the string into words:** Ignore the extra spaces and extract only the words.
- **Reverse the order of the words:** Once we have the words, reverse their order.
- **Join the words into a single string:** After reversing the words, join them back into a single string with a single space between them.

Approach: Splitting, reversing, and joining

The steps are as follows:

1. **Remove extra spaces:** First, we need to split the string based on spaces and ignore any extra spaces. Python's **`split()`** method handles this by splitting on whitespace and removing extra spaces automatically.
2. **Reverse the words:** Once we have the words, reversing them is straightforward using Python's slicing.
3. **Join the words:** After reversing the words, we join them back into a single string using **`join()`**.

   a. **Code implementation:**

```
def reverse_words(s):
    # Step 1: Split the string into words, ignoring extra spaces
```

```
    words = s.split()

    # Step 2: Reverse the list of words
    reversed_words = words[::-1]

    # Step 3: Join the words back into a single string
    return ' '.join(reversed_words)
```

   b. **Time complexity**: *O(n)*, where n is the length of the string **s**.

   c. **Space complexity**: *O(n)*, where n is the number of characters in the input string.

The step-by-step explanation is as follows:

1. **Splitting the string:** Use Python's **split()** method to break the string into words, automatically removing extra spaces. For example:

```
s = "  the sky is   blue  "
words = s.split()  # ['the', 'sky', 'is', 'blue']
```

2. **Reversing the words:** Reverse the list of words using Python's slicing:

```
reversed_words = words[::-1]  # ['blue', 'is', 'sky', 'the']
```

3. **Joining the words:** Finally, join the reversed words with a single space between them:

```
result = ' '.join(reversed_words)  # "blue is sky the"
```

   a. **Example walkthrough:** Let us walk through an example step by step.

   - **Given input:**

```
s = "  the sky is   blue  "
```

      i. **Split the string:** After splitting the string, the result is:

```
words = ['the', 'sky', 'is', 'blue']
```

      ii. **Reverse the words:** Reverse the list of words:

```
reversed_words = ['blue', 'is', 'sky', 'the']
```

      iii. **Join the words:** Join the reversed words into a single string:

```
result = "blue is sky the"
```

   Thus, the final output is **blue is sky the**.

Dig deeper

The edge cases are as follows:

- **Empty string:** If the input string is empty, the result should also be an empty string.

```
s = ""  # Output: ""
```

- **String with only spaces:** If the input string contains only spaces, the result should be an empty string.

```
s = "     "  # Output: ""
```

- **String with one word:** If the input string contains only one word, the result should be the same word.

```
s = "hello"  # Output: "hello"
```

The time and space complexity are explained as follows:

- **Time complexity**: *O(n)*, where n is the number of characters in the string **`s`**. We process each character when splitting, reversing, and joining the words.
- **Space complexity**: *O(n)*, as we store the words in a list, and the final result is also a string of length n.

How to approach this problem in an interview:

- **Clarify the problem:** Ensure that you understand the task is to reverse the order of the words in the string and remove any extra spaces.
- **Brute-force solution:** Mention that a brute-force solution would involve manually parsing the string character by character, but using Python's built-in **`split()`** and **`join()`** methods simplifies the solution.
- **Optimal approach:** Explain how splitting the string into words, reversing the list of words, and joining them back together achieves the desired result in *O(n)* time.
- **Edge cases:** Discuss how the solution handles edge cases, such as empty strings, strings with only spaces, or strings with one word.
- **Time and space complexity:** Emphasize that this solution runs in *O(n)* time and *O(n)* space, which is optimal for this problem.

The key takeaways for interviews are as follows:

- **Efficient string manipulation**: This problem is an excellent test of your ability to manipulate strings efficiently.
- **Built-in methods**: Using built-in methods like **`split()`**, **`join()`**, and list slicing demonstrates your familiarity with Python's standard library and efficient problem-solving techniques.
- **Edge case handling**: Be sure to explain how your solution handles different edge cases, such as empty strings and strings with only spaces.

Problem 38: Find the longest common prefix

Problem statement: Given an array of strings, write a function to find the **longest common prefix (LCP)** among all the strings. If there is no common prefix, return an empty string "".

For example:

- **Input**:

  ```
  strs = ["flower", "flow", "flight"]
  ```

- **Output**:

  ```
  "fl"
  ```

Another example:

- **Input**:

  ```
  strs = ["dog", "racecar", "car"]
  ```

- **Output**:

  ```
  ""
  ```

Understanding the problem: In this problem, you are given an array of strings, and the goal is to find the LCP shared by all the strings. A **prefix** is the starting substring that is common across all the strings.

For example, in the array ["flower", "flow", "flight"], the LCP is "fl", as it is the common starting substring in all three words. If no such common prefix exists, the output will be an empty string.

We will use a straightforward approach to solve this problem. The steps are as follows:

1. **Start with the first string as a reference:** Assume the first string in the array is the LCP and compare it with all the other strings.
2. **Gradually shorten the prefix:** Compare the reference string with each subsequent string, character by character. If a mismatch is found, reduce the length of the prefix.
3. **Return the final common prefix:** After comparing the reference string with all other strings, the remaining prefix will be the LCP.

Approach: Compare characters

The steps are as follows:

1. **Initial prefix:** Assume the first string in the array is the LCP.
2. **Compare each string:** For each string in the array, check if it starts with the current prefix. If it does not, remove the last character from the prefix and repeat until a match is found or the prefix becomes empty.

   a. **Code implementation:**

   ```
   def longest_common_prefix(strs):
       if not strs:
   ```

```
        return ""

    # Start with the first string as the reference prefix
    prefix = strs[0]

    # Compare the prefix with each string
    for string in strs[1:]:
        # Shorten the prefix until it matches the current string
        while not string.startswith(prefix):
            prefix = prefix[:-1]
            if not prefix:
                return ""

    return prefix
```

b. **Time complexity**: *O(n * m)*, where n is the number of strings and m is the length of the shortest string in the array.

c. **Space complexity**: *O(1)*, as we are only using a constant amount of extra space.

The step-by-step explanation is as follows:

1. **Initialize the prefix:** Assume the first string is the LCP.

   `prefix = "flower"`

2. **Compare the prefix with each string:** Start comparing the prefix with each string in the array.

   a. Compare "flower" with "flow". Since "flower" does not start with "flow", reduce the prefix to "flow".

   b. Compare "flow" with "flight". Since "flow" does not start with "fl", reduce the prefix to "fl", which is the LCP for all strings.

3. **Return the prefix:** After comparing all the strings, the final value of prefix is "fl", which is returned as the result.

   a. **Example walkthrough:** Let us walk through an example step by step.

   b. **Given input:**

      `strs = ["flower", "flow", "flight"]`

   c. **The steps of the code are:**

      i. **Initialize the prefix:** The first string "flower" is assumed to be the LCP.

         `prefix = "flower"`

      ii. **Compare with "flow":** "flow" does not start with "flower", so shorten the prefix until it does → prefix = "flow"

         `prefix = "flow"`

iii. **Compare with "flight":** "flight" does not start with "flow", so shorten prefix until it does → prefix = "fl"

```
prefix = "fl"
```

iv. **Return the final prefix:** The LCP is "fl", so the function returns "fl".

Dig deeper

The edge cases are as follows:

- **Empty array:** If the input array is empty, return an empty string.

  ```
  strs = []  # Output: ""
  ```

- **No common prefix:** If there is no common prefix among the strings, return an empty string.

  ```
  strs = ["dog", "racecar", "car"]  # Output: ""
  ```

- **One string in the array:** If the array contains only one string, that string itself is the LCP.

  ```
  strs = ["alone"]  # Output: "alone"
  ```

- **Identical strings:** If all the strings are identical, return the string itself as the LCP.

  ```
  strs = ["test", "test", "test"]  # Output: "test"
  ```

The time and space complexity are explained as follows:

- **Time complexity**: $O(n * m)$, where n is the number of strings and m is the length of the shortest string. In the worst case, we have to compare each character of every string.
- **Space complexity**: $O(1)$, since no additional data structures are used apart from the input strings.

How to approach this problem in an interview:

- **Clarify the problem:** Make sure you understand that the task is to find the LCP among an array of strings. If there is no common prefix, return an empty string.
- **Brute-force solution:** Mention that a brute-force solution would compare each character of the strings one by one, but that could be inefficient. Instead, comparing prefixes is more optimal.
- **Optimal approach:** Explain how you use the first string as a reference and then shorten the prefix as you compare it with each string in the array. This approach efficiently finds the common prefix in $O(n * m)$ time.
- **Edge cases:** Discuss how the solution handles edge cases like an empty array, no common prefix, or an array with identical strings.

- **Time and space complexity:** Emphasize that this solution runs in *O(n * m)* time and uses *O(1)* space, which is optimal for this problem.

The key takeaways for interviews are as follows:

- **String manipulation**: This problem is a good test of your ability to manipulate and compare strings efficiently.
- **Prefix matching**: Using prefix matching with a reference string demonstrates your understanding of string comparison and optimization techniques.
- **Edge case handling**: Make sure to explain how your solution handles edge cases, especially when there is no common prefix.

Problem 39: Minimum window substring

Problem statement: Given two strings **s** and **t**, return the minimum window in **s** that contains all the characters of **t**. If there is no such window, return an empty string "". If there is such a window, it should contain all characters in t, including duplicates, in any order.

For example:

- **Input**:

  `s = "ADOBECODEBANC"`

  `t = "ABC"`

- **Output**:

  "BANC"

Another example:

- **Input**:

  `s = "a"`

  `t = "a"`

- **Output**:

  "a"

Understanding the problem: The problem asks you to find the smallest substring in string **s** that contains all the characters of string **t**. The substring must contain at least one occurrence of each character in **t**, and the order of the characters does not matter.

For instance, in the example where s = "ADOBECODEBANC" and t = "ABC", the minimum window in s that contains all the characters in t is "BANC".

We will solve this problem using a **sliding window** approach. The step-by-step solution is as follows:

1. **Expand the window:** Move the right end of the window to include characters from s until the window contains all the characters from t.

2. **Shrink the window:** Once the window contains all the characters from t, move the left end to minimize the window size.
3. **Track the smallest window:** During the process, keep track of the smallest window that satisfies the condition.

Approach: Sliding window

The steps are as follows:

1. **Track character frequency:** Use a dictionary to keep track of the frequency of characters in **t**. For each character in **s**, we check if it is in **t** and adjust the window accordingly.
2. **Expand and shrink the window:** Expand the window by moving the right pointer. When the window contains all characters in **t**, try to shrink it by moving the left pointer to minimize the window size.
3. **Store the smallest valid window:** Keep track of the length and the start of the smallest valid window, and update it as you find smaller windows.
    a. **Code implementation:** From collections import **Counter**:

```
def min_window(s, t):
    if not s or not t:
        return ""

    # Dictionary to count the frequency of characters in t
    char_count_t = Counter(t)
    required = len(char_count_t)

    # Left and right pointers for the window
    l, r = 0, 0

    # Dictionary to count the characters in the current window
    window_counts = {}
    formed = 0

    # Result tuple: (window length, left, right)
    ans = float("inf"), None, None

    while r < len(s):
        # Add the character from the right pointer
        char = s[r]
        window_counts[char] = window_counts.get(char, 0) + 1

        # Check if this character matches the frequency in t
        if char in char_count_t and window_counts[char] == char_
count_t[char]:
            formed += 1

        # Try to shrink the window from the left
```

```
            while l <= r and formed == required:
                char = s[l]

                # Save the smallest window
                if r - l + 1 < ans[0]:
                    ans = (r - l + 1, l, r)

                # Remove the character from the left
                window_counts[char] -= 1
                if char in char_count_t and window_counts[char] <
char_count_t[char]:
                    formed -= 1

                l += 1

            # Expand the window by moving the right pointer
            r += 1

        # Return the smallest window or an empty string if no valid
window is found
        return "" if ans[0] == float("inf") else s[ans[1]:ans[2] + 1]
```

b. **Time complexity**: *O(n)*, where n is the length of the string **s**. Both left and right pointers move through the string only once.

c. **Space complexity**: *O(t)*, where *t* is the number of unique characters in string *t*.

The step-by-step explanation is as follows:

1. **Track character frequencies:** Use the **Counter** from the collections module to store the frequency of each character in **t**. For example:

   ```
   t = «ABC»
   char_count_t = Counter(t)  # {'A': 1, 'B': 1, 'C': 1}
   ```

2. **Sliding window:** Use two pointers **l** and **r,** to define the window. Initially, both pointers are at the beginning of the string **s**. The right pointer **r** expands the window, and the left pointer **l** shrinks the window when the condition is met.

3. **Expand the window:** Expand the window by moving the right pointer **r**. For each character at position **r**, add it to the **window_counts** dictionary. If this character completes one of the required characters in t, increment the formed count.

4. **Shrink the window:** When all the characters in t are found in the window (**formed == required**), try to shrink the window from the left. If shrinking makes the window smaller while still containing all characters of t, update the result.

5. **Track the minimum window:** During the process, keep track of the smallest window that satisfies the condition. Return the substring representing the smallest window at the end.

a. **Example walkthrough:** Let us walk through an example step by step.

- **Given input:**

```
s = "ADOBECODEBANC"
t = "ABC"
```

- The steps of the code are as follows:

  i. **Initialize:**
     - `char_count_t = {'A': 1, 'B': 1, 'C': 1}`
     - `window_counts = {}`, `required = 3, formed = 0`
     - `l = 0, r = 0, ans = (inf, None, None)`

  ii. **Expand the window:**
     - Move the right pointer **r** and add characters to the window.
     - When the window contains all characters of **t**, check the window size and update **ans**.
     - For example:
       - At **r = 5**, the window is "ADOBEC", and it contains all the characters of t. Update **ans** to (6, 0, 5).
       - At **r = 12**, the window is "BANC", which is a smaller valid window. Update **ans** to (4, 9, 12).

  iii. **Shrink the window:** Shrink the window by moving the left pointer **l** to minimize the window size while still containing all the characters of **t**.

  iv. **Return the smallest window:** The final result is "BANC", the smallest window containing all characters of **t**.

Dig deeper

The edge cases are as follows:

- **Empty string:** If either **s** or **t** is empty, return an empty string.

```
s = "", t = "A"  # Output: ""
```

- **No valid window:** If there is no window in **s** that contains all the characters of **t**, return an empty string.

```
s = "ADOBECODEBANC", t = "XYZ"  # Output: ""
```

- **Exact match:** If **t** is exactly the same as a substring in **s**, return that substring.

```
s = "AA", t = "AA"  # Output: "AA"
```

The time and space complexity are explained as follows:

- **Time complexity**: *O(n)*, where n is the length of **s**. We traverse the string with two pointers, each moving at most n times.
- **Space complexity**: *O(t + s)*, where t is the number of unique characters in t and s is the number of unique characters in s.

How to approach this problem in an interview:

- **Clarify the problem:** Make sure you understand that the problem's goal is to find the minimum window in s that contains all characters of t.
- **Brute-force approach:** Mention that a brute-force solution would involve checking all possible substrings, but this would be inefficient.
- **Sliding window approach:** Explain how the sliding window approach allows you to efficiently expand and shrink the window, maintaining a count of characters and minimizing the window size when all characters are found.
- **Edge cases:** Discuss how the solution handles edge cases, such as when t is larger than s, or when no valid window exists.
- **Time and space complexity:** This solution runs in *O(n)* time and *O(t + s)* space, which is optimal for this problem.

The key takeaways for interviews are as follows:

- **Sliding window technique**: This problem is a classic example of the sliding window technique, which is a common interview topic.
- **Efficient character tracking**: Using dictionaries to track character frequencies demonstrates your ability to optimize solutions for problems involving strings.
- **Edge case handling**: Explain how your solution handles different edge cases, such as empty strings or no valid windows.

Problem 40: Valid parentheses

Problem statement: Given a string s containing just the characters '(', ')', '{', '}', '[', and ']', determine if the input string is valid.

An input string is valid if:

- Open brackets must be closed by the same type of brackets.
- Open brackets must be closed in the correct order.
- Every closing bracket has a corresponding open bracket of the same type.

For example:

- **Input**:
  ```
  s = "({[]})"
  ```
- **Output**:
  ```
  True
  ```
- **Explanation:** Every opening bracket has a corresponding closing bracket in the correct order.

Understanding the problem: The valid parentheses problem is a common coding challenge that tests your understanding of stacks and proper bracket matching. The goal is to check if a string of brackets is balanced, which is essential in parsing tasks, compilers, and expression validation. A stack data structure is ideal for this problem due to its **Last In, First Out** (**LIFO**) nature, which helps track the most recent unmatched opening bracket.

The step-by-step solution is as follows.

Approach 1: Brute-force

Repeatedly replace pairs of valid brackets in the string until none remain. If the string becomes empty, it is valid.

Code example:

```
def is_valid(s):
    while '()' in s or '{}' in s or '[]' in s:
        s = s.replace('()', '').replace('{}', '').replace('[]', '')
    return s == ''
```

The details are as follows:

- **Time complexity**: $O(n^2)$, as each replacement can take $O(n)$ and could occur $n/2$ times.
- **Space complexity**: $O(n)$, due to string immutability and intermediate copies.
- **Notes**: While this works for small inputs, it is inefficient for large strings.

Approach 2: Optimized using stack

Use a stack to track open brackets. For every closing bracket, check if it matches the top of the stack. If it does, pop it. If not, the string is invalid.

Code example:

```
def is_valid(s):
    stack = []
    bracket_map = {')': '(', '}': '{', ']': '['}
```

```
for char in s:
    if char in bracket_map.values():
        stack.append(char)
    elif char in bracket_map:
        if not stack or stack[-1] != bracket_map[char]:
            return False
        stack.pop()
    else:
        return False
return not stack
```

The details are as follows:

- **Time complexity**: *O(n)*, where n is the length of the string.
- **Space complexity**: *O(n)*, for storing opening brackets in the stack.

The step-by-step explanation is as follows:

1. **Initialize a stack:** We use a list as a stack to keep track of opening brackets.
2. **Iterate through the string:** For each character:
   a. If it is an opening bracket, push it to the stack.
   b. If it is a closing bracket, check if the stack is empty or the top of the stack does not match the corresponding opening bracket. If so, return False.
   c. Otherwise, pop the matched opening bracket.
3. **Final check:** After processing all characters, if the stack is empty, return True. Otherwise, return False.

   Example walkthrough: Let us walk through an example step by step:

   - **Given input**:

     ```
     s = "({[]})"
     ```

   - The steps of the code are as follows:
     i. Stack = []
     ii. Read '(': Push → Stack = ['(']
     iii. Read '{': Push → Stack = ['(', '{']
     iv. Read '[': Push → Stack = ['(', '{', '[']
     v. Read ']': Match with '[' → Pop → Stack = ['(', '{']
     vi. Read '}': Match with '{' → Pop → Stack = ['(']
     vii. Read ')': Match with '(' → Pop → Stack = []
     viii. Final stack is empty → Valid → Output: True

Dig deeper

The edge cases are as follows:

- **Empty string:** If **s** is empty, it will be considered valid.

  ```
  s = "" # Output: True
  ```

- **Only one char:** If **s** contains only one character, either an opening or a closing bracket, it will be considered valid.

  ```
  s = "(" # Output: True
  ```

- **Mismatched:** If there is a mismatched type or order in **s**, consider it invalid.

  ```
  s = "(["  # Output: False
  ```

How to approach this problem in an interview:

- **Explain the goal:** Validate if brackets are balanced and properly ordered.
- **Brute-force approach:** Explain the string replacement method and its limitations.
- **Stack approach:** Emphasize the LIFO nature of stacks and how they solve the problem efficiently.
- **Edge cases:** Address empty strings, unmatched brackets, etc.
- **Time and space complexity:** To justify efficiency.

The key takeaways for interviews are as follows:

- **Stack approach**: Ideal for matching problems due to its LIFO property.
- **Balanced expressions**: Understanding how to validate expressions is a common interview topic.
- **Optimization**: Moving from brute-force to stack demonstrates algorithmic thinking.

Join our Discord space

Join our Discord workspace for latest updates, offers, tech happenings around the world, new releases, and sessions with the authors:

https://discord.bpbonline.com

Section 4
Searching and Sorting Algorithms

Introduction

Welcome to *Section 4,* where we explore the fascinating world of searching and sorting algorithms. These algorithms are among the most fundamental concepts in computer science and programming. No matter if you are building a simple application or developing a highly scalable system, understanding how to search through data efficiently and sort that data is crucial.

Imagine you are trying to find a specific book in a massive library, or you need to organize hundreds of files by date. Searching and sorting are not just tasks developers face during coding interviews; they are essential skills in real-world software development. From web applications that rank search results to algorithms that power recommendations on your favorite streaming platform, efficient searching and sorting are at the heart of it all.

In this section, we will look further into **binary search**, one of the most efficient search algorithms for sorted data. We will also explore classic sorting algorithms like **merge sort** and **quick sort,** and more specialized ones like **bucket sort** and **radix sort**. You will gain a strong understanding of how these algorithms work, their time complexities, and when to use them.

Why searching and sorting matter: In every coding interview and technical assessment, you will likely encounter problems that require you to search for a specific element or sort a list of data. It is no coincidence that these algorithms are the foundation of most coding challenges.

Interviewers want to see if you can think critically about processing and organizing data efficiently.

Efficient searching and sorting can drastically reduce the time required to perform a task. For example, using binary search in a sorted list allows you to find an element in *O(log n)* time rather than *O(n)* if you search through every element. Sorting a dataset before performing operations on it can simplify problems, and knowing which sorting algorithm to use for a given situation is a valuable skill.

Objectives

We will start with binary search, a simple yet powerful search algorithm that operates on sorted data. You will learn how to implement it iteratively and recursively and understand why it is much more efficient than a linear search.

From there, we will look at sorting algorithms. You will explore the strengths and weaknesses of each algorithm, from the classic merge sort and quick sort to more specialized sorts like **heap sort**, bucket sort, and radix sort. These sorting algorithms are not just theoretical; understanding how to implement and optimize them will be critical in interviews and real-world projects.

We will also cover *divide-and-conquer algorithms like merge sort, which breaks* down problems into smaller, more manageable pieces, and quick sort, one of the fastest algorithms for sorting data in practice.

Challenges ahead: Throughout this section, you will work on coding challenges that build your skills in searching and sorting. You will implement algorithms like binary search and use them to solve problems like finding the *Kth Largest Element in an Array*. You will also tackle more advanced sorting challenges like the *Dutch National Flag Problem,* where you will learn how to sort arrays based on specific criteria in linear time.

Each challenge is designed to deepen your understanding of these essential algorithms. You will implement the algorithms, learn to *analyze their time complexity*, and understand why certain algorithms are better suited for specific tasks.

Practical applications: Algorithms like merge sort and quick sort are often used in databases, search engines, and file systems. You will see these algorithms in action when optimizing data retrieval or processing large datasets. For instance, a streaming service might use these sorting techniques to rank content, and search engines use similar algorithms to quickly display the most relevant results.

Understanding these algorithms will allow you to write efficient, optimized code. You will be able to choose the suitable algorithm for the job, improving the performance of your applications and setting yourself apart as a developer who knows how to optimize solutions.

The real-world examples are as follows:

- **E-commerce platforms**: Sorting algorithms display products based on price, ratings, or relevance.
- **Search engines**: Search algorithms like binary search help retrieve search results quickly from sorted datasets.
- **Data processing**: Algorithms like **counting sort** and radix sort are often used in applications that handle massive amounts of data and need fast sorting mechanisms.
- **Game development**: In gaming, searching and sorting algorithms optimize leaderboards, inventory systems, and pathfinding algorithms.

Engagement through challenges:

Each challenge in this section is designed to simulate real-world problems you will face in interviews and on the job. You will work on problems like finding the *Top K Frequent Elements* in an array or implementing efficient sorting algorithms that can handle large amounts of data. As you solve these problems, you will gain the confidence to face any coding challenge involving searching and sorting algorithms.

By finishing this section, you will have mastered essential algorithms that are a staple of coding interviews and professional development. You can implement these algorithms and understand their underlying mechanics, time complexity, and when to use each.

Problem 41: Binary search implementation

Problem statement: Given a sorted array of integers, write a function to find the index of a given target value. If the target exists in the array, return its index. Otherwise, return -1.

For example:

- **Input**:

  ```
  arr = [1, 3, 5, 7, 9, 11, 13, 15]
  target = 7
  ```

- **Output**:

  ```
  3 # The target 7 is found at index 3
  ```

Another example:

- **Input**:

  ```
  arr = [2, 4, 6, 8, 10, 12]
  target = 5
  ```

- **Output**:

  ```
  -1 # Target 5 is not found in the array
  ```

Understanding the problem: Binary search is a highly efficient algorithm to search for an element in a sorted array. Unlike linear search, which checks each element one by one, binary search divides the search space in half each time, significantly reducing the number of comparisons.

In binary search, we use two pointers: one starting at the beginning (left) and one at the end (right) of the array. We then calculate the middle index (mid) and compare the middle element with the target:

1. If the middle element matches the target, we return the index.
2. If the target is less than the middle element, we adjust the right pointer to search in the left half.
3. If the target is greater than the middle element, we adjust the left pointer to search in the right half.

This process continues until the target is found or the search space is exhausted.

Approach: Iterative binary search

The steps are as follows:

1. **Start with pointers:** Set the left pointer to the beginning of the array (0) and the right pointer to the end (len(arr) - 1).
2. **Calculate the middle:** In each iteration, calculate the middle index:
   `mid = (left + right) // 2`
3. **Compare the middle element with the target:**
   a. If the middle element is equal to the target, return the index.
   b. If the target is smaller, move the right pointer to mid - 1.
   c. If the target is larger, move the left pointer to mid + 1.
4. **Return result:** If the left pointer exceeds the right pointer, the target is not in the array, so return -1.

Code implementation: Iterative approach:

```
def binary_search(arr, target):
    left, right = 0, len(arr) - 1

    while left <= right:
        mid = (left + right) // 2

        # Check if the middle element is the target
        if arr[mid] == target:
            return mid

        # If target is smaller, search the left half
```

```
        elif target < arr[mid]:
            right = mid - 1

        # If target is larger, search the right half
        else:
            left = mid + 1

    # Target not found
    return -1
```

Example walkthrough: Let us walk through an example step by step.

- **Given input:**

  ```
  arr = [1, 3, 5, 7, 9, 11, 13, 15]
  target = 7
  ```

- **Step**: Initial pointers:

  ```
  left = 0, right = 7
  Calculate mid = (0 + 7) // 2 = 3
  arr[mid] = arr[3] = 7, which is equal to the target.
  Return mid = 3.
  ```

  The result is 3, meaning the target 7 is found at index 3.

The time and space complexity are explained as follows:

- **Time complexity**: *O(log n)*, where n is the number of elements in the array. The search space is halved in every step, making this one of the most efficient search algorithms.
- **Space complexity**: *O(1)*, as no additional data structures are used.

Alternative approach: Recursive binary search

In addition to the iterative approach, binary search can also be implemented recursively. The recursive version works similarly by reducing the search space in each recursive call.

Code implementation: Recursive approach:

```
def recursive_binary_search(arr, target, left, right):
    # Base case: if the search space is exhausted
    if left > right:
        return -1

    # Calculate the middle index
    mid = (left + right) // 2

    # Check if the middle element is the target
    if arr[mid] == target:
        return mid
```

```
    # If target is smaller, search the left half
    elif target < arr[mid]:
        return recursive_binary_search(arr, target, left, mid - 1)

    # If target is larger, search the right half
    else:
        return recursive_binary_search(arr, target, mid + 1, right)
```

In this approach, we use recursion to keep breaking down the array into smaller segments until we find the target or the search space is exhausted. The time and space complexity are explained as follows:

- **Time complexity:** *O(log n).*
- **Space complexity**: *O(log n),* due to the recursive call stack.

How to approach this problem in an interview:

- **Clarify the problem:** Ensure that the input array is sorted, and discuss whether you can use an iterative or recursive approach.
- **Discuss time complexity:** Explain why binary search is more efficient than a linear search, especially for large datasets. Mention that binary search runs in *O(log n)* time, which is optimal for this problem.
- **Edge cases:** Discuss edge cases like an empty array, a single-element array, or when the target is not present in the array.
- **Space complexity:** Mention that the iterative approach uses *O(1)* space, whereas the recursive approach requires *O(log n)* space due to the call stack.

Dig deeper

The edge cases are as follows:

- **Empty array:** If the input array is empty, return -1.

  ```
  arr = []  # Output: -1
  ```

- **Target not found:** If the target is not present in the array, return -1.

  ```
  arr = [1, 2, 3], target = 4  # Output: -1
  ```

- **Single-element array:** If the array has only one element, the algorithm should still work.

  ```
  arr = [5], target = 5  # Output: 0
  ```

- **All elements are the same:** If all elements in the array are the same, the algorithm will still find the target if it exists.

  ```
  arr = [5, 5, 5, 5], target = 5  # Output: any valid index, e.g., 0
  ```

The key takeaways for interviews are as follows:

- **Binary search**: This is a fundamental search algorithm that often appears in technical interviews. It tests your understanding of searching, pointers, and how to reduce time complexity by halving the search space.
- **Iterative vs recursive**: Be ready to discuss both iterative and recursive approaches and explain their pros and cons.
- **Time and space complexity**: Emphasize that binary search is efficient, running in *O(log n)* time and using minimal space (*O(1)* iteratively, *O(log n)* recursively).

Problem 42: Merge sort

Problem statement: Given an unsorted array of integers, write a function that sorts the array in ascending order using the merge sort algorithm.

For example:

- **Input**:
  `arr = [12, 11, 13, 5, 6, 7]`
- **Output**:
  `[5, 6, 7, 11, 12, 13]`

Another example:

- **Input**:
  `arr = [3, 7, 2, 9, 1]`
- **Output**:
  `[1, 2, 3, 7, 9]`

Understanding the problem: Merge sort is a **divide and conquer** algorithm that splits the array into smaller subarrays, sorts them, and then merges them back together to form a sorted array. Unlike algorithms like bubble sort or insertion sort, which work in $O(n^2)$ time, merge sort works efficiently in *O(n log n)* time.

Here is how it works:

- **Divide** the array into two halves.
- **Recursively** sort each half.
- **Merge** the two sorted halves into a single sorted array.

Approach: Divide and conquer

Merge sort works by continually splitting the array in half until each subarray contains only one element (which is considered sorted). Then, it merges these sorted subarrays back together. The steps are as follows:

1. **Split the array:** Repeatedly divide the array into two halves until you reach arrays of size one.
2. **Sort the subarrays:** Recursively sort each half of the array.
3. **Merge the subarrays:** Merge two sorted subarrays into one sorted array. During the merging step, compare the smallest elements from each subarray and build a new sorted array.

Code implementation: Merge sort:

```
def merge_sort(arr):
    if len(arr) > 1:
        # Find the middle of the array
        mid = len(arr) // 2

        # Divide the array elements into two halves
        left_half = arr[:mid]
        right_half = arr[mid:]

        # Recursively sort both halves
        merge_sort(left_half)
        merge_sort(right_half)

        # Merge the sorted halves
        i = j = k = 0

        # Copy data to the temporary arrays left_half[] and right_half[]
        while i < len(left_half) and j < len(right_half):
            if left_half[i] < right_half[j]:
                arr[k] = left_half[i]
                i += 1
            else:
                arr[k] = right_half[j]
                j += 1
            k += 1

        # Checking if any element was left
        while i < len(left_half):
            arr[k] = left_half[i]
            i += 1
            k += 1

        while j < len(right_half):
            arr[k] = right_half[j]
            j += 1
            k += 1
```

Example walkthrough: Let us walk through an example step by step.

Given input:

```
arr = [12, 11, 13, 5, 6, 7]
```

The steps are as follows:

1. **Divide the array:** The array is divided into two halves:
   - **Left half**: [12, 11, 13]
   - **Right half**: [5, 6, 7]
2. **Recursively sort each half:**
   - For the left half:
     - [12, 11, 13] is divided into [12] and [11, 13].
     - [11, 13] is further divided and then merged back as [11, 13].
     - Finally, [12] and [11, 13] are merged into [11, 12, 13].
   - For the right half:
     - [5, 6, 7] is divided into [5] and [6, 7].
     - [6, 7] is already sorted and merged back with [5] as [5, 6, 7].
3. **Merge the sorted halves:** Now, we merge [11, 12, 13] and [5, 6, 7]. During the merging process, we compare the smallest elements from both arrays and place them in the correct order. The final sorted array is:
   ```
   [5, 6, 7, 11, 12, 13]
   ```

The time and space complexity are explained as follows:

- **Time complexity:** O(n log n):
  - The time complexity of merge sort is *O(n log n)* because it divides the array into two halves at each step (log n levels of division) and requires linear time (*O(n)*) to merge the divided arrays at each level.
- **Space complexity:** O(n):
  - Merge sort requires *O(n)* additional space for the temporary arrays used during the merging process.

The step-by-step explanation is as follows:

1. **Base case:** If the array has one or fewer elements, it is already sorted, so we return.
2. **Divide the array:** Split the array into two halves by finding the middle index.
3. **Recursive sorting:** Recursively apply merge sort to both halves of the array.
4. **Merge the arrays:** The merging process involves comparing the elements of the two sorted halves and combining them into a single sorted array.

The edge cases are as follows:

- **Empty array**: If the input array is empty, return an empty array.
- **Single element**: If the array has only one element, it is already sorted, so no further processing is needed.

Merge sort vs. other sorting algorithms:

- **Merge sort vs. quick sort:** Merge sort has a guaranteed time complexity of *O(n log n)*, while quick sort can degrade to $O(n^2)$ in the worst case. However, merge sort requires additional space *(O(n))*, whereas quick sort is an in-place sorting algorithm with *O(log n)* space complexity.
- **Merge sort vs. bubble sort:** Merge sort is much faster than bubble sort, which runs in $O(n^2)$ time. Bubble sort repeatedly swaps adjacent elements until the array is sorted, making it inefficient for large arrays.
- **Merge sort for linked lists:** Merge sort is often the algorithm of choice for sorting linked lists because it does not require random access to elements (which is inefficient in linked lists) and can be implemented in *O(n log n)* time.

Some real-world applications of merge sort are as follows:

- **Sorting large datasets**: Merge sort's *O(n log n)* time complexity makes it ideal for sorting large datasets, especially in external sorting, where the data is too large to fit into memory.
- **Linked list sorting**: Merge sort is often preferred for sorting linked lists because of its ability to work efficiently without random access to elements.
- **Parallel processing**: Merge sort's divide-and-conquer approach makes it suitable for parallel processing, where the array can be divided into smaller parts and sorted concurrently.

Dig deeper

The edge cases are as follows:

- **Empty array:** If the input array is empty, return an empty array.

  ```
  arr = []  # Output: []
  ```

- **Single-element array:** If the array has only one element, it is already sorted.

  ```
  arr = [1]  # Output: [1]
  ```

- **Sorted array:** If the array is already sorted, merge sort will still divide and merge the elements, but will maintain the sorted order.

  ```
  arr = [1, 2, 3, 4]  # Output: [1, 2, 3, 4]
  ```

How to approach this problem in an interview:

- **Clarify the problem:** Make sure you understand the input and expected output. Ask about edge cases like an empty array or a single-element array.
- **Explain the time complexity:** Discuss how merge sort works in $O(n \log n)$ time and why it is more efficient than $O(n^2)$ algorithms like bubble sort and insertion sort.
- **Discuss the space complexity:** Mention that merge sort uses $O(n)$ space due to the temporary arrays used for merging.
- **Compare with other algorithms:** Be ready to explain when to use merge sort instead of quick sort or other sorting algorithms, especially in scenarios where stability (maintaining the relative order of equal elements) and guaranteed time complexity are important.

Some key takeaways for interviews are as follows:

- **Divide and conquer**: Merge sort is a classic example of a divide and conquer algorithm. Make sure to explain how dividing the problem into smaller subproblems helps solve it efficiently.
- **Stable sorting**: Merge sort is a stable sorting algorithm, meaning that it preserves the relative order of equal elements, which can be important in certain applications.
- **Time and space complexity**: Be clear about merge sort's time complexity ($O(n \log n)$) and space complexity ($O(n)$), and discuss when it is the best choice for sorting.

Problem 43: Quick sort

Problem statement: Given an unsorted array of integers, write a function that sorts the array in ascending order using the quick sort algorithm.

For example:

- **Input**:
  ```
  arr = [10, 7, 8, 9, 1, 5]
  ```
- **Output**:
  ```
  [1, 5, 7, 8, 9, 10]
  ```

Another example:

- **Input:**
  ```
  arr = [12, 4, 7, 9, 2]
  ```
- **Output:**
  ```
  [2, 4, 7, 9, 12]
  ```

Understanding the problem: Quick sort is another divide and conquer algorithm, much like merge sort. However, unlike merge sort, which divides the array in half, quick sort selects a **pivot** element and partitions the array into two subarrays, one with elements smaller than the pivot and the other with elements larger than the pivot. It recursively applies the same strategy to the subarrays.

Approach: Divide and conquer with pivot selection

The steps are as follows:

1. **Choose a pivot:** Select a pivot element from the array. The choice of pivot can vary:
    - First element
    - Last element
    - Random element
    - Median element
2. **Partition the array:** Rearrange the array so that all elements smaller than the pivot are on the left and all elements larger than the pivot are on the right.
3. **Recursive sorting:** Apply quick sort recursively to the two subarrays (left and right of the pivot).
4. **Base case:** The base case is when the subarray has only one element, which is inherently sorted.

Code implementation: Quick sort:

```
def quick_sort(arr):
    # Base case: if the array has 1 or 0 elements, it's already sorted
    if len(arr) <= 1:
        return arr

    # Choose the pivot (here we use the last element as the pivot)
    pivot = arr[len(arr) - 1]

    # Partition the array
    left = [x for x in arr[:-1] if x <= pivot]
    right = [x for x in arr[:-1] if x > pivot]

    # Recursively sort the left and right parts and return the combined result
    return quick_sort(left) + [pivot] + quick_sort(right)
```

Example walkthrough: Let us walk through an example step by step.

Given input:

```
arr = [10, 7, 8, 9, 1, 5]
```

The steps are as follows:

1. **Choose a pivot**: We choose the last element, 5, as the pivot.
2. **Partition the array:** Rearrange the array so that all elements smaller than 5 are on the left and those larger are on the right:
   - **Left**: [1]
   - **Right**: [10, 7, 8, 9]
3. **Recursively sort each subarray:**
   - **Sort the left subarray**: [1] (already sorted).
   - **Sort the right subarray**:
     - **Pivot**: 9, Left: [7, 8], Right: [10]
     - Recursively continue sorting until all subarrays are sorted.
4. **Merge the results:** Combine the sorted subarrays:
   `[1, 5, 7, 8, 9, 10]`

The time and space complexity are explained as follows:

- **Time complexity:**
  - **Average case**: $O(n \log n)$:
    - In most cases, quick sort has a time complexity of $O(n \log n)$ because the partitioning process divides the array into two roughly equal halves, and it takes linear time to partition the array at each level.
  - **Worst case**: $O(n^2)$:
    - The worst-case occurs when the pivot consistently picks the smallest or largest element, resulting in unbalanced partitions. For example, if the array is already sorted, the partitioning step will be inefficient, leading to $O(n^2)$ time.
- **Space complexity:** $O(\log n)$ due to the recursive call stack. Quick sort is an in-place sorting algorithm, meaning it does not require additional space for the sorted elements, unlike merge sort, which uses $O(n)$ space.

The step-by-step explanation is as follows:

1. **Base case:** If the array has one or fewer elements, it is already sorted.
2. **Choose the pivot:** The last element is chosen as the pivot in our implementation, though other strategies can also be used.
3. **Partition the array:** Split the array into two subarrays: elements smaller than or equal to the pivot go into one subarray, and elements greater than the pivot go into the other.

4. **Recursively sort each subarray:** Apply quick sort to both subarrays until the base case is reached.
5. **Combine the results:** Merge the sorted subarrays and the pivot to get the final sorted array.

Pivot selection strategies

The choice of pivot can significantly impact the performance of quick sort. Here are some common strategies:

- **First or last element:** This is simple to implement, but can lead to poor performance if the array is already sorted or reverse-sorted.
- **Random pivot:** Choosing a random element as the pivot helps reduce the likelihood of encountering the worst-case scenario.
- **Median-of-three:** Choose the median of the first, middle, and last elements as the pivot. This strategy helps avoid poor pivot choices.

Quick sort vs. merge sort:

- **Time complexity**: Both quick sort and merge sort have an average time complexity of $O(n \log n)$, but quick sort is typically faster in practice due to lower constant factors.
- **Space complexity**: Quick sort is an in-place algorithm with $O(\log n)$ space complexity, whereas merge sort requires $O(n)$ additional space for the merging process.
- **Worst case**: merge sort guarantees $O(n \log n)$ time complexity, while quick sort can degrade to $O(n^2)$ in the worst case.

Some real-world applications of quick sort are as follows:

- **Efficient sorting**: Quick sort is one of the fastest sorting algorithms in practice and is used in systems like the C++ STL **`sort()`** function.
- **Database systems**: Quick sort is often used in database systems to efficiently sort large datasets.
- **Memory-constrained environments**: Since quick sort is an in-place sorting algorithm, it is ideal for environments where memory usage needs to be minimized.

Dig deeper

The edge cases are as follows:

- **Empty array:** If the input array is empty, return an empty array.
  ```
  arr = []  # Output: []
  ```
- **Single-element array:** If the array has only one element, it is already sorted.
  ```
  arr = [1]  # Output: [1]
  ```

- **Already sorted array:** If the array is already sorted, quick sort can degrade to $O(n^2)$ depending on the pivot selection.

```
arr = [1, 2, 3, 4]  # Output: [1, 2, 3, 4]
```

- **Array with duplicate elements:** Quick sort handles arrays with duplicate elements by placing them in the correct position relative to the pivot.

```
arr = [4, 4, 4, 2, 1]  # Output: [1, 2, 4, 4, 4]
```

How to approach this problem in an interview:

- **Clarify the problem:** Confirm that the input array is unsorted and discuss the choice of pivot. Also, clarify if an in-place sort is required.
- **Discuss pivot selection:** Talk about different strategies for selecting a pivot and how they affect performance. Mention that choosing the right pivot reduces the likelihood of the worst-case scenario.
- **Compare quick sort with other sorting algorithms:** Be prepared to discuss how quick sort compares to other sorting algorithms like merge sort and why quick sort is generally preferred in practice.
- **Edge cases:** Mention how your solution handles edge cases like empty arrays, single-element arrays, and arrays with duplicates.

The key takeaways for interviews are as follows:

- **Pivot selection**: Understanding the importance of selecting a good pivot is crucial for optimizing quick sort's performance.
- **In-place sorting**: Quick sort is an in-place sorting algorithm, making it ideal for memory-constrained applications.
- **Time complexity**: While quick sort has an average time complexity of $O(n \log n)$, be sure to discuss the worst-case scenario and how to mitigate it by choosing a good pivot.
- **Comparison with merge sort**: Quick sort is often faster in practice due to its smaller constant factors, but merge sort is a more stable choice when worst-case guarantees are required.

Problem 44: Find the Kth largest element in an array

Problem statement: Given an array of integers, return the *Kth largest element* in the array.

Note that it is the Kth largest element in sorted order, not the Kth distinct element.

For example:

- **Input:**
  ```
  arr = [3, 2, 1, 5, 6, 4]
  k = 2
  ```
- **Output:**
  ```
  5
  ```

Another example:

- **Input:**
  ```
  arr = [7, 10, 4, 3, 20, 15]
  k = 3
  ```
- **Output:**
  ```
  10
  ```

Understanding the problem: The task is to find the *Kth largest element* in the given array. For instance, if we have an array [3, 2, 1, 5, 6, 4] and we are looking for the second largest element, the output should be 5 (since 6 is the largest and 5 is the second largest).

This problem can be solved using several methods, ranging from simple sorting to more efficient techniques like using a heap (priority queue).

Approach 1: Sorting the array

The simplest approach is to sort the array in *descending order* and then access the *Kth element*. Since sorting takes *O(n log n)*, this is a straightforward solution, but may not be the most efficient for large arrays.

Code implementation: Sorting approach:

```
def find_kth_largest(arr, k):
    # Sort the array in descending order
    arr.sort(reverse=True)

    # Return the Kth largest element
    return arr[k-1]
```

Example walkthrough: Let us walk through an example step by step.

Given input:

```
arr = [3, 2, 1, 5, 6, 4]
k = 2
```

The steps are as follows:

1. **Sort the array:** Sorting the array in descending order gives:
   ```
   [6, 5, 4, 3, 2, 1]
   ```

2. **Access the Kth element:** Since k = 2, the second largest element in the sorted array is 5.
3. **Final output:**

   ```
   5
   ```

The time and space complexity is explained as follows:

- **Time complexity:** *O(n log n)* due to the sorting step.
- **Space complexity:** *O(1)* if the sort is done in place; otherwise, *O(n)* if a new array is created.

Approach 2: Using a min-heap (optimal approach)

Instead of sorting the entire array, we can use a **min-heap** (or priority queue) to efficiently find the Kth largest element.

Here is the strategy:

1. Build a min-heap of size k.
2. Iterate through the array and push elements into the heap. If the heap grows larger than k, remove the smallest element (this ensures that only the k largest elements remain in the heap).
3. At the end of the iteration, the root of the heap will be the Kth largest element.

This approach has a time complexity of *O(n log k)*, which is more efficient than sorting for large arrays.

Code implementation: Min-heap approach:

```
import heapq

def find_kth_largest(arr, k):
    # Create a min-heap of the first k elements
    heap = arr[:k]
    heapq.heapify(heap)

    # Process the remaining elements
    for num in arr[k:]:
        if num > heap[0]:
            heapq.heappushpop(heap, num)

    # The root of the heap is the Kth largest element
    return heap[0]
```

Example walkthrough: Min-heap approach:

Let us go through an example with the array [3, 2, 1, 5, 6, 4] and k = 2.

1. **Build a min-heap:** Create a heap from the first two elements:
    - **Heap**: [2, 3]
2. **Process the remaining elements:**
    - For element 1, no change to the heap (1 is smaller than 2).
    - For element 5, push it into the heap and pop the smallest element: Heap: [3, 5]
    - For element 6, push it into the heap and pop the smallest element: Heap: [5, 6]
    - For element 4, no change to the heap (4 is smaller than 5).
3. **Return the Kth largest element:** The root of the heap (smallest element in the heap) is 5, which is the 2nd largest element in the array.
4. **Final output:**

    ```
    5
    ```

The time and space complexity are explained as follows:

- **Time complexity:** *O(n log k)*, where n is the number of elements in the array and k is the size of the heap.
- **Space complexity:** *O(k)* for storing the heap.

Dig deeper

The edge cases are as follows:

- **Empty array:** If the array is empty, return None or raise an exception, as there is no Kth largest element.
- **Array with fewer than K elements:** If the array has fewer than k elements, return None or raise an error because finding the Kth largest element is not possible.

    ```
    arr = [1, 2]
    k = 3
    # Output: None (or error)
    ```

- **Array with duplicates:** The algorithm handles duplicate elements correctly by treating them as separate elements when counting.

    ```
    arr = [3, 3, 3, 3]
    k = 1
    # Output: 3
    ```

How to approach this problem in an interview:

- **Clarify the problem:** Make sure the interviewer wants the *Kth largest element* in sorted order and not the Kth distinct element.

- **Explain the brute force approach:** Start by discussing the sorting approach, which is simple but has *O(n log n)* time complexity.
- **Introduce the min-heap approach:** Discuss how the min-heap allows you to solve the problem in *O(n log k)* time, which is more efficient for large arrays. Mention that you can optimize space by only keeping track of the K largest elements.
- **Edge cases:** Bring up edge cases like an empty array or when k is larger than the length of the array.

The key takeaways for interviews are as follows:

- **Heap-based approach:** Understanding the min-heap approach to this problem shows that you know how to optimize time complexity beyond simple sorting.
- **Comparing sorting and heaps:** Be prepared to explain why a min-heap is more efficient for large datasets compared to sorting.
- **Edge case awareness:** Mention edge cases like arrays with fewer elements than k and handle these gracefully in your code.

Problem 45: Sort colors (Dutch National Flag Problem)

Problem statement: Given an array containing only the integers 0, 1, and 2, sort the array so that all 0s come first, followed by all 1s, and then all 2s. This problem is also known as the **Dutch National Flag Problem** due to its three-color sorting challenge.

For example:

- **Input**:

  `arr = [2, 0, 2, 1, 1, 0]`

- **Output**:

  `[0, 0, 1, 1, 2, 2]`

Another example:

- **Input**:

  `arr = [2, 1, 0]`

- **Output**:

  `[0, 1, 2]`

Understanding the problem: We are tasked with sorting an array consisting only of 0s, 1s, and 2s in linear time and constant space. A straightforward approach would be to count the number of 0s, 1s, and 2s, and then rewrite the array accordingly. However, we will explore an optimal approach that uses *three pointers* to sort the array in a single pass, in-place, without extra memory.

Approach: Three pointers

The **Dutch National Flag** algorithm involves using three pointers:

- **low**: This pointer will track the position for placing 0s.
- **mid**: This pointer will traverse the array.
- **high**: This pointer will track the position for placing 2s.

The goal is to maintain three sections within the array:

- The part before low contains only 0s.
- The part after high contains only 2s.
- The part between low and high is still being evaluated, and mid will traverse through it.

Code implementation: Three-pointer approach:

```
def sort_colors(arr):
    # Initialize pointers
    low, mid, high = 0, 0, len(arr) - 1

    # Traverse through the array
    while mid <= high:
        if arr[mid] == 0:
            # Swap 0 to the front
            arr[low], arr[mid] = arr[mid], arr[low]
            low += 1
            mid += 1
        elif arr[mid] == 1:
            # 1 is already in the right place, just move mid
            mid += 1
        else:
            # Swap 2 to the end
            arr[high], arr[mid] = arr[mid], arr[high]
            high -= 1

    return arr
```

Example walkthrough: Let us walk through an example step by step.

Given input:

```
arr = [2, 0, 2, 1, 1, 0]
```

The steps are as follows:

1. **Initial pointers:** low = 0, mid = 0, high = 5
2. **First iteration:**
    - Current value at mid = 2
    - Swap **`arr[mid]`** with **`arr[high]`**
    - Decrement high to 4

      `arr = [0, 0, 2, 1, 1, 2]`
3. **Second iteration:**
    - Current value at mid = 0
    - Swap **`arr[mid]`** with **`arr[low]`**
    - Increment both low and mid

      `arr = [0, 0, 2, 1, 1, 2]`
4. **Continue traversal:** The algorithm continues adjusting low, mid, and high until the entire array is sorted.
    - Final output:

      `[0, 0, 1, 1, 2, 2]`

The time and space complexity is explained as follows:

- **Time complexity**: *O(n)* because the array is traversed only once, where n is the number of elements in the array.
- **Space complexity:** *O(1)* since we sort the array in place without using additional memory.

The step-by-step explanation is as follows:

1. **Base case:** If the array has fewer than two elements, it is already sorted, so no need to do anything.
2. **Three pointers:** We use three pointers to keep track of the positions for 0s, 1s, and 2s:
    - **low**: Tracks the next position to place a 0.
    - **mid**: The current element being evaluated.
    - **high**: Tracks the next position to place a 2.
3. **Swap and adjust pointers:**
    - If the current element is 0, swap it with the element at low and move both low and mid pointers forward.
    - If the current element is 1, just move mid forward since 1 is already in its correct place.

- If the current element is 2, swap it with the element at high and move high backward. Leave mid unchanged until the element is evaluated.

Alternate approach: Counting sort

Another approach is to count the number of 0s, 1s, and 2s in the array and then overwrite the array based on the counts.

1. Count the occurrences of 0, 1, and 2.
2. Rewrite the array based on these counts.

```
def sort_colors(arr):
    count = [0, 0, 0]  # counts for 0s, 1s, and 2s

    for num in arr:
        count[num] += 1

    # Overwrite the array with sorted elements
    index = 0
    for i in range(count[0]):
        arr[index] = 0
        index += 1
    for i in range(count[1]):
        arr[index] = 1
        index += 1
    for i in range(count[2]):
        arr[index] = 2
        index += 1

    return arr
```

The time and space complexity are as follows:

- **Time complexity:** *O(n)*
- **Space complexity**: *O(1)*

However, this approach requires two passes over the array (one for counting, one for writing), whereas the three-pointer solution works in a single pass.

Dig deeper

The edge cases are as follows:

- **Empty array:** If the input array is empty, simply return an empty array.
  ```
  arr = []  # Output: []
  ```
- **Array with all the same elements:** If the array contains only 0s, 1s, or 2s, the output will be the same as the input.
  ```
  arr = [1, 1, 1, 1]  # Output: [1, 1, 1, 1]
  ```

- **Already sorted array:** If the array is already sorted, the algorithm will still process it but leave it unchanged.

  ```
  arr = [0, 1, 2]  # Output: [0, 1, 2]
  ```

How to approach this problem in an interview:

- **Clarify the problem:** Confirm that the array consists of only three distinct values (0, 1, 2) and that you need to sort it in linear time.
- **Explain the brute force approach:** Start by discussing the counting sort method. Although it is a valid solution, it requires two passes over the array, which is not as optimal as the one-pass solution.
- **Introduce the three-pointer approach:** Discuss how the Dutch National Flag problem can be solved using three pointers to maintain a partitioned array in a single pass.
- **Edge cases:** Be ready to handle edge cases such as empty arrays or arrays containing all 0s, 1s, or 2s.

The key takeaways for interviews are as follows:

- **Three-pointer technique:** This approach demonstrates your understanding of in-place algorithms and how to minimize time complexity by avoiding extra passes over the array.
- **Problem-solving approach:** By explaining how you divide the array into sections and adjust pointers accordingly, you show a methodical approach to solving array problems.
- **Edge case awareness:** Handling edge cases like an empty array or already sorted arrays is crucial in interviews.

Problem 46: Top K frequent elements

Problem statement: Given a non-empty array of integers, return the K most frequent elements.

For example:

- **Input**:

  ```
  arr = [1, 1, 1, 2, 2, 3]
  k = 2
  ```

- **Output**:

  ```
  [1, 2]
  ```

Another example:

- **Input**:

  ```
  arr = [1]
  k = 1
  ```

- **Output:**

  `[1]`

Understanding the problem: We are asked to find the K *most frequent elements* from the given array. For instance, in the array [1, 1, 1, 2, 2, 3] with k = 2, the most frequent elements are 1 (appearing 3 times) and 2 (appearing 2 times). The result should be [1, 2].

This is a classic problem that can be efficiently solved using a **hashmap** (to count frequencies) and a **heap** (to extract the top K frequent elements).

Approach 1: Using a hashmap and heap

We can break the solution into two steps:

1. **Count the frequency of each element** in the array using a hashmap (or Python's **`collections.Counter`**).
2. **Use a min-heap** (priority queue) to keep track of the top K frequent elements.

In Python, the **heapq** library implements a min-heap, so we can use that to maintain the top K elements based on their frequency.

Code implementation: Hashmap and min-heap:

```
import heapq
from collections import Counter

def top_k_frequent(arr, k):
    # Step 1: Count frequencies
    freq_map = Counter(arr)

    # Step 2: Use a heap to keep the top K frequent elements
    heap = []

    # Iterate over the frequency map
    for num, freq in freq_map.items():
        heapq.heappush(heap, (freq, num))  # Push (frequency, element)

        # If the heap size exceeds k, remove the smallest element
        if len(heap) > k:
            heapq.heappop(heap)

    # Extract the elements from the heap
    return [num for freq, num in heap]
```

Example walkthrough: Let us walk through the example step by step.

Given input:

```
arr = [1, 1, 1, 2, 2, 3]
k = 2
```

The steps are as follows:

1. **Count frequencies:** Using Counter, we get the frequency of each element:

   `{1: 3, 2: 2, 3: 1}`

2. **Build the min-heap:**
   - Push (3, 1) into the heap.
   - Push (2, 2) into the heap.
   - Push (1, 3) into the heap. Since the heap now has more than k = 2 elements, pop the smallest one (which is (1, 3)).

3. **Extract the top K elements:** The remaining heap contains (3, 1) and (2, 2). Extract the elements:

   `[1, 2]`

   - **Final output:**

     `[1, 2]`

The time and space complexity is explained as follows:

- **Time complexity:** *O(n log k)*, where n is the number of elements in the array, and k is the number of top frequent elements we need to return. The log k comes from heap operations.
- **Space complexity:** *O(n)* for storing the frequency map and *O(k)* for the heap.

The step-by-step explanation is as follows:

1. **Counting frequencies:** We start by counting how frequently each element appears in the array. This step can be easily achieved using Python's **`collections.Counter`** or by manually iterating through the array and maintaining a hashmap.
2. **Maintaining a min-heap:** The key part of this solution is using a heap to store the most frequent elements. A min-heap is used because we want to maintain the top K elements. Whenever the heap size exceeds k, we remove the smallest element (the least frequent).
3. **Extracting results:** After processing all elements, the heap will contain the K most frequent elements. We then extract these elements from the heap and return them.

Alternate approach: Bucket sort

If we want to avoid using a heap, we can use bucket sort to solve this problem. In this approach:

- We count the frequency of each element.
- We create *buckets* where each bucket corresponds to a frequency, and we place elements into the bucket that corresponds to their frequency.
- Finally, we gather the top K elements from the highest frequency buckets.

Code implementation: Bucket sort:

```
from collections import Counter

def top_k_frequent(arr, k):
    # Step 1: Count frequencies
    freq_map = Counter(arr)

    # Step 2: Create a list of empty lists (buckets)
    bucket = [[] for _ in range(len(arr) + 1)]

    # Step 3: Populate the buckets
    for num, freq in freq_map.items():
        bucket[freq].append(num)

    # Step 4: Gather the top K frequent elements
    result = []
    for i in range(len(bucket) - 1, 0, -1):
        for num in bucket[i]:
            result.append(num)
            if len(result) == k:
                return result
```

Example walkthrough: Bucket sort:

Let us walk through an example using the bucket sort approach.

Given input:

```
arr = [1, 1, 1, 2, 2, 3]
k = 2
```

The steps are as follows:

1. **Count frequencies:** Using `Counter`, we get the frequency of each element:

   `{1: 3, 2: 2, 3: 1}`

2. **Populate buckets:** Create a list of empty lists (buckets) with a size of *len(arr) + 1 = 7.* Place elements into their respective buckets based on their frequency:

   `bucket = [[], [3], [2], [1], [], [], []]`

3. **Gather the top K elements:** Start from the highest frequency bucket and gather the elements until we have k = 2 elements:

   `result = [1, 2]`

Final output:

```
[1, 2]
```

The time and space complexity are as follows:

- **Time complexity:** *O(n)*, where n is the number of elements. This approach is more efficient than using a heap when we need to handle very large arrays because it avoids the *O(log k)* factor of heap operations.
- **Space complexity:** *O(n)* due to the use of buckets.

Dig deeper

The edge cases are as follows:

- **Array with one element:** If the array contains only one element, return that element:
```
arr = [1], k = 1
# Output: [1]
```
- **Array with all elements the same**: If all elements in the array are the same, the result will be that element:
```
arr = [1, 1, 1, 1], k = 1
# Output: [1]
```
- **Array with all elements having the same frequency:** If multiple elements have the same frequency, return any k of them:
```
arr = [1, 2, 3], k = 2
# Output: [1, 2] or [2, 3]
```

How to approach this problem in an interview:

- **Clarify the problem:** Confirm whether the interviewer expects you to find the top K most frequent elements and whether elements with the same frequency can be returned in any order.
- **Explain the brute force approach:** Start by explaining a simpler brute-force method (e.g., sorting based on frequency) before diving into more optimal solutions.
- **Introduce the optimal solution:** Discuss both the heap-based approach and the bucket sort approach. Highlight the trade-offs between them in terms of time and space complexity.
- **Edge cases:** Be prepared to handle cases like arrays with only one element, or where all elements have the same frequency.

The key takeaways for interviews are as follows:

- **Heap-based approach:** Understanding how to use a heap for this problem demonstrates your knowledge of priority queues and how to optimize for time complexity.
- **Bucket sort:** The bucket sort approach is more efficient in some cases and shows your ability to adapt algorithms for specific constraints.

- **Problem-solving strategy:** In interviews, being able to explain multiple approaches and discuss their trade-offs is crucial. Make sure to highlight why you chose a specific solution.

Problem 47: Heap sort algorithm

Problem statement: Implement the heap sort algorithm to sort an array of integers in ascending order.

For example:

- **Input:**

  `arr = [3, 6, 1, 5, 9, 8]`

- **Output:**

  `[1, 3, 5, 6, 8, 9]`

Another example:

- **Input:**

  `arr = [4, 10, 3, 5, 1]`

- **Output:**

  `[1, 3, 4, 5, 10]`

Understanding the problem: Heap sort is a *comparison-based sorting algorithm* that uses a *binary heap data structure.* It first builds a max-heap from the input array and then repeatedly swaps the first element (the largest) with the last element of the unsorted part of the array, reducing the heap's size each time.

Heap sort is efficient, with a time complexity of *O(n log n)*, and it is an *in-place sorting algorithm,* meaning it requires only a constant amount of extra memory space. However, unlike merge sort or quick sort, heap sort is not stable, meaning that the relative order of equal elements may not be preserved.

Approach: Heap sort algorithm

The algorithm can be divided into two main parts:

- **Building a max-heap:** A max-heap is a binary tree in which the parent node is greater than or equal to its child nodes. This ensures that the largest element is always at the root.

- **Sorting the array:** Once the max-heap is built, the largest element (at the root) is swapped with the last element of the heap. The heap size is reduced, and the heap property is restored for the remaining elements. This process is repeated until the entire array is sorted.

Code implementation: Heap sort:

```
def heapify(arr, n, i):
    largest = i
    left = 2 * i + 1
    right = 2 * i + 2

    # Check if the left child exists and is greater than the root
    if left < n and arr[left] > arr[largest]:
        largest = left

    # Check if the right child exists and is greater than the current largest
    if right < n and arr[right] > arr[largest]:
        largest = right

    # If the largest element is not the root, swap and heapify the affected
subtree
    if largest != i:
        arr[i], arr[largest] = arr[largest], arr[i]
        heapify(arr, n, largest)

def heap_sort(arr):
    n = len(arr)

    # Step 1: Build a max-heap
    for i in range(n // 2 - 1, -1, -1):
        heapify(arr, n, i)

    # Step 2: Extract elements one by one from the heap
    for i in range(n - 1, 0, -1):
        arr[i], arr[0] = arr[0], arr[i]  # Swap the root (largest) with the
last element
        heapify(arr, i, 0)  # Heapify the reduced heap

    return arr
```

Example walkthrough: Let us walk through an example step by step.

Given input:

```
arr = [4, 10, 3, 5, 1]
```

The steps are as follows:

1. **Build a max-heap:** Start by heapifying the array to build a max-heap:
    - **Initial array**: [4, 10, 3, 5, 1]
    - **After building the max-heap**: [10, 5, 3, 4, 1]
2. **Swap and heapify:** Swap the root (largest) element with the last element in the array, and then heapify the reduced heap:

- **After the first swap:** [1, 5, 3, 4, 10]
- **Heapify the reduced array**: [5, 4, 3, 1, 10]

3. **Repeat the process:** Continue swapping the root with the last unsorted element and heapifying the reduced heap:
   - **After second swap**: [1, 4, 3, 5, 10]
   - **Heapify**: [4, 1, 3, 5, 10]
   - **After third swap**: [3, 1, 4, 5, 10]
   - **Heapify**: [3, 1, 4, 5, 10]
   - **After fourth swap**: [1, 3, 4, 5, 10]
   - **Heapify**: [1, 3, 4, 5, 10]

Final output:

```
[1, 3, 4, 5, 10]
```

The time and space complexity are as follows:

- **Time complexity:** The time complexity of heap sort is *O(n log n)*, where n is the number of elements. Building the heap takes *O(n)* time, and extracting the elements (with heapify) takes *O(log n)* for each of the n elements.
- **Space complexity:** *O(1)* because heap sort is an in-place algorithm. It requires no additional memory except for a few extra variables.

The step-by-step explanation is as follows:

1. **Heapify function:** The heapify function ensures that the subtree rooted at a given index satisfies the max-heap property. If the root is smaller than one of its children, the largest child becomes the new root, and the heapify process is repeated for the affected subtree.
2. **Building a max-heap:** We start from the last non-leaf node and apply the heapify function to ensure the entire tree is a valid max-heap.
3. **Extracting elements:** After building the heap, the largest element is at the root (index 0). We swap this element with the last element of the unsorted portion of the array, reduce the heap size, and heapify the remaining unsorted portion.

The applications of heap sort are as follows:

- **Priority queues:** The heap data structure is commonly used to implement priority queues, where the highest (or lowest) priority element is always extracted first.
- **Sorting large datasets:** Heap sort is efficient for sorting large datasets when memory is limited because it does not require extra space like merge sort or quick sort's recursion stack.

Heap sort vs. quick sort

Both heap sort and quick sort have a time complexity of *O(n log n)*, but there are differences:

- **Heap sort** is not as cache-friendly as quick sort because of its non-sequential memory access pattern.
- **Quick sort** is generally faster in practice due to better locality of reference, but has a worst-case time complexity of $O(n^2)$ if the pivot selection is poor.
- **Heap sort** is always *O(n log n)* but may be slower than quick sort on average due to constant factors.

Dig deeper

The edge cases are as follows:

- **Empty array:** If the input array is empty, the output is also an empty array:
  ```
  arr = []
  # Output: []
  ```
- **Array with one element:** If the input array contains only one element, it is already sorted:
  ```
  arr = [1]
  # Output: [1]
  ```
- **Array with repeated elements:** Heap sort handles arrays with repeated elements effectively:
  ```
  arr = [5, 5, 5, 5]
  # Output: [5, 5, 5, 5]
  ```

How to approach this problem in an interview:

- **Explain heap sort concepts:** Start by explaining the concept of a heap (max-heap or min-heap) and how it relates to sorting.
- **Discuss time and space complexity:** Mention that heap sort has a time complexity of *O(n log n)* and space complexity of *O(1)*, making it efficient for large datasets.
- **Edge cases and stability:** Be ready to handle questions about edge cases, such as an empty array, and discuss the fact that heap sort is not stable.

The key takeaways for interviews are as follows:

- **Heapify and max-heap:** Understanding how heapify works and how a max-heap is built is crucial. In interviews, explaining heap structure and the heapify process will demonstrate your understanding of the algorithm.

- **In-place sorting:** Heap sort's in-place nature (constant extra space) is a major advantage. In scenarios where memory is constrained, heap sort is preferred over quick sort or merge sort.
- **Versatility of heaps:** Highlight that heaps are not only useful for sorting but also form the basis of many other algorithms, such as priority queues and finding the Kth largest element.

Problem 48: Bucket sort algorithm

Problem statement: Implement the bucket sort algorithm to sort an array of floating-point numbers between 0 and 1 in ascending order.

For example:

- **Input**:
  `arr = [0.78, 0.17, 0.39, 0.72, 0.94, 0.21, 0.12, 0.23]`
- **Output**:
  `[0.12, 0.17, 0.21, 0.23, 0.39, 0.72, 0.78, 0.94]`

Another example:

- **Input**:
  `arr = [0.9, 0.1, 0.2, 0.4, 0.6]`
- **Output**:
  `[0.1, 0.2, 0.4, 0.6, 0.9]`

Understanding the problem: Bucket sort is a *distribution-based sorting algorithm* that works well when the input is uniformly distributed over a range. In this case, we will assume the input is an array of floating-point numbers between 0 and 1. The algorithm works by dividing the input array into several "buckets," sorting the individual buckets, and then combining them to get the final sorted array.

Bucket sort is typically efficient when the input is uniformly distributed over a known range, making it ideal for numbers like floating-point values between 0 and 1.

Approach: Bucket sort algorithm

The algorithm can be broken down into the following steps:

1. **Create buckets:** Divide the range (0 to 1) into **n** equally spaced buckets (where **n** is the number of elements in the array).
2. **Distribute elements into buckets:** Place each element in its appropriate bucket based on its value. The idea is that elements closer in value will end up in the same bucket.
3. **Sort individual buckets:** Sort each bucket using an efficient sorting algorithm (like insertion sort or even Python's built-in Timsort).

4. **Concatenate the buckets:** Finally, combine the sorted buckets into one array.

Code implementation: Bucket sort:

```
def bucket_sort(arr):
    n = len(arr)
    if n == 0:
        return arr

    # Step 1: Create empty buckets
    buckets = [[] for _ in range(n)]

    # Step 2: Distribute elements into buckets
    for num in arr:
        # Determine the bucket index based on the value
        index = int(num * n)
        buckets[index].append(num)

    # Step 3: Sort individual buckets
    for i in range(n):
        buckets[i].sort()

    # Step 4: Concatenate the sorted buckets
    sorted_array = []
    for bucket in buckets:
        sorted_array.extend(bucket)

    return sorted_array
```

Example walkthrough: Let us walk through an example step by step.

Given input:

```
arr = [0.78, 0.17, 0.39, 0.72, 0.94, 0.21, 0.12, 0.23]
```

The steps are as follows:

1. **Create empty buckets:** Create an empty list of buckets. Since the array has 8 elements, we will create 8 buckets:

   ```
   buckets = [[], [], [], [], [], [], [], []]
   ```

2. **Distribute elements into buckets:** Each element is placed into its corresponding bucket based on its value:

   ```
   0.78 -> bucket[6]
   0.17 -> bucket[1]
   0.39 -> bucket[3]
   0.72 -> bucket[5]
   0.94 -> bucket[7]
   0.21 -> bucket[1]
   ```

```
0.12 -> bucket[0]
0.23 -> bucket[1]
```

a. Resulting buckets:

```
[[0.12], [0.17, 0.21, 0.23], [], [0.39], [0.72], [0.78], [], [0.94]]
```

3. **Sort individual buckets:** Sort each bucket individually:

```
[[0.12], [0.17, 0.21, 0.23], [], [0.39], [0.72], [0.78], [], [0.94]]
```

4. **Concatenate the sorted buckets:** Combine the sorted elements from each bucket:

```
[0.12, 0.17, 0.21, 0.23, 0.39, 0.72, 0.78, 0.94]
```

Final output:

`[0.12, 0.17, 0.21, 0.23, 0.39, 0.72, 0.78, 0.94]`

The time and space complexity are as follows:

- **Time complexity:** $O(n + k)$, where n is the number of elements, and k is the number of buckets. Sorting within each bucket can take time, but since the number of elements per bucket is typically small, the overall time complexity remains efficient.
- **Space complexity:** $O(n + k)$ for the extra space used by the buckets.

The step-by-step explanation is as follows:

1. **Creating buckets:** The array is divided into n buckets, where each bucket represents a range of values (between 0 and 1 in this case). The number of buckets is typically equal to the size of the array.
2. **Distributing elements:** The elements are placed into their corresponding buckets based on their values. Elements closer in value will end up in the same bucket, which helps in reducing the number of comparisons during sorting.
3. **Sorting each bucket:** Since the number of elements in each bucket is small, sorting each bucket (using insertion sort or any other efficient algorithm) is fast.
4. **Concatenating buckets:** Once all the buckets are sorted, the elements are concatenated to form the final sorted array.

When to use bucket sort

Bucket sort is particularly useful when:

- The input is uniformly distributed over a known range (like numbers between 0 and 1).
- You need a *linear-time sorting algorithm* and can afford the extra space for buckets.
- You want to avoid the *O(n log n)* complexity of comparison-based sorts like quick sort and merge sort.

Some real-world applications are as follows:

- **Sorting floating-point numbers:** Bucket sort is often used to sort floating-point numbers, especially when they are uniformly distributed over a range (such as 0 to 1).
- **Distributed systems:** Bucket sort can be adapted for parallel processing or distributed systems, where each processor or node is responsible for sorting its own bucket.
- **Graphics and image processing:** In some graphics applications, bucket sort is used for efficiently sorting pixel intensities or colors.

Dig deeper

The edge cases are as follows:

- **Empty array:** If the array is empty, the output will also be an empty array:
```
arr = []
# Output: []
```
- **Array with one element:** If the array contains only one element, it is already sorted:
```
arr = [0.5]
# Output: [0.5]
```
- **Array with all elements the same:** If all elements in the array are the same, the result will be the same array:
```
arr = [0.3, 0.3, 0.3]
# Output: [0.3, 0.3, 0.3]
```

How to approach this problem in an interview:

- **Explain bucket sort concepts**: Start by explaining what bucket sort is and how it works. Discuss how the input range is divided into buckets and how the elements are distributed across the buckets.
- **Edge cases:** Be ready to handle edge cases like an empty array or an array with all the same elements.
- **Compare with other algorithms:** Discuss how bucket sort compares with other sorting algorithms like quick sort and merge sort. Highlight that bucket sort is efficient for uniformly distributed inputs.
- **Real-world use cases:** Mention when bucket sort is used in practice, such as in sorting floating-point numbers or for parallel processing.

The key takeaways for interviews are as follows:

- **Efficiency in certain cases:** Bucket sort is particularly efficient for uniformly distributed inputs over a known range. Highlight how this makes it ideal for floating-point numbers.

- **Space vs. time trade-off:** While bucket sort can achieve linear time complexity, it requires extra space for the buckets. Depending on the problem's constraints, this trade-off may or may not be suitable.
- **Customizability:** Explain that bucket sort can be adapted for various types of data and can even be used in distributed systems where a different processor or node sorts each bucket.

Problem 49: Counting sort algorithm

Problem statement: Implement the **counting sort** algorithm to sort a given array of non-negative integers in ascending order.

For example:

- **Input**:
  ```
  arr = [4, 2, 2, 8, 3, 3, 1]
  ```
- **Output**:
  ```
  [1, 2, 2, 3, 3, 4, 8]
  ```

Another example:

- **Input**:
  ```
  arr = [10, 7, 12, 15, 7, 8, 7]
  ```
- **Output**:
  ```
  [7, 7, 7, 8, 10, 12, 15]
  ```

Understanding the problem: Counting sort is a *non-comparison-based sorting algorithm*. It is efficient when the range of input values is known and not significantly larger than the number of elements. Unlike algorithms like quick sort or merge sort, counting sort does not compare elements directly. Instead, it counts the occurrences of each distinct element in the input array.

Once the counts are recorded, the algorithm reconstructs the sorted array by iterating over the counted values and placing each number in its correct position.

Approach: Counting sort algorithm

The algorithm can be divided into the following steps:

1. **Count occurrences:** Create a count array where each index represents a unique element in the input array, and the value at that index represents the number of times that element appears.
2. **Modify the count array:** Adjust the count array so that each element at each index stores the sum of the previous counts. This modification helps to place elements directly in their correct position in the output array.

3. **Build the output array:** Using the modified count array, place each element from the input array into the correct position in the output array.

Code implementation: Counting sort:

```
def counting_sort(arr):
    if len(arr) == 0:
        return arr

    # Step 1: Find the maximum element in the array
    max_value = max(arr)

    # Step 2: Create a count array to store the count of each element
    count = [0] * (max_value + 1)

    # Step 3: Count each element in the input array
    for num in arr:
        count[num] += 1

    # Step 4: Modify the count array so that each element contains the actual
position of the element
    for i in range(1, len(count)):
        count[i] += count[i - 1]
    # Step 5: Build the output array
    output = [0] * len(arr)
    for num in reversed(arr):
        output[count[num] - 1] = num
        count[num] -= 1

    return output
```

Example walkthrough: Let us walk through an example step by step.

Given input:

```
arr = [4, 2, 2, 8, 3, 3, 1]
```

The steps are as follows:

1. **Find the maximum element:** The largest element in the array is 8:
   `max_value = 8`
2. **Create the count array:** Initialize a count array of size *max_value + 1* (i.e., 9 in this case) to store the count of each element:
   `count = [0, 0, 0, 0, 0, 0, 0, 0, 0]`
3. **Count the occurrences:** Iterate over the input array and count the occurrences of each element:
   ```
   arr = [4, 2, 2, 8, 3, 3, 1]
   count = [0, 1, 2, 2, 1, 0, 0, 0, 1]
   ```

4. **Modify the count array:** Modify the count array so that each element contains the sum of previous counts:

   ```
   count = [0, 1, 3, 5, 6, 6, 6, 6, 7]
   ```

5. **Build the output array:** Using the modified count array, build the sorted output array:

   ```
   output = [1, 2, 2, 3, 3, 4, 8]
   ```

Final output:

```
[1, 2, 2, 3, 3, 4, 8]
```

The time and space complexity are as follows:

- **Time complexity:** $O(n + k)$, where n is the number of elements and k is the range of input values (the maximum value in the array). This is because we need to count each element and then modify the count array, both of which take linear time.
- **Space complexity:** $O(n + k)$ for the extra space required by the count array and the output array.

The step-by-step explanation is as follows:

1. **Counting the elements:** The first step of the algorithm involves counting how many times each element appears in the input array. For example, in the array [4, 2, 2, 8, 3, 3, 1], the number 2 appears twice, so its count in the count array will be 2.
2. **Modifying the count array:** After counting the elements, we modify the count array to store cumulative sums, which will help in placing each element at its correct position in the output array.
3. **Building the output array:** The final step is to traverse the input array from right to left and use the count array to place each element in its correct position in the output array. This ensures that the relative order of equal elements is preserved, making counting sort a *stable sorting algorithm*.

When to use counting sort

Counting sort is particularly useful when:

- The range of input values is relatively small compared to the number of elements (i.e., k is not significantly larger than n).
- You need a *linear-time sorting algorithm* for non-negative integers.

The real-world applications are as follows:

- **Data analysis:** Counting sort is useful in applications where the range of possible values is small, such as sorting grades or age groups.
- **Counting occurrences:** Counting sort is ideal for counting occurrences, for example, counting how many times each element appears in a dataset.

Dig deeper

The edge cases are as follows:

- **Empty array:** If the array is empty, the output will also be an empty array:

```
arr = []
# Output: []
```

- **Array with one element:** If the array contains only one element, it is already sorted:

```
arr = [5]
# Output: [5]
```

- **Array with identical elements:** If all elements in the array are the same, the result will be the same array:

```
arr = [3, 3, 3, 3]
# Output: [3, 3, 3, 3]
```

How to approach this problem in an interview:

- **Explain counting sort concepts:** Start by explaining the basic idea behind counting sort: counting the occurrences of each element and using the counts to place elements in their correct positions.
- **Highlight time and space complexity:** Emphasize that counting sort has a time complexity of $O(n + k)$, where n is the number of elements and k is the range of input values. Mention that it requires additional space for the count array.
- **Edge cases:** Be prepared to handle questions about edge cases, like an empty array or an array with only one element.

The key takeaways for interviews are as follows:

- **Efficient for limited range:** Counting sort is highly efficient for arrays with a limited range of values (small k), and it runs in linear time, making it faster than comparison-based algorithms in such cases.
- **Stable sorting algorithm:** Since counting sort preserves the relative order of equal elements, it is a stable sorting algorithm, which can be an important property in certain applications.
- **Space complexity trade-off:** While counting sort is efficient in terms of time complexity, it does require extra space for the count array, which can be a drawback if the range of values (k) is very large.

Problem 50: Radix sort algorithm

Problem statement: Implement the radix sort algorithm to sort a list of non-negative integers in ascending order.

For example:

- **Input**:
  `arr = [170, 45, 75, 90, 802, 24, 2, 66]`
- **Output**:
  `[2, 24, 45, 66, 75, 90, 170, 802]`

Another example:

- **Input**:
  `arr = [101, 201, 11, 999, 120, 34, 19]`
- **Output**:
  `[11, 19, 34, 101, 120, 201, 999]`

Understanding the problem: Radix sort is a *non-comparison-based sorting algorithm* that sorts numbers by processing individual digits. It sorts the elements *digit by digit*, starting from the **least significant digit** (**LSD**) to the **most significant digit** (**MSD**). The algorithm requires a stable sorting algorithm (like counting sort) as an intermediate step to ensure that the order of elements with equal digits is preserved.

Radix sort is most efficient when all elements are integers, making it ideal for sorting large numbers of integers where comparison-based algorithms like quick sort may not perform as well.

Approach: Radix sort algorithm

Radix sort can be broken down into the following steps:

1. **Find the maximum number:** Determine the largest number in the array to know how many digits the largest number has. The algorithm will sort the array based on each digit, from the least significant to the most significant.
2. **Sort by each digit:** Use counting sort as a subroutine to sort the numbers based on each digit (ones, tens, hundreds, etc.). Counting sort is stable, meaning that it preserves the relative order of numbers with the same digit in a particular place value.
3. **Repeat for each place value:** Repeat the sorting process for every digit, starting from the least significant digit (ones place) to the most significant digit.

Code implementation: Radix sort:

```
def counting_sort_for_radix(arr, exp):
    n = len(arr)

    # Output array to store sorted numbers
    output = [0] * n

    # Count array to store the occurrences of digits (0-9)
```

```
    count = [0] * 10

    # Count occurrences of digits in the current place value (exp)
    for i in range(n):
        index = arr[i] // exp
        count[index % 10] += 1

    # Modify the count array to store actual positions of digits
    for i in range(1, 10):
        count[i] += count[i - 1]

    # Build the output array
    for i in reversed(range(n)):
        index = arr[i] // exp
        output[count[index % 10] - 1] = arr[i]
        count[index % 10] -= 1

    # Copy the sorted numbers back to the original array
    for i in range(n):
        arr[i] = output[i]

def radix_sort(arr):
    # Step 1: Find the maximum number to know the number of digits
    max_value = max(arr)

    # Step 2: Perform counting sort for each digit, starting from the least
significant digit
    exp = 1  # Initialize exp to 1 (1's place)
    while max_value // exp > 0:
        counting_sort_for_radix(arr, exp)
        exp *= 10  # Move to the next place value (10's place, 100's place,
etc.)
```

Example walkthrough: Let us walk through an example step by step.

Given input:

`arr = [170, 45, 75, 90, 802, 24, 2, 66]`

The steps are as follows:

1. **Find the maximum number:** The largest number is 802, which has three digits:

   `max_value = 802`

2. **Sort by the least significant digit (1's place):** Perform counting sort on the ones place:

   `arr = [170, 90, 802, 2, 24, 45, 66, 75]`

3. **Sort by the tens digit (10's place):** Perform counting sort on the tens place:
   ```
   arr = [802, 2, 24, 45, 66, 75, 170, 90]
   ```
4. **Sort by the hundreds digit (100's place):** Perform counting sort on the hundreds place:
   ```
   arr = [2, 24, 45, 66, 75, 90, 170, 802]
   ```

Final output:

```
[2, 24, 45, 66, 75, 90, 170, 802]
```

The time and space complexity are as follows:

- **Time complexity:** $O(d * (n + k))$, where n is the number of elements, k is the range of digits (0–9), and d is the number of digits in the largest number. This is more efficient than comparison-based sorting algorithms when d is small compared to n log n.
- **Space complexity:** $O(n + k)$ for the extra space required by the output and count arrays used in counting sort.

The step-by-step explanation is as follows:

- **Counting sort for each digit:** Radix sort uses counting sort as a subroutine to sort the elements based on each digit. This ensures that the sorting process for each place value is stable, which is critical for radix sort to work correctly.
- **Processing place values:** The algorithm starts by sorting the elements based on the least significant digit (ones place) and works its way up to the most significant digit (tens place, hundreds place, etc.).
- **Stable sorting:** Radix sort is a stable algorithm, meaning that it preserves the relative order of elements with the same digit. This is why it is important to use counting sort, which is also a stable sorting algorithm.

When to use radix sort

Radix sort is particularly useful when:

- The input consists of numbers with a small range of digits (such as 3-digit or 4-digit numbers).
- You need a *linear-time sorting algorithm* that does not rely on comparisons.

The real-world applications are as follows:

- **Sorting large integers:** Radix sort is commonly used to sort large integers, especially when the number of digits is small compared to the number of elements.
- **Distributed systems:** Radix sort can be adapted for parallel processing or distributed systems, where each processor or node sorts a specific digit position.

- **Digital data:** Radix sort is often used in digital data processing, where data can be divided into fixed-length segments or fields.

Dig deeper

The edge cases are as follows:

- **Empty array:** If the array is empty, the output will also be an empty array:
```
arr = []
# Output: []
```
- **Array with one element:** If the array contains only one element, it is already sorted:
```
arr = [5]
# Output: [5]
```
- **Array with identical elements:** If all elements in the array are the same, the result will be the same array:
```
arr = [7, 7, 7, 7]
# Output: [7, 7, 7, 7]
```

How to approach this problem in an interview:

- **Explain radix sort concepts:** Begin by explaining that radix sort sorts elements by processing digits individually, from the least significant digit to the most significant digit.
- **Discuss time complexity:** Highlight that radix sort has a time complexity of $O(d * (n + k))$, where d is the number of digits, n is the number of elements, and k is the range of digits (usually 0–9).
- **Edge cases:** Be prepared to handle questions about edge cases, like an empty array or an array with only one element.

The key takeaways for interviews are as follows:

- **Efficiency for large integers:** Radix sort is highly efficient for sorting large sets of integers, especially when the number of digits is small compared to the total number of elements.
- **Stable sorting algorithm:** Radix sort is a stable sorting algorithm, which means it preserves the relative order of equal elements.
- **Not comparison-based:** Radix sort does not rely on comparisons between elements, making it faster than comparison-based algorithms like quick sort or merge sort in specific cases.

Join our Discord space

Join our Discord workspace for latest updates, offers, tech happenings around the world, new releases, and sessions with the authors:

https://discord.bpbonline.com

SECTION 5
Recursion and Backtracking

Introduction

Welcome to the fascinating world of **recursion** and **backtracking**, two of the most powerful tools in a programmer's toolkit. This section will take you on an exciting journey through problems that require you to think deeply about breaking down tasks into smaller, repeatable steps and exploring various possibilities to find optimal solutions.

Imagine you are solving a maze. You do not know which path will lead to the exit, so you try one path, and if it does not work, you backtrack and try another. This is the essence of backtracking. Similarly, recursion is like peeling an onion; you keep peeling layer by layer (or solving smaller parts of a problem) until you reach the core, and then you work your way back up, solving the whole problem as you go.

Why recursion and backtracking matter: At first, these concepts might seem challenging, but mastering them will significantly boost your problem-solving skills. Recursion, in particular, is an essential topic for interviews and understanding how computers solve problems. It allows you to express solutions to complex problems elegantly by breaking them down into smaller, more manageable tasks.

Backtracking, on the other hand, teaches you to approach problems systematically. This technique is perfect for solving problems where you must explore all possible solutions but want to eliminate paths that do not lead to a valid result. Problems like the *N-queens* or *Sudoku solver* are classic examples of where backtracking shines.

Recursion and backtracking problems are highly favored in coding interviews because they test both your logical thinking and your ability to handle challenging scenarios. Companies like *Google*, *Facebook*, and *Amazon* frequently ask recursion and backtracking questions, so understanding these concepts is crucial for acing technical interviews.

Objectives

This section will take you through some of the most common and challenging problems related to recursion and backtracking:

- We will begin with recursion by solving problems like finding the **factorial** of a number and generating the **Fibonacci sequence**. These will give you a solid foundation for understanding how recursion works by calling a function from within.
- Next, we will tackle problems like generating **subsets** of a set, *permutations of a string*, and solving the N-queens problem. These problems require you to explore multiple paths, make decisions at each step, and backtrack when a particular path does not lead to the correct solution.
- You will also look at more advanced problems, like solving a Sudoku puzzle or finding all valid **IP addresses** from a string. These problems are perfect examples of where backtracking is essential; you will need to explore every possible solution, but efficiently eliminate invalid options as soon as you spot them.

Challenges ahead: This section will challenge your ability to break down problems and solve them step by step. At first, recursion may seem like magic; a function calling itself can be mind-bending. However, once you understand how it works under the hood (especially how the **call stack** manages recursive calls), you will find that recursion is a powerful tool for solving complex problems.

Similarly, backtracking will test your ability to explore all options systematically. Problems like the N-queens problem require you to place queens on a chessboard such that no two queens can attack each other. You will try one configuration; if it does not work, you will backtrack and try another. This method teaches you to think about multiple solutions simultaneously and quickly discard invalid ones.

Engagement through challenges: This section is full of problems that are not only fun but also deeply satisfying to solve. Each problem presents a challenge that can feel overwhelming at first, but as you work through it, breaking it down piece by piece, you will find that the solution gradually emerges.

Recursion and backtracking also teach you to write more efficient and elegant code. You will learn to stop brute-forcing your way through problems and instead rely on smart algorithms that can find solutions much faster.

Mastering interview challenges: Interviewers love recursion and backtracking problems because they reveal how well you can solve complex problems systematically. Whether it is generating all permutations of a string, solving the Sudoku puzzle, or determining the **subset sum**, these problems will push you to think critically and analytically.

By the end of this section, you will be prepared to solve recursion and backtracking problems in interviews and in real-world programming challenges where exploring multiple possibilities is necessary.

Problem 51: Factorial of a number (recursion)

Problem statement: Write a recursive function to calculate the factorial of a given non-negative integer n. The factorial of a number is the product of all positive integers less than or equal to n.

For example:

- **Input**:
  ```
  n = 5
  ```
- **Output**:
  ```
  120  # (5 * 4 * 3 * 2 * 1)
  ```

Another example:

- **Input**:
  ```
  n = 3
  ```
- **Output**:
  ```
  6  # (3 * 2 * 1)
  ```

Understanding the problem: The factorial of a number n is defined as:

*n! = n * (n-1) * (n-2) * .... * 1*

Factorials grow very quickly. For instance:

- 5! = 120
- 10! = 3,628,800

The base case for factorial is 0! = 1, because the factorial of 0 is defined to be 1.

Approach: Recursion

Recursion is a natural way to solve this problem because the definition of factorial is inherently recursive:

*n! = n * (n-1)!*

We can use this definition directly to write a recursive function. The key is to:

- **Identify the *base case*:** When n is 0, the function should return 1.
- **Identify the *recursive case*:** When n is greater than 0, return *n * factorial(n - 1)*.

Code implementation: Factorial using recursion:

```
def factorial(n):
    # Base case: If n is 0, return 1
    if n == 0:
        return 1
    else:
        # Recursive case: n * factorial of (n-1)
        return n * factorial(n - 1)
```

Example walkthrough: Let us walk through an example to see how recursion works step by step.

Given input:

```
n = 5
```

The steps are as follows:

1. **First call:**
   ```
   factorial(5)
   ```
   The function calls itself recursively with n = 4.
2. **Second call:**
   ```
   factorial(4)
   ```
   The function calls itself recursively with n = 3.
3. **Third call:**
   ```
   factorial(3)
   ```
   The function calls itself recursively with n = 2.
4. **Fourth call:**
   ```
   factorial(2)
   ```
   The function calls itself recursively with n = 1.
5. **Fifth call:**
   ```
   factorial(1)
   ```
   The function calls itself recursively with n = 0.
6. **Base case:**
   ```
   factorial(0)
   ```
   The base case is reached, and the function returns 1.

   The function then unwinds, multiplying the results as it goes back up the recursion stack:

   - *factorial(1) = 1 * factorial(0) = 1*

- *factorial(2) = 2 * factorial(1) = 2*
- *factorial(3) = 3 * factorial(2) = 6*
- *factorial(4) = 4 * factorial(3) = 24*
- *factorial(5) = 5 * factorial(4) = 120*

The time and space complexity are as follows:

- **Time complexity:** *O(n)*, because the function makes n recursive calls, where n is the input number.
- **Space complexity:** *O(n)*, because the recursion stack grows with each call, and in the worst case, the depth of the stack is n.

The step-by-step explanation is as follows:

1. **Base case:** The base case is crucial for stopping the recursion. Without the base case, the function would keep calling itself indefinitely, causing a *stack overflow*. In our case, the base case is when n = 0, where the factorial is defined to be 1.

2. **Recursive case:** The recursive case is where the function calls itself with a smaller argument, n - 1. This reduces the problem size at each step until it eventually reaches the base case.

3. **Unwinding the stack:** After the base case is reached, the function unwinds, multiplying the results of each recursive call. This is how the final factorial value is computed.

When to use recursion for factorial

Recursion is particularly useful for problems like factorial because it directly mirrors the mathematical definition. However, it is important to note that recursion may not be the most efficient approach for very large values of n. For large n, you might encounter issues with stack overflow or performance limitations due to deep recursion. In such cases, an *iterative approach* might be preferred.

Iterative approach to factorial

An iterative solution avoids the potential stack overflow problem by using a simple loop to calculate the factorial:

```
def factorial_iterative(n):
    result = 1
    for i in range(2, n + 1):
        result *= i
    return result
```

This version runs in *O(n)* time, just like the recursive version, but has *O(1)* space complexity, making it more efficient in terms of memory usage.

How to approach this problem in an interview:

- **Explain recursion:** In an interview, explain how recursion mirrors the definition of factorial and clearly walk through the base case and recursive case. It is crucial to demonstrate a recursive problem-solving mindset.
- **Discuss edge cases:** Be sure to handle edge cases like n = 0 and negative inputs if the interviewer asks about them. For negative inputs, you could either return an error or indicate that factorial is undefined for negative numbers.
- **Iterative approach:** Be prepared to offer an iterative solution if asked. Highlight the differences in space complexity and the potential drawbacks of deep recursion.

Dig deeper

The edge cases are as follows:

- **n = 0:** The factorial of 0 is 1, which is defined by convention.
- **n = 1:** The factorial of 1 is also 1.
- **Negative inputs:** Factorial is not defined for negative numbers. If the interviewer asks, you can handle this by returning an error message or None:

```
def factorial(n):
    if n < 0:
        return None  # Undefined for negative numbers
    elif n == 0:
        return 1
    else:
        return n * factorial(n - 1)
```

Some real-world applications are as follows:

- **Combinatorics:** Factorials are used in combinatorics to calculate permutations and combinations. For example, the number of ways to arrange n objects in a sequence is n!.
- **Probability:** Factorials are essential in calculating probabilities in statistics, especially in problems involving combinations and permutations.

How interviewers might challenge you

Interviewers may ask you to:

- Implement both recursive and iterative solutions.
- Optimize the recursive solution to handle larger inputs (for example, using memoization).
- Handle edge cases like negative inputs and large numbers.

Problem 52: Fibonacci sequence (recursion)

Problem statement: Write a recursive function to generate the *n-th Fibonacci number*. The Fibonacci sequence is a series of numbers where each number is the sum of the two preceding ones, usually starting with 0 and 1.

For example:

- **Input**:
  ```
  n = 6
  ```
- **Output**:
  ```
  8  # (0, 1, 1, 2, 3, 5, 8)
  ```

Another example:

- **Input:**
  ```
  n = 10
  ```
- **Output**:
  ```
  55  # (0, 1, 1, 2, 3, 5, 8, 13, 21, 34, 55)
  ```

Understanding the problem: The Fibonacci sequence is defined as follows:

```
F(0)=0 , F(1)=1
For n >= 2:
F(n) = F(n-1) + F(n-2)
So the sequence looks like this:
0, 1, 1, 2, 3, 5, 8, 13, 21, 34, 55, …
```

The problem asks you to compute the n-th Fibonacci number, where the position starts from 0.

Approach: Recursion

A natural way to compute the Fibonacci sequence is through recursion because the value of the n-th Fibonacci number depends on the values of the (n-1)-th and (n-2)-th Fibonacci numbers. This recursive relationship allows us to express the solution in a clean, elegant way:

- **Base case:** The base cases are when n = 0 and n = 1, where the values of the Fibonacci sequence are 0 and 1, respectively.
- **Recursive case:** For n >= 2, the function calls itself recursively to compute the values of F(n-1) and F(n-2).

Code implementation: Fibonacci using recursion:

```
def fibonacci(n):
    # Base case: Return n if n is 0 or 1
```

```
    if n == 0 or n == 1:
        return n
    else:
        # Recursive case: Return the sum of the two preceding numbers
        return fibonacci(n - 1) + fibonacci(n - 2)
```

Example walkthrough: Let us walk through the recursive process step by step for n = 6.

Given input:

```
n = 6
```

The steps are as follows:

1. **First call:**

   `fibonacci(6)`

   The function calls **`fibonacci(5)`** and **`fibonacci(4)`**.

2. **Second call (left branch):**

   `fibonacci(5)`

   The function calls **`fibonacci(4)`** and **`fibonacci(3)`**.

3. **Third call (left branch):**

   `fibonacci(4)`

   The function calls **`fibonacci(3)`** and **`fibonacci(2)`**.

4. **Fourth call (left branch):**

   `fibonacci(3)`

   The function calls **`fibonacci(2)`** and **`fibonacci(1)`**.

5. **Base cases:** The recursion eventually reaches the base cases for **`fibonacci(1)`** and **`fibonacci(0)`**.

   Once the base cases are reached, the function starts to return values and unwinds the recursive calls:

   - **`fibonacci(2) = 1`**
   - **`fibonacci(3) = 2`**
   - **`fibonacci(4) = 3`**
   - **`fibonacci(5) = 5`**
   - **`fibonacci(6) = 8`**

The time and space complexity are explained as follows:

- **Time complexity:** *O(2^n)*, because the function makes two recursive calls at each step, leading to an exponential number of calls as n increases.
- **Space complexity:** *O(n)*, because the recursion depth is proportional to n, and each recursive call takes up space on the call stack.

Optimized approach: Memoization

The recursive solution, while simple and elegant, has an exponential time complexity due to overlapping subproblems (the same Fibonacci numbers are recomputed multiple times). We can optimize this using **memoization**, where we store the results of Fibonacci numbers in a cache and reuse them when needed.

Here is how to implement the Fibonacci sequence using memoization:

```
def fibonacci_memo(n, memo={}):
    # Base case: Return n if n is 0 or 1
    if n == 0 or n == 1:
        return n

    # Check if the result is already in the memo dictionary
    if n not in memo:
        # Store the result in memo after computing
        memo[n] = fibonacci_memo(n - 1, memo) + fibonacci_memo(n - 2, memo)

    return memo[n]
```

Iterative approach to Fibonacci

An iterative solution avoids recursion altogether, making it more efficient for larger values of n:

```
def fibonacci_iterative(n):
    if n == 0:
        return 0
    elif n == 1:
        return 1

    a, b = 0, 1
    for _ in range(2, n + 1):
        a, b = b, a + b
    return b
```

This version has *O(n)* time complexity and *O(1)* space complexity, making it far more efficient for large values of n.

How to approach this problem in an interview:

- **Explain the recursive solution:** Walk the interviewer through the recursive approach, highlighting the base cases and the recursive relation between F(n), F(n-1), and F(n-2).
- **Identify optimization:** Recognize that the recursive approach has overlapping subproblems, leading to inefficiency. Mention that you can optimize it using memoization or an iterative approach.

- **Handle large inputs:** If the interviewer asks for a solution that handles large values of n, use the iterative approach or memoization to avoid stack overflow and reduce the time complexity.

Dig deeper

The edge cases are as follows:

- **n = 0:** The Fibonacci sequence starts with *F(0) = 0*.
- **n = 1:** The second Fibonacci number is *F(1) = 1*.
- **Negative inputs:** In some implementations, Fibonacci is only defined for non-negative integers. You could handle this by returning an error or None for negative inputs.

The real-world applications are as follows:

- **Computer graphics:** Fibonacci numbers appear in natural patterns and are sometimes used in computer graphics to create visually appealing designs, such as spiral patterns.
- **Dynamic programming:** The Fibonacci problem is often used to introduce **dynamic programming** concepts, where you store solutions to subproblems and reuse them to avoid redundant calculations.
- **Data structures:** Fibonacci heaps, a special type of data structure, use Fibonacci numbers to achieve faster amortized running times for certain operations.

How interviewers might challenge you

Interviewers might ask you to:

- Implement both recursive and iterative solutions.
- Optimize the recursive solution using memoization.
- Handle large inputs efficiently using an iterative approach.
- Discuss the **call stack** and how recursion is managed under the hood.

Problem 53: Generate all subsets of a set (power set)

Problem statement: Given a set of distinct integers, return all possible subsets (the power set). The solution set must not contain duplicate subsets.

For example:

- **Input:**

  ```
  nums = [1, 2, 3]
  ```

- **Output**:

  `[[], [1], [2], [3], [1,2], [1,3], [2,3], [1,2,3]]`

Understanding the problem: The **power set** of a given set is the collection of all possible subsets, including the empty set and the set itself. For a set of size n, the number of subsets is 2^n. This is because each element can either be included or excluded from a subset, leading to 2 possibilities for each element.

For example, the power set of the set {1, 2, 3} is:

`{}, {1}, {2}, {3}, {1,2}, {1,3}, {2,3}, {1,2,3}`

Approach: Backtracking

A natural way to generate all subsets is by using **backtracking**, where we systematically explore all possible ways to include or exclude each element. Backtracking allows us to build the solution incrementally and explore all the possible combinations.

Code implementation: Power set using backtracking:

We will use a recursive function that takes the current subset and the index of the next element to consider. At each step, we have two choices: either include the current element in the subset or skip it. Once we reach the end of the array, we add the current subset to the final result.

```
def subsets(nums):
    result = []

    def backtrack(current_subset, index):
        # Add the current subset to the result
        result.append(list(current_subset))

        # Explore further subsets by including or excluding the next element
        for i in range(index, len(nums)):
            # Include nums[i] in the current subset
            current_subset.append(nums[i])
            # Move to the next element
            backtrack(current_subset, i + 1)
            # Backtrack: Remove nums[i] to explore other subsets
            current_subset.pop()

    backtrack([], 0)
    return result
```

Example walkthrough: Let us walk through an example step by step to understand the backtracking process.

Given input:

```
nums = [1, 2, 3]
```

The steps are as follows:

1. We start with the empty subset [].
2. We explore adding 1 to the subset:
    - Subset: [1]
    - Then, we explore adding 2:
        - Subset: [1, 2]
        - Then, we explore adding 3: Subset: [1, 2, 3]
        - Backtrack to [1, 2]
    - Backtrack to [1]:
        - Then, we explore adding 3: Subset: [1, 3]
        - Backtrack to [1]
3. Backtrack to [] and explore adding 2:
    - Subset: [2]
        - Then, we explore adding 3: Subset: [2, 3]
        - Backtrack to [2]
4. Backtrack to [] and explore adding 3:
    - Subset: [3]
    - Backtrack to []

The final result is:

```
[[], [1], [2], [3], [1,2], [1,3], [2,3], [1,2,3]]
```

The time and space complexity are as follows:

- **Time complexity:** *O(2^n)*, where n is the number of elements in the input set. We generate all possible subsets, and for each subset, we perform constant-time operations like adding to the result.
- **Space complexity:** *O(2^n)*, because we are storing all subsets in the result list, which contains 2^*n* subsets.

Optimized approach: Iterative method

Another way to generate the power set is using an iterative approach. We start with an empty set, and for each element in the input set, we add it to all the existing subsets.

Here is the iterative implementation:

```
def subsets_iterative(nums):
    result = [[]]
```

```
    for num in nums:
        result += [curr + [num] for curr in result]
    return result
```

Example walkthrough (iterative approach): Let us go through the example again using the iterative approach.

Input:

```
nums = [1, 2, 3]
```

The steps are as follows:

1. Start with the empty subset:
   `result = [[]]`
2. Add 1 to all subsets in the result:
   `result = [[], [1]]`
3. Add 2 to all subsets in the result:
   `result = [[], [1], [2], [1, 2]]`
4. Add 3 to all subsets in the result:
   `result = [[], [1], [2], [1, 2], [3], [1, 3], [2, 3], [1, 2, 3]]`

The final result is the same as the recursive approach.

The time and space complexity are as follows:

- **Time complexity:** *O(n · 2^n)*. For each of the n elements, we duplicate all existing subsets (which grow to 2^*n* total).
- **Space complexity:** *O(2^n)* to store all subsets (plus *O(n)* temporary space while building).

How to approach this problem in an interview:

- **Explain the recursive approach:** Walk through the backtracking solution, explaining how recursion helps explore all possible subsets by including or excluding each element.
- **Iterative approach:** If time permits, suggest the iterative approach as an alternative. The iterative method may be easier to grasp and does not involve recursion.
- **Complexity analysis:** Be prepared to explain the time and space complexity, emphasizing that the number of subsets grows exponentially with the size of the input.

Dig deeper

The edge cases are as follows:

- **Empty set:** The power set of an empty set is just the empty set:

  ```
  nums = []
  # Output: [[]]
  ```

- **Single-element set:** The power set of a single-element set includes the empty set and the element itself:

  ```
  nums = [1]
  # Output: [[], [1]]
  ```

Some real-world applications are as follows:

- **Subset problems in combinatorics:** Subsets are frequently used in combinatorial problems where you need to explore all combinations of elements, such as finding all possible team combinations from a group of people.
- **Decision making:** In some decision-making processes, subsets can represent different configurations or choices, and generating all subsets allows for the exploration of all possible outcomes.

How interviewers might challenge you

Interviewers may ask you to:

- Implement both the recursive and iterative solutions.
- Handle large input sets and discuss ways to optimize space usage.
- Adapt the solution to exclude or include specific conditions, such as subsets of a specific length.

Problem 54: Permutations of a set

Note: **This problem is different from Problem 53 (Power set), where you generated all possible subsets.**

In this problem, you must generate *all possible permutations*, i.e., *all possible orderings* of the elements, rather than combinations or subsets.

Problem statement: Given a set of distinct integers, return all possible permutations.

For example:

- **Input:**

  ```
  nums = [1, 2, 3]
  ```

- **Output**:

  `[[1, 2, 3], [1, 3, 2], [2, 1, 3], [2, 3, 1], [3, 1, 2], [3, 2, 1]]`

Understanding the problem: The permutations of a set represent all possible orderings of its elements. Unlike subsets, the order of elements matters in permutations. For a set of size *n*, the total number of permutations is *n! (n factorial).*

For example, the permutations of the set {1, 2, 3} are:

`[1,2,3], [1,3,2], [2,1,3], [2,3,1], [3,1,2], [3,2,1]`

Approach: Backtracking

A natural way to generate all permutations is by using **backtracking**, where we build permutations by exploring all elements that have not yet been used in the current position.

Code implementation: Permutations using backtracking:

```
def permute(nums):
    result = []
    used = [False] * len(nums)

    def backtrack(current_permutation):
        if len(current_permutation) == len(nums):
            result.append(current_permutation[:])
            return

        for i in range(len(nums)):
            if not used[i]:
                used[i] = True
                current_permutation.append(nums[i])
                backtrack(current_permutation)
                current_permutation.pop()
                used[i] = False

    backtrack([])
    return result
```

Example walkthrough: Let us walk through an example step by step to understand the backtracking process.

Given input:

```
nums = [1, 2, 3]
```

The steps are as follows:

1. We start with the empty set [].
2. Add 1 → `[1]` → add 2 → `[1,2]` → add 3 → `[1,2,3]` → save

3. Backtrack → `[1,3]` → add 2 → `[1,3,2]` → save
4. Repeat with starting 2 → `[2,1,3]`, etc.
5. Continue until all permutations are generated.

The time and space complexity are as follows:

- **Time complexity:** *O(n!)*, where n is the length of the input list. Each element can be placed in each position, leading to n! permutations.
- **Space complexity:** *O(n)*, for the recursion stack and temporary data structures. Result storage is *O(n!)*.

Iterative approach: with insertion

In this approach, we build permutations iteratively by inserting each element into every possible position of existing permutations.

Here is the iterative implementation:

```
def permute_iterative(nums):
    result = [[]]
    for num in nums:
        new_result = []
        for perm in result:
            for i in range(len(perm)+1):
                new_result.append(perm[:i] + [num] + perm[i:])
        result = new_result
    return result
```

Example walkthrough (iterative approach): Let us go through the example again using the iterative approach.

Input:

```
nums = [1, 2, 3]
```

1. Start with the empty set: result = [[]]
2. Add 1 → result: [[1]]
3. Add 2 → insert into all positions → [[2,1],[1,2]]
4. Add 3 → insert into all positions → [[3,2,1],[2,3,1],[2,1,3],[3,1,2],[1,3,2],[1,2,3]]

Dig deeper

The edge cases are as follows:

- **Empty set:** Input: [] → Output: [[]]

- **Single-element set:** Input: [1] → Output: [[1]].
- **Large input set:** Input: [1, 2, 3, 4] → 24 permutations.

Some real-world applications are as follows:

- Generating all possible configurations, such as travel routes (Traveling Salesman Problem).
- Task scheduling or arranging items in different orders.
- Puzzle solving (e.g., Sudoku permutations).

How interviewers might challenge you

Interviewers might ask you to:

- Implement both the recursive and iterative solutions.
- How to generate permutations of a specific length.

Problem 55: Combination sum

Problem statement: Given an array of distinct integers candidates and a target integer target, return all unique combinations of candidates where the chosen numbers sum up to target. The same number may be used multiple times.

The solution set must not contain duplicate combinations.

For example:

- **Input**:
  `candidates = [2, 3, 6, 7], target = 7`
- **Output**:
  `[[2, 2, 3], [7]]`

Another example:

- **Input**:
  `candidates = [2, 3, 5], target = 8`
- **Output**:
  `[[2, 2, 2, 2], [2, 3, 3], [3, 5]]`

Understanding the problem: The problem requires us to find all possible combinations of numbers from the candidates array that sum up to a given target. We can reuse the numbers as many times as needed, but the resulting combinations must be unique.

Approach: Backtracking

We will use backtracking to explore all possible combinations. At each step, we will choose whether to include a number from the candidates' list and reduce the target accordingly. We continue this process until the target becomes 0, which indicates that a valid combination has been found.

The key steps are as follows:

1. Start with an empty combination and a given target.
2. For each number in the candidates list, explore two options:
   a. Include the number in the current combination and reduce the target.
   b. Skip the number and move to the next one.
3. If the target reaches 0, add the current combination to the result list.
4. Backtrack to explore other possibilities by removing the last included number and trying other combinations.

Code implementation: Combination sum using backtracking:

```
def combination_sum(candidates, target):
    result = []

    def backtrack(remaining, current_combination, start):
        # Base case: If the remaining target is 0, add the current combination
to the result
        if remaining == 0:
            result.append(list(current_combination))
            return
        # Explore each candidate starting from the current index
        for i in range(start, len(candidates)):
            candidate = candidates[i]
            # If the candidate is greater than the remaining target, break (no
point in continuing)
            if candidate > remaining:
                break
            # Include the candidate in the combination
            current_combination.append(candidate)
            # Recursively try to reach the target by reducing the remaining value
            backtrack(remaining - candidate, current_combination, i)
            # Backtrack by removing the last included candidate
            current_combination.pop()

    # Sort the candidates to ensure the combinations are generated in order
    candidates.sort()
```

```
    backtrack(target, [], 0)
    return result
```

Example walkthrough: Let us walk through an example step by step.

- **Input**:
  ```
  candidates = [2, 3, 6, 7]
  target = 7
  ```

The steps are as follows:

1. We start with an empty combination and a target of 7.
2. We explore each candidate starting from the first element:
   a. Include 2: Current combination: [2], Remaining target: 5
   b. Include another 2: Current combination: [2, 2], Remaining target: 3
   c. Include another 2: Current combination: [2, 2, 2], Remaining target: 1
      i. **Backtrack**: The remaining target is less than the smallest candidate, so we backtrack.
3. Try adding 3 to the combination [2, 2]:
   a. Current combination: [2, 2, 3], Remaining target: 0
      i. **Valid combination found**: Add [2, 2, 3] to the result.
4. Try adding 7 directly to the empty combination:
   a. Current combination: [7], Remaining target: 0
      i. **Valid combination found**: Add [7] to the result.

The final result is:

```
[[2, 2, 3], [7]]
```

The time and space complexity is as follows:

- **Time complexity:** The time complexity is $O(2^n)$, where n is the size of the input array candidates. The function explores all possible combinations of candidates that could sum to the target.
- **Space complexity:** *O(target)*, because the depth of the recursion tree depends on the target value. In the worst case, the depth is proportional to the target.

Optimized approach: Early stopping

An optimization we can make is to **sort** the candidate list and **break** early in the recursive function if the current candidate is greater than the remaining target. This avoids unnecessary recursion and improves performance.

Here is the optimized implementation:

```
def combination_sum_optimized(candidates, target):
    result = []

    def backtrack(remaining, current_combination, start):
        if remaining == 0:
            result.append(list(current_combination))
            return
        for i in range(start, len(candidates)):
            candidate = candidates[i]
            if candidate > remaining:
                break
            current_combination.append(candidate)
            backtrack(remaining - candidate, current_combination, i)
            current_combination.pop()

    candidates.sort()
    backtrack(target, [], 0)
    return result
```

How to approach this problem in an interview:

- **Explain backtracking:** Start by explaining how backtracking works to explore all possible combinations of the candidates array. Mention the recursive nature of the solution and the importance of the base case (when the remaining target becomes 0).
- **Complexity analysis:** Discuss the time complexity and why the solution explores all potential combinations, leading to an exponential number of recursive calls.
- **Optimizations:** Mention how sorting the candidates and early stopping (breaking when the candidate is greater than the remaining target) improves performance.

Dig deeper

The edge cases are as follows:

- **Empty candidates array:** If the candidates array is empty, the result should be an empty list because there are no possible combinations.

  ```
  candidates = []
  target = 7
  # Output: []
  ```

- **Target is smaller than the smallest candidate:** If the target is smaller than the smallest candidate, no combination can sum up to the target.
- **No valid combinations:** If there are no valid combinations, the function should return an empty list.

Some real-world applications are as follows:

- **Resource allocation:** This problem can be applied to resource allocation problems where you need to find all combinations of resources that sum up to a given target.
- **Subset sum problems:** The combination sum problem is closely related to the *subset sum problem*, which has applications in areas like knapsack problems, decision-making, and financial planning.
- **Game development:** In certain games, you might need to combine items or powers in various ways to reach a goal, which is similar to finding combinations that sum up to a target.

How interviewers might challenge you

Interviewers may ask you to:

- Implement both the recursive and iterative solutions.
- Modify the solution to handle repeated elements in the candidates list, ensuring no duplicate combinations are generated.
- Discuss how to optimize the solution for large input arrays and targets.

Problem 56: N-queens problem

Problem statement: The N-queens problem is a classic puzzle in which you are tasked with placing N queens on an N x N chessboard such that no two queens attack each other. A queen can attack another queen if they are placed in the same row, column, or diagonal.

Your task is to write a function that returns all possible configurations of the chessboard where N queens can be placed safely.

For example, for N = 4, there are two possible configurations:

```
[
  [«.Q..»,  // Solution 1
   «...Q»,
   «Q...»,
   «..Q.»],

  [«..Q.»,  // Solution 2
   «Q...»,
   "...Q",
   ".Q.."]
]
```

Understanding the problem: The challenge of the N-queens problem is ensuring that no two queens threaten each other. Queens can attack in three directions:

- Same row
- Same column
- Same diagonal

For example, if a queen is placed on the first row, first column, you cannot place any other queen on:

- The same row (row 1).
- The same column (column 1).
- Any diagonal that passes through that position.

Approach: Backtracking

We will use backtracking to solve this problem. The idea is to place a queen in the first row, then move to the second row and try placing another queen in a safe spot. If placing a queen leads to a conflict, we backtrack and try a different position. We repeat this process until we either find a solution or exhaust all possibilities.

The key steps are as follows:

1. Place a queen on the first available row.
2. For each valid position in the next row, check if placing a queen results in a valid configuration (no queen can attack another).
3. If a valid configuration is found, recursively place queens in the remaining rows.
4. If no valid configuration is possible in a row, backtrack by removing the last placed queen and try a different position.

Code implementation: N-queens using backtracking:

```
def solve_n_queens(n):
    result = []

    # Helper function to check if placing a queen at (row, col) is valid
    def is_valid(board, row, col):
        # Check the same column
        for i in range(row):
            if board[i][col] == 'Q':
                return False
        # Check the upper left diagonal
        for i, j in zip(range(row - 1, -1, -1), range(col - 1, -1, -1)):
            if board[i][j] == 'Q':
                return False
        # Check the upper right diagonal
        for i, j in zip(range(row - 1, -1, -1), range(col + 1, n)):
            if board[i][j] == 'Q':
```

```
            return False
        return True

    # Helper function to backtrack and find all solutions
    def backtrack(board, row):
        if row == n:
            # Found a valid configuration, add it to the result
            result.append(["".join(row) for row in board])
            return
        for col in range(n):
            if is_valid(board, row, col):
                board[row][col] = 'Q'  # Place a queen
                backtrack(board, row + 1)  # Move to the next row
                board[row][col] = '.'  # Backtrack and remove the queen

    # Initialize an empty board
    board = [["." for _ in range(n)] for _ in range(n)]
    backtrack(board, 0)
    return result
```

Example walkthrough: Let us walk through an example where N = 4. The steps are as follows:

1. Start with an empty board:

   ```
   ....
   ....
   ....
   ....
   ```

2. Place a queen in the first row, first column:

   ```
   Q...
   ....
   ....
   ....
   ```

3. Move to the second row and try placing a queen. The first column is blocked, so place it in the second column:

   ```
   Q...
   .Q..
   ....
   ....
   ```

4. Move to the third row. Both the first and second columns are blocked, but the third column is free:

   ```
   Q...
   .Q..
   ..Q.
   ....
   ```

5. Move to the fourth row, but there is no valid place to put a queen. Backtrack and remove the last placed queen:

   ```
   Q...
   .Q..
   ....
   ....
   ```

6. Try placing the third queen in the fourth column instead:

   ```
   Q...
   .Q..
   ....Q
     ....
   ```

7. No valid place for the fourth queen in the last row, so backtrack again and continue the process until all solutions are found.

   The final result for N = 4 is:

   ```
   [
     [«.Q..»,  // Solution 1
      «...Q»,
      «Q...»,
      «..Q.»],

     [«..Q.»,  // Solution 2
      «Q...»,
      "...Q",
      ".Q.."]
   ]
   ```

The time and space complexity is explained as follows:

- **Time complexity:** *O(N!)*, where N is the number of queens. This is because the solution explores all possible arrangements of queens on the board.
- **Space complexity:** *(N^2)*, since we store the board as a 2D list and recursively track the state of the board.

Optimized approach: Column and diagonal checks

To optimize the solution, instead of checking the validity of a queen's placement for each column and diagonal every time, we can use **sets** to keep track of the columns and diagonals that already have queens. This reduces the time spent in the **is_valid** function.

```
def solve_n_queens_optimized(n):
    result = []
    columns = set()
    pos_diagonals = set()  # (r + c)
```

```
    neg_diagonals = set()  # (r - c)

    def backtrack(row, board):
        if row == n:
            result.append(["".join(row) for row in board])
            return
        for col in range(n):
            if col in columns or (row + col) in pos_diagonals or (row - col)
in neg_diagonals:
                continue
            # Place the queen
            columns.add(col)
            pos_diagonals.add(row + col)
            neg_diagonals.add(row - col)
            board[row][col] = 'Q'
            # Move to the next row
            backtrack(row + 1, board)
            # Backtrack: Remove the queen
            columns.remove(col)
            pos_diagonals.remove(row + col)
            neg_diagonals.remove(row - col)
            board[row][col] = '.'

    board = [["." for _ in range(n)] for _ in range(n)]
    backtrack(0, board)
    return result
```

How to approach this problem in an interview:

- **Explain backtracking:** Start by explaining the backtracking approach. Mention that we try placing a queen in each row and use recursion to check if placing the queen leads to a valid configuration.
- **Optimization:** Explain the optimization of using sets to track columns and diagonals. This reduces the time complexity of checking the validity of each queen's placement.
- **Complexity discussion:** Be prepared to discuss the time complexity and why generating all possible configurations takes *O(N!)*.

Dig deeper

The edge cases are as follows:

- **Small values of N:**
    - For *N* = *1*, there is only one possible solution:

    - [["Q"]]
    - For $N = 2$ and $N = 3$, there are no possible solutions, as it is impossible to place queens without them attacking each other.

- **Large N:** For larger values of N, the solution can become computationally expensive due to the factorial time complexity. Optimizations using sets help mitigate this.

The real-world applications are as follows:

- **Constraint satisfaction problems:** The N-queens problem is an example of a *constraint satisfaction problem*. Such problems are common in fields like AI, where the goal is to find a solution that satisfies a set of constraints.
- **Scheduling and resource allocation:** The principles of the N-queens problem can be applied to scheduling and resource allocation tasks, where you need to place resources (like employees or machines) in a way that avoids conflicts.

How interviewers might challenge you

Interviewers may ask you to:

- Implement both the basic and optimized solutions.
- Discuss alternative approaches or optimizations.
- Extend the problem to other types of puzzles or constraint satisfaction problems.

Problem 57: Subset sum

Problem statement: Given a set of positive integers and a target sum, determine if there exists a subset whose sum equals the target sum. Return True if such a subset exists, otherwise return False.

For example:

- **Input**:
```
nums = [3, 34, 4, 12, 5, 2], target = 9
```
- **Output**:
```
True  # Subset [4, 5] sums up to 9.
```

Understanding the problem: The *subset sum problem* is a well-known problem in computer science and is often used in coding interviews. It asks whether there exists a subset of numbers from a given set that adds up to a specified target sum.

The challenge involves finding the right subset of numbers to achieve this target sum while ensuring the solution is efficient enough to handle larger datasets. This problem has many applications in real life, including financial portfolio optimization, resource allocation, and even scheduling.

Approach: Backtracking

We can solve the subset sum problem using backtracking. This method explores all possible subsets of the given set. At each step, we decide whether to include or exclude a particular element from the subset and recursively check if the subset sum equals the target.

The steps are as follows:

1. Start with an empty subset and check the sum.
2. Recursively include or exclude each element.
3. Return True if any subset sums to the target.

Code implementation: Subset sum using backtracking:

```
def subset_sum(nums, target):
    def backtrack(index, current_sum):
        # Base case: If the current sum equals the target, return True
        if current_sum == target:
            return True
        # If we've processed all elements or exceeded the target, return False
        if index >= len(nums) or current_sum > target:
            return False

        # Option 1: Include the current number
        include = backtrack(index + 1, current_sum + nums[index])
        # Option 2: Exclude the current number
        exclude = backtrack(index + 1, current_sum)

        # Return True if either option results in the target sum
        return include or exclude

    return backtrack(0, 0)
```

Example walkthrough: Let us break down the example *nums = [3, 34, 4, 12, 5, 2]* and *target =* 9. The steps are:

1. Start with an empty subset ([]) and a sum of 0.
2. For each number in the list:
    - **Include**: Add the number to the subset.
    - **Exclude**: Skip the number and move to the next one.
3. Keep track of the current subset sum and check if it matches the target at any point.

    For example:

    - Start with 3: *Current sum* = 3

- Add 4: *Current sum = 7*
- Add 2: *Current sum = 9* (Target found)

The output is True.

The time and space complexity is explained as follows:

- **Time complexity:** *O(2^n)*, where n is the number of elements in the input list. This is because we explore all possible subsets (including/excluding each element).
- **Space complexity:** *O(n)*, due to the recursion depth as we explore different subsets.

Optimized approach: Dynamic programming

To avoid recalculating results multiple times, we can use **dynamic programming** (**DP**). DP stores previously computed values, allowing us to solve the problem more efficiently.

Code implementation: Subset sum using dynamic programming:

```
def subset_sum_dp(nums, target):
    # Create a DP table with dimensions (n+1) x (target+1)
    dp = [[False] * (target + 1) for _ in range(len(nums) + 1)]

    # A sum of 0 can always be achieved with the empty subset
    for i in range(len(nums) + 1):
        dp[i][0] = True

    # Fill the DP table
    for i in range(1, len(nums) + 1):
        for j in range(1, target + 1):
            if nums[i - 1] > j:
                dp[i][j] = dp[i - 1][j]  # Can't include current element
            else:
                dp[i][j] = dp[i - 1][j] or dp[i - 1][j - nums[i - 1]]  #
Include or exclude current element

    return dp[len(nums)][target]
```

The explanation of the DP approach is as follows:

- **DP table initialization:** A DP table *dp[i][j]* is used, where *i* represents the elements considered and *j* represents the sum we want to achieve. *dp[i][j]* is True if it is possible to form sum *j* with the first *i* elements.
- **Base case:** A sum of 0 can always be achieved by selecting the empty subset.
- **Recursive relation:** For each element *nums[i-1]*, you either:
    - Exclude the element, keeping the same sum *j*.

   - Include the element, updating the sum to *j - nums[i-1]*.
- **Result**: The answer is found in *dp[len(nums)][target]*, which tells us if the subset sum is achievable.

Example walkthrough: Dynamic programming:

For *nums = [3, 34, 4, 12, 5, 2]* and *target* = 9, the DP table looks like this:

	0	1	2	3	4	5	6	7	8	9
0	T	F	F	F	F	F	F	F	F	F
1	T	F	F	T	F	F	F	F	F	F
2	T	F	F	T	F	F	F	F	F	F
3	T	F	T	T	T	F	F	F	F	F
4	T	F	T	T	T	T	F	F	F	F
5	T	F	T	T	T	T	F	T	T	T
6	T	F	T	T	T	T	F	T	T	T

In this example, the DP table shows that the sum 9 is achievable by including 4 and 5, as *dp[6][9]* is True.

The time and space complexity of the DP approach are as follows:

- **Time complexity:** *O(n * target)*, where n is the number of elements and target is the sum we are aiming for. This is much faster than the backtracking approach.
- **Space complexity:** *O(n * target)*, because we store the DP table with dimensions *(n+1) x (target+1)*.

Some real-world applications are as follows:

- **Resource allocation:** Subset sum can be applied to resource allocation problems, such as determining the optimal allocation of resources within constraints (e.g., budget or capacity limits).
- **Financial planning:** In finance, the subset sum problem is used to determine if a combination of investments can achieve a specific target return.

Dig deeper

The edge cases are as follows:

- **Target sum of zero:** If the target sum is 0, the answer is always True, as the empty subset sums to 0.
- **Negative numbers:** This solution assumes positive integers. If negative numbers are allowed, modifications to the algorithm are required.

How to approach this problem in an interview:

- **Explain the brute force approach:** Start with the backtracking approach. This will show that you understand the base case and how the problem can be solved by exploring all subsets.
- **Discuss the dynamic programming approach:** Move on to explain the more optimized DP solution, which reduces time complexity. Interviewers often look for how well candidates can optimize their code.
- **Analyze complexity:** Be prepared to explain both time and space complexity, and highlight why the DP approach is a better fit for larger input sizes.

Problem 58: Word search

Problem statement: Given a 2D board of characters and a word, determine if the word exists in the board. The word can be constructed from letters of sequentially adjacent cells, where "adjacent" cells are horizontally or vertically neighboring. The same letter cell may not be used more than once.

For example:

- **Input**:
```
board = [
    ['A', 'B', 'C', 'E'],
    ['S', 'F', 'C', 'S'],
    ['A', 'D', 'E', 'E']
]
word = "ABCCED"
```
- **Output**:
```
True  # The word "ABCCED" can be formed from adjacent cells.
```

Understanding the problem: In the *word search problem*, we need to determine whether a word can be formed by navigating through a grid of letters. The challenge lies in ensuring that you only move horizontally or vertically, and no cell is used more than once. The problem is often used in interviews to test candidates' understanding of **depth-first search** (**DFS**) and backtracking.

Approach: Depth-first search (DFS) with backtracking

We can solve this problem using **DFS and backtracking**. DFS will allow us to explore each potential path on the board, and backtracking will help revert to previous states when we determine that a path does not lead to the solution.

The steps are as follows:

1. Start from any cell that matches the first character of the word.
2. Perform DFS to check all possible directions (up, down, left, and right).
3. If a letter is found, continue searching in adjacent cells.
4. If the word is found, return True. If no path works, backtrack and try the next possible cell.

Code implementation: Word search using DFS and backtracking:

```
def exist(board, word):
    rows, cols = len(board), len(board[0])

    def dfs(r, c, i):
        # Base case: if we've found the entire word
        if i == len(word):
            return True
        # If out of bounds or the current cell doesn't match the current
letter
        if r < 0 or c < 0 or r >= rows or c >= cols or board[r][c] != word[i]:
            return False

        # Temporarily mark the cell as visited by modifying its value
        temp, board[r][c] = board[r][c], '#'

        # Explore all four directions: up, down, left, right
        found = (dfs(r + 1, c, i + 1) or  # down
                 dfs(r - 1, c, i + 1) or  # up
                 dfs(r, c + 1, i + 1) or  # right
                 dfs(r, c - 1, i + 1))    # left

        # Restore the original value after backtracking
        board[r][c] = temp

        return found

    # Start the search from every cell in the board
    for row in range(rows):
        for col in range(cols):
            if board[row][col] == word[0] and dfs(row, col, 0):
                return True

    return False
```

Example walkthrough: Let us walk through an example with *board = [['A', 'B', 'C', 'E'], ['S', 'F', 'C', 'S'], ['A', 'D', 'E', 'E']]* and *word = "ABCCED"*. The steps are as follows:

1. Start from the first cell, A (position (0,0)). It matches the first letter of the word.

2. Explore adjacent cells. Move right to B (position (0,1)), which matches the next letter.
3. Continue moving right to C (position (0,2)), which matches.
4. Now move down to C (position (1,2)), then down to E (position (2,2)), and finally left to D (position (2,1)), successfully matching the entire word "ABCCED".

The result is True.

The time and space complexity are explained as follows:

- **Time complexity:** *O(m * n * 4^L)*, where m and n are the dimensions of the board and L is the length of the word. In the worst case, we perform DFS from every cell and explore up to 4 possible directions for each letter in the word.
- **Space complexity:** *O(L)*, where L is the length of the word. This space is used by the recursion stack during the DFS.

Optimized approach: Early termination

We can slightly optimize this solution by returning False early if the length of the word exceeds the number of available cells or if the board does not contain all the letters in the word.

Dig deeper

The edge cases are as follows:

- **Word longer than the number of cells:** If the length of the word exceeds the number of cells in the board, it is impossible to find the word, so return False immediately.
- **Empty board or empty word:** If the board or the word is empty, return False.
- **Multiple paths:** Ensure that multiple paths are explored, but only the first successful path is returned as True.

How to approach this problem in an interview:

- **Clarify the constraints:** Ask the interviewer about edge cases, such as empty boards or words, and whether diagonal movements are allowed (typically, they are not).
- **Discuss DFS and backtracking:** Begin with the DFS approach, explaining how it will search each possible path recursively. Then introduce backtracking, which allows you to revert to previous states when a path does not work.
- **Optimize if possible:** Mention any potential optimizations, such as pruning the search early if the word cannot possibly fit on the board.
- **Test with examples:** Be ready to walk through your solution with examples like the one provided above.

Some real-world applications are as follows:

- **Word search puzzles:** This problem is the foundation for creating and solving word search puzzles, where users need to find words hidden in grids of letters.
- **Pathfinding**: The DFS approach is commonly used in pathfinding problems, such as navigating mazes or finding routes on maps.
- **Pattern matching:** Variations of the word search problem are used in pattern recognition tasks, where patterns must be identified in large data grids.

Challenges in interviews

The word search problem tests several skills:

- **DFS and backtracking**: Key techniques for exploring possible solutions.
- **Handling edge cases**: Ensuring that your code works for all input scenarios.
- **Efficiency**: DFS can be slow for large grids, so understanding time complexity is critical.

You may also be asked to extend the problem, such as allowing diagonal movements or modifying the grid in real-time.

Problem 59: Sudoku solver

Problem statement: Given a partially filled 9x9 Sudoku board, write a function to fill in the empty cells. Each cell can contain numbers between 1 and 9, and no two numbers in the same row, column, or 3x3 subgrid can be the same.

The Sudoku board is represented as a 2D list where empty cells are denoted by the character '.'.

For example:

```
board = [
  ['5', '3', '.', '.', '7', '.', '.', '.', '.'],
  ['6', '.', '.', '1', '9', '5', '.', '.', '.'],
  ['.', '9', '8', '.', '.', '.', '.', '6', '.'],
  ['8', '.', '.', '.', '6', '.', '.', '.', '3'],
  ['4', '.', '.', '8', '.', '3', '.', '.', '1'],
  ['7', '.', '.', '.', '2', '.', '.', '.', '6'],
  ['.', '6', '.', '.', '.', '.', '2', '8', '.'],
  ['.', '.', '.', '4', '1', '9', '.', '.', '5'],
  ['.', '.', '.', '.', '8', '.', '.', '7', '9']
]
```

Understanding the problem: The Sudoku solver problem requires filling the board while maintaining the rules of Sudoku:

1. Each number from 1 to 9 must appear exactly once in each row.
2. Each number from 1 to 9 must appear exactly once in each column.
3. Each number from 1 to 9 must appear exactly once in each 3x3 subgrid.

This problem is a great example of using backtracking to explore possible configurations. Backtracking helps us systematically try each number in empty cells, undoing incorrect attempts, and continuing until the board is fully solved.

Approach: Backtracking

To solve the Sudoku puzzle, we will use backtracking:

1. **Find an empty cell**: Scan the board to find the next empty cell (denoted by '.').
2. **Try filling with numbers 1-9**: For each empty cell, attempt to place digits 1 through 9.
3. **Check validity**: Before placing a number, check if it is valid in the current row, column, and subgrid.
4. **Recursion**: If the placement is valid, recursively try to fill the next empty cell.
5. **Backtrack**: If placing a number leads to an invalid state, undo the placement and try the next number.

Code implementation: Sudoku solver using backtracking:

```
def solve_sudoku(board):
    def is_valid(board, row, col, num):
        # Check the row
        for i in range(9):
            if board[row][i] == num:
                return False
        # Check the column
        for i in range(9):
            if board[i][col] == num:
                return False
        # Check the 3x3 subgrid
        start_row, start_col = 3 * (row // 3), 3 * (col // 3)
        for i in range(start_row, start_row + 3):
            for j in range(start_col, start_col + 3):
                if board[i][j] == num:
                    return False
        return True

    def solve(board):
        for row in range(9):
            for col in range(9):
```

```
            if board[row][col] == '.':
                for num in map(str, range(1, 10)):  # Try digits 1-9
                    if is_valid(board, row, col, num):
                        board[row][col] = num
                        if solve(board):
                            return True
                        board[row][col] = '.'  # Backtrack
                return False  # If no valid number found, return False
    return True  # Sudoku is solved

solve(board)
```

Example walkthrough: Let us walk through how the code works using the given example board:

1. Start by finding the first empty cell, which is at position (0,2).
2. Try placing numbers 1 through 9 in this cell. After checking, we find that placing 1 is invalid because it conflicts with a number in the same row or subgrid. The same applies to 2 and 3.
3. Place 4, which is valid. Move to the next empty cell.
4. Continue this process recursively. If a number placement leads to a dead-end where no number can be placed, the algorithm backtracks, undoing previous placements until it finds the correct configuration.

The algorithm eventually fills the entire board correctly.

The time and space complexity is explained as follows:

- **Time complexity:** *O(9^(n))*, where n is the number of empty cells. In the worst case, the algorithm attempts to place numbers 1 through 9 in each empty cell, resulting in exponential time complexity.
- **Space complexity:** *O(n)*, where n is the number of empty cells. This is due to the recursion stack used during backtracking.

Optimized approach: Early termination and efficiency

Though backtracking can be slow for larger inputs, we can optimize the algorithm by:

- **Pre-filling data structures:** Use data structures to store the numbers already present in each row, column, and subgrid. This avoids scanning the entire board repeatedly.
- **Early termination:** If a number cannot be placed in any cell early on, terminate the search.

Dig deeper

The edge cases are as follows:

- **Already solved board:** If the board is already solved, the algorithm returns immediately without making any changes.
- **Invalid board:** If the board violates Sudoku rules (e.g., has duplicates in a row), backtracking will detect this, and the function will return without finding a solution.
- **Minimal clue board:** Boards with very few numbers (clues) can take significantly longer to solve because there are more possibilities to explore. These boards can often test the efficiency of your algorithm.

How to approach this problem in an interview:

- **Explain backtracking:** Backtracking is a fundamental algorithmic technique used for exploring possibilities. In an interview, be sure to explain how backtracking works, including the recursive exploration of possibilities and the rollback (undo) mechanism when a solution does not work.
- **Code the base case first:** Start with a simple case, such as checking if a number can be placed in a particular cell, and build up from there. Then, introduce the recursive backtracking logic.
- **Discuss time complexity:** Be prepared to discuss why the solution has exponential time complexity and how the backtracking method ensures that the problem is solved efficiently.

Some real-world applications are as follows:

- **Puzzle solvers:** The backtracking technique used to solve Sudoku can also be applied to other types of puzzles, such as crossword puzzles, N-queens, and pathfinding problems.
- **Constraint satisfaction problems (CSPs):** Sudoku is an example of a CSP, where you must satisfy specific constraints (e.g., each row, column, and subgrid must contain unique digits). Backtracking is commonly used to solve CSPs in AI and optimization.
- **Algorithmic thinking:** Solving Sudoku using backtracking helps you understand how to approach problems systematically and optimize solutions for complex challenges.

Some challenges in interviews are as follows:

- **Edge cases:** Be prepared for interviewers to ask about edge cases, such as invalid Sudoku boards or minimal clue boards. Discuss how your solution can handle these cases efficiently.
- **Backtracking logic:** Interviewers may ask you to explain how backtracking works in detail. Be ready to walk through the algorithm with an example, showing how the solution explores possibilities and revises decisions when necessary.

- **Optimization:** If the interviewer challenges you to optimize your code, suggest improvements like pre-filling data structures for faster lookups or terminating the search early if a valid solution is impossible.

Practice exercise

To strengthen your understanding of backtracking and Sudoku solving, try solving Sudoku puzzles with varying difficulty levels. Practice writing code for:

- Detecting invalid Sudoku boards.
- Generating Sudoku boards.
- Optimizing the Sudoku solver by storing row, column, and subgrid constraints in hash sets for quick lookups.

Problem 60: Restore IP addresses

Problem statement: Given a string containing only digits, return all possible valid IP address combinations that can be formed by inserting three dots into the string. An IP address is valid if:

- It consists of exactly four integers (each between 0 and 255), separated by dots.
- Each integer should not contain leading zeros, unless the integer is exactly 0.

For example:

- **Input**:
  `"25525511135"`
- **Output**:
  `["255.255.11.135", "255.255.111.35"]`

Understanding the problem: In the *Restore IP Addresses* problem, you are given a string of digits, and your task is to insert three dots in different positions to generate all possible valid IP addresses.

The challenge lies in ensuring that each segment of the IP address (separated by dots) is valid. A valid segment must:

- Be between 0 and 255.
- Have no leading zeros (e.g., 01 is not valid, but 0 is).

Approach: Backtracking

To solve this problem, we can use backtracking:

1. **Try inserting dots**: We explore different ways of placing three dots in the string to divide it into four segments.

2. **Validate each segment**: Each segment must satisfy the conditions of being a valid IP address component (i.e., between 0 and 255, no leading zeros).

3. **Recursion and backtracking**: We recurse by adding dots and checking each segment. If a segment is invalid, we backtrack and try a different position for the dot.

Code implementation: Restore IP addresses using backtracking:

```
def restore_ip_addresses(s):
    def is_valid(segment):
        # Check if the segment is between 0 and 255 and has no leading zeros
        return len(segment) == 1 or (segment[0] != '0' and int(segment) <= 255)

    def backtrack(start, dots, path):
        # If we have placed 3 dots and the remaining part is valid, add the result
        if dots == 3:
            segment = s[start:]
            if is_valid(segment):
                result.append(path + segment)
            return

        # Try placing a dot after 1, 2, or 3 digits
        for i in range(start, min(start + 3, len(s))):
            segment = s[start:i + 1]
            if is_valid(segment):
                backtrack(i + 1, dots + 1, path + segment + '.')

    result = []
    if len(s) > 12:  # Too long to be a valid IP address
        return result
    backtrack(0, 0, "")
    return result
```

Example walkthrough: Let us walk through the example with input s = "25525511135":

1. Start by trying different ways of placing dots:
    a. First, place a dot after the first segment (255). The segment is valid because it is between 0 and 255.
    b. Then place a dot after the next segment (255). This is also valid.
    c. Finally, place a dot after 11. Now, check if the remaining segment (135) is valid.

5. The resulting valid IP address is 255.255.11.135.

6. Continue exploring other possible dot placements:
    a. Another valid IP address is 255.255.111.35.

The time and space complexity are explained as follows:

- **Time complexity:** *O(1)*, since the length of the string is fixed (at most 12 characters). We are only processing strings of limited length, so the time complexity is constant.
- **Space complexity:** *O(1)*, because the recursion depth is limited by the number of characters in the string (at most 12).

Optimized approach: Pruning invalid segments early

We can optimize the solution by pruning invalid segments as early as possible:

- If a segment starts with a 0, it is invalid unless it is exactly "0".
- If a segment exceeds 255, it is invalid.

These optimizations ensure that we do not explore unnecessary paths in the backtracking process.

Dig deeper

The edge cases are as follows:

- **String length too short or too long:** If the string has fewer than 4 or more than 12 characters, it is impossible to form a valid IP address, and we should return an empty result immediately.
- **Leading zeros:** Handle cases like "001", which are invalid IP address segments because of leading zeros. The only valid zero is "0".
- **All digits the same:** A string like "111111111111" would result in multiple valid IP addresses because it can be split in different ways to form valid segments.

How to approach this problem in an interview:

- **Clarify the requirements:** Ask the interviewer to clarify the rules for IP address validity, such as whether leading zeros are allowed or if segments must be exactly between 0 and 255.
- **Explain backtracking:** Be sure to explain how backtracking is used to explore different ways of placing dots, and how the solution ensures that all possible valid IP addresses are found.
- **Optimize and discuss time complexity:** Mention optimizations, such as pruning invalid segments early, and explain why the time complexity is *O(1)* due to the limited string length.

- **Test with examples:** Be prepared to walk through a few examples, such as s = *"123456789"*, and demonstrate how your code handles various cases.

Some real-world applications are as follows:

- **IP address parsing:** The solution to this problem is similar to how IP addresses are parsed from network packets in networking software.
- **String parsing in general:** The technique of splitting strings and validating segments is useful in many applications, such as parsing dates, phone numbers, or structured data formats.

Interview tips

When solving the IP address restoration problem in an interview, consider these tips:

- **Communicate**: Explain your thought process as you explore different dot placements.
- **Handle edge cases**: Make sure your code handles strings that are too short or too long and avoids invalid segments with leading zeros.
- **Iterate quickly**: Be ready to implement the base solution quickly, then refine it by adding optimizations like pruning invalid segments early.

Challenge yourself

Once you have mastered the basic IP address restoration problem, challenge yourself by:

- Modifying the problem to allow IP addresses of varying segment lengths (e.g., IPv6).
- Optimizing the solution further by avoiding recursion and using iteration to place dots.
- Solving similar string parsing problems to practice your backtracking and string manipulation skills.

Join our Discord space

Join our Discord workspace for latest updates, offers, tech happenings around the world, new releases, and sessions with the authors:

https://discord.bpbonline.com

SECTION 6
Dynamic Programming

Introduction

Welcome to the world of **dynamic programming (DP)**, one of the most powerful and elegant techniques in computer science. If you have ever wondered how to approach problems that involve making a series of decisions where each decision affects the next, then DP is the tool you have been waiting for. This section is your gateway to mastering this technique, which is a favorite in technical interviews and often seen as a critical skill for top-tier coding jobs.

Dynamic programming can be a bit intimidating at first, but think of it as solving problems by breaking them down into simpler sub-problems. It is like solving a puzzle one piece at a time, remembering the solutions to smaller parts so you do not have to solve the same part repeatedly. This is what makes DP efficient; by remembering solutions, or **memoization**, it avoids the redundancy seen in more brute-force approaches.

Imagine you are climbing a staircase with a certain number of steps, and each time, you can either take one step or two steps. If you try to brute-force every possible way to reach the top, you will end up with a lot of repeated calculations. However, if you can remember how many ways there are to reach the last step and the second-to-last step, you can easily compute the total. This is the essence of DP: solving big problems by solving small, similar ones first.

Why DP matters: In interviews, DP is frequently tested because it demonstrates your ability to optimize solutions and think critically. It is not just about coding; it is about recognizing patterns, breaking problems down into their essential parts, and using previous solutions to build toward the final answer.

Many of the world's most complex problems, from finance to artificial intelligence, can be optimized using DP. Whether you are calculating the shortest path, maximizing profit, or counting the number of possible solutions to a problem, DP is a tool you will reach for again and again.

Objectives

In this section, you will tackle some of the most common and important DP problems. We will start with basic problems like the *climbing stairs problem*, which helps you understand how to approach a DP problem from scratch. You will learn to recognize the *overlapping subproblems* and how to use a *memoization table* or a *recursive approach* to store previously computed results.

Next, you will move on to more complex challenges, such as the **longest common subsequence** and the famous *0/1 Knapsack problem*. These problems test your ability to make decisions based on constraints, like choosing which items to pack in a knapsack to maximize profit, given limited capacity.

The problems in this section are not only useful for interviews but are also a window into how real-world applications solve optimization problems. From *coin change* to *house robber*, you will gain insight into how to break down big, seemingly impossible problems into manageable parts and use DP to solve them efficiently.

Engagement through challenges: Each problem in this section will stretch your understanding of DP and challenge your ability to come up with efficient solutions. We will begin with problems that can be solved in *O(n)* time and space complexity, like the *climbing stairs* and *house robber*, and gradually move on to more intricate problems that require *2D arrays* or *recursive solutions* with **backtracking**.

As you progress, you will see how DP applies to a wide range of problems, whether it is finding the *maximum area* in a matrix or determining how many ways you can *decode a string*. Each problem builds on the last, and by the end of this section, you will be confident in applying DP to any challenge that comes your way.

Challenges ahead: This section is designed to challenge not just your ability to write code but also your problem-solving mindset. You will face some of the trickiest interview questions, like the **longest increasing subsequence (LIS)** and the *Edit Distance* problem, which are favorites of companies like Google and Facebook. These challenges will test your ability to balance multiple constraints and optimize solutions efficiently.

You will also encounter problems that deal with grids, such as *Unique Paths* and *Maximal Square*, which are commonly used to test your spatial reasoning and ability to work with 2D data structures.

DP's magic: The true magic of DP lies in its ability to take brute-force approaches and transform them into efficient, scalable solutions. Without DP, many of the problems in this section would take exponential time to solve. With DP, however, you will learn how to break problems down, store solutions to sub-problems, and reduce the time complexity significantly.

For example, the *Coin Change problem*, which asks how many ways you can make a certain amount of money using various coin denominations, could be solved through brute force, but it would take too long. By using DP, you will quickly learn how to find the optimal solution in a fraction of the time.

Some real-world applications of DP are as follows:

- **Finance and economics**: DP is used to solve problems like portfolio optimization, where you need to maximize returns based on a set of constraints.
- **Route optimization**: Algorithms like Dijkstra's and Bellman-Ford, which are used for finding the shortest path in graphs, are based on DP principles.
- **Game development**: Many games use DP to solve problems related to pathfinding, resource management, and decision-making in AI characters.
- **Data compression**: Techniques like the **Lempel-Ziv-Welch** (**LZW**) algorithm, used in ZIP compression, are based on DP.
- **Bioinformatics**: DP is essential in solving alignment problems for DNA sequencing and protein structure prediction.

Engagement through practice: By the end of each chapter, you will find exercises and additional challenges to test your understanding of DP concepts. These problems will help you solidify what you have learned and push your problem-solving abilities even further.

Problem 61: Climbing stairs

Problem statement: You are climbing a staircase, and it takes n steps to reach the top. Each time, you can either climb 1 or 2 steps. In how many distinct ways can you reach the top?

For example:

- **Input**: n = 3
- **Output**: 3 Explanation: There are three ways to climb to the top:

  1 step + 1 step + 1 step

  1 step + 2 steps

  2 steps + 1 step

Understanding the problem: The *climbing stairs* problem is a classic example of DP. Each time, you are faced with the option of taking either 1 step or 2 steps, and the goal is to find how many different ways you can climb n stairs. This is a combinatorial problem that is often compared to the Fibonacci sequence.

Let us break down the problem:

- If you are on step i, you could have come from step i-1 or i-2. Therefore, the total number of ways to reach step i is the sum of the ways to reach steps i-1 and i-2.
- This is very similar to the Fibonacci sequence, where *Fib(i) = Fib(i-1) + Fib(i-2)*.

This recurrence relation gives us the basis for solving this problem using DP.

Approach 1: DP with tabulation

One approach to solving this problem is to use a *bottom-up DP* approach, where we build up a solution by solving for smaller subproblems first. We use a table (**dp** array) to store the number of ways to reach each step:

- **Base cases:**
  - If n = 1, there is only 1 way to climb the stairs (take 1 step).
  - If n = 2, there are 2 ways to climb the stairs (either take two 1-steps, or take one 2-step).
- **Recurrence relation:** The number of ways to reach step i is the sum of the ways to reach step i-1 and i-2.

Code implementation: DP solution:

```
def climb_stairs(n):
    # Base case for n = 1 or n = 2
    if n == 1:
        return 1
    if n == 2:
        return 2

    # DP array to store the number of ways to reach each step
    dp = [0] * (n + 1)
    dp[1] = 1  # 1 way to reach step 1
    dp[2] = 2  # 2 ways to reach step 2

    # Build the dp array from step 3 to n
    for i in range(3, n + 1):
        dp[i] = dp[i - 1] + dp[i - 2]

    # The answer is stored in dp[n]
    return dp[n]
```

Example walkthrough: Let us walk through an example with n = 5:

1. Initialize *dp = [0, 1, 2, 0, 0, 0]*.

2. For step 3, calculate *dp[3] = dp[2] + dp[1] = 2 + 1 = 3.*
3. For step 4, calculate *dp[4] = dp[3] + dp[2] = 3 + 2 = 5.*
4. For step 5, calculate *dp[5] = dp[4] + dp[3] = 5 + 3 = 8.*

At the end, *dp[5] = 8,* which means there are 8 distinct ways to climb 5 stairs.

Approach 2: Optimized space complexity

The solution above uses *O(n)* space to store the entire **dp** array. However, we only need the last two values to compute the next value. We can reduce the space complexity to *O(1)* by storing just the previous two results.

Code implementation: Optimized space solution:

```
def climb_stairs_optimized(n):
    if n == 1:
        return 1
    if n == 2:
        return 2

    # Variables to store the last two steps
    prev1, prev2 = 1, 2

    # Calculate the number of ways for each step from 3 to n
    for i in range(3, n + 1):
        current = prev1 + prev2
        prev1, prev2 = prev2, current

    return prev2
```

The time and space complexity are explained as follows:

- **Time complexity:** *O(n)* because we are iterating through the stairs from 1 to n.
- **Space complexity:** *O(1)* for the optimized space solution, since we are only using two variables to store the previous results.

Dig deeper

The edge cases are as follows:

- **n = 1:** If there is only one step, the answer is 1.
- **n = 2:** If there are two steps, the answer is 2 because you can either take two 1-steps or one 2-step.
- **n = 0:** If there are no steps, there is no way to climb, so the answer is 0.

How to approach this problem in an interview:

- **Explain the base case:** Always start by explaining the base case. For n = 1 or n = 2, describe the number of ways you can climb the stairs. This helps set the foundation for your solution.
- **Introduce the recurrence relation:** Talk about how each step i can be reached from i-1 or i-2 and how this leads to the recurrence relation *dp[i] = dp[i-1] + dp[i-2]*.
- **Optimize:** If the interviewer asks for optimization, be ready to discuss the space-optimized solution where you only store the last two steps instead of the entire `dp` array.
- **Time complexity:** Explain why the solution runs in $O(n)$ time and why it is an efficient approach for this problem.

Some real-world applications are as follows:

- **Fibonacci sequences:** The *climbing stairs* problem is essentially a variant of the Fibonacci sequence, which appears in various real-world phenomena, from population growth models to the branching patterns of trees.
- **Pathfinding:** In robotics or game development, finding the number of distinct ways to reach a destination with specific movement constraints is a common problem that can be solved using similar techniques.
- **Dynamic decision making:** The principles of this problem can be applied in finance, logistics, and operations management, where decision-making over multiple stages is required.

The interview tips are as follows:

- **Communicate your thought process:** Clearly explain the thought process behind your solution, focusing on the recurrence relation and how the problem is broken down into subproblems.
- **Handle edge cases:** Make sure to address edge cases like $n = 1$ and $n = 2$, as they help demonstrate your attention to detail and problem-solving completeness.
- **Optimize when asked:** If the interviewer asks for an optimized solution, show how you can reduce space complexity by only storing the last two steps.

Practice exercises

- **Variations of the climbing stairs problem:** Modify the problem so that you can take either 1, 2, or 3 steps at a time. How does the recurrence relation change? Implement a solution.
- **Generalizing to multiple steps:** Generalize the problem where you can take any number of steps between 1 and k. Implement a solution using DP.

Problem 62: House robber

Problem statement: You are a professional robber planning to rob houses along a street. Each house has a certain amount of money stashed, but the houses are arranged in a line, and adjacent houses have security systems connected. This means that if two adjacent houses are robbed, the alarms will go off.

Given an integer array **`nums`** representing the amount of money in each house, return the maximum amount of money you can rob without triggering the alarms.

For example:

- **Input**: `nums = [1, 2, 3, 1]`
- **Output**: **4**
- **Explanation**: Rob house 1 (money = 1) and then rob house 3 (money = 3), which gives you a total of 4.

Understanding the problem: The *house robber* problem is about maximizing the amount of money you can steal from non-adjacent houses. Since you cannot rob two adjacent houses, you need to make a strategic decision at each house: either rob it or skip it. The goal is to find the optimal sequence of house robberies that gives you the maximum profit.

This problem can be framed as a DP problem, where:

- **Decision-making**: For each house, decide whether to rob it (and skip the next) or skip it (and move to the next house).
- **Optimal substructure**: The maximum amount you can rob up to a certain house depends on the decisions made at previous houses.
- **Overlapping subproblems**: The decision to rob or skip a house is based on subproblems (decisions made for earlier houses).

Approach 1: DP with tabulation

We can solve the house robber problem using a *bottom-up DP* approach. We maintain a **`dp`** array where each entry **`dp[i]`** represents the maximum amount of money that can be robbed up to house **`i`**.

1. **Base cases:**
   a. If there is only one house, the maximum money you can rob is the money in that house.
   b. If there are two houses, the maximum money you can rob is the maximum of the two amounts.

2. **Recurrence relation:** For each house **i**, you have two choices:
    a. Rob the current house i and add its value to **dp[i-2]** (since you must skip the adjacent house).
    b. Skip the current house i, and take the value of **dp[i-1]** (the best you can do without robbing house **i**).

Thus, the recurrence relation is: **dp[i] = max(dp[i-1], dp[i-2] + nums[i])**.

Code implementation: DP solution:

```
def rob(nums):
    n = len(nums)

    # Handle base cases
    if n == 0:
        return 0
    if n == 1:
        return nums[0]
    if n == 2:
        return max(nums[0], nums[1])

    # DP array to store the maximum money that can be robbed up to house i
    dp = [0] * n
    dp[0] = nums[0]
    dp[1] = max(nums[0], nums[1])

    # Fill the dp array
    for i in range(2, n):
        dp[i] = max(dp[i-1], dp[i-2] + nums[i])

    # The result will be stored in dp[n-1]
    return dp[n-1]
```

Example walkthrough: Let us walk through an example with **nums = [2, 7, 9, 3, 1]**:

1. Initialize **dp = [0] * 5**.
2. Set base cases: **dp[0] = 2, dp[1] = max(2, 7) = 7**.
3. For house 3: **dp[2] = max(dp[1], dp[0] + nums[2]) = max(7, 2 + 9) = 11**.
4. For house 4: **dp[3] = max(dp[2], dp[1] + nums[3]) = max(11, 7 + 3) = 11**.
5. For house 5: **dp[4] = max(dp[3], dp[2] + nums[4]) = max(11, 11 + 1) = 12**.

Thus, the maximum amount of money you can rob is **dp[4] = 12**.

Approach 2: Optimized space complexity

Instead of maintaining a **dp** array, we can reduce the space complexity by only storing the last two values, as those are the only ones we need to calculate the next value.

Code implementation: Optimized space solution:

```
def rob_optimized(nums):
    n = len(nums)

    # Handle base cases
    if n == 0:
        return 0
    if n == 1:
        return nums[0]
    if n == 2:
        return max(nums[0], nums[1])

    # Variables to store the last two results
    prev1 = nums[0]
    prev2 = max(nums[0], nums[1])
    # Calculate the maximum money for each house from 2 to n-1
    for i in range(2, n):
        current = max(prev2, prev1 + nums[i])
        prev1, prev2 = prev2, current
    return prev2
```

The time and space complexity are as follows:

- **Time complexity:** *O(n)*, where n is the number of houses, since we are iterating through the list once.
- **Space complexity:** *O(1)* for the optimized solution, as we are only storing two variables (**prev1** and **prev2**).

Dig deeper

The edge cases are as follows:

- **No houses:** If there are no houses (**nums = []**), the result should be 0.
- **One house:** If there is only one house, the result is simply the amount of money in that house (**nums[0]**).
- **Two houses:** If there are two houses, the result is the maximum amount between the two (**max(nums[0], nums[1])**).

How to approach this problem in an interview:

- **Explain the base case:** Start by explaining the simplest cases, one house and two houses. This sets a foundation for the interviewer to understand the problem.

- **Introduce the recurrence relation:** Discuss how the decision to rob a house or skip it depends on the previous two houses. This helps the interviewer understand the DP approach.
- **Space optimization:** If asked to optimize space, show how you can reduce space complexity by storing only the last two results instead of the entire `dp` array.
- **Time complexity:** Be ready to explain why the solution is $O(n)$ and how it efficiently solves the problem in linear time.

Some real-world applications are as follows:

- **Investment strategies:** Similar to the house robber problem, investment strategies often require you to make decisions that maximize profit while avoiding adjacent investments that might not be feasible together.
- **Resource allocation:** In project management or manufacturing, resources may need to be allocated optimally, but certain resources may conflict with one another, similar to robbing non-adjacent houses.

The interview tips are as follows:

- **Communicate your thought process:** Clearly explain how the decision-making process works and why you chose to rob or skip a house based on previous results.
- **Handle edge cases:** Address special cases like empty arrays, one house, or two houses to demonstrate your thoroughness.
- **Optimization:** If asked for an optimized solution, present the space-optimized approach where you only store two variables instead of the entire `dp` array.

Challenge yourself

- **Circular houses:** Modify the problem so that the first and last houses are adjacent (i.e., the houses form a circle). This requires a different approach since the first and last houses cannot be robbed together.
- **House robber III:** Explore a more advanced version of this problem where the houses are arranged in a binary tree, and you need to decide which nodes to rob while skipping their immediate children.

Problem 63: LIS

Problem statement: Given an unsorted array of integers, find the length of the LIS.

A subsequence is a sequence derived from another sequence by deleting some or no elements without changing the order of the remaining elements. An increasing subsequence is one in which each subsequent element is greater than the previous one.

For example:

- **Input**: nums = [10, 9, 2, 5, 3, 7, 101, 18]
- **Output**: 4
- **Explanation**: There are multiple increasing subsequences, such as [10, 101], [2, 5, 7, 101], [2, 3, 7, 101], but the LIS is [2, 3, 7, 101], which has a length of 4.

Understanding the problem: The LIS problem asks you to find the longest subsequence in a given array such that the elements of the subsequence are sorted in strictly increasing order. This is a common DP problem.

Let us break down the problem:

- You are not required to sort the entire array, just identify the longest subsequence where the numbers increase.
- For each element in the array, you need to check if you can extend an increasing subsequence up to that point.

Approach 1: DP with tabulation

We can solve this problem using DP. The key idea is to use an array **dp** where **dp[i]** represents the length of the LIS that ends at index **i**.

Base case: Each element is, by itself, an increasing subsequence of length 1. Therefore, initialize the **dp** array with 1 for each element.

1. **Recurrence relation:** For each element **nums[i]**, check all previous elements **nums[j]** (where j<i). If **nums[i] > nums[j]**, then **nums[i]** can extend the increasing subsequence ending at **nums[j]**. In that case, update **dp[i]** as:

   dp[i] = max(dp[i], dp[j] + 1)

2. **Final result:** The length of the LIS is the maximum value in the **dp** array.

Code implementation: DP solution:

```
def length_of_lis(nums):
    if not nums:
        return 0

    # Initialize the dp array where each element starts with length 1
    dp = [1] * len(nums)

    # Fill the dp array
    for i in range(1, len(nums)):
        for j in range(i):
            if nums[i] > nums[j]:
                dp[i] = max(dp[i], dp[j] + 1)
```

```
    # The answer is the maximum value in the dp array
    return max(dp)
```

Example walkthrough: Let us walk through the example with **`nums = [10, 9, 2, 5, 3, 7, 101, 18]`**:

1. Initialize **`dp = [1, 1, 1, 1, 1, 1, 1, 1]`** (each element is its own subsequence).
2. For index 3 (**`nums[3] = 5`**):
    a. Compare with **`nums[0] = 10`**, no update (5 is not greater than 10).
    b. Compare with **`nums[1] = 9`**, no update.
    c. Compare with **`nums[2] = 2`**, update **`dp[3] = max(dp[3], dp[2] + 1) = 2`**.
3. Continue this process for each element.

By the end, the **`dp`** array will be:

`dp = [1, 1, 1, 2, 2, 3, 4, 4].`

The maximum value in **`dp`** is **4**, meaning the LIS has a length of 4.

The time and space complexity are explained as follows:

- **Time complexity:** $O(n^2)$, where n is the length of the input array. This is because we have two nested loops iterating through the array.
- **Space complexity:** $O(n)$, where n is the length of the input array. We are using an array dp of size n to store the lengths of the LISs.

Approach 2: Optimized solution using binary search

The DP approach has a time complexity of $O(n^2)$, which can be inefficient for large inputs. We can optimize this to $O(n \log n)$ by using **binary search**.

In this approach, we maintain an array lis (LIS), which we update as we iterate through the input array:

1. For each element in **`nums`**, use binary search to find the position where this element can either extend or replace an element in **`lis`**.
2. If the element is larger than all elements in **`lis`**, append it to **`lis`**.
3. If the element is smaller than or equal to an element in **`lis`**, replace the first element in lis that is greater than or equal to the current element.

Code implementation: Binary search solution:

```
import bisect

def length_of_lis_optimized(nums):
```

```
lis = []

for num in nums:
    # Find the index where num can be placed
    pos = bisect.bisect_left(lis, num)

    # If num is larger than any element in lis, append it
    if pos == len(lis):
        lis.append(num)
    else:
        # Otherwise, replace the existing element
        lis[pos] = num

return len(lis)
```

Explanation of the optimized approach: Let us go through an example with **`nums = [10, 9, 2, 5, 3, 7, 101, 18]`**:

1. Start with an empty **`lis = []`**.
2. For **`nums[0] = 10`**, append 10 to **`lis`**.
    a. **`lis = [10]`**.
3. For **`nums[1] = 9`**, replace 10 with 9 (since 9 < 10).
    a. **`lis = [9]`**.
4. Continue this process for each element. At the end, the array **`lis`** will be:
    a. **`lis = [2, 3, 7, 18]`**.

The length of **`lis`** is **4**, which is the length of the LIS.

The time and space complexity are explained as follows:

- **Time complexity:** *O(n log n)* due to the binary search operation for each element.
- **Space complexity:** *O(n),* where n is the length of the input array, as we are using an array lis to store the increasing subsequence.

Dig deeper

How to approach this problem in an interview:

- **Explain the DP approach first:** Start by explaining the DP solution with $O(n^2)$ complexity. This is a straightforward approach and shows that you understand the fundamentals.
- **Introduce the binary search optimization:** If the interviewer asks for optimization, explain how binary search can reduce the time complexity to *O(n log n)* by keeping track of the LIS and updating it efficiently.

- **Discuss the trade-offs:** Mention the trade-offs between the two approaches in terms of time complexity and ease of understanding.

Some real-world applications are as follows:

- **Stock prices:** The LIS can represent the longest period where stock prices are increasing consecutively. Investors may use this to identify potential profitable trends.
- **Job promotions:** In a career path, the LIS might represent the longest period of career growth (in terms of promotions or salary increases).

The interview tips are as follows:

- **Edge cases:** Always mention edge cases like an empty array, an array with one element, or an array with all equal elements.
- **Optimization:** Be ready to discuss both the DP and the optimized binary search approaches, as this shows your ability to improve solutions.
- **Communicate clearly:** Make sure to explain why each solution works and how you derived the recurrence relation or optimization strategy.

Problem 64: Longest common subsequence (LCS)

Problem statement: Given two strings `text1` and `text2`, return the length of their longest common subsequence. If there is no common subsequence, return 0.

A subsequence is a sequence that appears in the same relative order, but not necessarily consecutively. A common subsequence is a subsequence that is common to both strings.

For example:

- **Input**: `text1 = "abcde", text2 = "ace"`
- **Output**: `3`
- **Explanation**: The longest common subsequence is "ace", which has a length of 3.

Understanding the problem: The LCS problem is about finding the longest subsequence that appears in both given strings. The subsequence does not have to be contiguous, but the relative order of characters must be preserved.

For example:

- In the strings "abcde" and "ace", the longest common subsequence is "ace".

The challenge lies in efficiently finding this subsequence by comparing both strings while maintaining the order of characters.

Approach: DP

We can solve the LCS problem using DP. The idea is to build a 2D table **dp** where **dp[i][j]** represents the length of the longest common subsequence between the substrings **text1[0:i]** and **text2[0:j]**. The steps are as follows:

1. **Base case:** If either string is empty, the longest common subsequence is 0.
2. **Recurrence relation:**
   a. If the characters **text1[i-1]** and **text2[j-1]** match, then **dp[i][j] = dp[i-1][j-1] + 1**. This means the current characters contribute to the LCS, so we add 1 to the previous LCS.
   b. If they do not match, then we take the maximum of **dp[i-1][j]** and **dp[i][j-1]**. This means we skip either the current character in **text1** or **text2**.

Code implementation: DP solution:

```
def longest_common_subsequence(text1, text2):
    m, n = len(text1), len(text2)

    # Initialize a 2D dp array with size (m+1) x (n+1)
    dp = [[0] * (n + 1) for _ in range(m + 1)]

    # Fill the dp array
    for i in range(1, m + 1):
        for j in range(1, n + 1):
            if text1[i - 1] == text2[j - 1]:
                dp[i][j] = dp[i - 1][j - 1] + 1
            else:
                dp[i][j] = max(dp[i - 1][j], dp[i][j - 1])

    # The length of the longest common subsequence will be in dp[m][n]
    return dp[m][n]
```

Example walkthrough: Let us walk through the example with text1 = "abcde" and **text2 = "ace"**:

1. Initialize the **dp** table:

```
dp = [[0, 0, 0, 0],
      [0, 0, 0, 0],
      [0, 0, 0, 0],
      [0, 0, 0, 0],
      [0, 0, 0, 0],
      [0, 0, 0, 0]]
```

2. Compare each character:

a. At **i = 1, j = 1:text1[0] = "a"; text1[0] = "a"** and **text2[0] = "a"**. They match, so **dp[1][1] = dp[0][0] + 1 = 1**.

b. At **i = 1; j = 2; text1[0] = "a"** and text2[1] = "c". They do not match, so **dp[1][2] = max(dp[0][2], dp[1][1]) = max(0,1) = 1**

c. At **i = 2, j = 2:text1[1] = "b"** and **text2[1] = "c"**. They do not match, so **dp[2][2] = max(dp[1][2], dp[2][1]) = 1**.

d. At **i = 3, j = 3:text1[2] = "c"** and **text2[1] = "c"**. They match, so **dp[3][2] = dp[2][1] + 1 = 2**.

e. Continue filling the table using these rules. The final dp table looks like this:

```
dp = [[0, 0, 0, 0],
      [0, 1, 1, 1],
      [0, 1, 1, 1],
      [0, 1, 2, 2],
      [0, 1, 2, 2],
      [0, 1, 2, 3]]
```

3. The length of the longest common subsequence is **dp[5][3] = 3**.

The time and space complexity are as follows:

- **Time complexity:** *O(m * n)*, where m and n are the lengths of the two input strings. We fill the **dp** table of size m x n.
- **Space complexity:** *O(m * n)* for storing the **dp** table.

Optimization: Reducing space complexity

We can reduce the space complexity to *O(n)* by using only two rows in the **dp** array. Since we only need the values from the previous row to calculate the current row, we can overwrite one row at a time.

Code implementation: Optimized space solution:

```
def longest_common_subsequence_optimized(text1, text2):
    m, n = len(text1), len(text2)

    # Use only two rows for the dp array
    prev = [0] * (n + 1)
    curr = [0] * (n + 1)

    for i in range(1, m + 1):
        for j in range(1, n + 1):
            if text1[i - 1] == text2[j - 1]:
                curr[j] = prev[j - 1] + 1
            else:
```

```
            curr[j] = max(prev[j], curr[j - 1])
        prev, curr = curr, prev
    return prev[n]
```

Dig deeper

Some real-world applications are as follows:

- **Version control:** LCS is used in version control systems like Git to identify the differences between two files and find the longest common subsequences, which helps in merging and comparing changes.
- **DNA sequence matching:** In bioinformatics, LCS is used to compare DNA sequences to find similarities between them. DNA sequences can be thought of as strings, and the longest common subsequence helps determine how closely related two sequences are.
- **Text comparison tools:** Text comparison software, like plagiarism checkers, uses LCS to find the longest matching sequences between two documents.

How to approach this problem in an interview:

- **Explain the concept of LCS:** Start by explaining what a subsequence is and how the longest common subsequence is defined. Clarify that the subsequence does not need to be contiguous but must preserve the order of characters.
- **DP approach:** Discuss the DP approach, explaining how you use the dp table to store the length of the LCS up to each pair of indices in the two strings.
- **Space optimization:** If asked, present the optimized space solution using only two rows. This shows that you can improve the solution when required.

The interview tips are as follows:

- **Edge cases:** Mention edge cases like empty strings, where the result should be 0.
- **Communication:** Walk the interviewer through the recurrence relation and how the **dp** table is filled, providing clear examples.
- **Time and space complexity:** Be ready to discuss the time and space complexity, especially when moving to the optimized solution.

Real-world practice

- **Longest repeated subsequence:** Modify the problem to find the longest subsequence that appears twice in the same string. Try solving this as a follow-up challenge.
- **Small modifications:** What happens if you modify the problem to allow at most one character difference between the two subsequences? This requires tweaking the DP approach.

Problem 65: 0/1 Knapsack problem

Problem statement: Given n items, each with a weight and a value, determine the maximum value you can obtain by selecting items that do not exceed a given weight capacity W. You cannot split an item, meaning you must either take the entire item or leave it (0/1 choice).

For example:

- **Input**: `weights = [1, 2, 3]`, `values = [10, 15, 40]`, `W = 6`
- **Output**: `65`
- **Explanation**: The maximum value obtained is 65 by taking all three items, since their total weight (1+2+3=6) is within the Knapsack's capacity.

Understanding the problem: The *0/1 Knapsack problem* is one of the most classic problems in DP. You are given a set of items, each with a weight and a value, and you need to determine which items to include in a knapsack to maximize the total value without exceeding the knapsack's weight limit.

In this version of the knapsack problem, you can either take an item completely or leave it behind, hence the 0/1 nature of the problem.

Approach: DP

We can solve this problem using DP by building a 2D table **`dp`**, where **`dp[i][w]`** represents the maximum value that can be obtained by considering the first **`i`** items and a knapsack of capacity **`w`**. The steps are:

1. **Base case:** If there are no items to consider or the capacity of the knapsack is zero, the maximum value is 0. So, **`dp[i][0] = 0`** for all **`i`**, and **`dp[0][w] = 0`** for all **`w`**.
2. **Recurrence relation:**
    a. If the current item's weight is less than or equal to the current capacity **`w`**, we have two choices:
        i. **Include the current item**: The value would be **`dp[i-1][w - weight[i]] + value[i]`**.
        ii. **Exclude the current item**: The value would be dp[i-1][w].
        iii. Take the maximum of these two **`choices:dp[i][w] = max(dp[i-1][w], dp[i-1][w - weight[i]] + value[i]`**).
    b. If the current item's weight is greater than w, we cannot include it: **`dp[i][w] = dp[i-1][w]`**.

Code implementation: DP solution:

```
def knapsack(weights, values, W):
    n = len(weights)
```

```
    # Initialize the dp table with all zeros
    dp = [[0] * (W + 1) for _ in range(n + 1)]

    # Build the dp table
    for i in range(1, n + 1):
        for w in range(1, W + 1):
            if weights[i - 1] <= w:
                # Either take the current item or don't take it
                dp[i][w] = max(dp[i - 1][w], dp[i - 1][w - weights[i - 1]] +
values[i - 1])
            else:
                dp[i][w] = dp[i - 1][w]

    # The last cell of the dp table will contain the maximum value
    return dp[n][W]
```

Example walkthrough: Let us walk through the example with **`weights = [1, 2, 3]`**, **`values = [10, 15, 40]`**, and **`W = 6`**:

1. Initialize the **`dp`** table:

```
dp = [[0, 0, 0, 0, 0, 0, 0],  # 0 items considered
      [0, 0, 0, 0, 0, 0, 0],  # 1st item considered
      [0, 0, 0, 0, 0, 0, 0],  # 2nd item considered
      [0, 0, 0, 0, 0, 0, 0]]  # 3rd item considered
```

2. Fill the table by checking each item and weight combination:
   a. For the first item (weight = 1, value = 10):
      i. If W >= 1, we can include this item, so **`dp[1][1] = 10`**, and the rest follows: **`dp[1][2] = 10`**, **`dp[1][3] = 10`**, etc.
3. Continue for the second and third items, building the table as you consider each weight.
4. The final table looks like this:

```
dp = [[0, 0, 0, 0, 0, 0, 0],
      [0, 10, 10, 10, 10, 10, 10],
      [0, 10, 15, 25, 25, 25, 25],
      [0, 10, 15, 40, 50, 55, 65]]
```

The maximum value is 65, obtained by taking all three items.

The time and space complexity are as follows:

- **Time complexity:** *O(n * W)*, where n is the number of items and W is the capacity of the knapsack. We fill a 2D table of size *(n + 1) x (W + 1)*.
- **Space complexity:** *O(n * W)* for the **`dp`** table.

Optimization: Space optimization using 1D array

We can reduce the space complexity to *O(W)* by using a single 1D array instead of a 2D table. We update the array from right to left for each item to avoid overwriting needed values.

```
def knapsack_optimized(weights, values, W):
    n = len(weights)

    # Initialize the 1D dp array of size w+1
    dp = [0] * (W + 1)

    # loop each item
    for i in range(n):
       # Traverse in reverse, it will avoid using updated value in same 
iteration
         for w in range(W, weights[i]-1, -1):
              # either include the current item or skip it
             dp[w] = max(dp[w], dp[w - weights[i]] + values[i])
    # The last element will contain the maximum value
    return dp[n][W]
```

Dig deeper

Some real-world applications are as follows:

- **Resource allocation:** The knapsack problem models real-world scenarios like resource allocation, where you have limited resources (capacity) and need to maximize the benefits (value).
- **Budgeting:** In financial planning, the knapsack problem can be used to select investments or projects under a fixed budget to maximize returns.
- **Storage management:** In cloud computing, knapsack algorithms help in optimizing the allocation of limited storage resources while maximizing the stored data's value.

The interview tips are as follows:

- **Start with a greedy solution:** In interviews, you can mention the greedy approach first (taking the item with the highest value-to-weight ratio), but explain that it does not always give the optimal solution for the 0/1 Knapsack.
- **Explain DP clearly:** Walk the interviewer through the decision-making process at each step of building the `dp` table. Explain the trade-off between including and excluding an item.
- **Edge cases:** Be prepared to discuss edge cases, such as when all items weigh more than the knapsack's capacity or when all items have the same value.

Practice exercises

- **Fractional knapsack:** In the fractional knapsack problem, you can take fractions of items. Modify the solution to allow fractional weights.
- **Multi-dimensional knapsack:** What if there are multiple constraints (e.g., weight and volume)? Try solving the multi-dimensional knapsack problem.

Problem 66: Coin change

Problem statement: Given an integer array of coins representing the different denominations of coins and an integer amount representing a total amount of money, determine the fewest coins needed to make up that amount. If any combination of the coins cannot make up that amount, return -1.

For example:

- **Input**: `coins = [1, 2, 5]`, `amount = 11`
- **Output**: `3`
- **Explanation**: 11 can be made with three coins: 5 + 5 + 1.

Understanding the problem: The *Coin Change problem* is a classic DP problem where you must find the minimum number of coins required to make a given amount from a set of denominations. This problem can be solved using both recursive and DP approaches. Still, DP offers a more efficient solution with a time complexity of *O(n * amount)*, where n is the number of coin denominations.

The idea is to use DP to build a solution, starting with small amounts and incrementally solving for larger amounts using the smaller results.

Approach: DP

We solve the problem by maintaining a `dp` array where `dp[i]` represents the minimum number of coins needed to make up the amount `i`. We initialize `dp[0] = 0` because no coins are needed to make up the amount 0. For all other amounts, we initialize `dp[i] = amount + 1`, which is a value larger than the maximum possible result.

The recursive relation is simple: for each coin, we check if we can reduce the current amount by the coin's value and update the `dp[i]` with the minimum number of coins required.

The steps are as follows:

1. **Initialization**:
    a. `dp[0] = 0` because no coins are required to make up the amount 0.
    b. For all other amounts, initialize the `dp` array with amount + 1 (a placeholder for an unattainable amount).

2. **Recurrence relation:** For each coin in the **coins** array and for each amount **i** from coin to amount:
   a. Update **dp[i]** by checking the minimum number of coins required:
   b. **dp[i] = min(dp[i], dp[i - coin] + 1)**.
3. **Result:** If **dp[amount]** is still equal to amount + 1, return -1 (since it is unattainable); otherwise, return **dp[amount]**.

Code implementation: DP:

```
def coin_change(coins, amount):
    # Initialize dp array with amount + 1 (infeasible large number)
    dp = [amount + 1] * (amount + 1)
    dp[0] = 0  # Base case: no coins are needed to make amount 0

    # Fill dp array
    for coin in coins:
        for i in range(coin, amount + 1):
            dp[i] = min(dp[i], dp[i - coin] + 1)

    # If dp[amount] is still amount + 1, return -1 (unattainable)
    return dp[amount] if dp[amount] != amount + 1 else -1
```

Example walkthrough: Let us walk through the example with **coins = [1, 2, 5]** and **amount = 11**:

1. Initialize the **dp** array:

   dp = [0, inf, inf, inf, inf, inf, inf, inf, inf, inf, inf, inf]

   (Where **inf** represents amount + 1, which is unattainable initially.)
2. Process each coin:
   a. **For coin = 1:** We can make amounts 1, 2, 3, ... up to 11 by using 1-coin denominations: **dp = [0, 1, 2, 3, 4, 5, 6, 7, 8, 9, 10, 11]**.
   b. **For coin = 2**: We can improve some values using 2-coin denominations. For example: **dp[2] = 1** (instead of 2), **dp[3] = 2**, **dp[4] = 2**, and so on. **dp = [0, 1, 1, 2, 2, 3, 3, 4, 4, 5, 5, 6]**.
   c. **For coin = 5:** Using 5-coin denominations, we can further reduce some values. For example: **dp[5] = 1**, **dp[6] = 2**, **dp[7] = 2**, and so on. **dp = [0, 1, 1, 2, 2, 1, 2, 2, 3, 3, 2, 3]**.
3. The result is **dp[11] = 3**, meaning we need 3 coins to make 11 (5 + 5 + 1).

The time and space complexity are explained as follows:

- **Time complexity:** *O(n * amount),* where n is the number of coin denominations, and amount is the total amount. We iterate over each coin and each amount up to the target amount.
- **Space complexity:** *O(amount),* since we use a **dp** array to store results for each amount up to the target.

Dig deeper

Why DP works: DP is the best approach for this problem because it avoids the inefficiencies of brute-force. The brute-force approach would try every possible combination of coins, resulting in an exponential time complexity. Instead, DP builds up the solution from smaller subproblems and ensures that each subproblem is solved only once, making the solution efficient.

The edge cases are as follows:

- **Impossible to make the amount:** If no combination of coins can make up the given amount, the algorithm returns 1. For example, if **`coins = [2]`** and **`amount = 3`**, it is impossible to make 3, so the output is 1.
- **Exact match:** If the amount is exactly one of the coin denominations, the algorithm returns 1. For example, if **`coins = [1, 5, 10]`** and **`amount = 10`**, the result is 1.
- **Large amounts:** The DP approach can handle large amounts efficiently, but if the amount is extremely large and the coins are few, the **dp** array will need a lot of space. You may need to optimize space usage in such cases.

How to approach this problem in an interview:

- **Explain the problem:** Clearly state that the goal is to find the minimum number of coins to make up the given amount.
- **Naive approach:** Briefly mention the brute-force approach of trying every possible combination of coins, then explain why this approach is inefficient.
- **DP:** Introduce the DP approach and explain how you build the solution from smaller subproblems.
- **Edge cases:** Discuss edge cases, like when the amount cannot be formed or when there is an exact match.

Some real-world applications are as follows:

- **Currency exchange**: The coin change problem can be applied to currency exchange systems, where you need to give the customer the least number of coins or bills.
- **Resource allocation:** In logistics, this problem can model resource allocation when you have limited types of resources and need to distribute them efficiently.

- **Making change in cash transactions:** This problem directly applies to making change in cash transactions, where the goal is to minimize the number of coins or bills used.

Practice exercises

- **Unlimited coin supply:** What if you have an unlimited supply of coins and want to minimize the number of coins used? Modify the algorithm to handle this scenario.
- **Limited coin supply:** What if you have a limited supply of each type of coin? Can you adapt the DP approach to handle this?

Problem 67: Partition equal subset sum

Problem statement: Given a non-empty array of positive integers, determine if the array can be partitioned into two subsets such that the sum of the elements in both subsets is equal.

For example:

- **Input**: `nums = [1, 5, 11, 5]`
- **Output**: `True`
- **Explanation**: The array can be partitioned as [1, 5, 5] and [11], both of which have a sum of 11.

Understanding the problem: This problem is a variation of the *0/1 Knapsack problem*. The task is to determine if the given array can be split into two subsets whose sums are equal. If the total sum of the array is odd, the answer is immediately False, as we cannot split an odd number into two equal subsets. Otherwise, we need to check if there exists a subset with a sum equal to *total_sum // 2*.

This subset sum problem can be solved using DP by treating it as a decision-making process where, for each element, we decide whether to include it in the subset or not.

Approach: DP

To solve this problem, we aim to check if there is a subset of the given array that sums to *total_sum // 2*. The process involves:

1. **Initial check:** If the sum of the array is odd, return False because an odd number cannot be split evenly into two subsets.
2. **Subset sum problem:** The problem reduces to finding if there exists a subset of the array that sums to *total_sum // 2*. We use a DP approach similar to the knapsack problem to check this.
3. **DP array:** We create a Boolean `dp` array where `dp[i]` is True if a subset sum of i can be achieved, and False otherwise. Initialize `dp[0] = True` because a sum of 0 can always be achieved by selecting no elements.

4. **Filling the DP array:** For each element in the array, update the **dp** array by checking if including the current element enables us to achieve a new subset sum.

The steps to solve are as follows:

1. **Initialize the DP array:**
   a. Initialize a Boolean **dp** array of size *target + 1*, where *target = total_sum // 2*.
   b. Set **dp[0] = True** because a sum of 0 can always be achieved by selecting no elements.
2. **Iterate through the array:** For each element in **nums**, update the **dp** array from target down to the current number, ensuring that we check for each subset sum only once.
3. **Return the result:** If **dp[target]** is True, it means we can achieve a subset sum equal to target, and therefore the array can be partitioned into two equal subsets. Otherwise, return False.

Code implementation: DP solution:

```
def can_partition(nums):
    total_sum = sum(nums)

    # If the total sum is odd, we can't split it equally
    if total_sum % 2 != 0:
        return False
    target = total_sum // 2
    dp = [False] * (target + 1)
    dp[0] = True # Base case: A sum of 0 can always be achieved

    # Update dp array for each number in nums
    for num in nums:
        for i in range(target, num - 1, -1):
            dp[i] = dp[i] or dp[i - num]

    return dp[target]
```

Example walkthrough: Let us walk through the example **nums = [1, 5, 11, 5]**:

1. **Calculate total sum:**

   `total_sum = 1 + 5 + 11 + 5 = 22.`

   Since 22 is even, we proceed. The target is *target = total_sum // 2 = 11*.
2. **Initialize the DP array:**

   `dp = [True, False, False, False, False, False, False, False, False, False, False, False].`
3. **Iterate through the array:**
   a. **For num = 1:** Update **dp[1] = True** since we can form a subset sum of 1.

b. **For num = 5:** Update **`dp[6] = True, dp[5] = True`.**

c. **For num = 11:** Update **`dp[11] = True`** since we can form a subset sum of 11.

d. **For num = 5 again**: Further updates will not change the result, as we already achieved a subset sum of 11.

4. **Check the result:** Since **`dp[11] = True`**, the array can be partitioned into two subsets with equal sums. The result is True.

The time and space complexity is as follows:

- **Time complexity:** *O(n * target)*, where n is the number of elements in **`nums`** and **`target`** is *total_sum // 2*. We iterate through each element and update the **`dp`** array.
- **Space complexity:** *O(target)*, since we only need a 1D array of size *target + 1*.

Why this solution works: The DP approach works because it efficiently checks all possible subset sums up to *target = total_sum // 2*. By iterating over the array in reverse and updating the **`dp`** array, we ensure that each number is considered only once, and we avoid overcounting any subset sums.

Dig deeper

The edge cases are as follows:

- **Empty array:** If **`nums`** is empty, the result is False, as there is no way to form two non-empty subsets.
- **All elements are the same:** If all elements in **`nums`** are the same and the total sum is even, the result will be True because we can always split the array into two equal subsets.
- **Odd total sum:** If the total sum of the array is odd, the result is immediately False since an odd number cannot be split into two equal integers.

How to approach this problem in an interview:

- **Explain the problem clearly:** Mention that the task is to check if the array can be partitioned into two subsets with equal sums.
- **DP approach:** Explain how you reduce the problem to a subset sum problem and use DP to solve it. Be sure to mention the space and time complexities of the solution.
- **Edge cases:** Be prepared to discuss edge cases, such as when the array is empty or the total sum is odd.

Some real-world applications are as follows:

- **Resource allocation:** The partition problem models scenarios where resources need to be split evenly between two tasks or groups.

- **Load balancing:** This problem can be used to model load balancing problems, where tasks need to be divided evenly among servers to ensure optimal performance.
- **Team formation:** When forming teams with equal skill levels or weights, this problem helps decide how to split members into two equal groups.

Practice exercises

- **Subset sum problem:** Extend this problem by finding the exact subset that adds up to *total_sum // 2*.
- **Three-partition problem:** Modify the problem to check if the array can be split into three equal subsets.

Problem 68: Edit distance (Levenshtein distance)

Problem statement: Given two strings `word1` and `word2`, calculate the minimum number of operations required to convert `word1` into `word2`. The allowed operations are:

1. Insert a character
2. Delete a character
3. Replace a character

For example:

- **Input**: `word1 = "horse", word2 = "ros"`
- **Output**: `3`
- **Explanation**:
  - Replace 'h' with 'r'
  - Remove 'o'
  - Remove 'e'

Understanding the problem: The *Edit Distance*, also known as the *Levenshtein Distance*, measures how dissimilar two strings are by counting the minimum number of operations required to transform one string into another. The three operations allowed are insertions, deletions, and replacements. Each operation has a cost of 1, and our task is to find the minimum total cost.

This problem can be solved using DP to efficiently compute the minimum number of operations.

Approach: DP

We can use a 2D DP table to store the edit distance between all prefixes of **word1** and **word2**. The idea is to compute the edit distance for smaller problems (substrings) and use those results to build up the solution for the larger problem.

The steps are as follows:

1. **Define the DP table:** Let **dp[i][j]** be the minimum number of operations required to convert the first **i** characters of **word1** into the first **j** characters of **word2**.

2. **Base case:**

   a. If **i == 0**, it means **word1** is empty, so the only way to convert it into **word2** is to insert all **j** characters of **word2**. Hence, **dp[0][j] = j**.

   b. If **j == 0**, it means **word2** is empty, so the only way to convert **word1** into **word2** is to delete all **i** characters of **word1**. Hence, **dp[i][0] = i**.

3. **Recurrence relation:**

   a. If the characters **word1[i-1]** and **word2[j-1]** are the same, then no operation is needed, so **dp[i][j] = dp[i-1][j-1]**.

   b. If the characters are different, we have three options:

      i. Insert a character into **word1** to match **word2: dp[i][j-1] + 1**

      ii. Delete a character from **word1: dp[i-1][j] + 1**

      iii. Replace a character in **word1** with the character in **word2**: **dp[i-1][j-1] + 1**

   c. Take the minimum of these three values: **dp[i][j] = min(dp[i][j-1] + 1, dp[i-1][j] + 1, dp[i-1][j-1] + 1**).

4. **Final result:** After filling in the DP table, the result will be in **dp[m][n]**, where **m** is the length of **word1** and **n** is the length of **word2**.

Code implementation: DP solution:

```
def min_distance(word1, word2):
    m, n = len(word1), len(word2)

    # Create a DP table with (m+1) x (n+1) size
    dp = [[0] * (n + 1) for _ in range(m + 1)]

    # Initialize base cases
    for i in range(m + 1):
        dp[i][0] = i  # Deleting all characters in word1
    for j in range(n + 1):
        dp[0][j] = j  # Inserting all characters in word2

    # Fill the DP table
```

```
    for i in range(1, m + 1):
        for j in range(1, n + 1):
            if word1[i - 1] == word2[j - 1]:
                dp[i][j] = dp[i - 1][j - 1]  # No change needed if characters
match
            else:
                dp[i][j] = min(
                    dp[i - 1][j] + 1,    # Delete
                    dp[i][j - 1] + 1,    # Insert
                    dp[i - 1][j - 1] + 1 # Replace
                )
    return dp[m][n]
```

Example walkthrough: Let us walk through the example with **`word1 = "horse"`** and **`word2 = "ros"`**:

1. **Initial setup**: Initialize the **`dp`** table:
   ```
   dp = [
     [0, 1, 2, 3],
     [1, 0, 0, 0],
     [2, 0, 0, 0],
     [3, 0, 0, 0],
     [4, 0, 0, 0],
     [5, 0, 0, 0]
   ]
   ```
2. **Fill the table:**
   a. Compare h with r, o with r, and so on, updating the table based on the recurrence relation.
   b. After processing all characters:
   ```
   dp = [
     [0, 1, 2, 3],
     [1, 1, 2, 3],
     [2, 2, 2, 2],
     [3, 3, 3, 2],
     [4, 4, 4, 3],
     [5, 5, 4, 3]
   ]
   ```
3. **Result:** The minimum number of operations to convert "horse" to "ros" is **`dp[5][3] = 3`**. The three operations are:
   a. Replace 'h' with 'r'.

b. Remove 'r' at index 2.

c. Remove 'e'.

The time and space complexity is explained as follows:

- **Time complexity:** *O(m * n)*, where m and n are the lengths of **word1** and **word2**. We fill a DP table of size *(m+1) x (n+1)*.
- **Space complexity:** *O(m * n)* for the DP table.

Dig deeper

Why DP works: The DP solution works by building up solutions to smaller subproblems. For each prefix of **word1** and **word2**, we compute the minimum number of operations required to convert one prefix into the other. This approach ensures that we avoid recomputing subproblems and efficiently solve the problem by storing intermediate results.

The edge cases are as follows:

- **One string is empty:** If one of the strings is empty, the result is the length of the other string because we must insert or delete all characters.
- **Identical strings:** If **word1** and **word2** are the same, the result is 0 because no operations are needed.
- **Single character difference:** If the strings differ by just one character, the result is 1 (either an insert, delete, or replace operation).

How to approach this problem in an interview:

- **Explain the problem:** Start by clearly stating that the goal is to calculate the minimum number of operations (insert, delete, or replace) to convert one string into another.
- **DP approach:** Introduce the DP solution and explain how the **dp** table is used to store intermediate results. Walk through the recurrence relation and the base cases.
- **Edge cases:** Discuss edge cases such as one string being empty or both strings being identical.

Some real-world applications are as follows:

- **Spell checkers:** Edit distance algorithms are used in spell checkers to suggest the correct spelling of a word by calculating the edit distance between the misspelled word and dictionary words.
- **DNA sequence comparison:** In bioinformatics, edit distance is used to compare DNA sequences, where the operations (insert, delete, replace) represent mutations in the genetic code.
- **Version control systems:** Edit distance algorithms help in determining the differences between file versions in version control systems like Git.

Practice exercises

- **Multiple operations:** Modify the problem to include other operations, such as swapping two adjacent characters, and adjust the DP solution accordingly.
- **Weighted edit distance:** What if each operation had a different cost? For example, deleting a character might cost more than inserting one. Modify the solution to account for varying operation costs.

Problem 69: Word break problem

Problem statement: Given a string s and a dictionary of words **`wordDict`**, determine if s can be segmented into a space-separated sequence of one or more dictionary words.

For example:

- **Input**: `s = "leetcode", wordDict = ["leet", "code"]`
- **Output**: `True`
- **Explanation**: The string can be segmented as "leet code".

Understanding the problem: The *Word Break problem* asks us to determine if a given string can be segmented into valid words from a dictionary. Essentially, the task is to decide if the entire string can be constructed using a combination of words from the provided word dictionary.

The problem can be visualized as a decision-making process where we try to break the string into valid words at different points, checking if the remaining portion of the string can also be broken down in the same way.

Approach: DP

This problem can be efficiently solved using DP. The idea is to build a Boolean array **`dp[]`** where each **`dp[i]`** represents whether the substring **`s[0:i]`** can be segmented into words from the dictionary.

The steps to solve are as follows:

1. **Initialize the DP table:**
    a. Create a Boolean **`dp[]`** array of size *len(s) + 1*, where **`dp[i]`** is True if the substring **`s[0:i]`** can be segmented, and False otherwise.
    b. Set **`dp[0] = True`** as the base case because an empty string can always be segmented.
2. **Iterate over substrings:** For each position **`i`** in the string, check all possible substrings **`s[j:i]`** where **`j < i`**. If **`dp[j]`** is True and **`s[j:i]`** is a word in the dictionary, set **`dp[i] = True`**.

3. **Final result:** After processing all characters of s, the result will be **dp[len(s)]**, which indicates whether the entire string can be segmented.

Code implementation: DP solution:

```
def word_break(s, wordDict):
    word_set = set(wordDict)  # Convert wordDict to a set for faster lookups
    dp = [False] * (len(s) + 1)
    dp[0] = True  # Base case: Empty string can always be segmented

    # Fill the dp array
    for i in range(1, len(s) + 1):
        for j in range(i):
            if dp[j] and s[j:i] in word_set:
                dp[i] = True
                break  # No need to check further if dp[i] is True

    return dp[len(s)]
```

Example walkthrough: Let us walk through the example **s = "leetcode", wordDict = ["leet", "code"]**:

1. **Initial setup:** Convert the word dictionary to a set for faster lookups: **word_set = {"leet", "code"}**. Initialize the **dp** array:

   `dp = [True, False, False, False, False, False, False, False, False]`

2. **Fill the DP array:**

   a. **For i = 4:** We check the substring s[0:4] = "leet", which is in word_set. So, **dp[4] = True**.

   b. **For i = 8:** We check the substring s[4:8] = "code", which is in word_set. Since **dp[4] = True**, we set **dp[8] = True**.

3. **Final DP array:** After processing all characters of s, the **dp** array looks like this:

   `dp = [True, False, False, False, True, False, False, False, True]`

4. **Result:** Since **dp[8] = True**, the string can be segmented as "leet code", and the result is True.

The time and space complexity are explained as follows:

- **Time complexity:** *O(n^2)* where n is the length of the string **s**. For each index **i**, we check all previous substrings, resulting in a quadratic time complexity. However, the lookup in **wordDict** is *O(1)* due to the use of a set.

- **Space complexity:** *O(n)*, where n is the length of the string **s**. We use an array of size n + 1 to store the DP results.

Dig deeper

Why this solution works: The DP approach works by breaking the problem down into smaller subproblems. By building up solutions for all substrings of s, we can efficiently check if the entire string can be segmented. Using a Boolean `dp[]` array ensures that we only compute each subproblem once, making the solution both time and space-efficient.

The edge cases are as follows:

- **Empty string:** If **s** is an empty string, the result is True, as an empty string can always be segmented.
- **No valid segmentation:** If none of the words in `wordDict` match any part of s, the result will be False.
- **Dictionary with overlapping words:** If `wordDict` contains overlapping words (e.g., ["a", "abc"]), the algorithm still works as it checks all possible substrings.

How to approach this problem in an interview:

- **Explain the problem clearly:** Start by explaining that the goal is to check if the string can be broken down into valid words from the dictionary.
- **DP approach:** Discuss how the DP table is used to store the results of subproblems (whether substrings can be segmented) and walk through the recurrence relation.
- **Edge cases:** Be prepared to discuss how the algorithm handles cases like empty strings and dictionaries with overlapping words.

Some real-world applications are as follows:

- **Text segmentation:** This problem models real-world applications where text needs to be segmented, such as splitting a continuous stream of text (e.g., Chinese or Japanese) into individual words.
- **Natural language processing:** Word break algorithms are used in NLP to break down large chunks of text into smaller, meaningful units.
- **Search engines:** Search engines often need to break down queries into smaller components, and this algorithm helps in determining the valid breakdown of search terms.

Practice exercises

- **Word break II:** Extend the problem by finding all possible segmentations of s into valid words from `wordDict`.
- **Longest word break:** Modify the problem to find the longest valid segmentation of the string using words from the dictionary.

Problem 70: Maximal square in a matrix

Problem statement: Given a 2D binary matrix filled with 0s and 1s, find the largest square containing only 1s and return its area.

For example:

- **Input**:

  ```
  matrix = [
    ["1", "0", "1", "0", "0"],
    ["1", "0", "1", "1", "1"],
    ["1", "1", "1", "1", "1"],
    ["1", "0", "0", "1", "0"]
  ]
  ```

- **Output**: **4**
- **Explanation**: The largest square is a 2x2 square containing all 1s, so the area is 2 x 2 = 4.

Understanding the problem: The *Maximal Square problem* asks us to find the largest square submatrix in a binary matrix (where each entry is either 0 or 1) that contains only 1s. We are not only required to find this square, but also return its area.

The problem can be visualized as finding the largest possible block of 1s in the matrix that forms a perfect square.

Approach: DP

We can solve this problem using DP. The idea is to maintain a 2D DP table where each cell represents the size of the largest square that can be formed with that cell as the bottom-right corner.

The steps to solve are as follows:

1. **Define the DP table:** Let **dp[i][j]** be the size of the largest square that can be formed with the cell (i, j) as its bottom-right corner.
2. **Transition relation:** If **matrix[i][j]** is 1, the value of **dp[i][j]** depends on the values of the cells to the left, top, and top-left of **dp[i][j]**:

   ```
   dp[i][j] = min(dp[i-1][j], dp[i][j-1], dp[i-1][j-1]) + 1
   ```
3. **Base case:** Initialize the first row and first column of the DP table directly from the matrix. If a cell contains 1, it can only form a square of size 1.
4. **Final result:** The result will be the maximum value in the **dp** table, as it represents the largest square that can be formed in the matrix. The area of the square is simply the square of this value.

Code implementation: DP solution:

```
def maximal_square(matrix):
    if not matrix:
        return 0

    rows = len(matrix)
    cols = len(matrix[0])

    # Create a DP table with (rows + 1) x (cols + 1) size
    dp = [[0] * (cols + 1) for _ in range(rows + 1)]

    max_square_length = 0

    # Fill the DP table
    for i in range(1, rows + 1):
        for j in range(1, cols + 1):
            if matrix[i - 1][j - 1] == "1":
                dp[i][j] = min(dp[i - 1][j], dp[i][j - 1], dp[i - 1][j - 1]) +
1
                max_square_length = max(max_square_length, dp[i][j])

    # The area of the largest square
    return max_square_length ** 2
```

Example walkthrough: Let us walk through the example matrix:

```
matrix = [
  ["1", "0", "1", "0", "0"],
  ["1", "0", "1", "1", "1"],
  ["1", "1", "1", "1", "1"],
  ["1", "0", "0", "1", "0"]
]
```

The steps are as follows:

1. **Initial setup:** Create a DP table initialized to all zeroes:

   ```
   dp = [
     [0, 0, 0, 0, 0, 0],
     [0, 0, 0, 0, 0, 0],
     [0, 0, 0, 0, 0, 0],
     [0, 0, 0, 0, 0, 0],
     [0, 0, 0, 0, 0, 0]
   ]
   ```

2. **Filling the DP table:**

   a. For **`i = 1, j = 1`**: Since **`matrix[0][0]`** is 1, set **`dp[1][1] = 1`**.

   Similarly, update other cells accordingly, checking for the minimum value of the surrounding cells.

b. After filling in the table, the final DP table looks like this:

```
dp = [
  [0, 0, 0, 0, 0, 0],
  [0, 1, 0, 1, 0, 0],
  [0, 1, 0, 1, 1, 1],
  [0, 1, 1, 1, 2, 2],
  [0, 1, 0, 0, 1, 0]
]
```

3. **Result:** The largest value in the DP table is 2, meaning the largest square has a side length of 2. Therefore, the area is $2 \times 2 = 4$.

The time and space complexity are explained as follows:

- **Time complexity:** $O(m * n)$, where m is the number of rows and n is the number of columns in the matrix. We iterate through all cells of the matrix and update the DP table.

- **Space complexity:** $O(m * n)$ for the DP table. This can be optimized to $O(n)$ by using a single row of the DP table at a time, as each row depends only on the previous row.

Dig deeper

Why this solution works: The DP solution works by leveraging previously computed values to find the size of the largest square at each cell. By examining the minimum of the top, left, and top-left cells, we ensure that we only expand the square when all three surrounding cells can also form part of a square.

The edge cases are as follows:

- **Empty matrix:** If the matrix is empty, the result is 0 because there is no square to be found.

- **Matrix with no 1s:** If the matrix contains only 0s, the result is 0 because no square of 1s can be formed.

- **Single cell matrix:** If the matrix is a single cell containing 1, the result is 1.

How to approach this problem in an interview:

- **Explain the problem clearly:** Start by explaining that the goal is to find the largest square of 1s in the binary matrix and return its area.

- **DP approach:** Discuss the DP approach and how the **dp** table stores the size of the largest square at each cell. Walk through the recurrence relation.

- **Edge cases:** Be prepared to handle cases like empty matrices and matrices with no 1s.

Some real-world applications are as follows:

- **Image processing:** The maximal square problem can be used in image processing to find the largest area of connected pixels in binary images.
- **Urban planning:** This problem can also model scenarios in urban planning where we need to find the largest square plot of land that satisfies certain conditions.

Practice exercises

- **Maximal rectangle:** Extend the problem to find the largest rectangle containing only 1s in a binary matrix.
- **Connected components:** Modify the problem to find the number of connected components of 1s in the matrix.

Problem 71: Palindromic substrings count

Problem statement: Given a string **s**, your task is to count how many substrings of **s** are palindromes.

A **palindrome** is a string that reads the same forward and backward. For example:

- **Input**: **"abc"**
  - **Output**: **3** (The palindromic substrings are: "a", "b", "c")
- **Input**: **"aaa"**
  - **Output**: **6** (The palindromic substrings are: "a", "a", "a", "aa", "aa", "aaa")

Understanding the problem: In this problem, we need to identify all the palindromic substrings within a given string **s**. Palindromic substrings are those that are the same when read both forward and backward. For example, in the string "madam", both "m", "a", and "madam" are palindromic substrings.

The task is to count all such substrings in the string.

Approach 1: Expanding around the center

One of the most efficient ways to solve this problem is by expanding around each possible "center" of the string. Every palindrome has a center, and we can expand around this center to find all palindromes. A palindrome can either have:

- A single center (for odd-length palindromes), or
- Two centers (for even-length palindromes).

The steps to solve are as follows:

1. **Treat each character as a center:** Every single character in the string can be the center of an odd-length palindrome.

2. **Check for even-length palindromes:** We also need to check for palindromes that have two characters as their center (even-length palindromes).
3. **Expand around the center:** For each center, expand outward as long as the characters on both sides are equal. This ensures we count all palindromic substrings.

Code implementation: Expanding around the center:

```
def count_palindromic_substrings(s):
    def expand_around_center(left, right):
        count = 0
        while left >= 0 and right < len(s) and s[left] == s[right]:
            count += 1
            left -= 1
            right += 1
        return count

    total_palindromes = 0

    # Expand around each character (odd-length palindromes)
    for i in range(len(s)):
        total_palindromes += expand_around_center(i, i)  # Odd length

    # Expand around each pair of characters (even-length palindromes)
    for i in range(len(s) - 1):
        total_palindromes += expand_around_center(i, i + 1)  # Even length

    return total_palindromes
```

Example walkthrough: Let us walk through an example where **`s = "aaa"`**:

1. **Expand around each center:**
    a. **For i = 0:** Expand around the center **`s[0] = "a"`**. The substring "a" is a palindrome.
    b. **For i = 1:** Expand around the center **`s[1] = "a"`**. The substrings "a" and "aa" are palindromes.
    c. **For i = 2:** Expand around the center **`s[2] = "a"`**. The substrings "a" and "aaa" are palindromes.
2. **Result:** The total number of palindromic substrings is 6.

The time and space complexity are explained as follows:

- **Time complexity:** $O(n^2)$, where n is the length of the string. For each character, we expand around the center, which takes $O(n)$ time for each center.
- **Space complexity:** $O(1)$, since we are only using a constant amount of extra space.

Dig deeper

Why this solution works: The *expand around center* technique works because it allows us to efficiently check all possible palindromes by using each character (and pairs of characters) as the center of the palindrome. This method avoids the need to check all possible substrings individually, which would be computationally expensive.

The edge cases are as follows:

- **Empty string:** If **s** is an empty string, the result is 0 because there are no palindromic substrings.
- **Single character:** If s contains only one character, the result is 1 because a single character is always a palindrome.
- **All characters are the same:** If all characters in the string are the same (e.g., s = "aaaa"), the result will be large because every substring will be a palindrome.

How to approach this problem in an interview:

- **Explain the problem clearly:** Start by explaining that the task is to count all substrings of s that are palindromes.
- **Expanding around center:** Discuss how the "expand around center" technique works by treating each character (and pairs of characters) as potential centers of palindromes.
- **Edge cases:** Be prepared to discuss edge cases like empty strings, single characters, and strings with all the same characters.

Some real-world applications are as follows:

- **DNA sequence analysis:** In bioinformatics, palindromic sequences are important in DNA analysis. This algorithm can be used to find and count palindromic regions in DNA sequences.
- **Text analysis:** Palindromic substrings are used in cryptography and text analysis to find symmetric patterns in strings.
- **Pattern recognition:** This problem can be applied to pattern recognition tasks where symmetric patterns need to be identified in data.

Practice exercises

- **Longest palindromic substring:** Extend this problem to find the longest palindromic substring in **s**.
- **Palindrome partitioning:** Modify the problem to partition the string into the minimum number of palindromic substrings.

Problem 72: Unique paths in a grid

Problem statement: You are given a grid with m rows and n columns. You are currently at the top-left corner of the grid (position (0, 0)), and your goal is to reach the bottom-right corner of the grid (position (m-1, n-1)). You can only move either down or right at any point in time.

Write a function to calculate how many unique paths there are from the top-left to the bottom-right.

For example:

- **Input:** `m = 3, n = 7`
- **Output:** `28`

Understanding the problem: In this problem, you need to determine how many ways you can move from the top-left corner to the bottom-right corner of a grid, but there is a catch: you can only move *right* or *down*. This restriction simplifies the problem and allows us to focus on the number of possible routes within the grid.

Imagine the grid as a maze, but instead of walls, you are limited by movement direction. Each step takes you either one cell to the right or one cell down, and the goal is to count all the unique paths that reach the bottom-right corner.

Approach 1: DP

This problem can be efficiently solved using **DP** by breaking it down into smaller subproblems.

The steps to solve are as follows:

1. **Define the DP table:** Let **`dp[i][j]`** represent the number of unique paths to reach cell (i, j) from the top-left corner (0, 0).
2. **Base case:**
   a. There is only *one way* to reach any cell in the first row, as you can only move right.
   b. Similarly, there is only one way to reach any cell in the first column, as you can only move down.
3. **Transition relation:** The number of paths to reach a cell (i, j) is the sum of the number of paths to reach the cell directly above it (**`dp[i-1][j]`**) and the cell directly to the left (**`dp[i][j-1]`**):
   ```
   dp[i][j] = dp[i-1][j] + dp[i][j-1]
   ```
4. **Final result:** The value at **`dp[m-1][n-1]`** will give us the total number of unique paths to reach the bottom-right corner of the grid.

Code implementation: DP solution:

```
def unique_paths(m, n):
    # Create a DP table with m rows and n columns
    dp = [[1] * n for _ in range(m)]

    # Fill the DP table
    for i in range(1, m):
        for j in range(1, n):
            dp[i][j] = dp[i - 1][j] + dp[i][j - 1]

    # The result is in the bottom-right corner of the table
    return dp[m - 1][n - 1]
```

Example walkthrough: Let us walk through an example with a 3 x 3 grid (m = 3, n = 3):

1. **Initial setup:** Initialize the DP table with 1s for the first row and the first column, as there is only one way to reach those cells:

   ```
   dp = [
       [1, 1, 1],
       [1, 0, 0],
       [1, 0, 0]
   ]
   ```

2. **Filling the DP table:**

   a. **For i = 1, j = 1:** The number of ways to reach this cell is **`dp[0][1] + dp[1][0] = 1 + 1 = 2`**.

   b. **For i = 1, j = 2:** The number of ways to reach this cell is **`dp[0][2] + dp[1][1] = 1 + 2 = 3`**.

   Continue this process for all cells:

   ```
   dp = [
       [1, 1, 1],
       [1, 2, 3],
       [1, 3, 6]
   ]
   ```

3. **Result**: The number of unique paths to reach the bottom-right corner is **`dp[2][2] = 6`**.

The time and space complexity are explained as follows:

- **Time complexity:** *O(m * n)*, where *m* is the number of rows and *n* is the number of columns in the grid. We iterate through every cell of the DP table.
- **Space complexity:** *O(m * n)* for the DP table. This can be optimized to *O(n)* by using a single row of the DP table at a time, as each row depends only on the previous row.

Dig deeper

Why this solution works: This DP approach works because we systematically build the solution for larger grids based on smaller subproblems. By considering how we can reach each cell based on the cells directly above and to the left, we can efficiently calculate the total number of paths.

The edge cases are as follows:

- **Single row or single column:** If there is only one row or one column, there is only one path because you can only move in one direction.
- **Square grids:** The approach works for both rectangular and square grids. The dimensions of the grid do not affect the generality of the solution.
- **Minimal grid (1x1):** If $m = 1$ and $n = 1$, there is only one path since you are already at the destination.

How to approach this problem in an interview:

- **Explain the problem clearly:** Start by explaining the goal: to find how many unique paths exist from the top-left to the bottom-right corner, moving only down or right.
- **DP approach:** Discuss the DP solution and how each cell's value is calculated based on the sum of the top and left cells.
- **Edge cases:** Be prepared to handle single-row, single-column, and minimal grid cases.

Some real-world applications are as follows:

- **Robot navigation:** This problem models real-world scenarios like robot navigation in a grid, where the robot can only move in certain directions.
- **Pathfinding in games:** Pathfinding algorithms in video games or simulations often involve counting possible routes, similar to this problem.
- **Logistics and planning:** In logistics, counting unique paths can help optimize delivery routes or plan movement in grid-based systems.

Practice exercises

- **Obstacle grid:** Modify the problem to handle obstacles in the grid (represented by 0s). Find how many unique paths exist if some cells are blocked.
- **Minimum path sum:** Extend the problem to find the path that minimizes the sum of the values in the grid as you move from the top-left to the bottom-right.

Problem 73: Jump game problem

Problem statement: You are given an array of non-negative integers **`nums`**, where each element represents the maximum jump length you can make from that position. Your task is to determine if you can reach the last index of the array starting from the first index.

For example:

- **Input**: **`nums = [2, 3, 1, 1, 4]`**
  - **Output**: **`True`** (We can jump from 0 → 1 → 4)
- **Input**: **`nums = [3, 2, 1, 0, 4]`**
  - **Output**: **`False`** (We cannot jump past the 0 at index 3)

Understanding the problem: Imagine you are playing a game where each position in the array is like a stepping stone, and the number on each stone represents how far you can jump from that position. You want to see if you can jump from the first stone to the last stone. If at any point, you land on a stone that does not allow you to jump far enough, the game is over.

Approach 1: Greedy algorithm

This problem can be solved using a *greedy algorithm*. The key idea is to keep track of the *farthest position* you can reach at any point in time. As you move through the array, you check if you can continue moving forward based on the current element's jump distance.

The steps to solve are as follows:

1. **Initialize the farthest reach:** Start by keeping track of the farthest position you can reach, initialized to 0 (since you are starting at the first position).
2. **Iterate through the array:** For each index **`i`**, check if you can reach it (i.e., **`i <= farthest`**). If you can, update your farthest reach to **`max(farthest, i + nums[i])`**.
3. **Check if you reach the last index:** If at any point your farthest reach is greater than or equal to the last index, return True. If the loop finishes and you have not reached the last index, return False.

Code implementation: Greedy approach:

```
def can_jump(nums):
    farthest = 0
    for i in range(len(nums)):
        if i > farthest:
            return False
        farthest = max(farthest, i + nums[i])
    return farthest >= len(nums) - 1
```

Example walkthrough: Let us walk through an example with `nums = [2, 3, 1, 1, 4]`:

1. **Initial setup:** `farthest = 0` (You start at index 0).
2. **Iterate through the array:**
   a. **For i = 0:** The farthest we can jump is `max(0, 0 + 2) = 2`. Now, `farthest = 2`.
   b. **For i = 1:** The farthest we can jump is `max(2, 1 + 3) = 4`. Now, `farthest = 4`. We have reached the last index, so we return True.

The time and space complexity are explained as follows:

- **Time complexity:** *O(n)*, where n is the number of elements in the array. We make a single pass through the array.
- **Space complexity:** *O(1)*, since we are only using a constant amount of extra space to track the farthest position.

Dig deeper

Why this solution works: This greedy algorithm works because we always prioritize making the farthest jump possible at every step. By continuously updating the farthest position we can reach, we can determine whether it is possible to jump all the way to the last index.

The edge cases are as follows:

- **Single-element array:** If `nums` has only one element, the result is always True because you are already at the last index.
- **Array with zeros:** If `nums` contains zeros but the zeros are placed in such a way that they do not block the path (e.g., `nums = [2, 0, 0, 1, 4]`), you can still reach the last index.
- **All zeros:** If all elements are zeros except the first, you cannot reach the last index unless the array size is 1.

How to approach this problem in an interview:

- **Explain the problem clearly:** Start by explaining that you are checking if it is possible to jump from the first index to the last, based on the values in the array.
- **Greedy approach:** Discuss how the greedy approach helps you calculate the farthest position you can reach and how that helps in deciding whether you can reach the last index.
- **Edge cases:** Be prepared to discuss edge cases like a single-element array, arrays with zeros, and cases where jumping is impossible.

Some real-world applications are as follows:

- **Video games:** This problem can be applied to pathfinding in video games, where you need to determine if a player can reach the end of a level, given certain movement restrictions.
- **Networking:** The problem is similar to determining if a signal can reach the end of a series of network nodes, where each node has a limited range.

Practice exercises

- **Minimum jumps to reach the end:** Modify the problem to calculate the minimum number of jumps required to reach the last index.
- **Jump game II:** Consider a variation where you must find the minimum number of jumps required to reach the end of the array.

Problem 74: Decode ways (Ways to decode a string)

Problem statement: You are given a string s containing only digits (0-9), where each digit or pair of digits represents a letter:

`1 -> A, 2 -> B, ..., 26 -> Z`

Your task is to determine how many ways you can decode the string **`s`**.

For example:

- **Input: "12"**
  - **Output: 2** (It can be decoded as "AB" (1 -> A, 2 -> B) or "L" (12 -> L))
- **Input: "226"**
  - **Output: 3** (It can be decoded as "BZ", "VF", or "BBF")

Understanding the problem: The problem is asking us to find how many different ways we can decode a string of digits, where each digit or pair of digits represents a letter from the alphabet. The challenge comes from figuring out the valid ways to group digits together. For example, "226" can be split as "2 2 6", "22 6", or "2 26".

The decoding follows specific rules:

- A single digit (1-9) maps directly to a letter (1 -> A, 2 -> B, etc.).
- A pair of digits (10-26) maps to letters as well (10 -> J, 26 -> Z).
- Any leading zero or an isolated 0 is not valid (e.g., 0 cannot map to any letter by itself).

Approach 1: DP

To solve this problem efficiently, we can use a DP approach. The key observation here is that the number of ways to decode a string up to index **i** depends on the previous one or two digits. This allows us to break the problem down into smaller subproblems and build the solution incrementally.

The steps to solve are as follows:

1. **Define the DP table:** Let **dp[i]** represent the number of ways to decode the string up to **index i-1** in **s**. Our goal is to compute **dp[len(s)]**, which will give the total number of ways to decode the string.
2. **Base case:** There is only **one way** to decode an empty string, so **dp[0] = 1**.
3. **Transition relation:** To fill **dp[i]**, we consider two possibilities:
    a. **Single digit**: If the digit at **index i-1** is between 1 and 9, then it can be decoded as a single character. In this case, **dp[i] += dp[i-1]**.
    b. **Two digits**: If the two digits at indices **i-2** and **i-1** form a number between 10 and 26, then it can be decoded as a pair. In this case, **dp[i] += dp[i-2]**.

Code implementation: DP solution:

```
def num_decodings(s):
    if not s or s[0] == '0':
        return 0

    n = len(s)
    dp = [0] * (n + 1)
    dp[0] = 1  # Base case: One way to decode an empty string
    dp[1] = 1  # One way to decode a string if the first digit is valid

    for i in range(2, n + 1):
        # Single digit decoding (s[i-1])
        if s[i-1] != '0':
            dp[i] += dp[i-1]

        # Two-digit decoding (s[i-2:i])
        if 10 <= int(s[i-2:i]) <= 26:
            dp[i] += dp[i-2]

    return dp[n]
```

Example walkthrough: Let us walk through an example with s = "226":

1. **Initial setup:** Initialize the DP table:

    ```
    dp = [1, 1, 0, 0]
    ```

2. **Filling the DP table:**

   a. For `i = 2`: We check the single digit (`s[1] = 2`, valid) and the two digits (`s[0:2] = 22`, `valid`):

      i. `dp[2] += dp[1]` (single digit) → `dp[2] = 1`

      ii. `dp[2] += dp[0]` (two digits) → `dp[2] = 2`

   b. For `i = 3`: We check the single digit (`s[2] = 6`, valid) and the two digits (`s[1:3] = 26`, valid):

      i. `dp[3] += dp[2]` (single digit) → `dp[3] = 2`

      ii. `dp[3] += dp[1]` (two digits) → `dp[3] = 3`

   Final **dp** table:

   ```
   dp = [1, 1, 2, 3]
   ```

3. **Result:** The number of ways to decode "226" is dp[3] = 3.

The time and space complexity are explained as follows:

- **Time complexity:** *O(n)*, where *n* is the length of the string **s**. We iterate over each character of the string once.
- **Space complexity:** *O(n)* for the DP table. This can be optimized to *O(1)* by using just two variables to track the previous states.

Dig deeper

Why this solution works: This DP approach works because it breaks the problem down into smaller subproblems that depend on either the previous one or two digits. By systematically building up the number of ways to decode the string, we can solve the problem efficiently.

The edge cases are as follows:

- **Empty string:** If s is an empty string, there is only one way to decode it (an empty string), so the result is 1.
- **Leading zeros:** If s starts with 0, the result is 0 because no valid decoding starts with 0.
- **All zeros:** If s contains isolated zeros (e.g., 1002), the result is 0 because 0 cannot be decoded alone.

How to approach this problem in an interview:

- **Explain the problem clearly:** Start by explaining that the task is to count how many different ways you can decode the string, where digits map to letters.
- **DP approach:** Discuss how the number of ways to decode the string up to a certain index depends on the previous one or two digits.

- **Edge cases:** Be prepared to handle cases like empty strings, leading zeros, and cases where decoding is impossible.

The real-world applications are as follows:

- **Message decoding:** This problem models real-world scenarios like decoding secret messages, where each number or pair of numbers represents a different letter or instruction.
- **Cryptography:** Similar to message decoding, this problem can be applied to cryptographic systems where numbers are mapped to letters or symbols.

Practice exercises

- **Decode ways II:** Modify the problem to handle cases where * can represent any digit from 1-9.
- **Longest palindromic subsequence:** Extend the problem to find the longest palindromic subsequence in a string.

Problem 75: Minimum path sum in a grid

Problem statement: You are given a 2D grid filled with non-negative numbers. Your task is to find the path from the top-left corner to the bottom-right corner of the grid that minimizes the sum of all numbers along its path. You can only move either down or right at any point in time.

For example:

- **Input:**

```
grid = [[1, 3, 1],
        [1, 5, 1],
        [4, 2, 1]]
```

- **Output**: 7 The minimum path is 1 → 3 → 1 → 1 → 1, and the sum is 7.

Understanding the problem: The problem asks us to find the path with the smallest sum from the top-left to the bottom-right of a grid. You can only move in two directions: either down or right. As you move along the grid, you accumulate the values from each cell you pass through, and you want to minimize the total sum of the numbers in those cells.

Approach: DP

To solve this problem efficiently, we can use DP. The key idea is to track the minimum path sum at each cell as we move through the grid.

The steps to solve are as follows:

1. **Define the DP table:** Let **dp[i][j]** represent the minimum sum to reach cell (i, j) from the top-left corner. The goal is to compute **dp[m-1][n-1]** (where m is the number of rows and n is the number of columns).

2. **Base case:** The minimum path sum to reach the top-left corner is simply the value of the first cell, so **dp[0][0] = grid[0][0]**.

3. **Transition relation:** To calculate **dp[i][j]**, we have two options: move from the cell above (**dp[i-1][j]**) or from the cell to the left (**dp[i][j-1]**). The minimum path sum to reach (i, j) is the minimum of these two values, plus the value of the current cell:

   dp[i][j] = grid[i][j] + min(dp[i-1][j], dp[i][j-1]).

4. **Edge cases:** If you are on the first row (i = 0), you can only move from the left, and if you are on the first column (j = 0), you can only move from above.

Code implementation: DP solution:

```
def min_path_sum(grid):
    m, n = len(grid), len(grid[0])
    # Initialize the dp table
    dp = [[0] * n for _ in range(m)]

    # Base case: starting point
    dp[0][0] = grid[0][0]

    # Fill the first row (can only move right)
    for j in range(1, n):
        dp[0][j] = dp[0][j-1] + grid[0][j]

    # Fill the first column (can only move down)
    for i in range(1, m):
        dp[i][0] = dp[i-1][0] + grid[i][0]

    # Fill the rest of the dp table
    for i in range(1, m):
        for j in range(1, n):
            dp[i][j] = grid[i][j] + min(dp[i-1][j], dp[i][j-1])

    return dp[m-1][n-1]
```

Example walkthrough: Let us walk through an example with the grid:

```
grid = [[1, 3, 1],
        [1, 5, 1],
        [4, 2, 1]]
```

The steps are as follows:

1. **Initial setup:** Initialize the DP table with zeros:

   ```
   dp = [[0, 0, 0],
         [0, 0, 0],
         [0, 0, 0]]
   ```

2. **Base case:**

   `Set dp[0][0] = grid[0][0] = 1.`

3. **Fill the first row:** Fill the first row where we can only move right:

   ```
   dp = [[1, 4, 5],
         [0, 0, 0],
         [0, 0, 0]]
   ```

4. **Fill the first column:** Fill the first column where we can only move down:

   ```
   dp = [[1, 4, 5],
         [2, 0, 0],
         [6, 0, 0]]
   ```

5. **Fill the rest of the table:** Now, fill the rest of the DP table using the minimum path sum formula:

   ```
   dp = [[1, 4, 5],
         [2, 7, 6],
         [6, 8, 7]]
   ```

6. **Result:** The minimum path sum is **`dp[2][2] = 7`**.

The time and space complexity are explained as follows:

- **Time complexity:** *O(m * n)*, where *m* is the number of rows and *n* is the number of columns in the grid. We iterate over each cell of the grid once.
- **Space complexity:** *O(m * n)* for the DP table. This can be optimized to *O(n)* by keeping only the current and previous rows in memory.

Dig deeper

Why this solution works: This DP approach works because we break down the problem into smaller subproblems (finding the minimum path sum for each cell) and build up the solution incrementally. By tracking the minimum path sum at each cell, we can determine the optimal solution to reach the bottom-right corner.

The edge cases are as follows:

- **Single cell grid:** If the grid has only one cell, the result is simply the value of that cell.
- **Empty grid:** If the grid is empty, the result should be 0.

How to approach this problem in an interview:

- **Explain the problem clearly:** Start by explaining that you are finding the minimum path sum from the top-left corner to the bottom-right corner of a grid, where you can only move down or right.
- **DP approach:** Discuss how you will calculate the minimum path sum for each cell based on the previous cell (either from above or to the left).
- **Edge cases:** Be prepared to discuss cases like a single-cell grid or an empty grid.

Some real-world applications are as follows:

- **Robotics and pathfinding:** This problem models real-world pathfinding problems in robotics, where the goal is to navigate through a grid while minimizing energy or cost.
- **Logistics and routing:** In logistics, this problem can be applied to finding the optimal path through a grid-like city, minimizing travel time or distance.

Practice exercises

- **Minimum path sum with obstacles:** Modify the problem to handle obstacles (cells that cannot be traversed).
- **Unique paths with a minimum sum:** Extend the problem to count how many unique paths lead to the minimum path sum.

Join our Discord space

Join our Discord workspace for latest updates, offers, tech happenings around the world, new releases, and sessions with the authors:

https://discord.bpbonline.com

SECTION 7
Graphs and Trees

Introduction

In this section, we look at **graphs** and **trees**, two vital data structures frequently appearing in coding interviews. Graphs represent relationships between objects, while trees are a specific graph type that organizes data hierarchically. Navigating a network of cities, finding connections in a social media graph, or organizing file systems, graphs, and trees are foundational to problem-solving.

Graphs can be complex, with interconnected nodes and edges representing relationships. They challenge you to think beyond linear structures, exploring connections and finding optimal solutions, like the shortest path in a maze or detecting cycles in a network. Trees, on the other hand, simplify hierarchical data organization. Common interview problems involving binary trees, tree traversals, and decision-making processes make them essential knowledge for any aspiring software engineer.

As you tackle the challenges in this section, you will learn to traverse, search, and manipulate graphs and trees efficiently. Each coding problem will sharpen your skills in handling these intricate data structures, preparing you for questions asked by top tech companies.

Objectives

The objective of this section is to help you develop a strong understanding of graphs and trees, two fundamental data structures widely used in both interviews and real-world applications. You will learn how to represent graphs using adjacency lists and matrices, and implement essential algorithms such as **depth-first search** (**DFS**), **breadth-first search** (**BFS**), cycle detection, and shortest path finding. For trees, you will explore binary trees, **binary search trees** (**BST**), and various traversal techniques, including in-order, pre-order, and post-order traversals. By working through practical coding problems, you will gain the skills to efficiently traverse, search, and manipulate graphs and trees, enabling you to solve complex problems with confidence. This section will prepare you for technical interviews by sharpening your ability to handle non-linear data structures and think critically about hierarchical and networked relationships between data.

Problem 76: BFS and DFS

Problem statement: Given an undirected graph represented as an adjacency list, implement both BFS and DFS starting from a given source node. Return the order of the nodes visited during the traversal for each search method.

For example:

- **Input**:
    - o An adjacency list representing the graph.
    - o A starting node.
- **Output**: A list of nodes visited in the order of traversal for both BFS and DFS.

Understanding the problem: Graphs represent a collection of nodes (or vertices) connected by edges. The goal of this problem is to explore a graph using two common traversal techniques:

- **BFS** traverses the graph level by level. Starting from the source node, it first visits all the neighbors of the source before moving on to their neighbors. This ensures that nodes closer to the source are visited first. BFS is typically implemented using a **queue**.
- **DFS**, in contrast, explores the graph as deep as possible along each branch before backtracking. DFS explores one path fully before checking the next. It is often implemented using a **stack** or recursion.

Your task is to implement both algorithms and return the order of the nodes visited for each. These traversal techniques are widely used in problems involving connectivity, pathfinding, and searching in graphs.

Step-by-step explanation

BFS explores all nodes at the present depth before moving on to nodes at the next depth level. It starts with the source node, visits all its neighbors, and then proceeds to the neighbors of those neighbors.

The steps are as follows:

1. Initialize a queue to keep track of the nodes to visit.
2. Add the starting node to the queue and mark it as visited.
3. Dequeue a node from the queue, visit it, and enqueue all its unvisited neighbors.
4. Repeat this process until the queue is empty.

Example BFS traversal: Consider the following undirected graph as an adjacency list:

```
graph = {
    'A': ['B', 'C'],
    'B': ['D', 'E'],
    'C': ['F'],
    'D': [],
    'E': [],
    'F': []
}
```

Let us perform BFS starting from node A:

1. Start with node A. Queue = [A]
2. Visit A and enqueue its neighbors B and C. Queue = [B, C]
3. Visit B and enqueue its neighbors D and E. Queue = [C, D, E]
4. Visit C and enqueue its neighbor F. Queue = [D, E, F]
5. Visit D. Queue = [E, F]
6. Visit E. Queue = [F]
7. Visit F. Queue = []

BFS result: A → B → C → D → E → F

DFS

DFS explores as deeply as possible along one branch before backtracking. It fully explores one path, then backtracks and tries other paths from the last visited node.

The steps are as follows:

1. Initialize a stack (or use recursion) and a *visited set* to keep track of visited nodes.

2. Push the starting node onto the stack and mark it as visited.
3. Pop the node from the stack, visit it, and push all its unvisited neighbors onto the stack.
4. Repeat this process until the stack is empty.

Example DFS traversal: Using the same graph:

```
graph = {
    'A': ['B', 'C'],
    'B': ['D', 'E'],
    'C': ['F'],
    'D': [],
    'E': [],
    'F': []
}
```

Let us perform DFS starting from node A:

1. Start with node A. Stack = [A]
2. Visit A, and push its neighbors B and C. Stack = [B, C]
3. Visit B, and push its neighbors D and E. Stack = [D, E, C]
4. Visit D. Stack = [E, C]
5. Backtrack to B, and visit E. Stack = [C]
6. Backtrack to A, and visit C. Stack = [F]
7. Visit F. Stack = []

DFS result: A → B → D → E → C → F

Implementation

For BFS:

```
from collections import deque

def bfs(graph, start):
    visited = set()
    queue = deque([start])
    result = []

    while queue:
        node = queue.popleft()
        if node not in visited:
            result.append(node)
            visited.add(node)
            for neighbor in graph[node]:
```

```
                if neighbor not in visited:
                    queue.append(neighbor)
    return result
```

For DFS:

```
def dfs(graph, start, visited=None):
    if visited is None:
        visited = set()
    result = []

    def dfs_recursive(node):
        if node not in visited:
            result.append(node)
            visited.add(node)
            for neighbor in graph[node]:
                if neighbor not in visited:
                    dfs_recursive(neighbor)

    dfs_recursive(start)
    return result
```

The time and space complexity are explained as follows:

- **BFS:**
    - **Time complexity**: *O(V + E)*, where *V* is the number of vertices and *E* is the number of edges. Each vertex and edge is processed once.
    - **Space complexity**: *O(V)*, as you need to store the visited nodes and the queue.
- **DFS:**
    - **Time complexity**: *O(V + E)*, similar to BFS since each node and edge is processed once.
    - **Space complexity**: *O(V)*, either due to the recursion stack or an explicit stack used for backtracking.

Dig deeper

The complexity analysis is as follows:

- **BFS** is ideal when you need to find the shortest path in an unweighted graph, as it visits all nodes at the current level before going deeper.
- **DFS** is more suitable when you need to explore deep paths or backtrack, such as in pathfinding and decision-making problems.

The edge cases are as follows:

- **Disconnected graph**: If the graph is disconnected, BFS and DFS will only visit nodes reachable from the starting node.
- **Self-loops**: Ensure self-loops (a node connected to itself) do not cause infinite loops.
- **Cyclic graphs**: Handle cycles properly by marking nodes as visited.
- **Empty graph**: If there are no nodes or edges, the result will be empty.

Interview insights

In technical interviews, BFS and DFS are crucial tools for solving various problems, such as:

- **Pathfinding**: BFS is often used to find the shortest path in an unweighted graph.
- **Cycle detection**: DFS can help identify cycles in directed and undirected graphs.
- **Connected components**: Both BFS and DFS can be used to find all connected components in a graph.
- **Tree traversal**: DFS is commonly used in problems related to binary trees, such as pre-order, in-order, and post-order traversals.

Practice problem: Write a function using BFS to find the shortest path in a 2D grid from the top-left corner to the bottom-right corner. Return the path or indicate that no path exists.

Problem 77: Find the shortest path in a maze

Problem statement: Given a 2D grid representing a maze, where 0 represents an open space and 1 represents a wall, write a function to find the shortest path from the top-left corner (0, 0) to the bottom-right corner (*m-1, n-1*) of the grid. You can only move up, down, left, or right. If there is no valid path, return -1.

For example:

- **Input:** A 2D grid of size m x n where each cell is either 0 (open path) or 1 (wall).
- **Output:** The length of the shortest path from the top-left corner to the bottom-right corner. Return -1 if no valid path exists.

Understanding the problem: This problem asks us to navigate a maze from the top-left corner to the bottom-right corner and find the shortest path. The grid contains open spaces (0) and walls (1), and we need to determine the minimum number of steps to reach the destination.

In this maze problem, the most efficient way to find the shortest path in an unweighted grid is to use BFS. BFS is ideal for exploring all possible moves level by level, ensuring that once we reach the destination, we have used the fewest steps possible.

Approach 1: BFS

BFS explores all possible directions from the current position, ensuring that you find the shortest path to the destination. We will use a queue to explore all valid moves (up, down, left, right) from the starting point (0, 0).

The step-by-step explanation is as follows:

1. **Initialize the BFS queue**: Start from the top-left corner (0, 0) and enqueue the starting position along with the number of steps taken (initially 0).
2. **Explore neighbors**: For each cell in the queue, check its neighbors (up, down, left, and right) to see if they are valid and open (0).
3. **Track visited cells**: Keep track of the cells you have visited to avoid revisiting them and getting stuck in an infinite loop.
4. **Reach destination**: When you reach the bottom-right corner, return the number of steps taken.
5. **No path found**: If the queue is empty and you have not reached the destination, return 1, indicating no valid path exists.

Code example:

```
from collections import deque

def shortest_path_in_maze(maze):
    rows, cols = len(maze), len(maze[0])

    # Directions for moving up, down, left, right as (dx, dy) coordinate
offsets
    # Define direction as (0,1)-> right, (1,0)->down, (0,-1)->left,
(-1,0)->right
    directions = [(0, 1), (1, 0), (0, -1), (-1, 0)]

    # Check if the start or end point is blocked
    if maze[0][0] == 1 or maze[rows-1][cols-1] == 1:
        return -1

    # Initialize BFS queue with starting position (0, 0) and step count 0
    queue = deque([(0, 0, 0)])  # (row, col, steps)
    visited = set((0, 0))

    while queue:
        x, y, steps = queue.popleft()

        # If we've reached the bottom-right corner, return the steps
        if x == rows - 1 and y == cols - 1:
            return steps
```

```
        # Explore the four possible directions
        for dx, dy in directions:
            nx, ny = x + dx, y + dy

            if 0 <= nx < rows and 0 <= ny < cols and (nx, ny) not in visited
and maze[nx][ny] == 0:
                queue.append((nx, ny, steps + 1))
                visited.add((nx, ny))

    # If no path is found, return -1
    return -1
```

Step-by-step explanation

Let us walk through the mage:

```
maze = [[0, 0, 1]
        [1, 0, 0]
        [1, 1, 0] ]
```

We want to react cell (2,2) starting from cell (0,0), moving only through zeros (open paths).

The steps are as follows:

1. Start at (0, 0) , step 0
2. Move to (0, 1) , step 1
3. Move to (1, 1), step 2
4. Move to (1, 2), step 3
5. Move to (2, 2), step 4

The minimum number of step to reach the bottom corner is 4.

Approach 2: DFS with backtracking (inefficient)

DFS can also be used to solve this problem, but it will not guarantee the shortest path. DFS explores one path fully before backtracking to explore other paths. Since DFS does not explore all neighbors at each level, it can lead to a non-optimal solution in this case.

Code example (DFS):

```
def dfs(maze, x, y, visited):
    if x == len(maze) - 1 and y == len(maze[0]) - 1:
        return 0  # Reached the destination

    visited.add((x, y))
```

```
    directions = [(0, 1), (1, 0), (0, -1), (-1, 0)]
    min_path = float('inf')

    for dx, dy in directions:
        nx, ny = x + dx, y + dy
        if 0 <= nx < len(maze) and 0 <= ny < len(maze[0]) and (nx, ny) not in
visited and maze[nx][ny] == 0:
            path_length = dfs(maze, nx, ny, visited)
            if path_length != -1:
                min_path = min(min_path, path_length + 1)

    visited.remove((x, y))

    return min_path if min_path != float('inf') else -1
```

DFS is less efficient than BFS for this problem, and its usage is not recommended in interviews for shortest pathfinding problems.

Dig deeper

The complexity analysis is as follows:

- **Time complexity**: *O(m * n),* where m is the number of rows and n is the number of columns in the grid. In the worst case, every cell is visited once.
- **Space complexity**: *O(m * n),* due to the space required for the queue and the set of visited nodes.

The edge cases to consider are as follows:

- **No path exists**: If the grid is fully blocked or there is no possible way to reach the destination, return -1.
    - **Example**: `maze = [[1, 1], [1, 1]]` → Output: `-1`
- **Starting or ending blocked**: If either the starting point or the destination is blocked by a wall (1), return -1 immediately.
    - **Example**: `maze = [[1, 0], [0, 0]]` → Output: `-1`
- **Small grid**: Consider cases with very small grids, such as 1x1 or 2x2.
- **Example**: `maze = [[0]]` → Output: `1`

How to tackle this in an interview:

- **Clarify the problem**: Ask the interviewer about edge cases and constraints, such as whether the maze can have blocked start/end points, or if there can be cycles in the maze.
- **Start with BFS**: Explain why BFS is the most efficient solution for this problem (finding the shortest path in an unweighted grid). Briefly mention that DFS would be inefficient.

- **Discuss complexity**: Always discuss the time and space complexity. Make sure to show that you understand the trade-offs between BFS and DFS.
- **Handle edge cases**: Think of scenarios where the maze is fully blocked, has no solution, or starts/ends with a wall. Address these cases upfront in your solution.

Some edge case examples are as follows:

- **Case 1**: Fully blocked maze.
  ```
  maze = [[1, 1], [1, 1]]
  shortest_path_in_maze(maze)  # Output: -1
  ```
- **Case 2**: Small grid with an open path.
  ```
  maze = [[0]]
  shortest_path_in_maze(maze)  # Output: 1
  ```

Practice problem: Given a grid where 0 represents open spaces and 1 represents walls, write a function that calculates the shortest path from any given starting point to any destination point in the grid. Use BFS to solve the problem, and handle cases where no valid path exists.

Problem 78: Cycle detection in a graph

Problem statement: Given a graph represented as an adjacency list, write a function to detect whether there is a cycle in the graph. The graph can be directed or undirected. A cycle occurs when a sequence of edges forms a closed loop, returning to the same node.

Understanding the problem: In a graph, a cycle means starting from a node, following a series of edges, and eventually returning to the same node. Detecting cycles is essential in various scenarios, like preventing infinite loops in networking and dependency resolution in tasks.

There are two primary types of graphs:

- **Directed graph**: The edges have a direction (from one node to another).

  Example:
  ```
  graph_directed = {
        0: [1, 2],
        1: [0],
        2: [0]
        }
  ```
- **Undirected graph**: The edges do not have a direction, meaning they connect two nodes in both directions.

  Example:
  ```
  graph_undirected = {
        0: [1],
        1: [2],
  ```

```
2: [0]
}
```

The approach to cycle detection differs slightly depending on the type of graph. Let us focus on both cases, starting with undirected graphs.

Approach 1: Cycle detection in an undirected graph using DFS

For undirected graphs, we can use DFS to detect cycles. The key idea is to traverse the graph and track visited nodes. If we encounter a visited node that is not the parent of the current node, we have found a cycle.

The step-by-step explanation is as follows:

1. **DFS traversal**: Start DFS from any unvisited node. Mark nodes as visited.
2. **Tracking parent nodes**: While traversing, keep track of the parent node of each node. This helps differentiate between legitimate edges and back edges (which indicate a cycle).
3. **Back edge detection**: If DFS visits an already visited node that is not the parent of the current node, a cycle exists.

Code example for an undirected graph:

```
def has_cycle_undirected(graph):
    def dfs(node, parent):
        visited.add(node)
        for neighbor in graph[node]:
            if neighbor not in visited:
                if dfs(neighbor, node):
                    return True
            elif neighbor != parent:
                return True
        return False

    visited = set()

    # Check for cycles starting from each node
    for node in graph:
        if node not in visited:
            if dfs(node, -1):  # Start DFS with no parent (-1)
                return True
    return False
```

The explanation is as follows:

- The **dfs** function traverses the graph recursively. If we encounter a visited node that is not the parent, we return True (cycle detected).
- The outer loop ensures we handle disconnected components of the graph.

Approach 2: Cycle detection in a directed graph using DFS and recursion stack

For directed graphs, cycle detection requires a slightly different approach. We need to track the recursion stack (the path we are currently exploring) because revisiting a node in the recursion stack indicates a cycle.

The step-by-step explanation is as follows:

1. **DFS traversal**: Use DFS to traverse the graph.
2. **Recursion stack**: Maintain a recursion stack to track the nodes currently being explored. If a node is revisited and is already in the recursion stack, a cycle exists.

Code example for directed graph:

```
def has_cycle_directed(graph):
    def dfs(node):
        visited.add(node)
        rec_stack.add(node)

        for neighbor in graph[node]:
            if neighbor not in visited:
                if dfs(neighbor):
                    return True
            elif neighbor in rec_stack:
                return True

        rec_stack.remove(node)
        return False

    visited = set()
    rec_stack = set()

    # Start DFS from every node to cover disconnected components
    for node in graph:
        if node not in visited:
            if dfs(node):
                return True
    return False
```

The explanation is as follows:

- We use a recursion stack (**`rec_stack`**) to track nodes currently in the recursive DFS call. If we encounter a node already in the stack, a cycle exists.
- We return True if a cycle is found, and False otherwise.

Approach 3: Cycle detection using union-find (disjoint set)

For undirected graphs, another efficient way to detect cycles is to use the **union-find** (or disjoint set) algorithm. This algorithm groups nodes into sets, and a cycle exists if two nodes in the same set are connected.

The step-by-step explanation is as follows:

1. **Union-find**: Maintain a disjoint set (group of nodes) for the graph.
2. **Union operation**: Each time an edge connects two nodes, check if they are in the same set. If they are, a cycle exists.
3. **Path compression and union by rank**: Optimize the union-find operations to make the algorithm faster.

Code example (union-find):

```
class UnionFind:
    def __init__(self, n):
        self.parent = list(range(n))
        self.rank = [1] * n

    def find(self, u):
        if self.parent[u] != u:
            self.parent[u] = self.find(self.parent[u])
        return self.parent[u]

    def union(self, u, v):
        root_u = self.find(u)
        root_v = self.find(v)

        if root_u == root_v:
            return False
        if self.rank[root_u] > self.rank[root_v]:
            self.parent[root_v] = root_u
        elif self.rank[root_u] < self.rank[root_v]:
            self.parent[root_u] = root_v
        else:
            self.parent[root_v] = root_u
```

```
            self.rank[root_u] += 1
        return True

def has_cycle_union_find(edges, n):
    uf = UnionFind(n)
    for u, v in edges:
        if not uf.union(u, v):
            return True
    return False
```

The explanation is as follows:

- This code uses a union-find data structure to detect cycles. If two nodes are already in the same set, adding an edge between them forms a cycle.
- **Time complexity**: *O(E * logV)* – where *E* is the number of edges, and V is the number of vertices.

Dig deeper

The complexity analysis is as follows:

- **Time complexity:**
  - **DFS approach**: *O(V + E)*, where *V* is the number of vertices, and *E* is the number of edges.
  - **Union-find**: *O(E * logV)*, where *E* is the number of edges.
- **Space complexity**: *O(V)* for both approaches to store visited nodes and the recursion stack or parent sets.

The edge cases to consider are as follows:

- **Disconnected graph**: The graph may contain multiple disconnected components, so you must check each component for cycles.
  - **Example**: `graph = {0: [1], 2: [3]}` → Output: `False`
- **Single node**: A single node with no edges should not be considered a cycle.
  - **Example**: `graph = {0: []}` → Output: `False`
- **Graph with no edges**: A graph with no edges (all nodes are isolated) should not have any cycles.
  - **Example**: `graph = {0: [], 1: [], 2: []}` → Output: `False`

How to tackle this in an interview:

- **Clarify the problem**: Ensure that the interviewer specifies whether the graph is directed or undirected. This will determine which approach you use.

- **Choose the right approach**: For undirected graphs, DFS and union-find are good options. For directed graphs, stick with DFS and the recursion stack.
- **Discuss complexity**: Explain the time and space complexity of your solution, and be ready to discuss the pros and cons of each approach.
- **Consider edge cases**: Think about cases where the graph is disconnected, contains isolated nodes, or has no edges.

Some edge case examples are as follows:

- **Case 1**: Disconnected graph with no cycles:

```
graph = {0: [1], 1: [0], 2: []}
has_cycle_undirected(graph)  # Output: False
```

- **Case 2**: Simple cycle in an undirected graph:

```
graph = {0: [1], 1: [0, 2], 2: [1]}
has_cycle_undirected(graph)  # Output: True
```

The key takeaways for interviews are as follows:

- Start by clarifying whether the graph is directed or undirected.
- For undirected graphs, explain DFS or union-find. For directed graphs, stick with DFS and the recursion stack.
- Be ready to discuss both the time and space complexity of your solution.
- Be clear in explaining edge cases, especially in disconnected graphs or graphs with no edges.

Problem 79: Find all paths between two nodes in a graph

Problem statement: Given a directed graph and two nodes, start and end, write a function to find all possible paths from start to end. The graph is represented as an adjacency list.

Understanding the problem: In this problem, the goal is to find *all possible paths* from one node to another in a directed graph. Unlike the shortest path problem, we need to explore every possible path between two nodes, which could include multiple ways to reach the destination.

The key points are as follows:

- The graph is *directed*, meaning each edge has a direction.
- We want to find *all paths* from the start node to the end node, not just the shortest one.
- The paths should be *distinct* and may vary in length.

For example:

- **Input:**
  - o A directed graph is represented as an adjacency list.
  - o Two nodes, start and end, for which we need to find all possible paths.
- **Output**: A list of lists where each inner list represents a path from start to end.

Approach 1: DFS to explore all paths

DFS is the ideal approach for exploring all possible paths in a graph because it allows us to traverse down one path until we reach the destination or a dead-end, then backtrack and explore the next path.

The step-by-step explanation is as follows:

1. **DFS traversal**: Start from the start node, and explore all its neighbors.
2. **Path tracking**: Keep track of the current path being explored. If we reach the end node, add this path to the list of valid paths.
3. **Backtracking**: After reaching a dead-end or the end node, backtrack to explore other potential paths.

Code example:

```
def find_all_paths(graph, start, end):
    def dfs(node, path):
        path.append(node)

        if node == end:
            # If the current node is the destination, add the path to the results
            all_paths.append(list(path))
        else:
            # Explore all neighbors
            for neighbor in graph.get(node, []):
                dfs(neighbor, path)

        # Backtrack: remove the current node from the path
        path.pop()

    all_paths = []
    dfs(start, [])
    return all_paths
```

The explanations are as follows:

- **DFS function**: We recursively traverse each node in the graph. If the node equals end, the current path is added to **all_paths**. After exploring each neighbor, we backtrack by removing the current node from the path.

- **Base case**: When **node == end**, we append the current path to the result.

Example:

```
graph = {
    'A': ['B', 'C'],
    'B': ['D', 'E'],
    'C': ['F'],
    'D': [],
    'E': ['F'],
    'F': []
}

# Find all paths from A to F
print(find_all_paths(graph, 'A', 'F'))
```

Output:

```
[['A', 'B', 'E', 'F'], ['A', 'C', 'F']]
```

The explanation is as follows:

- There are two paths from node A to node F:
  - A -> B -> E -> F
  - A -> C -> F
- The DFS explores all possible paths and backtracks to ensure no paths are missed.

Approach 2: Using BFS to find all paths

Though DFS is more suited to this problem, BFS can also be used. However, BFS will traverse the graph level by level, which can lead to more memory usage since it keeps track of every node and all possible paths at each level.

The step-by-step explanation is as follows:

1. **BFS traversal**: Use a queue to explore nodes level by level, starting from the start node.
2. **Path tracking**: Each time we visit a node, keep track of the path that led to it. If we reach the end node, add this path to the list of valid paths.

Code example (BFS):

```
from collections import deque

def find_all_paths_bfs(graph, start, end):
    queue = deque([[start]])
    all_paths = []

    while queue:
        path = queue.popleft()
```

```
        node = path[-1]

        if node == end:
            all_paths.append(path)
        else:
            for neighbor in graph.get(node, []):
                new_path = list(path)
                new_path.append(neighbor)
                queue.append(new_path)

    return all_paths
```

The explanation is as follows:

- **Queue**: The BFS uses a queue to store paths, and at each level, we extend the current path by appending neighbors of the node.
- **Level-by-level exploration**: BFS explores all nodes level by level, ensuring that all paths are considered.

Dig deeper

The complexity analysis is as follows:

- **Time complexity:**
  - **DFS**: *O(V + E)*, where *V* is the number of vertices and *E* is the number of edges.
  - **BFS**: *O(V + E)*, but BFS may use more memory to track nodes at each level.
- **Space complexity:**
  - **DFS**: *O(V)* due to the recursion stack.
  - **BFS**: *O(V * P)*, where *P* is the number of paths stored in the queue.

The edge cases to consider are as follows:

- **No paths exist**: The start node may not have a valid path to the end node.
  - **Example**: `graph = {1: [2], 2: [3], 3: []}` for start = 1 and end = 4.
  - **Output**: `[]`
- **Multiple paths**: The graph may have several paths, and the algorithm must explore all of them.
  - **Example**: `graph = {1: [2, 3], 2: [4], 3: [4], 4: []}`.
  - **Output**: `[[1, 2, 4], [1, 3, 4]]`
- **Cyclic graph**: The graph may have cycles, so the algorithm should handle cycles carefully to avoid infinite loops.
  - **Solution**: Maintain a visited set or backtrack properly during DFS.

Some edge case examples are as follows:

- **Case 1:** No path exists:

```
graph = {0: [1], 1: [2], 2: []}
print(find_all_paths(graph, 0, 3))  # Output: []
```

- **Case 2**: Multiple paths:

```
graph = {0: [1, 2], 1: [3], 2: [3], 3: []}
print(find_all_paths(graph, 0, 3))  # Output: [[0, 1, 3], [0, 2, 3]]
```

How to tackle this in an interview:

- **Clarify the graph type**: Ask whether the graph is directed or undirected and whether it contains cycles.
- **Explain your approach**: Discuss the difference between DFS and BFS, and why DFS might be more suitable for this problem due to its depth-first nature.
- **Consider edge cases**: Mention edge cases like disconnected graphs, cycles, or nodes with no neighbors.
- **Optimize**: Be ready to explain why DFS is more memory-efficient than BFS, especially when there are many possible paths.

An edge case example is as follows:

Disconnected graph: If the graph is disconnected and the start node cannot reach the end node, your function should return an empty list.

- `graph = {1: [2], 3: [4]}`
- `start = 1, end = 4`

Output: `[]`

The key takeaways for interviews are as follows:

- **Explain DFS vs. BFS**: Make sure you explain why DFS is often preferred for finding all paths, but also mention how BFS could be used.
- **Edge cases**: Handle cases like disconnected nodes, cycles, and graphs with no edges.
- **Time and space complexity**: Be ready to discuss the complexities of both approaches and why DFS might use less memory.

Problem 80: Connected components in a graph

Problem statement: Given an undirected graph, write a function to find all connected components in the graph. A connected component is a set of vertices where there is a path between every pair of vertices. Vertices in different connected components have no path connecting them.

Understanding the problem: A *connected component* in an undirected graph is a subset of the graph in which every vertex is reachable from every other vertex, and no vertices outside of the subset are reachable from any vertex within the subset. In simpler terms, it is a "cluster" of nodes that are connected to each other but disconnected from the rest of the graph.

The key points to remember are as follows:

- The graph is *undirected*, meaning edges between nodes have no direction.
- We want to find all distinct connected components in the graph.

For example:

- **Input**: An undirected graph represented as an adjacency list or adjacency matrix.
- **Output**: A list of lists where each inner list represents the nodes in one connected component.

Approach 1: DFS to find connected components

We can solve this problem by performing a DFS (or BFS) on the graph. Each time we find an unvisited node, we run a DFS from that node to discover all the nodes in its connected component. Once the DFS finishes, we move on to the next unvisited node and repeat the process.

The step-by-step explanation is as follows:

1. **Initialization**: Create a visited set to keep track of all visited nodes. Also, create a list of components to store all the connected components.
2. **DFS traversal**: For each unvisited node, perform a DFS to explore all nodes in its connected component and mark them as visited.
3. **Store components**: After each DFS, add the set of nodes discovered to the components list.
4. **Repeat**: Repeat this process for all unvisited nodes.

Code example:

```
def find_connected_components(graph):
    def dfs(node, component):
        visited.add(node)
        component.append(node)

        for neighbor in graph.get(node, []):
            if neighbor not in visited:
                dfs(neighbor, component)

    visited = set()
    components = []
```

```
    for node in graph:
        if node not in visited:
            component = []
            dfs(node, component)
            components.append(component)

    return components
```

The explanation is as follows:

- **DFS function**: We recursively visit each neighbor of the current node, adding each unvisited neighbor to the current component. Once the DFS completes, we add the component to the components list.
- **Visited set**: The visited set ensures we do not revisit nodes in already discovered connected components.

Example:

```
graph = {
    1: [2],
    2: [1, 3],
    3: [2],
    4: [5],
    5: [4]
}

# Find connected components
print(find_connected_components(graph))
```

Output:

```
[[1, 2, 3], [4, 5]]
```

Explanation: There are two connected components in the graph:

- 1, 2, 3 form one connected component because they are all reachable from each other.
- 4, 5 form another connected component because they are connected but disconnected from the rest of the graph.

Approach 2: BFS

Alternatively, we can use BFS instead of DFS to find connected components. BFS explores the graph level by level, starting from an unvisited node and visiting all reachable nodes.

The step-by-step explanation is as follows:

1. **Queue**: Use a queue to perform BFS starting from any unvisited node.
2. **Component tracking**: Track all nodes visited in each BFS traversal and mark them as visited.

3. **Repeat**: After completing one BFS traversal, move to the next unvisited node and repeat.

Code example (BFS):

```
from collections import deque

def find_connected_components_bfs(graph):
    visited = set()
    components = []

    for node in graph:
        if node not in visited:
            component = []
            queue = deque([node])
            visited.add(node)

            while queue:
                current = queue.popleft()
                component.append(current)

                for neighbor in graph.get(current, []):
                    if neighbor not in visited:
                        visited.add(neighbor)
                        queue.append(neighbor)

            components.append(component)

    return components
```

The explanation is as follows:

- **BFS function**: We use a queue to explore all nodes level by level, marking each node as visited. Once a BFS completes, we add the component to the components list.
- **Visited Set**: Keeps track of all nodes we have already visited to avoid revisiting nodes in already discovered components.

Dig deeper

The complexity analysis is explained as follows:

- **Time complexity:**
  - **DFS**: $O(V + E)$, where V is the number of vertices and E is the number of edges.
  - **BFS**: $O(V + E)$ – BFS also runs in linear time relative to the number of vertices and edges.

- **Space complexity:**
  - **DFS**: *O(V)* due to the recursion stack and the visited set.
  - **BFS**: *O(V)* due to the queue and the visited set.

The edge cases to consider are as follows:

- **Empty graph**: If the graph is empty, there are no connected components.
  - **Example**: `graph = {}`
  - **Output**: `[]`
- **Single node**: If the graph has only one node with no edges, that node forms a connected component by itself.
  - **Example**: `graph = {1: []}`
  - **Output**: `[[1]]`
- **Disconnected nodes**: If the graph consists of isolated nodes (no edges), each node will be its own connected component.
  - **Example**: `graph = {1: [], 2: [], 3: []}`
  - **Output**: `[[1], [2], [3]]`

How to tackle this problem:

- **Clarify the graph type**: Confirm whether the graph is directed or undirected and if cycles exist.
- **Explain DFS vs. BFS**: Be ready to explain the difference between using DFS and BFS for finding connected components. Typically, DFS is simpler for this task, but both approaches work equally well.
- **Edge cases**: Discuss how your solution handles edge cases, such as an empty graph or isolated nodes.
- **Optimization**: In cases of sparse graphs, using an adjacency list (as we did) is more memory-efficient than using an adjacency matrix.

Key takeaways for interviews:

- **Explain DFS/BFS clearly**: Be ready to discuss why DFS or BFS is used to find connected components.
- **Edge case consideration**: Make sure to handle empty graphs, isolated nodes, and other edge cases.
- **Time complexity**: Understanding the time complexity (*O(V + E)*) is crucial when discussing the efficiency of your solution in the interview.

Problem 81: Find the lowest common ancestor (LCA) of a binary tree

Problem statement: Given a binary tree and two nodes p and q, find their LCA. The lowest common ancestor is defined as the lowest node in the tree that has both p and q as descendants (where we allow a node to be a descendant of itself).

Understanding the problem: In a binary tree, the LCA of two nodes p and q is the deepest node that is an ancestor of both. It is important to note that p and q can be descendants of the same node, and one of them can also be the LCA if the other node is in its subtree.

The key points are as follows:

- The binary tree is not necessarily a BST.
- Both nodes p and q are guaranteed to exist in the tree.

For example:

- Input:
    - A binary tree is represented by the root node.
    - Two nodes, p and q, for which you need to find the LCA.
- **Output**: The node that is the lowest common ancestor of p and q.

Approach 1: Recursive DFS

We can solve this problem by performing a recursive DFS traversal of the binary tree. The idea is to search for nodes p and q in the left and right subtrees of each node. If both nodes are found in different subtrees, the current node is their LCA. If both nodes are found in the same subtree, continue the search in that subtree.

The step-by-step explanation is as follows:

1. **Base case**: If the current node is **None**, return None. This happens when we reach a leaf node and do not find **p** or **q**.
2. **Return early**: If the current node is **p** or **q**, return the current node. This means we have found one of the nodes we are looking for.
3. **Recursive search**: Recursively search the left and right subtrees for **p** and **q**.
4. **Check for LCA**: If both the left and right subtrees return non-null values, the current node is the LCA, because **p** and **q** are found in different subtrees.
5. **Continue the search**: If only one subtree returns a non-null value, that means both **p** and **q** are located in that subtree, so return the non-null value.

Code example:

```
class TreeNode:
    def __init__(self, val=0, left=None, right=None):
        self.val = val
        self.left = left
        self.right = right

def lowest_common_ancestor(root, p, q):
    if not root:
        return None

    if root == p or root == q:
        return root

    left = lowest_common_ancestor(root.left, p, q)
    right = lowest_common_ancestor(root.right, p, q)

    if left and right:
        return root

    return left if left else right
```

The explanation is as follows:

- **Base case**: If the current node is **None** or we have found either **p** or **q**, return the current node.
- **Recursive search**: We recursively search the left and right subtrees to find **p** and **q**.
- **LCA check**: If both left and right are non-null, it means that **p** and **q** are found in different subtrees, so the current node is their LCA.
- **Return the result**: If only one of left or right is non-null, return the non-null value, indicating that both **p** and **q** are in that subtree.

Example:

```
# Example binary tree
       3
      / \
     5   1
    / \ / \
   6  2 0  8
     / \
    7   4

root = TreeNode(3)
root.left = TreeNode(5)
root.right = TreeNode(1)
root.left.left = TreeNode(6)
```

```
root.left.right = TreeNode(2)
root.right.left = TreeNode(0)
root.right.right = TreeNode(8)
root.left.right.left = TreeNode(7)
root.left.right.right = TreeNode(4)

p = root.left  # Node 5
q = root.left.right.right  # Node 4

# Find LCA
print(lowest_common_ancestor(root, p, q).val)
```

Output:

```
5
```

Explanation: In this binary tree, 5 is the parent of 4, so 5 is the lowest common ancestor of 5 and 4.

Approach 2: Iterative solution using parent pointers

Another approach is to store the parent pointers of each node while traversing the tree. Once we have the parent pointers, we can trace the path from both **p** and **q** to the root and then find the last common node on both paths, which will be their LCA.

The step-by-step explanation is as follows:

1. **Parent map**: Traverse the tree and store the parent of each node in a dictionary.
2. **Trace ancestors**: Trace the ancestors of **p** by following its parent pointers back to the root and store them in a set.
3. **Find LCA**: Trace the ancestors of **q**, and the first ancestor that is also in p's set is the LCA.

Code example:

```
def lowest_common_ancestor_iterative(root, p, q):
    parent = {root: None}
    stack = [root]

    while p not in parent or q not in parent:
        node = stack.pop()

        if node.left:
            parent[node.left] = node
            stack.append(node.left)

        if node.right:
            parent[node.right] = node
            stack.append(node.right)
```

```
ancestors = set()

while p:
    ancestors.add(p)
    p = parent[p]

while q not in ancestors:
    q = parent[q]

return q
```

The explanation is as follows:

- **Parent map**: We create a map that stores the parent of each node. This allows us to trace the path of both **p** and **q** to the root.
- **Trace ancestors**: First, we trace the ancestors of **p** and store them in a set.
- **Find LCA**: Then, we trace q's ancestors until we find the first common ancestor, which is the LCA.

Dig deeper

The complexity analysis is as follows:

- **Time complexity:**
    - **Recursive DFS**: *O(n)*, where n is the number of nodes in the tree. We visit each node once.
    - **Iterative parent pointer**: *O(n)* for building the parent map and tracing the ancestors.
- **Space complexity:**
    - **Recursive DFS:** *O(h)*, where h is the height of the tree, due to the recursion stack.
    - **Iterative parent pointer**: *O(n)* for storing the parent pointers and ancestors.

The edge cases to consider are as follows:

- **Nodes are the same**: If **p** and **q** are the same node, the LCA is the node itself.
    - **Example**: **p = q = 5**.
    - **Output**: **5**.
- **Root is the LCA**: If **p** or **q** is the root, the LCA is the root.
    - **Example**: In the example above, if **p = 3** and **q = 5**, the LCA is 3.
- **Deeply nested tree**: The tree may have a long chain of nodes (linked list-like structure).
    - Handle cases where the tree is skewed.

How to approach this problem:

1. **Clarify the problem**: Make sure to clarify if the binary tree is a BST or just a regular binary tree, as this affects the approach.
2. **Discuss recursive vs. iterative**: Be prepared to discuss both recursive and iterative solutions and the trade-offs between them.
3. **Explain complexity**: Always explain the time and space complexity of your approach, especially when recursion is involved.
4. **Edge cases**: Mention edge cases like when **p** and **q** are the same node or when one node is the root of the tree.

The edge case examples are as follows:

- **Same node**: When **p** and **q** are the same.

```
p = root.left  # Node 5
q = root.left  # Node 5
print(lowest_common_ancestor(root, p, q).val)  # Output: 5
```

- **Root as LCA**: When the root is the common ancestor of **p** and **q**.

```
p = root.left  # Node 5
q = root.right  # Node 1
print(lowest_common_ancestor(root, p, q).val)  # Output: 3
```

The key takeaways for interviews are as follows:

- Be clear about your approach (recursive DFS vs. iterative with parent pointers).
- Always consider edge cases, such as when nodes are the same or when one node is the root.
- Be prepared to discuss the time and space complexity of your solution and why it is optimal for the given problem.

Problem 82: Maximum depth of a binary tree

Problem statement: Given a binary tree, find its maximum depth. The maximum depth is the number of nodes along the longest path from the root node down to the farthest leaf node.

Understanding the problem: The maximum depth (also called the height) of a binary tree is the longest path from the root to any leaf node. A leaf node is a node with no children. For example, in a balanced binary tree, the maximum depth is equal to the number of levels in the tree. In an unbalanced binary tree, the longest branch will determine the depth of the branch.

The key points are as follows:

- **Binary tree**: A tree structure where each node has at most two children (left and right).
- **Maximum depth**: The length of the path from the root node to the deepest leaf node.

For example:

- **Input**: A binary tree represented by its root node.
- **Output**: An integer representing the maximum depth of the binary tree.

Approach 1: Recursive DFS

A common approach to this problem is to use recursion. The idea is to recursively calculate the depth of the left and right subtrees and return the greater of the two depths plus one (to account for the root).

The step-by-step explanation is as follows:

1. **Base case**: If the current node is `None`, return 0. This is because an empty tree has a depth of 0.
2. **Recursive case**: For each node, recursively find the maximum depth of its left and right subtrees.
3. **Return the depth**: The depth of the current node is 1 (itself) plus the maximum depth of its left and right subtrees.

Code example:

```
class TreeNode:
    def __init__(self, val=0, left=None, right=None):
        self.val = val
        self.left = left
        self.right = right

def max_depth(root):
    if not root:
        return 0
    left_depth = max_depth(root.left)
    right_depth = max_depth(root.right)
    return max(left_depth, right_depth) + 1
```

The explanation is as follows:

- **Base case**: If the current node is `None`, return 0.
- **Recursive call**: For each node, we recursively compute the depth of its left and right children.
- **Return the result**: The depth of the current node is 1 (itself) plus the maximum of the left and right subtree depths.

Example:

```
# Example binary tree
root = TreeNode(3)
```

```
root.left = TreeNode(9)
root.right = TreeNode(20)
root.right.left = TreeNode(15)
root.right.right = TreeNode(7)

# Find the maximum depth
print(max_depth(root))  # Output: 3
```

Explanation: The maximum depth of the tree is 3 because the longest path is from the root 3 → 20 → 15 or 7.

Approach 2: Iterative DFS using a stack

We can also solve this problem iteratively using a stack. In this approach, we perform a DFS traversal of the tree using a stack and keep track of the depth at each node.

The step-by-step explanation is as follows:

1. **Stack initialization**: Use a stack where each element is a tuple (node, depth). The node is the current node, and depth is the depth of that node.
2. **Iterate through the stack**: Pop a node from the stack, check its left and right children, and update the maximum depth encountered.
3. **Update maximum depth**: Keep track of the maximum depth while traversing the tree.

Code example:

```
def max_depth_iterative(root):
    if not root:
        return 0

    stack = [(root, 1)]
    max_depth = 0

    while stack:
        node, depth = stack.pop()
        if node:
            max_depth = max(max_depth, depth)
            stack.append((node.left, depth + 1))
            stack.append((node.right, depth + 1))

    return max_depth
```

The explanation is as follows:

- **Stack**: We use a stack to perform DFS, starting with the root node at depth 1.
- **Update depth**: For each node, we update the maximum depth if the current depth is greater than the previous maximum.
- **Iterative traversal**: We continue this process until all nodes have been visited.

Approach 3: BFS

Another approach is to use BFS and traverse the tree level by level. The depth is the number of levels in the tree.

The step-by-step explanation is as follows:

1. **Queue initialization**: Use a queue to store the nodes of the current level.
2. **Level-by-level traversal**: For each node, add its left and right children to the queue. Once all nodes of a level have been processed, increment the depth counter.
3. **Return the depth**: The number of levels traversed is the depth of the tree.

Code example:

```
from collections import deque

def max_depth_bfs(root):
    if not root:
        return 0

    queue = deque([root])
    depth = 0

    while queue:
        level_size = len(queue)
        for i in range(level_size):
            node = queue.popleft()
            if node.left:
                queue.append(node.left)
            if node.right:
                queue.append(node.right)
        depth += 1
    return depth
```

The explanation is as follows:

- **Queue**: We use a queue to perform BFS, starting with the root node at level 1.
- **Level-by-level traversal**: We process all nodes of a level before moving to the next level.
- **Update depth**: For each level processed, we increment the depth counter.

Dig deeper

The complexity analysis is as follows:

- **Time complexity:**
  - **Recursive DFS**: *O(n)*, where n is the number of nodes in the tree. We visit each node once.

  - **Iterative DFS**: $O(n)$, as we also visit each node once using a stack.
  - **BFS**: $O(n)$, as we visit each node once using a queue.
- **Space complexity:**
  - **Recursive DFS**: $O(h)$, where h is the height of the tree due to the recursion stack.
  - **Iterative DFS**: $O(h)$, where h is the height of the tree due to the stack.
  - **BFS**: $O(n)$, because we store all nodes of a level in the queue.

The edge cases to consider are as follows:

- **Empty tree**: If the binary tree is empty (**`root = None`**), the maximum depth is 0.
  - **Example**: **`root = None`**
  - **Output**: **`0`**
- **Single node**: If the binary tree has only one node, the maximum depth is 1.
  - **Example**: **`root = TreeNode(1)`**
  - **Output**: **`1`**
- **Balanced vs. unbalanced trees**: In a balanced tree, the depth is proportional to the number of levels, while in an unbalanced tree, the depth can vary significantly depending on the longest branch.

How to approach this problem:

1. **Clarify the problem**: Make sure to confirm whether the tree is binary, balanced, or unbalanced. This affects the depth.
2. **Recursive vs. iterative**: Be ready to discuss both recursive and iterative approaches and their trade-offs.
3. **Time and space complexity**: Always explain the complexity of your solution. Iterative solutions often have lower space complexity compared to recursion in deeply nested trees.
4. **Edge cases**: Think about edge cases like an empty tree or a single-node tree. Always mention these in interviews to show that you are thorough.

Some edge case examples are as follows:

- **Empty tree:**
```
root = None
print(max_depth(root))  # Output: 0
```
- **Single node:**
```
root = TreeNode(1)
print(max_depth(root))  # Output: 1
```

- **Balanced tree:**

```
root = TreeNode(3)
root.left = TreeNode(9)
root.right = TreeNode(20)
print(max_depth(root))  # Output: 2
```

The key takeaways for interviews are as follows:

- **Clarify the type of tree**: Is it binary or balanced? This can affect the solution.
- **Understand the trade-offs**: Be prepared to discuss the differences between recursive DFS, iterative DFS, and BFS.
- **Think about edge cases**: Always address cases like empty trees or single-node trees in your solution.

Problem 83: Invert a binary tree

Problem statement: Given the root of a binary tree, invert the tree and return its root. Inverting a binary tree means swapping the left and right children of every node in the tree.

For example, this is what happens when a binary tree is inverted:

- **Original tree**:

```
        4
      / \\
     2    7
   / \\ / \\
  1   3 6   9
```

- **Inverted tree**:

```
        4
      / \\
     7    2
   / \\ / \\
  9   6 3   1
```

Understanding the problem: Inverting a binary tree is conceptually simple: for each node, you swap its left and right child. This operation is recursive, as each node's left and right children are themselves binary trees, which need to be inverted as well. Think of this as a mirror reflection of the binary tree.

The key points are as follows:

- **Input**: The root of a binary tree.
- **Output**: The root of the inverted binary tree.
- The inversion can be done using either recursion or iteration.

Approach 1: Recursive DFS

The recursive approach follows a simple idea: for every node in the tree, swap its left and right children and then recursively invert the subtrees.

The step-by-step explanation is as follows:

1. **Base case**: If the current node is **None**, return None. This means we have reached a leaf node.
2. **Recursive case**: Swap the left and right children of the current node.
3. **Inversion**: Recursively call the invert function on the swapped children.

Code example:

```
class TreeNode:
    def __init__(self, val=0, left=None, right=None):
        self.val = val
        self.left = left
        self.right = right

def invert_tree(root):
    if not root:
        return None
    root.left, root.right = root.right, root.left  # Swap children
    invert_tree(root.left)  # Recursively invert left subtree
    invert_tree(root.right)  # Recursively invert right subtree
    return root
```

The explanation is as follows:

- **Base case**: If the node is **None**, return.
- **Recursive call**: Swap the left and right children, and recursively call **invert_tree** on both the left and right subtrees.

Approach 2: Iterative DFS using a stack

We can also use an iterative approach to invert the binary tree using a stack to perform DFS. The idea is to push nodes onto the stack, swap their children, and then continue to push the swapped children onto the stack.

The step-by-step explanation is as follows:

1. **Stack initialization**: Start with the root node on the stack.
2. **Process each node**: For each node popped from the stack, swap its left and right children.

3. **Continue the inversion**: Push the children onto the stack and continue the process until all nodes are inverted.

Code example:

```
def invert_tree_iterative(root):
    if not root:
        return None

    stack = [root]
    while stack:
        node = stack.pop()
        if node:
            node.left, node.right = node.right, node.left  # Swap children
            stack.append(node.left)
            stack.append(node.right)

    return root
```

The explanation is as follows:

- **Stack**: We use a stack to perform DFS. For each node, we swap its children and push them onto the stack.
- **Inversion**: The stack continues to store nodes that need to be processed until the entire tree is inverted.

Approach 3: BFS using a queue

Another iterative approach involves BFS. Instead of a stack, we use a queue to process each node level by level, swapping the children at each step.

The step-by-step explanation is as follows:

1. **Queue initialization**: Start with the root node in a queue.
2. **Process each level**: For each node in the queue, swap its children, then add the children to the queue.
3. **Continue until done**: Repeat until the entire tree is inverted.

Code example:

```
from collections import deque

def invert_tree_bfs(root):
    if not root:
        return None

    queue = deque([root])
    while queue:
```

```
        node = queue.popleft()
        if node:
            node.left, node.right = node.right, node.left  # Swap children
            queue.append(node.left)
            queue.append(node.right)

    return root
```

The explanation is as follows:

- **Queue**: We use a queue to perform BFS. For each node, we swap its children and add them to the queue.
- **Level-by-level inversion**: This approach processes the tree level by level, inverting each node's children as it goes.

Dig deeper

The complexity analysis is as follows:

- **Time complexity:**
    - **Recursive DFS**: *O(n)*, where n is the number of nodes in the tree. We visit each node once.
    - **Iterative DFS**: *O(n)*, as we also visit each node once using a stack.
    - **BFS**: *O(n)*, as we visit each node once using a queue.
- **Space complexity:**
    - **Recursive DFS**: *O(h)*, where h is the height of the tree due to the recursion stack.
    - **Iterative DFS**: *O(h)*, where h is the height of the tree due to the stack.
    - **BFS**: *O(n)*, because we store all nodes of a level in the queue.

The edge cases to consider are as *f*:

- **Empty tree**: If the binary tree is empty (**`root = None`**), return None.
    - **Example**: **`root = None`**
    - **Output**: **`None`**
- **Single-node tree**: If the binary tree has only one node, the inverted tree will be the same as the original.
    - **Example**: **`root = TreeNode(1)`**
    - **Output**: **`TreeNode(1)`**
- **Balanced vs. unbalanced trees**: Both types of trees can be inverted using the same approach. Inverting an unbalanced tree will result in a different structure compared to a balanced one.

How to approach this problem:

1. **Clarify the problem**: Ask if you are allowed to use iterative or recursive solutions. Clarify if the tree can be empty.
2. **Recursive vs. iterative**: Be ready to discuss both recursive and iterative approaches. Each has its trade-offs.
3. **Efficiency**: While both approaches have the same time complexity, iterative solutions are often preferred when recursion depth could be an issue (e.g., very deep trees).
4. **Edge cases**: Make sure to consider cases like an empty tree or a tree with only one node. Always mention these in interviews.

Some edge case examples are as follows:

- **Empty tree:**

```
root = None
print(invert_tree(root))  # Output: None
```

- **Single node:**

```
root = TreeNode(1)
print(invert_tree(root))  # Output: TreeNode(1)
```

- **Balanced tree:**

```
root = TreeNode(4)
root.left = TreeNode(2)
root.right = TreeNode(7)
print(invert_tree(root))  # Output: Inverted tree
```

The key takeaways for interviews are as follows:

- **Understand the problem**: Ask clarifying questions about tree structures.
- **Recursive vs. iterative**: Explain the trade-offs between recursion and iteration. Mention stack depth limits for recursion.
- **Time and space complexity**: Be sure to analyze the complexity of your solution and be ready to discuss how it scales with larger inputs.
- **Edge cases**: Discuss edge cases like an empty tree or a tree with only one node.

Problem 84: Serialize and deserialize a binary tree

Problem statement: Serialization is the process of converting a data structure into a format that can be easily stored or transmitted (such as a string or file). Deserialization is the reverse process, converting the stored format back into the original data structure.

Given the root of a binary tree, design an algorithm to serialize the tree into a string and then deserialize that string back into the original tree structure.

Understanding the problem: Imagine you need to save a binary tree to a file or send it over the internet. To do that, you need to convert the tree into a string (serialization). Later, when you want to use the tree again, you will need to recreate the tree from that string (deserialization).

The key points are as follows:

- **Input**: The root of a binary tree.
- **Output**: A serialized string (for serialization) and the root of the original tree (for deserialization).

This problem involves two tasks:

- **Serialize** the tree by converting it into a string.
- **Deserialize** the string back into the tree.

Approach 1: BFS

One of the most common ways to serialize a binary tree is using BFS (or level-order traversal). For each node, we record its value in the serialized string. If a node is None (indicating no child), we add a placeholder (like "null") to represent it. For deserialization, we can reverse the process by reading the values from the serialized string and reconstructing the tree.

The step-by-step explanation is as follows:

- **Serialization:**
    1. Start with the root node and initialize an empty queue.
    2. For each node in the queue, record its value in the string. If the node is `None`, append "null".
    3. Add the node's left and right children to the queue (even if they are None).
    4. Continue until all nodes are processed.
- **Deserialization:**
    1. Start by reading the first value in the serialized string and setting it as the root.
    2. Initialize a queue and process the serialized values level by level.
    3. For each node, read its left and right children from the serialized string.
    4. Reconstruct the tree as you process the nodes.

Code example:

```
from collections import deque

class TreeNode:
```

```
    def __init__(self, val=0, left=None, right=None):
        self.val = val
        self.left = left
        self.right = right

def serialize(root):
    if not root:
        return "null"

    result = []
    queue = deque([root])

    while queue:
        node = queue.popleft()
        if node:
            result.append(str(node.val))
            queue.append(node.left)
            queue.append(node.right)
        else:
            result.append("null")

    return ",".join(result)

def deserialize(data):
    if data == "null":
        return None

    values = data.split(",")
    root = TreeNode(int(values[0]))
    queue = deque([root])
    i = 1

    while queue:
        node = queue.popleft()

        if values[i] != "null":
            node.left = TreeNode(int(values[i]))
            queue.append(node.left)
        i += 1

        if values[i] != "null":
            node.right = TreeNode(int(values[i]))
            queue.append(node.right)
        i += 1

    return root
```

Approach 2: DFS

An alternative method is to use DFS (preorder traversal) for serialization and deserialization. In preorder traversal, we visit the root node first, then recursively visit the left and right subtrees.

The step-by-step explanation is as follows:

- **Serialization:**
    1. Start at the root and recursively serialize the left and right subtrees.
    2. If a node is **None**, append "null" to the serialized string.
- **Deserialization:**
    1. Start by reading the first value in the serialized string and setting it as the root.
    2. Recursively rebuild the left and right subtrees from the serialized string.

Code example:

```
def serialize_dfs(root):
    def dfs(node):
        if not node:
            return "null,"
        return str(node.val) + "," + dfs(node.left) + dfs(node.right)

    return dfs(root)

def deserialize_dfs(data):
    def dfs(nodes):
        val = nodes.pop(0)
        if val == "null":
            return None
        node = TreeNode(int(val))
        node.left = dfs(nodes)
        node.right = dfs(nodes)
        return node

    node_list = data.split(",")
    return dfs(node_list)
```

Dig deeper

The complexity analysis is as follows:

- **Time complexity:**
    - **BFS or DFS:** *O(n)*, where n is the number of nodes in the tree. We visit each node once during serialization and deserialization.

- **Space complexity:**
  - **BFS**: *O(n)*, due to the queue used to store the nodes.
  - **DFS**: *O(n)*, due to the recursion stack and list of node values.

The edge cases to consider are as follows:

- **Empty tree**: If the tree is empty (**`root = None`**), the serialized string should be "null".
  - **Example**: **`root = None`**
  - **Output**: **`"null"`**
- **Single node tree**: If the tree contains only one node, the serialization should reflect that.
  - **Example**: **`root = TreeNode(1)`**
  - **Output**: **`"1,null,null"`**
- **Unbalanced tree**: The algorithm should handle both balanced and unbalanced trees.
  - **Example**: **`root = TreeNode(1, left=TreeNode(2), right=TreeNode(3, left=TreeNode(4)))`**

How to approach this problem:

1. **Clarify the problem**: Make sure you understand whether the interviewer expects BFS, DFS, or either. Also, clarify the format of the serialized string (e.g., use of commas, spaces, or another delimiter).
2. **Recursive vs. iterative**: Be ready to discuss both recursive DFS and iterative BFS approaches. Each has its pros and cons, and the interviewer may want you to explore both.
3. **Time and space complexity**: Always explain the complexity of your solution. For large trees, both BFS and DFS have similar time complexities, but their space usage might differ based on the tree's structure.
4. **Edge cases**: Always discuss how your solution handles edge cases like empty trees, single-node trees, or unbalanced trees.

Some edge case examples are as follows:

- **Empty tree:**

```
root = None
print(serialize(root)) # Output: "null"
print(deserialize("null")) # Output: None
```

- **Single node:**

```
root = TreeNode(1)
print(serialize(root)) # Output: "1,null,null"
print(deserialize("1,null,null")) # Output: TreeNode(1)
```

- **Unbalanced tree:**

```
root = TreeNode(1)
root.left = TreeNode(2)
root.right = TreeNode(3)
root.right.left = TreeNode(4)
print(serialize(root))  # Output: "1,2,null,null,3,4,null,null,null"
print(deserialize("1,2,null,null,3,4,null,null,null"))  # Output:
original tree
```

Key takeaways for interviews:

- **Be ready to explain** both the serialization and deserialization processes in detail.
- **Discuss edge cases**, such as an empty tree, a single-node tree, and unbalanced trees.
- **Offer both BFS and DFS approaches** if time permits, and be prepared to explain the differences between them.
- **Analyze the space complexity** carefully, especially for recursive DFS, where the recursion stack could grow large for deep trees.

Problem 85: Validate a BST

Problem statement: Given the root of a binary tree, write a function to check if it is a valid BST.

A valid BST is defined as follows:

- The left subtree of a node contains only nodes with values less than the node's value.
- The right subtree of a node contains only nodes with values greater than the node's value.
- Both the left and right subtrees must also be BSTs.

Understanding the problem: A BST is a binary tree in which each node follows certain rules:

- **Left subtree**: All the nodes in the left subtree have values *less than* the node's value.
- **Right subtree**: All the nodes in the right subtree have values *greater than* the node's value.
- **Recursion**: Both the left and right subtrees must themselves be valid BSTs.

Your task is to check whether a given binary tree adheres to these properties.

The key points to consider are as follows:

- **Input**: The root of a binary tree.
- **Output**: True if the tree is a valid BST, False otherwise.

Approach 1: Inorder traversal

One approach to solving this problem is to perform an *inorder traversal* of the tree. In an inorder traversal, we visit nodes in the following order: left subtree, current node, right subtree.

For a BST, an inorder traversal should produce nodes in *ascending order*.

The step-by-step explanation is as follows:

1. Traverse the tree using inorder traversal.
2. Keep track of the previous node value.
3. If any node is smaller than or equal to the previous node, the tree is not a valid BST.

Code example:

```
class TreeNode:
    def __init__(self, val=0, left=None, right=None):
        self.val = val
        self.left = left
        self.right = right

def is_valid_bst(root):
    def inorder(node, prev):
        if not node:
            return True
        if not inorder(node.left, prev):
            return False
        if prev[0] is not None and node.val <= prev[0]:
            return False
        prev[0] = node.val
        return inorder(node.right, prev)

    return inorder(root, [None])
```

The explanation is as follows:

- We use a helper function **inorder** that recursively traverses the left and right subtrees.
- We store the value of the last visited node in a list prev. If the current node's value is less than or equal to the previous value, the tree is not a valid BST.

The time and space complexity are explained as follows:

- **Time complexity**: *O(n)*, where n is the number of nodes in the tree. Each node is visited once.
- **Space complexity**: *O(n)* for the recursion stack in the worst case of a completely unbalanced tree.

Approach 2: Recursive min/max boundaries

Another approach is to use recursive validation by setting *minimum* and *maximum boundaries* for each node.

The step-by-step explanation is as follows:

1. Start at the root node with the entire range of valid values (initially, the range is (-∞, ∞)).
2. For each node:
   a. Check if the node's value is within the valid range.
   b. Recursively validate the left subtree with a new upper bound (the current node's value).
   c. Recursively validate the right subtree with a new lower bound (the current node's value).
3. If any node violates the bounds, the tree is not a valid BST.

Code example:

```
def is_valid_bst(root):
    def validate(node, low, high):
        if not node:
            return True
        if not (low < node.val < high):
            return False
        return (validate(node.left, low, node.val) and
                validate(node.right, node.val, high))

    return validate(root, float('-inf'), float('inf'))
```

The explanation is as follows:

- We define a helper function validate that takes a node and its allowed range of values (low and high).
- For each node, check if its value is within the range. If it is, recurse on the left and right children with updated bounds.

The time and space complexity are as follows:

- **Time complexity**: *O(n)*, where n is the number of nodes in the tree.
- **Space complexity**: *O(n)* for the recursion stack in the worst case of a completely unbalanced tree.

Approach 3: Iterative inorder traversal

We can also validate a BST using an *iterative inorder traversal* with the help of a stack. This approach avoids the recursion limit in cases where the tree is very deep.

The step-by-step explanation is as follows:

1. Use a stack to perform an iterative inorder traversal.
2. Keep track of the previous node's value.
3. For each node, check if its value is greater than the previous node's value. If not, the tree is not a valid BST.

Code example:

```
def is_valid_bst(root):
    stack = []
    prev = None

    while stack or root:
        while root:
            stack.append(root)
            root = root.left
        root = stack.pop()
        if prev is not None and root.val <= prev:
            return False
        prev = root.val
        root = root.right

    return True
```

The explanation is as follows:

- We simulate recursion using a stack and iterate through the tree in an inorder manner.
- Keep track of the previous node value and ensure that the current node's value is greater than the previous one.

The time and space complexity is as follows:

- **Time complexity**: *O(n),* where n is the number of nodes in the tree.
- **Space complexity**: *O(n),* due to the stack used for traversal.

Dig deeper

The edge cases to consider are as follows:

- **Empty tree**: An empty tree is considered a valid BST.
    - **Example: `root = None`**

  - **Output**: `True`
- **Single-node tree**: A tree with only one node is always a valid BST.
  - **Example**: `root = TreeNode(1)`
  - **Output**: `True`
- **Unbalanced tree**: Both balanced and unbalanced trees should be validated.
  - **Example**: `root = TreeNode(5, TreeNode(1), TreeNode(10, TreeNode(7), TreeNode(12)))`
- **Subtree violations**: Ensure the subtree rules are followed, especially for deeper levels.
  - **Example**: `root = TreeNode(10, TreeNode(5, TreeNode(15)))` (Invalid BST because 15 is in the wrong subtree)

How to approach this problem:

1. **Clarify the problem**: Make sure you understand whether the interviewer expects recursion or iteration, and discuss the tree structure with them. You can ask about edge cases like an empty tree or a single-node tree.
2. **Recursive vs. iterative**: Be prepared to discuss both recursive and iterative approaches. Each has trade-offs in terms of simplicity and performance.
3. **Time and space complexity**: Always mention the time and space complexity of your solution, especially for recursive approaches where the recursion depth might matter.
4. **Edge cases**: Discuss how your solution handles edge cases like unbalanced trees, empty trees, and invalid subtrees.

Some edge case examples are as follows:

- **Empty tree:**

```
root = None
print(is_valid_bst(root))  # Output: True
```

- **Single node:**

```
root = TreeNode(1)
print(is_valid_bst(root))  # Output: True
```

- **Invalid BST:**

```
root = TreeNode(10, TreeNode(5, TreeNode(15)))
print(is_valid_bst(root))  # Output: False
```

The key takeaways for interviews are as follows:

- Always clarify if recursion or iteration is preferred.
- Discuss both time and space complexities in detail.

- Consider all edge cases, including unbalanced trees and invalid subtrees.
- Be ready to optimize or provide alternative solutions (like iterative vs. recursive).

Problem 86: Symmetric tree problem

Problem statement: Given the root of a binary tree, write a function to check if the tree is *symmetric*. A tree is symmetric if it is a mirror reflection of itself.

For example, consider this binary tree:

```
      1
    /   \\
   2     2
  / \\   / \\
 3   4 4   3
```

This tree is symmetric because the left subtree is a mirror image of the right subtree.

Understanding the problem: In this problem, you need to determine whether a given binary tree is symmetric. A binary tree is symmetric if:

- The left subtree is the mirror image of the right subtree.
- The tree's root serves as the axis of symmetry.

The key points are as follows:

- **Input**: The root node of a binary tree.
- **Output**: True if the tree is symmetric, False otherwise.

Approach 1: Recursive mirror check

The most intuitive way to check if a tree is symmetric is to compare the *left subtree* and *right subtree* recursively, checking whether they are mirror images of each other.

The step-by-step explanation is as follows:

1. Start by comparing the left and right subtrees.
2. For the tree to be symmetric:
   a. The left subtree of the left node should be a mirror image of the right subtree of the right node.
   b. The right subtree of the left node should be a mirror image of the left subtree of the right node.
3. If at any point the values differ, the tree is not symmetric.
4. The recursion continues until all pairs of nodes are compared.

Code example (recursive):

```
class TreeNode:
    def __init__(self, val=0, left=None, right=None):
        self.val = val
        self.left = left
        self.right = right

def is_symmetric(root):
    # Helper function to compare two subtrees
    def is_mirror(left, right):
        # Base case: if both nodes are None, they are symmetric
        if not left and not right:
            return True
        # If one is None and the other is not, they are not symmetric
        if not left or not right:
            return False
        # Check if the values are the same and the subtrees are mirrors
        return (left.val == right.val and
                is_mirror(left.left, right.right) and
                is_mirror(left.right, right.left))

    # An empty tree is symmetric
    if not root:
        return True

    # Start comparing the left and right subtrees
    return is_mirror(root.left, root.right)
```

The explanation is as follows:

- The helper function **`is_mirror`** recursively checks if two subtrees are mirrors of each other.
- If both subtrees are empty (**`None`**), they are symmetric.
- If only one of them is empty, the tree is not symmetric.
- If the values are the same, we recursively check the subtrees.

The time and space complexity are as follows:

- **Time complexity**: *O(n)*, where n is the number of nodes in the tree, as we visit each node once.
- **Space complexity**: *O(h)*, where h is the height of the tree, due to the recursion stack.

Approach 2: Iterative approach using a queue

Another approach is to use an *iterative solution* with a queue. Instead of recursion, you can compare the nodes level by level.

The step-by-step explanation is as follows:

1. Use a queue to store pairs of nodes to be compared.
2. Initially, add the left and right children of the root to the queue.
3. For each pair of nodes:
   a. If both are None, continue.
   b. If only one is None or their values are different, the tree is not symmetric.
   c. Otherwise, enqueue their children in the opposite order to check for symmetry.
4. Repeat until the queue is empty.

Code example (iterative):

```
from collections import deque

def is_symmetric(root):
    # A tree is symmetric if the left and right subtrees are mirrors
    if not root:
        return True

    # Use a queue to store the pairs of nodes to compare
    queue = deque([(root.left, root.right)])

    while queue:
        left, right = queue.popleft()

        # If both are None, continue
        if not left and not right:
            continue
        # If one is None or values are different, the tree is not symmetric
        if not left or not right or left.val != right.val:
            return False
        # Enqueue the children in reverse order to check for mirror symmetry
        queue.append((left.left, right.right))
        queue.append((left.right, right.left))

    return True
```

The explanation is as follows:

- We use a queue to iteratively compare nodes.
- For each pair of nodes, we check their values and enqueue their children in reverse order to maintain symmetry.

The time and space complexity are as follows:

- **Time complexity**: *O(n)* – We visit each node once.
- **Space complexity**: *O(n)* – In the worst case, we need to store all the nodes in the queue.

Dig deeper

The edge cases to consider are as follows:

- **Empty tree**: An empty tree is symmetric.
  - **Example**: `root = None`
  - **Output**: `True`
- **Single-node tree**: A tree with only one node is symmetric.
  - **Example**: `root = TreeNode(1)`
  - **Output**: `True`
- **Asymmetric tree**: A tree with mismatched nodes on the left and right sides.

Example:

```
   1
  / \\
 2   2
  \\    \\
   3     3
```

Output: `False`

How to think about this problem:

1. **Clarify the problem**: Always confirm with the interviewer what they expect in terms of recursion or iteration.
2. **Recursive vs. iterative**: Be ready to explain both approaches. Recursive solutions are easier to write but may run into issues with very deep trees due to recursion limits.
3. **Time and space complexity**: Discuss the time and space complexity for both recursive and iterative approaches. Iteration tends to be more space-efficient in very deep trees.
4. **Edge cases**: Make sure to handle edge cases, including empty trees and single-node trees, and discuss them during the interview.

Some edge case examples are as follows:

- **Empty tree:**

```
root = None
print(is_symmetric(root))  # Output: True
```

- **Single node:**
```
root = TreeNode(1)
print(is_symmetric(root))  # Output: True
```
- **Asymmetric tree:**
```
root = TreeNode(1, TreeNode(2), TreeNode(2, None, TreeNode(3)))
print(is_symmetric(root))  # Output: False
```

The key takeaways for interviews are as follows:

- Clarify whether recursion or iteration is preferred by the interviewer.
- Clearly explain the time and space complexity of your solution.
- Be ready to handle edge cases and provide optimizations where necessary.
- Clearly communicate your approach step by step, especially when working through a recursive or iterative process.

Problem 87: Binary tree level order traversal

Problem statement: Given the root of a binary tree, return the *level order traversal* of its nodes' values. (i.e., from left to right, level by level).

For example, consider the binary tree as follows:

```
    3
   / \\
  9  20
    /  \\
   15   7
```

The level order traversal of this tree is:

```
[[3], [9, 20], [15, 7]]
```

Understanding the problem: Level order traversal is a way of visiting nodes level by level from top to bottom. For each level, we visit all the nodes from left to right. This is a common problem in binary tree traversal and is often solved using a BFS approach.

In the example above, we first visit the root node 3, then move on to the second level, which includes nodes 9 and 20, and finally, we visit the third level, which includes nodes 15 and 7.

The key points are as follows:

- **Input**: The root node of a binary tree.
- **Output**: A list of lists, where each list represents the values of nodes at that level, from left to right.

Approach 1: BFS with a queue

The easiest way to perform level order traversal is by using a **queue** to simulate the BFS process. We will visit all the nodes level by level and store the values in the correct order.

The step-by-step explanation is as follows:

1. Start by checking if the root is None. If the tree is empty, return an empty list.
2. Initialize a queue with the root node.
3. While the queue is not empty:
    a. Process each level of the tree by dequeuing nodes one by one.
    b. For each node, enqueue its left and right children (if they exist).
    c. Once all nodes at a level have been processed, store their values in a list.
4. Repeat the process for the next level until all levels are traversed.

Code example (BFS with queue):

```
from collections import deque

class TreeNode:
    def __init__(self, val=0, left=None, right=None):
        self.val = val
        self.left = left
        self.right = right

def level_order_traversal(root):
    if not root:
        return []

    # Initialize a queue for BFS
    queue = deque([root])
    result = []

    while queue:
        level = []
        # Process all nodes at the current level
        for _ in range(len(queue)):
            node = queue.popleft()
            level.append(node.val)

            # Enqueue left and right children
            if node.left:
                queue.append(node.left)
            if node.right:
                queue.append(node.right)
```

```
        # Add the current level to the result
        result.append(level)

    return result
```

The explanation is as follows:

- We use a queue to traverse each level of the tree.
- After processing each level, we store the node values in a list and move to the next level.

The time and space complexity are as follows:

- **Time complexity**: *O(n)*, where n is the number of nodes in the tree, since we visit each node once.
- **Space complexity**: *O(n)*, as we need space for the queue and result list.

Alternative approach: Recursive DFS with level tracking

While BFS is the most common way to solve this problem, we can also use DFS recursively, keeping track of the current level.

The step-by-step explanation is as follows:

1. Initialize a result list to hold the values at each level.
2. Define a recursive function that traverses the tree:
    a. If the current level does not exist in the result list, create a new list for it.
    b. Add the node's value to the corresponding level in the result list.
    c. Recursively call the function for the left and right children, incrementing the level.
3. Return the result list after all levels are processed.

Code example (recursive DFS):

```
def level_order_traversal_dfs(root):
    result = []

    def dfs(node, level):
        if not node:
            return

        # If the current level does not exist, create it
        if len(result) == level:
            result.append([])
```

```
        # Add the current node's value to the current level
        result[level].append(node.val)

        # Recur for the left and right children
        dfs(node.left, level + 1)
        dfs(node.right, level + 1)

    # Start DFS from the root
    dfs(root, 0)
    return result
```

The explanation is as follows:

- We recursively traverse the tree, keeping track of the current level.
- For each level, we store the node values in the result list.

The time and space complexity are as follows:

- **Time complexity**: *O(n)* – We visit each node once.
- **Space complexity**: *O(h)*, where h is the height of the tree, due to the recursion stack.

Dig deeper

The edge cases to consider are as follows:

- **Empty tre**: If the input tree is empty, return an empty list.
    - **Example**: `root = None`
    - **Output**: `[]`
- **Single-node tree**: A tree with only one node should return a single list with that node's value.
    - **Example**: `root = TreeNode(1)`
    - **Output**: `[[1]]`
- **Unbalanced tree**: The function should handle trees where one side is deeper than the other.
    - **Example**:

```
        1
       /
      2
     /
    3
```

    - **Output**: `[[1], [2], [3]]`

How to think about this problem:

1. **Clarify the problem**: Always clarify with the interviewer whether they expect a BFS or DFS solution.
2. **Iterative vs. recursive**: Be prepared to discuss both approaches. BFS is typically easier to implement for level order traversal, but recursion with DFS can also work well.
3. **Time and space complexity**: Make sure to explain the time and space complexity of your solution, especially with respect to the queue or recursion stack.
4. **Edge cases**: Mention how your solution handles edge cases, including empty trees and trees with only one node.

Some edge case examples are as follows:

- **Empty tree:**

  ```
  root = None
  print(level_order_traversal(root))  # Output: []
  ```

- **Single node:**

  ```
  root = TreeNode(1)
  print(level_order_traversal(root))  # Output: [[1]]
  ```

- **Unbalanced tree:**

  ```
  root = TreeNode(1, TreeNode(2, TreeNode(3)))
  print(level_order_traversal(root))  # Output: [[1], [2], [3]]
  ```

The key takeaways for interviews are as follows:

- **Clarify the problem** and confirm whether the interviewer expects a BFS or DFS solution.
- **Start with BFS** since it is a natural fit for level order traversal.
- **Time and space complexity** are both $O(n)$, which is optimal for this problem.
- Be prepared to handle **edge cases**, including empty trees and single-node trees.
- **Explain your thought process clearly**, and discuss any potential optimizations, such as limiting recursion depth in large trees.

Problem 88: Binary tree zigzag level order traversal

Problem statement: Given the root of a binary tree, return the *zigzag level order traversal* of its nodes' values. (i.e., from left to right, then right to left for the next level, and alternate between).

For example, consider the binary tree as follows:

```
    3
   / \\
  9  20
    /  \\
   15   7
```

The zigzag level order traversal of this tree is:

```
[[3], [20, 9], [15, 7]]
```

Understanding the problem: In this problem, we need to traverse the binary tree level by level, but with a twist: at each level, we alternate the direction in which we traverse. The first level is left-to-right, the second is right-to-left, the third is left-to-right again, and so on. This gives the traversal its "zigzag" pattern.

The key points to consider are as follows:

- **Input**: The root node of a binary tree.
- **Output**: A list of lists where each inner list contains the values of the nodes at a given level, traversed in zigzag order.

Approach 1: BFS with direction toggle

We can solve this problem by performing a BFS traversal using a queue, but with an extra flag to keep track of the direction (left-to-right or right-to-left) at each level.

The step-by-step explanation is as follows:

1. Start by checking if the root is None. If the tree is empty, return an empty list.
2. Initialize a queue with the root node and a Boolean flag **`left_to_right`** to control the traversal direction.
3. Process the nodes level by level:
    a. If **`left_to_right`** is True, process the level normally (left to right).
    b. If **`left_to_right`** is False, reverse the order of nodes before adding them to the result.
4. After processing each level, flip the **`left_to_right`** flag to alternate the direction for the next level.
5. Continue until all levels are processed.

Code example (BFS with direction toggle):

```
from collections import deque
class TreeNode:
```

```
    def __init__(self, val=0, left=None, right=None):
        self.val = val
        self.left = left
        self.right = right

def zigzag_level_order(root):
    if not root:
        return []
    # Initialize the queue for BFS
    queue = deque([root])
    result = []
    left_to_right = True  # Start with left-to-right traversal

    while queue:
        level = []
        for _ in range(len(queue)):
            node = queue.popleft()
            level.append(node.val)

            # Enqueue left and right children
            if node.left:
                queue.append(node.left)
            if node.right:
                queue.append(node.right)

        # If we are traversing right to left, reverse the current level
        if not left_to_right:
            level.reverse()

        # Add the level to the result and toggle the direction
        result.append(level)
        left_to_right = not left_to_right  # Toggle the direction for next level

    return result
```

The explanation is as follows:

- We use a queue to perform a BFS traversal.
- After processing each level, we check the **left_to_right** flag. If it is False, we reverse the list of node values for that level before adding it to the result.

The time and space complexity are as follows:

- **Time complexity**: *O(n)*, where n is the number of nodes in the tree. We visit each node once.
- **Space complexity**: *O(n)*, as we need space for the queue and result list.

Alternative approach: DFS with level tracking

Another approach is to use DFS recursively and track the level of each node. For odd levels, append the node values from left to right; for even levels, insert the values from right to left.

The step-by-step explanation is as follows:

1. Define a recursive DFS function that tracks both the node and its level.
2. If the current level does not exist in the result list, create a new list for that level.
3. If the level is odd, append the node's value; if the level is even, insert the value at the beginning of the list to reverse the order.
4. Recursively call the function for the left and right children, incrementing the level.
5. Return the result after all levels are processed.

Code example (recursive DFS):

```
def zigzag_level_order_dfs(root):
    result = []

    def dfs(node, level):
        if not node:
            return

        # Create a new level if it doesn't exist
        if len(result) == level:
            result.append([])

        # Insert the node's value based on the level's direction
        if level % 2 == 0:
            result[level].append(node.val)  # Left to right
        else:
            result[level].insert(0, node.val)  # Right to left

        # Recur for the left and right children
        dfs(node.left, level + 1)
        dfs(node.right, level + 1)

    dfs(root, 0)
    return result
```

The explanation is as follows:

- We recursively traverse the tree, keeping track of the level.
- For odd levels, we reverse the insertion order by using **`insert(0, node.val)`** to add the value at the front of the list.

The time and space complexity are as follows:

- **Time complexity**: *O(n)* – We visit each node once.
- **Space complexity**: *O(h)*, where h is the height of the tree due to the recursion stack.

Dig deeper

The edge cases to consider are as follows:

- **Empty tree**: If the input tree is empty, return an empty list.
  - **Example**: `root = None`
  - **Output**: `[]`
- **Single-node tree**: A tree with only one node should return a single list with that node's value.
  - **Example**: `root = TreeNode(1)`
  - **Output**: `[[1]]`
- **Unbalanced tree**: The function should handle trees where one side is deeper than the other.
  - **Example**:

```
    1
   /
  2
 /
3
```

  - **Output**: `[[1], [2], [3]]`

How to think about this problem:

- **Clarify the problem**: In an interview, clarify whether the tree has any specific properties (e.g., is it a BST or a regular binary tree?).
- **Iterative vs. recursive**: BFS is typically easier to implement for zigzag traversal, but DFS with level tracking is a valid alternative. Discuss both approaches if time allows.
- **Time and space complexity**: Always mention that both approaches have a time complexity of *O(n)*, but BFS uses a queue, while DFS uses recursion and stack space.
- **Edge cases**: Be prepared to discuss how your solution handles empty trees, single-node trees, and unbalanced trees.

The edge case examples are as follows:

- **Empty tree**:

```
root = None
print(zigzag_level_order(root))  # Output: []
```

- **Single node:**

```
root = TreeNode(1)
print(zigzag_level_order(root))  # Output: [[1]]
```

- **Unbalanced tree**:

```
root = TreeNode(1, TreeNode(2, TreeNode(3)))
print(zigzag_level_order(root))  # Output: [[1], [2], [3]]
```

The key takeaways for interviews are as follows:

- **Clarify the problem** and ensure you know whether BFS or DFS is preferred.
- **Start with BFS**, as it is a straightforward way to handle level order traversal.
- **Time and space complexity** are both *O(n)*, which is optimal for this problem.
- Consider how your solution handles **edge cases**, including empty and unbalanced trees.
- **Communicate your thought process clearly**, explaining why you chose a specific approach and any potential optimizations.

Problem 89: Count the number of islands (DFS/BFS)

Problem statement: Given a 2D grid map of '1's (land) and '0's (water), count the number of islands. An island is surrounded by water and is formed by connecting adjacent lands horizontally or vertically. You may assume all four edges of the grid are surrounded by water.

For example, consider the following grid:

```
[
  ['1', '1', '0', '0', '0'],
  ['1', '1', '0', '0', '0'],
  ['0', '0', '1', '0', '0'],
  ['0', '0', '0', '1', '1']
]
```

In this case, the output should be 3 because there are three islands.

Understanding the problem: This problem is essentially about finding connected components in a grid. Each island represents a connected component of adjacent '1's, and our goal is to count how many such components exist.

You can think of the grid as a graph where each cell represents a node, and there is an edge between two nodes if they are adjacent and both contain '1'. We need to explore all the connected components of '1's and count how many distinct groups we have.

The key points are as follows:

- **Input**: A 2D grid of '1's (land) and '0's (water).
- **Output**: The number of distinct islands (connected components of '1's).

Approach 1: DFS

We can use DFS to explore each island. Starting from any '1', we explore all connected '1's, marking them as visited by turning them into '0' to avoid counting the same island more than once. Each DFS call will completely explore one island.

The step-by-step explanation is as follows:

1. Traverse the grid cell by cell.
2. Whenever you encounter a '1', this marks the start of a new island. Perform a DFS to visit all adjacent land cells connected to this '1', marking them as '0' (visited).
3. Increase the island count each time you initiate a new DFS.
4. Return the total number of islands after processing all cells.

Code example (DFS):

```
def numIslands(grid):
    if not grid:
        return 0

    def dfs(grid, i, j):
        # Base case: if out of bounds or at water ('0'), return
        if i < 0 or i >= len(grid) or j < 0 or j >= len(grid[0]) or grid[i][j]
== '0':
            return

        # Mark the current cell as visited by setting it to '0'
        grid[i][j] = '0'

        # Visit all 4 adjacent cells (up, down, left, right)
        dfs(grid, i-1, j) # Up
        dfs(grid, i+1, j)  # Down
        dfs(grid, i, j-1)  # Left
        dfs(grid, i, j+1)  # Right

    island_count = 0

    for i in range(len(grid)):
        for j in range(len(grid[0])):
            if grid[i][j] == '1':  # Found an unvisited island
                dfs(grid, i, j)    # Perform DFS to visit the entire island
                island_count += 1  # Increase the island count

    return island_count
```

Explanation: This DFS approach explores each island, marks it as visited, and counts it.

Time complexity: *O(m × n)*, where m is the number of rows and n is the number of columns in the grid.

Space complexity: *O(m × n)* due to the recursion stack in the worst case.

Approach 2: BFS

We can also use BFS to solve this problem. Instead of recursively visiting each adjacent land cell, BFS uses a queue to iteratively explore all connected land cells level by level.

The step-by-step explanation is as follows:

1. Traverse the grid, and for each '1' found, initiate a BFS using a queue.
2. Mark the current land cell and its adjacent land cells as visited by turning them into '0'.
3. Increase the island count each time a BFS is initiated for a new island.

Code example BFS:

```
from collections import deque

def numIslands(grid):
    if not grid:
        return 0

    def bfs(grid, i, j):
        queue = deque([(i, j)])
        grid[i][j] = '0'

        while queue:
            x, y = queue.popleft()

            # Check all 4 adjacent directions
            for dx, dy in [(-1, 0), (1, 0), (0, -1), (0, 1)]:
                new_x, new_y = x + dx, y + dy

                if 0 <= new_x < len(grid) and 0 <= new_y < len(grid[0]) and
grid[new_x][new_y] == '1':
                    queue.append((new_x, new_y))
                    grid[new_x][new_y] = '0'  # Mark as visited

    island_count = 0

    for i in range(len(grid)):
        for j in range(len(grid[0])):
            if grid[i][j] == '1':  # Found an unvisited island
                bfs(grid, i, j)    # Perform BFS to visit the entire island
                island_count += 1  # Increase the island count

    return island_count
```

Explanation: This BFS approach explores the island iteratively using a queue and marks visited cells.

Time complexity: $O(m \times n)$, similar to DFS.

Space complexity: $O(min(m, n))$ due to the queue used for BFS traversal.

Dig deeper

How to think about this problem:

- **Recognize the connected component nature:** This problem is about finding connected components in a grid, similar to graph traversal problems. Recognizing that you can treat the grid like a graph helps you immediately think of DFS or BFS as potential solutions.
- **DFS vs. BFS:** Both DFS and BFS work for this problem, so be prepared to explain both approaches. Some interviewers may prefer one over the other, or they may ask you to implement both.
- **Edge cases:** Be sure to handle edge cases, such as an empty grid, a grid with no land ('1's), or a grid that is entirely land.

The edge cases to consider are as follows:

- **Empty grid**: If the grid is empty, the result should be 0.
  - **Example:** `[]` → s
- **No land**: If there are no '1's, the result should be 0.
  - **Example:** `[["0","0"],["0","0"]]` → `0`
- **Single island**: The entire grid could be a single connected island.
  - **Example:** `[["1","1"],["1","1"]]` → `1`

The key takeaways for interviews are as follows:

- Understand how grid problems can be treated as graph traversal problems.
- Be able to explain both DFS and BFS solutions.
- Be prepared to discuss the time and space complexities of your approach.
- Consider edge cases, such as an empty grid or grids with no land.

Problem 90: Alien dictionary problem

Problem statement: In an alien language, the letters are sorted in a specific order that is different from English. Given a list of words written in the alien language, return the order of the letters. If the order is invalid or cannot be determined, return an empty string.

For example, if the input is:

```
["wrt", "wrf", "er", "ett", "rftt"]
```

The output should be:

```
"wertf"
```

Understanding the problem: In this problem, we need to derive the order of the alien alphabet from a sorted list of words. The words in the list are sorted according to the alien dictionary's order of letters, and we must deduce that order.

Think of this problem as building a **graph** where each node is a letter, and there is a directed edge from one letter to another if one letter comes before another in the alien dictionary. The challenge is then to perform a **topological sort** on this graph to determine the order of the letters.

The key points are as follows:

- **Input**: A list of words written in alien language.
- **Output**: The order of the letters as a string.
- **Invalid case**: Return an empty string if the order cannot be determined or is invalid (like detecting a cycle in the graph).

Approach 1: Topological sort using BFS (Kahn's algorithm)

We can treat this problem as a graph problem where the nodes are letters, and the directed edges represent the precedence relationship between letters. Once we build the graph, we perform a topological sort to find the correct order of the letters.

The step-by-step explanation is as follows:

1. **Graph construction**: Build a graph where each node is a letter, and the directed edges between nodes represent the order of letters in the alien language.
    a. For each pair of adjacent words in the input list, find the first differing letter and add a directed edge between those two letters in the graph.
2. **Indegree array**: For each letter, we also maintain an indegree array that counts how many other letters must come before it.
3. **Topological sort (BFS)**: Once the graph is built, we perform a topological sort using BFS. Start with all letters that have an indegree of 0 (meaning no other letters must come before them). For each letter, remove it from the graph and reduce the indegree of its neighbors. If a neighbor's indegree becomes 0, add it to the queue.
4. **Detect cycles**: If there are still letters left in the graph after processing, that indicates a cycle, and we should return an empty string.

Code example:

```
from collections import defaultdict, deque

def alienOrder(words):
    # Step 1: Create a graph and indegree array
    graph = defaultdict(set)
    indegree = {char: 0 for word in words for char in word}

    # Step 2: Build the graph
    for i in range(len(words) - 1):
        word1, word2 = words[i], words[i + 1]
        min_len = min(len(word1), len(word2))

        # Check for invalid order like ["abc", "ab"]
        if len(word1) > len(word2) and word1[:min_len] == word2[:min_len]:
            return ""

        for j in range(min_len):
            if word1[j] != word2[j]:
                if word2[j] not in graph[word1[j]]:
                    graph[word1[j]].add(word2[j])
                    indegree[word2[j]] += 1
                break

    # Step 3: Topological sort using BFS (Kahn's Algorithm)
    queue = deque([char for char in indegree if indegree[char] == 0])
    result = []

    while queue:
        char = queue.popleft()
        result.append(char)

        for neighbor in graph[char]:
            indegree[neighbor] -= 1
            if indegree[neighbor] == 0:
                queue.append(neighbor)

    # Step 4: If result contains all characters, return as string, else return
""

    if len(result) == len(indegree):
        return "".join(result)
    else:
        return ""
```

Approach 2: Topological sort using DFS

We can also solve this problem using DFS to perform the topological sort. The key difference from BFS is that we start from any unvisited node, recursively visit all its neighbors, and then add the node to the output list. This ensures that nodes (letters) with no outgoing edges (i.e., those that appear later in the alien dictionary) are added to the result last.

The step-by-step explanation is as follows:

1. **Graph construction**: Same as in the BFS approach, we build a directed graph where nodes are letters and edges indicate their order.
2. **DFS for topological sort**: Perform a DFS on each unvisited node, and add nodes to a stack after visiting all their neighbors.
3. **Cycle detection**: Detect cycles during the DFS by checking if a node is currently being visited (i.e., backtracking to a previously visited node).

Code example DFS:

```
def alienOrder(words):
    graph = defaultdict(set)
    visited = {}  # 'visiting' (True) or 'visited' (False)
    result = []

    # Step 1: Build the graph
    for i in range(len(words) - 1):
        word1, word2 = words[i], words[i + 1]
        min_len = min(len(word1), len(word2))

        if len(word1) > len(word2) and word1[:min_len] == word2[:min_len]:
            return ""

        for j in range(min_len):
            if word1[j] != word2[j]:
                graph[word1[j]].add(word2[j])
                break

    # Step 2: DFS for topological sort
    def dfs(char):
        if char in visited:
            return visited[char]

        visited[char] = True  # Mark as visiting

        for neighbor in graph[char]:
            if dfs(neighbor):  # Cycle detected
```

```
            return True

        visited[char] = False  # Mark as visited
        result.append(char)
        return False

    # Visit all characters in the graph
    for char in {char for word in words for char in word}:
        if dfs(char):
            return ""  # Return empty string if cycle detected

    return "".join(result[::-1])
```

Explanation: We perform a DFS to construct the topological order of characters. If we encounter a cycle, we return an empty string.

Time complexity: *O(C)*, where *C* is the total number of characters in all words.

Space complexity: *O(C)* for the graph and recursion stack.

Dig deeper

How to think about this problem:

- **Topological sort and graph theory:** This problem is an excellent example of topological sorting. You must recognize that you are solving a *graph problem* where letters act as nodes and ordering constraints as edges.
- **Cycle detection:** Cycle detection is crucial in this problem. If there is a cycle in the graph (i.e., contradictory ordering constraints), the problem cannot be solved, and you must return an empty string.
- **BFS vs. DFS:** Both BFS and DFS are valid approaches. In an interview, you should be prepared to explain and implement both. DFS is more intuitive for many since it involves recursively visiting nodes, while BFS might be trickier but is a valid alternative.
- **Handling invalid input:** You must handle cases where one word is a prefix of another and the prefix is incorrectly ordered (e.g., "abc", "ab"). These cases should return an empty string since they violate the rules of the alien dictionary.

The edge cases to consider are as follows

- **Empty input**: If the input list is empty, return an empty string.
- **Single word**: If the input contains only one word, return all unique letters in that word.

   - **Example**: `["abc"]` → `"abc"`
- **Invalid prefix order**: If one word is a prefix of another but is longer, return an empty string.
   - **Example**: `["abc", "ab"]` → `""`

The key takeaways for interviews are as follows

- Recognize that this is a topological sort problem and explain your approach clearly.
- Be prepared to discuss both BFS and DFS approaches.
- Always check for cycles and invalid prefix order cases.
- Ensure you handle edge cases, such as empty input and single words.

Join our Discord space

SECTION 8

Advanced Topics and System Design

Introduction

In this final section of the book, we are exploring advanced topics and system design coding challenges. These types of problems often appear in high-level coding interviews for positions such as senior software engineers and technical leads. They require a deep understanding of Python's advanced features, data structures, and algorithms, and the ability to think in terms of *scalable system design*.

Here, we will tackle *complex coding challenges* focusing on real-world problems. We will start by implementing *advanced data structures* such as the **least recently used (LRU) cache** and **tries,** which are crucial for efficiently handling large datasets and optimizing memory use. You will learn how to solve problems that involve designing scalable systems, including a *Twitter clone,* a *URL shortener,* and a *message queue system.*

System design coding challenges are especially crucial for interviews, as they test not only your ability to write code but also your *problem-solving skills,* your understanding of *scalability,* and your ability to think about the architecture of large-scale systems.

Why these challenges matter: These advanced challenges test how well you can apply what you have learned throughout this book in more complex, *real-world scenarios.* You must consider *performance, efficiency,* and *scalability* while implementing your solutions. These problems require a *deep understanding* of Python's capabilities and will push you to think critically about the *best solutions.*

System design questions are often the most daunting part of technical interviews, especially for senior roles. The questions often focus on **architecting** efficient, scalable, and maintainable systems. Designing systems like a *Twitter clone* or *URL shortener* will test your ability to break down a large problem into manageable pieces and create an effective, optimized solution.

Objectives

You will learn the following:

- **Advanced data structures**: You will implement an LRU cache to efficiently manage memory and build a **trie** for fast prefix lookups in applications like autocomplete systems.
- **System design challenges**: You will design and implement real-world systems like a *message queue*, a *rate limiter*, and a *web crawler*. These challenges focus on *architecting solutions* that can scale to millions of users and handle large datasets.
- **Practical coding skills**: Each challenge will require you to *write clean, efficient code* and think about *time and space complexities*. You will practice balancing performance with readability, which is crucial in coding interviews.

Challenges ahead: These challenges are *advanced* and may take some time to grasp fully. Do not be discouraged if they seem difficult at first; the goal is to help you *think through complex problems* like an engineer. As you work through the problems, you will notice that they combine everything you have learned, from *data structures* to *algorithms* and *system design concepts*.

Each problem will be broken down into *easy-to-understand steps*, with multiple approaches when relevant. You will learn to explain your solutions effectively, a critical skill in coding interviews. Interviewers want to see that you can solve problems, understand the trade-offs involved, and reason about *scalability* and *performance*.

Preparing for your interview: By mastering the challenges in this section, you will be well-prepared for the *most challenging coding interviews* at top tech companies. These problems mimic the real-world scenarios you might face as a software engineer, where you need to design systems that can scale, manage large volumes of data, and handle complex performance issues.

Let us look at the first advanced coding challenge: *Implementing an LRU cache*. This common problem in interviews tests your ability to manage memory and implement an efficient caching mechanism.

Problem 91: Implement a least recently used (LRU) cache

Problem statement: Design and implement a data structure for an LRU cache. It should support the following operations:

- **get(key)**: Retrieve the value of the key if it exists in the cache; otherwise, return 1.
- **put(key, value)**: Insert or update the value if the key exists. When the cache reaches its capacity, it should invalidate the *least recently used* item before inserting a new one.

You are required to implement the LRU Cache with a fixed capacity. For example, if the cache size is 2 and we insert three items, the least recently used item will be removed from the cache.

Understanding the problem: The LRU cache is a commonly asked question in system design and algorithm interviews. It is used to keep track of the most recent data access and discard the least important data when the cache reaches its maximum capacity. You need to implement a data structure that supports constant-time *O(1)* operations for both retrieval and insertion.

Key points to note:

- **Cache**: A temporary storage mechanism that holds data for faster access.
- **Least recently used**: The cache removes the least accessed item when full.
- **Capacity**: The cache is limited in size. When new data is added beyond capacity, the oldest data must be evicted.

To implement this efficiently, we need a **doubly linked list** (to maintain the order of usage) and a **hash map** (for fast lookups).

Approach 1: Using a doubly linked list and a hash map

The step-by-step explanation is as follows:

1. **Doubly linked list:**
   a. The most recently accessed data is moved to the front.
   b. The least recently accessed data is at the end.
   c. We can remove items from the back (least recently used) and add new items to the front efficiently.
2. **Hash map:** The hash map will store key-value pairs, allowing us to access the data in constant time *O(1)*.
3. **Operations:**
   a. **Get(key):**
      i. Check if the key exists in the cache (hash map).
      ii. If it exists, move the node to the front (most recently used).
      iii. Return the value.
      iv. If the key does not exist, return 1.

b. **Put(key, value):**

   i. If the key already exists, update its value and move it to the front (most recently used).

   ii. If the key does not exist, insert it at the front.

   iii. If the cache is at capacity, remove the least recently used item (node at the end of the doubly linked list) before inserting the new item.

Code implementation:

```
class Node:
    def __init__(self, key=None, value=None):
        self.key = key
        self.value = value
        self.prev = None
        self.next = None

class LRUCache:
    def __init__(self, capacity: int):
        self.capacity = capacity
        self.cache = {}  # Hash map to store key and node reference
        self.head = Node()  # Dummy head node for doubly linked list
        self.tail = Node()  # Dummy tail node for doubly linked list
        self.head.next = self.tail
        self.tail.prev = self.head

    def _remove(self, node):
        """Helper function to remove a node from the linked list."""
        prev_node = node.prev
        next_node = node.next
        prev_node.next = next_node
        next_node.prev = prev_node

    def _add_to_front(self, node):
        """Helper function to add a node to the front (right after head)."""
        node.prev = self.head
        node.next = self.head.next
        self.head.next.prev = node
        self.head.next = node

    def get(self, key: int) -> int:
        if key in self.cache:
            node = self.cache[key]
            self._remove(node)  # Move node to front as it's recently used
            self._add_to_front(node)
```

```
            return node.value
        return -1

    def put(self, key: int, value: int) -> None:
        if key in self.cache:
            node = self.cache[key]
            node.value = value
            self._remove(node)
            self._add_to_front(node)
        else:
            if len(self.cache) >= self.capacity:
                # Remove least recently used node
                lru_node = self.tail.prev
                self._remove(lru_node)
                del self.cache[lru_node.key]
            new_node = Node(key, value)
            self._add_to_front(new_node)
            self.cache[key] = new_node
```

The explanation of the code is as follows:

- **Node class**: Defines each node in the doubly linked list, which holds the key and value, and references to the previous and next nodes.
- **LRUCache class**:
  - **init**: Initializes the cache, capacity, and doubly linked list with dummy head and tail nodes.
  - **get**: Checks if the key exists, retrieves its value, moves the node to the front (most recently used), and returns the value.
  - **put**: Adds a new key-value pair to the cache. If the cache is full, the least recently used node is evicted from the cache.
- **_remove and _add_to_front**: Helper methods to manage the doubly linked list, allowing nodes to be efficiently moved to the front or removed from the back.

The time and space complexity are explained as follows:

- **Time complexity:**
  - **get(key)**: *O(1)* because hash map lookups and doubly linked list updates are done in constant time.
  - **put(key, value)**: *O(1)* for the same reason as above.
- **Space complexity:** *O(n)*, where *n* is the capacity of the cache. We store up to *n* key-value pairs in the hash map and *n* nodes in the doubly linked list.

Dig deeper

The interview insights are as follows:

- **Data structures**: This problem combines two crucial data structures: hash maps for fast lookups and doubly linked lists for maintaining the order of usage. Explaining why both are needed will impress interviewers.
- **Edge cases**:
    - Handle cases where the cache is empty.
    - Handle when the cache reaches full capacity and must evict items.
    - Ensure that updates to existing keys refresh their status to "most recently used."
- **Alternative approaches**: Be prepared to discuss trade-offs between other potential data structures or solutions.

The edge cases to consider are as follows:

- **Cache miss**: If a key does not exist in the cache, get should return -1.
- **Cache full**: When adding a new item and the cache is at capacity, remove the least recently used item.
- **Update existing key**: If put is called with an existing key, it should update the value and move the key to the front.

The key takeaways for interviews are as follows:

- Demonstrate your ability to work with *multiple data structures*.
- Show your understanding of how to maintain *constant time complexity* for operations like **get** and **put**.
- Discuss how the cache system is used in *real-world applications* (e.g., databases, web browsers, etc.).

Problem 92: Design a Twitter clone (system design)

Problem statement: Design a simplified version of *Twitter* that supports the following key features:

1. **Post tweets**: Users can post tweets (short messages).
2. **Follow/unfollow users**: Users can follow and unfollow other users.
3. **View timeline**: A user can view a timeline that shows the recent tweets from the users they follow, in reverse chronological order.
4. **Like tweets**: Users can like tweets.

5. **Scalability**: The system should be scalable to support millions of users and tweets.

Understanding the problem: This is a classic *system design interview question* that tests your ability to build a social media platform similar to Twitter. We will focus on creating a system that efficiently handles large-scale user interactions, such as posting and viewing tweets, and managing user followings.

Let us break it down into components and discuss how to design a scalable architecture for this system.

The step-by-step approach is as follows:

1. **User Interface (UI):**
    a. **The UI allows users to interact with the platform**: Post tweets, follow/unfollow users, view their timeline, and like tweets.
    b. **Frontend technologies**: You could use *React* or *Vue.js* to build a responsive and interactive user interface.
2. **Backend (API Services):**
    a. The backend will handle requests for posting tweets, following/unfollowing users, retrieving timelines, and other actions.
    b. We will use RESTful APIs to design endpoints for the required functionalities (e.g., /postTweet, /follow, /timeline, etc.).
    c. **Backend technologies**: *Python (Flask, Django)* or *Node.js* can be used to build the backend API.
3. **Database design:**
    a. The database will store information about users, tweets, followers, and likes.
    b. **Data models**:
        i. **User table**: Contains user information (`user_id`, `username`, etc.).
        ii. **Tweet table**: Stores tweets (`tweet_id`, `user_id`, `timestamp`, `content`).
        iii. **Follow table**: Tracks who follows whom (`follower_id`, `followee_id`).
        iv. **Likes table**: Tracks which users liked which tweets (`user_id`, `tweet_id`).
    c. **Database technology**: SQL (PostgreSQL) or NoSQL (MongoDB).
4. **Timeline generation:**
    a. The timeline shows tweets from the users a person follows, sorted in reverse chronological order (newest first).
    b. **Fan-out on write**: When a user posts a tweet, the tweet is pushed to the timelines of all their followers.

   c. **Fan-out on read**: Alternatively, we can pull tweets from all the people the user follows when they request their timeline.

   d. **Optimization**: Store the recent tweets in a Redis cache for fast retrieval, especially for users with many followers.

5. **Caching:** For scalability, we can cache frequently accessed data (e.g., user profiles, popular tweets, timelines) using *Redis* or *Memcached* to reduce the load on the database.

6. **Load balancing:**

   a. Use **load balancers** to distribute traffic across multiple servers, ensuring that the system can handle a large number of users.

   b. **Content Delivery Networks (CDNs)**: Use CDNs to cache static content (like user profile images) close to users geographically for faster load times.

7. **Follow/unfollow mechanism:**

   a. A user can follow or unfollow others. This updates the Follow table, and when a user unfollows someone, their future tweets should no longer appear in the timeline.

   b. This operation should be performed efficiently with the help of database indexing and caching strategies.

8. **Likes feature:**

   a. Users can like tweets, and the system must store and display the number of likes for each tweet.

   b. The Likes table will track who liked which tweet, and you can use a counter for each tweet to display the number of likes.

The system design overview is as follows:

- **Posting a Tweet**
  - **API**: `/postTweet`
    - **Input**: `user_id`, `tweet_content`
    - **Process**: When a user posts a tweet, the system generates a new tweet ID and stores the tweet in the database.
    - **Fan-out**: The tweet is fanned out to the timelines of all followers (or stored for later retrieval based on timeline requests).
- **Follow/unfollow users:**
  - **API**: `/follow` and `/unfollow`
    - **Input**: `follower_id`, `followee_id`
    - **Process**: When a user follows or unfollows someone, update the Follow table in the database.

    - **Timeline update**: If a user unfollows another user, tweets from the unfollowed user should be removed from their timeline.

- **View timeline: API**: **`/timeline`**
  - **Input**: **`user_id`**
  - **Process**: Fetch the most recent tweets from the users the user follows. This can be done through either:
    - **Fan-out on write**: Tweets are pushed to followers' timelines when posted.
    - **Fan-out on read**: Tweets are pulled from followed users when a user requests their timeline.
  - **Caching**: Recent tweets can be cached for faster retrieval.
- **Like a tweet**
  - **API**: **`/likeTweet`**
    - **Input**: **`user_id`**, **`tweet_id`**
    - **Process**: Record the user's likes in the Likes table and update the like counter for the tweet.

Code example for posting and viewing a tweet

Here is an example of how the basic functionalities might look in Python using Flask:

```
from flask import Flask, request, jsonify
from datetime import datetime
from collections import defaultdict

app = Flask(__name__)

# In-memory storage (for simplicity)
users = {}  # user_id: username
tweets = defaultdict(list)  # user_id: list of tweets
follows = defaultdict(set)  # user_id: set of followees
timelines = defaultdict(list)  # user_id: list of recent tweets in timeline

# API to post a tweet
@app.route('/postTweet', methods=['POST'])
def post_tweet():
    user_id = request.json['user_id']
    content = request.json['content']
    tweet_id = len(tweets[user_id]) + 1
    timestamp = datetime.now()
    tweet = {'tweet_id': tweet_id, 'content': content, 'timestamp': timestamp}
```

```
    # Store tweet for the user
    tweets[user_id].append(tweet)

    # Fan-out to followers
    for follower in follows[user_id]:
        timelines[follower].append(tweet)

    return jsonify({"message": "Tweet posted successfully!"})

# API to view timeline
@app.route('/timeline', methods=['GET'])
def view_timeline():
    user_id = request.args.get('user_id')
    return jsonify({"timeline": timelines[user_id]})

# API to follow a user
@app.route('/follow', methods=['POST'])
def follow_user():
    user_id = request.json['user_id']
    followee_id = request.json['followee_id']
    follows[user_id].add(followee_id)
    return jsonify({"message": f"You are now following user {followee_id}!"})

# API to unfollow a user
@app.route('/unfollow', methods=['POST'])
def unfollow_user():
    user_id = request.json['user_id']
    followee_id = request.json['followee_id']
    if followee_id in follows[user_id]:
        follows[user_id].remove(followee_id)
        return jsonify({"message": f"You have unfollowed user {followee_
id}."})
    return jsonify({"message": f"You are not following user {followee_id}."})

if __name__ == "__main__":
    app.run(debug=True)
```

How to think about this problem:

- **Scalability:** Make sure to discuss how your system would handle millions of users and tweets. Use caching, load balancing, and database sharding for scalability.
- **Consistency**: How will your system ensure that users always see the latest tweets from those they follow? What happens if there is a delay in propagating tweets?
- **Real-time:** In a real-world scenario, Twitter works in real-time. Tweets should appear in users' timelines immediately after being posted.

- **Fault tolerance:** Discuss how you would ensure that the system can recover from failures or crashes without data loss.
- **Security:** Make sure that users cannot access or manipulate each other's data (e.g., tweets, followers).

The edge cases to consider are as follows:

- **What happens if a user posts a tweet while offline?**
    - You might need to handle offline operations and syncing.
- **What if a user has millions of followers?**
    - Fanning out to millions of timelines could be inefficient. You may need to implement lazy loading or caching for such users.
- **What happens if a user unfollows another user?**
    - How do you efficiently remove tweets from their timeline?

Problem 93: Design a URL shortener (system design)

Problem statement: You are tasked with designing a URL shortener, similar to services like **http://bit.ly/** or **TinyURL**. The system should take a long URL and generate a shortened URL. Additionally, when a user visits the shortened URL, they should be redirected to the original URL.

The system should support the following core features:

- **Shorten URL**: Given a long URL, return a shorter, unique URL.
- **Redirect to original URL**: When someone visits the shortened URL, they should be redirected to the original URL.
- **Scalability**: The system should handle millions of URL shortening requests and redirections.

Understanding the problem: The URL shortener is a popular system design question that tests your ability to handle mapping large amounts of data while ensuring scalability and low latency. The basic idea is to convert long URLs into shorter ones that are easier to share while still being able to map back to the original long URL.

Let us break down the problem:

- **Input**: A long URL (e.g., *https://www.example.com/some/long/path*).
- **Output**: A short URL (e.g., *https://short.ly/abc123*).
- **Scalability**: The system should support millions of users and be able to shorten millions of URLs without collisions (two long URLs mapping to the same short URL).

The step-by-step approach is as follows:

1. **Database design:**
    a. The primary task is to store the mapping between long URLs and their shortened versions.
    b. **Data models**:
        i. **URL table**: Contains fields for the short URL and the original long URL.
        ii. Example: *short_url: abc123, long_url: <https://www.example.com/some/long/path>*.
    c. You can use a relational database like *PostgreSQL* or a NoSQL database like *MongoDB* for fast reads and writes.
2. **Encoding mechanism:**
    a. To convert long URLs into short URLs, we need a mechanism to generate a unique short string (like abc123).
    b. Common methods include:
        i. **Base62 encoding**: A common technique where a unique ID is converted into a string using 62 characters (a-z, A-Z, 0-9). This allows us to represent a large number of unique URLs using fewer characters.
        ii. **Hashing**: Another approach is to use a hash function (like MD5 or SHA256) on the long URL and truncate the result to generate a short code. Hashing functions can create unique but deterministic short URLs.
3. **Short URL generation:**
    a. When a user requests to shorten a URL, the system generates a unique short code (e.g., abc123) using Base62 encoding or a hash function.
    b. The long URL is stored in the database, and the short code is returned to the user as the shortened URL.
4. **Redirection mechanism:**
    a. When a user visits the shortened URL (e.g., *https://short.ly/abc123*), the system looks up the corresponding long URL in the database and redirects the user to that URL.
    b. To ensure fast redirection, you can cache popular URLs using *Redis* or *Memcached*.
5. **Handling collisions:**
    a. One issue with hashing is that collisions can occur (i.e., two different URLs might generate the same short code). To handle this:
        i. You can check the database before assigning a short code to ensure there is no collision.

   ii. Alternatively, you can append random characters or numbers to the short code to avoid collisions.

6. **Scalability considerations:**
   a. **Sharding**: As the system grows, you may need to shard the database to handle a large number of URL mappings.
   b. **Caching**: Use **caching** (e.g., Redis) for frequently accessed short URLs to reduce the load on the database and improve response times.
   c. **Load balancing**: Implement load balancing to distribute traffic evenly across servers.

The system design overview is as follows:

- **Shorten a URL: API: `/shorten`**
  - **Input**: A long URL (e.g., *https://www.example.com/some/long/path*).
  - **Output**: A shortened URL (e.g., *https://short.ly/abc123*).
  - **Process**:
    - Generate a unique short code using Base62 encoding or a hashing function.
    - Store the mapping of the short URL and the long URL in the database.
    - Return the shortened URL to the user.
- **Redirect to original URL: API: `/abc123`**:
  - **Input**: A short URL (e.g., *https://short.ly/abc123*).
  - **Output**: Redirect to the long URL.
  - **Process**:
    - Retrieve the long URL from the database using the short code.
    - Redirect the user to the long URL.

Code example for shortening and redirecting URLs

Here is an example of how the basic functionalities might look in Python using Flask:

```
from flask import Flask, request, redirect, jsonify
import base64
import hashlib
import random

app = Flask(__name__)

# In-memory storage (for simplicity)
url_map = {}  # short_url: long_url
```

```
base_url = "<https://short.ly/>"

# Function to generate a short URL
def generate_short_url(long_url):
    # Use a hashing algorithm (e.g., MD5) and Base64 encode it
    hash_object = hashlib.md5(long_url.encode())
    short_url = base64.urlsafe_b64encode(hash_object.digest()[:6]).
decode('utf-8')
    return short_url

# API to shorten the URL
@app.route('/shorten', methods=['POST'])
def shorten_url():
    long_url = request.json['long_url']

    # Check if the URL is already shortened
    for short, long in url_map.items():
        if long == long_url:
            return jsonify({'short_url': base_url + short})

    # Generate a short URL
    short_url = generate_short_url(long_url)

    # Store the mapping
    url_map[short_url] = long_url

    return jsonify({'short_url': base_url + short_url})

# API to redirect to the original URL
@app.route('/<short_url>')
def redirect_to_long_url(short_url):
    long_url = url_map.get(short_url)
    if long_url:
        return redirect(long_url)
    else:
        return jsonify({'error': 'Short URL not found'}), 404

if __name__ == "__main__":
    app.run(debug=True)
```

How to think about this problem:

- **Efficiency:** Ensure that the process of shortening and retrieving URLs is fast. Consider the use of caching for frequently accessed URLs to reduce database load.
- **Scaling:** Think about how the system will scale as the number of users grows. The system should be able to handle millions of short URLs efficiently without collisions.

- **Data expiry:** URLs may not need to live forever. You can implement expiration dates for URLs, where shortened URLs expire after a certain period of inactivity to reduce the database size.

The edge cases to consider are as follows:

- **Duplicate URLs:** If a user repeatedly submits the same long URL, return the same short URL instead of generating a new one.
- **URL validity:** You can include validation to ensure that the input is a valid URL before shortening it.
- **Expired URLs:** If your system supports expiring URLs, make sure to handle requests for expired URLs gracefully (e.g., returning a "URL expired" message).

Problem 94: Implement a trie (prefix tree)

Problem statement: A trie (pronounced as "try") is a special data structure used to store strings. Unlike a binary tree, where nodes contain data, Trie nodes store individual characters. Tries are often used for searching words in dictionaries, autocomplete systems, and spell checkers.

Your task is to implement a trie that supports the following operations:

- **Insert**: Insert a word into the trie.
- **Search**: Search if a word exists in the trie.
- **StartsWith**: Return True if there is any word in the trie that starts with the given prefix.

Understanding the problem: The trie (also known as a prefix tree) is an efficient tree-like data structure commonly used for searching strings and their prefixes. Each node represents a single character, and words are formed by traversing down from the root node to a leaf node. The trie structure is particularly useful for problems where many words share common prefixes, like autocomplete.

Let us break down the problem:

- **Insert operation:**
  - We need to add a word to the trie, inserting one character at a time.
  - If the character already exists in the trie, we move to the next character.
  - If the character does not exist, we create a new node for it.
- **Search operation:**
  - To search for a word, we traverse the trie following the characters in the word.
  - If we find all characters and reach the end of the word, we return True.
  - If any character is missing, we return False.
- **StartsWith operation:** Similar to the search operation, but instead of checking for the entire word, we return True if the given prefix exists in the trie.

The step-by-step explanation is as follows:

1. **Trie node structure:**
   a. Each trie node contains a dictionary (or array) that stores references to its child nodes, representing the next possible characters.
   b. Additionally, a Boolean flag (**`is_end_of_word`**) is used to mark the end of a word.
2. **Insert operation:**
   a. Start at the root node.
   b. For each character in the word, check if the character exists in the current node's children. If not, create a new node for that character.
   c. After inserting all characters, mark the last node with **`is_end_of_word = True`**.
3. **Search operation:**
   a. Start at the root node.
   b. For each character in the word, move to the child node corresponding to that character. If the character does not exist, return False.
   c. If all characters are found, return True only if the last node marks the end of the word.
4. **StartsWith operation:** Similar to the search operation, but does not require checking **`is_end_of_word`**. Return True if all characters in the prefix are found.

Code example: Implementing a trie:

Here is how you can implement a trie in Python:

```
class TrieNode:
    def __init__(self):
        self.children = {}  # Dictionary to store child nodes
        self.is_end_of_word = False  # Marks the end of a word

class Trie:
    def __init__(self):
        self.root = TrieNode()  # Root node of the Trie

    def insert(self, word):
        current_node = self.root
        for char in word:
            if char not in current_node.children:
                current_node.children[char] = TrieNode()  # Create new node if
char doesn't exist
            current_node = current_node.children[char] # Move to the next
node
```

```
        current_node.is_end_of_word = True  # Mark the end of the word

    def search(self, word):
        current_node = self.root
        for char in word:
            if char not in current_node.children:
                return False  # Word not found
            current_node = current_node.children[char]
        return current_node.is_end_of_word  # Check if it's the end of the 
word

    def starts_with(self, prefix):
        current_node = self.root
        for char in prefix:
            if char not in current_node.children:
                return False  # Prefix not found
            current_node = current_node.children[char]
        return True  # Prefix exists
```

The time and space complexity analysis is as follows:

- **Insert operation:**
  - **Time complexity**: *O(n)*, where *n* is the length of the word being inserted. We need to traverse or create nodes for each character in the word.
  - **Space complexity**: *O(n)*, since each word may introduce new nodes for characters not seen before.
- **Search operation:**
  - **Time complexity**: *O(n)*, where *n* is the length of the word being searched.
  - **Space complexity**: *O(1)*, since no additional space is needed beyond the input word.
- **StartsWith operation:**
  - **Time complexity**: *O(n)*, where *n* is the length of the prefix.
  - **Space complexity**: *O(1)*, as we are not storing any additional data.

Approach 2: Optimized with arrays (Optional)

In the above solution, we used a dictionary to store children nodes. However, if the characters are restricted to lowercase letters (a-z), we can optimize the space usage by using an array of size 26 to store child references.

Code example:

```
class TrieNode:
    def __init__(self):
        self.children = [None] * 26  # Array of size 26 for lowercase letters
        self.is_end_of_word = False

class Trie:
    def __init__(self):
        self.root = TrieNode()

    def _char_to_index(self, char):
        return ord(char) - ord('a')  # Convert character to index (0-25)

    def insert(self, word):
        current_node = self.root
        for char in word:
            index = self._char_to_index(char)
            if current_node.children[index] is None:
                current_node.children[index] = TrieNode()
            current_node = current_node.children[index]
        current_node.is_end_of_word = True

    def search(self, word):
        current_node = self.root
        for char in word:
            index = self._char_to_index(char)
            if current_node.children[index] is None:
                return False
            current_node = current_node.children[index]
        return current_node.is_end_of_word

    def starts_with(self, prefix):
        current_node = self.root
        for char in prefix:
            index = self._char_to_index(char)
            if current_node.children[index] is None:
                return False
            current_node = current_node.children[index]
        return True
```

This version is more memory-efficient if we know the input is restricted to lowercase English letters.

How to think about this problem:

- **Clarify requirements:**
    - Ask whether the trie should be case-sensitive or case-insensitive.

  - Confirm if you are allowed to use a dictionary, or if an array-based solution is preferred (e.g., for optimizing space).

- **Explain time and space complexity:** Be sure to discuss both the time and space complexity of each operation. Tries are efficient for prefix-based searches, but the space complexity can grow significantly if many distinct characters are involved.
- **Edge cases to consider:** What happens if the word or prefix is an empty string? Ensure your solution handles these cases gracefully.
- **Explain alternative approaches:** While a trie is the optimal structure for prefix searches, you can mention that hash maps or sets could also solve the problem for specific use cases, though they would not be as efficient for prefix searches.

The edge cases to consider are as follows:

- **Empty string**: Handle cases where the input word or prefix is empty. The expected behavior should be clearly defined.
  - **Example**: `search("")` or `starts_with("")`.
- **Words with shared prefixes**: Ensure your trie can handle multiple words with common prefixes (e.g., "apple" and "app").
  - **Example**: Inserting "app" and "apple" should still allow both to be searchable independently.
- **Case sensitivity**: If the problem is case-sensitive, ensure that uppercase and lowercase letters are treated differently.
  - **Example**: Searching for "Apple" should not match "apple" if case-sensitive.

The key takeaways for interviews are as follows:

- **Why tries matter**: Tries are excellent for problems involving word searches, prefixes, and autocompletion. They provide an efficient solution for storing and searching in a large set of strings.
- **Handle edge cases**: Always consider edge cases like empty strings, prefixes of other words, and case sensitivity.
- **Explain optimizations**: Discuss how an array-based implementation can optimize space if the input set is limited to lowercase English letters.
- **Communicate clearly**: In an interview, it is essential to walk the interviewer through your thought process, explain the time and space complexity, and mention alternative approaches.

Problem 95: Design a message queue (system design)

Problem statement: Design and implement a basic message queue that allows multiple producers to send messages and multiple consumers to receive messages asynchronously. The queue should support operations like enqueue (send message) and dequeue (receive message), and ensure that each message is processed only once. Additionally, the system should handle concurrency efficiently.

Understanding the problem: Message queues are fundamental components in distributed systems. They decouple services, allowing them to communicate asynchronously and at their own pace. By introducing a message queue between services, you create a buffer that enables producers and consumers to operate independently. This system ensures reliable communication, especially in high-traffic or fault-tolerant systems.

The key concepts are as follows:

- **Producer**: A service that sends a message (enqueue).
- **Consumer**: A service that receives a message (dequeue).
- **Asynchronous communication**: The producer does not wait for the consumer to receive the message. Messages are processed in the background.
- **Concurrency**: Multiple producers and consumers can interact with the queue simultaneously.

The step-by-step explanation is as follows:

1. **Data structure:** You can use a simple queue (**First In, First Out** (**FIFO**)) to store messages. A list or deque from Python's collections module would be suitable for this task.
2. **Operations:**
    a. **Enqueue**: Add a message to the queue.
    b. **Dequeue**: Remove and return the message at the front of the queue for processing.
3. **Concurrency handling:** Multiple producers and consumers might access the queue simultaneously. You can handle this using thread locks (`threading.Lock` in Python) to ensure that no two operations (enqueue or dequeue) conflict.
4. **Message durability:** For real-world systems, message queues need to ensure message durability. This means storing the message reliably until it is consumed. In this example, we will assume the queue is in memory, but a more advanced system would use a database or persistent storage.

Code example:

```
import threading
from collections import deque

class MessageQueue:
    def __init__(self):
        self.queue = deque()  # FIFO queue
        self.lock = threading.Lock()  # Lock for concurrency

    def enqueue(self, message):
        with self.lock:  # Ensure exclusive access
            self.queue.append(message)
            print(f"Message Enqueued: {message}")

    def dequeue(self):
        with self.lock:  # Ensure exclusive access
            if len(self.queue) == 0:
                print("Queue is empty!")
                return None
            message = self.queue.popleft()  # Get the front message
            print(f"Message Dequeued: {message}")
            return message

# Example usage
queue = MessageQueue()

# Simulate multiple producers and consumers using threads
producer_thread = threading.Thread(target=queue.enqueue, args=("Hello, World!",))
consumer_thread = threading.Thread(target=queue.dequeue)

producer_thread.start()
consumer_thread.start()

producer_thread.join()
consumer_thread.join()
```

The explanation is as follows:

- The **MessageQueue** class encapsulates a basic FIFO queue using Python's deque.
- The enqueue method adds a message to the queue, and the dequeue method removes the oldest message.
- Thread locks are used to ensure that no two threads can modify the queue simultaneously, ensuring thread safety.

The time complexity is as follows:

- **Enqueue**: *O(1)* – Adding a message to the end of a deque is constant time.
- **Dequeue**: *O(1)* – Removing a message from the front of a deque is also constant time.

Approach 2: Advanced system design considerations

In a more complex scenario, the message queue needs to be distributed and durable. This might involve:

1. **Distributed message queues**: Systems like *Kafka* and *RabbitMQ* provide distributed, fault-tolerant message queuing. These systems manage concurrency, message durability, and high availability.
2. **Scaling producers and consumers**: In real-world applications, there are often many producers and consumers. A distributed message queue can scale horizontally to handle a higher volume of messages.
3. **Persistence**: Storing messages in a database ensures durability. In the event of a system crash, no messages are lost. For Python, you could use a relational database (like PostgreSQL) or a NoSQL database (like Redis) to store messages.

Example: Using Redis for message queuing

If durability is a concern, a solution could involve using a persistent storage system like Redis, which offers built-in support for lists (used as queues) and is optimized for speed.

Code example:

```
import redis

# Create a Redis connection
r = redis.Redis()

# Enqueue operation
def enqueue(message):
    r.rpush('message_queue', message)
    print(f»Message Enqueued: {message}»)

# Dequeue operation
def dequeue():
    message = r.lpop('message_queue')
    if message:
        print(f"Message Dequeued: {message.decode()}")
    else:
        print("Queue is empty!")

# Example usage
```

```
enqueue("Hello, Redis!")
dequeue()
```

The explanation is as follows:

- Redis's **rpush** adds an element to the end of the list, and **lpop** removes an element from the front, implementing a simple queue.
- Redis ensures message persistence, and you can use it across multiple producers and consumers on different machines.

The time complexity is as follows:

- **Enqueue**: *O(1)* – Adding an element to the list is constant time.
- **Dequeue**: *O(1)* – Removing an element from the list is constant time.

The edge cases to consider are as follows:

- **Empty queue**: Ensure the system handles cases where the queue is empty and a consumer tries to dequeue. In our implementation, the dequeue method returns None and prints a message if the queue is empty.
- **Concurrency issues**: If multiple producers and consumers are interacting with the queue simultaneously, locking mechanisms (like **threading.Lock**) or database transactions should ensure that operations do not conflict.
- **Persistence**: In a real-world scenario, you need to ensure that messages are not lost if the system crashes. Persistent message queues (e.g., Redis, Kafka) provide solutions for this.

The key takeaways for interviews are as follows:

- **Understanding message queues:** Message queues are used to decouple producers and consumers and ensure asynchronous communication between services. They are widely used in distributed systems for task scheduling, notifications, and more.
- **Concurrency and thread safety:** In a coding interview, understanding how to handle multiple threads and processes is essential. Make sure to explain how thread locks work and why they are necessary in this case.
- **Scaling considerations:** Discuss how a distributed message queue can handle more significant workloads and why systems like Kafka or RabbitMQ are preferred for high-scale systems.

Problem 96: Design a rate limiter (system design)

Problem statement: Design a rate-limiting system that restricts the number of requests a user can make to an API or service over a specific period. The system should prevent abuse, ensuring that no user can exceed a predefined limit of requests per minute, hour, or day. Implement rate-limiting using Python.

Understanding the problem: Rate limiting is a crucial technique for managing traffic to web services. It ensures that users do not overload your API or service by making excessive requests. In interviews, you may be asked to design and implement a rate limiter as part of a system design question.

The challenge here is to handle multiple users concurrently while ensuring that each user abides by the rate limits imposed.

The key concepts are as follows:

- **Request limit**: A maximum number of requests allowed within a specific time window (e.g., 100 requests per minute).
- **Time window**: The period during which the rate limit applies (e.g., 1 minute, 1 hour).
- **Sliding window**: A common approach to rate limiting, where requests are tracked over a rolling time window rather than fixed intervals.
- **User identification**: Each user should have a unique identifier to track their request count.

The step-by-step explanation is as follows:

1. **Data structure:** A dictionary (**`requests_log`**) where the key is the user ID, and the value is a list of timestamps representing when the user made requests.
2. **Operations:**
    a. **Track requests**: When a request comes in, add its timestamp to the list for that user.
    b. **Check rate limit**: Before processing a request, count how many requests the user has made in the current time window. If they exceed the limit, deny the request.
3. **Concurrency handling:** Use a thread-safe structure or locking mechanism if handling requests from multiple users simultaneously.

Code example: Sliding window approach:

```
import time
from collections import deque

class RateLimiter:
    def __init__(self, limit, time_window):
        self.limit = limit  # Maximum number of requests
        self.time_window = time_window  # Time window in seconds
        self.requests_log = {}  # Dictionary to store user requests
```

```
    def allow_request(self, user_id):
        current_time = time.time()

        # Initialize request log for the user if not present
        if user_id not in self.requests_log:
            self.requests_log[user_id] = deque()

        # Clean up old requests outside the current time window
        while self.requests_log[user_id] and self.requests_log[user_id][0] <
current_time - self.time_window:
            self.requests_log[user_id].popleft()

        # Check if the user has reached the request limit
        if len(self.requests_log[user_id]) < self.limit:
            # Allow the request and log the timestamp
            self.requests_log[user_id].append(current_time)
            print(f"Request allowed for user {user_id}.")
            return True
        else:
            # Deny the request
            print(f"Request denied for user {user_id}. Rate limit exceeded.")
            return False

# Example usage
limiter = RateLimiter(limit=5, time_window=60)  # 5 requests per minute

# Simulate user requests
user_id = "user123"
for i in range(7):
    limiter.allow_request(user_id)
    time.sleep(10)  # Simulate a delay between requests
```

The explanation is as follows:

- The **RateLimiter** class tracks the number of requests each user makes using a deque (double-ended queue). Each time a request comes in, the system checks if the user has exceeded the limit within the time window.
- Old requests that fall outside the time window are automatically removed to ensure the log stays up-to-date.
- The **allow_request** method either accepts or denies the request based on the current state of the user's request log.

The time complexity is as follows:

- **Enqueue request**: *O(1)* – Adding a timestamp to the deque is constant time.

- **Cleanup requests**: *O(n)* – Removing outdated requests from the deque requires scanning the timestamps, which takes linear time in the worst case.

Approach 2: Token bucket algorithm

The **token bucket** algorithm is another popular method for rate-limiting. It allows for bursts of traffic, where users can make several requests quickly as long as they have not exceeded the overall rate limit.

1. **Tokens**: The system generates tokens at a fixed rate (e.g., 1 token per second).
2. **Request handling**: Each request consumes a token. If no tokens are available, the request is denied.
3. **Bucket size**: The bucket holds a maximum number of tokens, representing the maximum burst capacity.

Code example: Token bucket:

```
import time

class TokenBucket:
    def __init__(self, capacity, refill_rate):
        self.capacity = capacity  # Max number of tokens
        self.tokens = capacity  # Current number of tokens
        self.refill_rate = refill_rate  # Tokens added per second
        self.last_refill_time = time.time()  # Last refill timestamp

    def allow_request(self):
        current_time = time.time()

        # Refill tokens based on time passed since last refill
        time_passed = current_time - self.last_refill_time
        refill_tokens = time_passed * self.refill_rate
        self.tokens = min(self.capacity, self.tokens + refill_tokens)
        self.last_refill_time = current_time

        if self.tokens >= 1:
            self.tokens -= 1
            print("Request allowed.")
            return True
        else:
            print("Request denied. No tokens available.")
            return False

# Example usage
bucket = TokenBucket(capacity=5, refill_rate=1)  # 5 tokens max, 1 token per
second
```

```
# Simulate user requests
for i in range(7):
    bucket.allow_request()
    time.sleep(0.5)  # Simulate delay between requests
```

The explanation is as follows:

- The **`TokenBucket`** class simulates a bucket of tokens that refills at a fixed rate. Each time a request is made, the system checks if tokens are available.
- If tokens are available, the request is allowed, and a token is consumed. If not, the request is denied.

The time complexity is explained as follows:

- **Allow request**: *O(1)* – Token checking and updating are constant time.

Advanced considerations for rate limiting

In a real-world scenario, rate limiting is implemented at a much larger scale and often requires additional features like:

- **Distributed rate limiting**: In microservice architectures, multiple servers may need to share rate-limiting information. Distributed databases like Redis can be used to store and sync rate-limiting data across multiple servers.
- **Per-API rate limiting**: Different APIs may have different rate limits. For example, a login API might be restricted more than a public API. Implementing a per-API rate limiter ensures that each endpoint has a unique limit.
- **Dynamic rate limits**: Some services offer dynamic rate limits based on the user's subscription plan or the time of day.

The edge cases to consider are as follows:

- **Multiple users**: Ensure that rate limiting works correctly for multiple users. Each user should have their own limit, tracked independently of other users.
- **System load**: High traffic to the rate-limiting system itself can cause bottlenecks. Consider how the system scales and maintains performance under load.
- **Sliding time windows**: The system should properly handle rolling or sliding windows, ensuring that requests made just before a window ends are treated fairly.

The key takeaways for interviews are as follows:

- **Why rate limiting:** Rate limiting prevents abuse and ensures fair usage of APIs and services. It is widely used in web applications and distributed systems to maintain stability.

- **Sliding window vs. token bucket:** Be ready to explain the differences between common rate-limiting algorithms like sliding window and token bucket. Each has its advantages, depending on the use case.
- **Scaling considerations:** If you are designing a rate limiter for a large-scale system, explain how you would implement distributed rate limiting across multiple servers.

Problem 97: Implement a web crawler

Problem statement: Design and implement a simple web crawler in Python. The web crawler should start at a given URL, fetch the page content, and then extract and crawl any hyperlinks found on that page. The crawler should continue this process until a specified depth or limit is reached. Ensure the crawler handles duplicate links, avoids revisiting the same page, and efficiently follows the links.

Understanding the problem: A web crawler, also known as a spider, is a program that systematically navigates the web by following links from one page to another. Web crawlers are the backbone of search engines like Google, which use them to index the entire internet. The goal here is to build a basic version that fetches pages, extracts links, and follows them to a limited depth.

In a coding interview, implementing a web crawler tests your understanding of:

- **Network requests**: Fetching web pages.
- **Parsing HTML**: Extracting hyperlinks from page content.
- **Data structures**: Using queues, sets, and dictionaries to manage the crawling process efficiently.

The step-by-step explanation is as follows:

1. **Making web requests:** To start, the crawler needs to fetch the content of web pages. Python's requests library is perfect for this. It allows you to send HTTP requests and retrieve the page content in a simple way.
2. **Extracting hyperlinks:** Once a page is fetched, you need to extract all the hyperlinks (`<a>` tags) from the page's HTML. The **BeautifulSoup** library is ideal for parsing HTML and extracting data.
3. **Handling multiple pages:** To crawl multiple pages, we need to keep track of:
    a. **Pages already visited**: To avoid crawling the same page multiple times.
    b. **Pages to visit**: A queue of URLs to crawl.
    c. **Depth of crawl**: Limit how far the crawler goes (e.g., crawl only 2 levels deep).
4. **Prevent infinite loops:** Crawling the web can lead to infinite loops if we keep visiting the same pages. Using a set to store already visited URLs prevents this issue.

Code example: Simple web crawler:

```
import requests
from bs4 import BeautifulSoup
from collections import deque

class WebCrawler:
    def __init__(self, start_url, max_depth):
        self.start_url = start_url
        self.max_depth = max_depth
        self.visited = set()  # Track visited URLs
        self.to_visit = deque([(start_url, 0)])  # URLs to visit, along with 
their depth

    def crawl(self):
        while self.to_visit:
            url, depth = self.to_visit.popleft()

            if depth > self.max_depth:
                continue

            if url not in self.visited:
                self.visited.add(url)
                print(f"Crawling: {url}, Depth: {depth}")

                links = self.fetch_links(url)
                for link in links:
                    if link not in self.visited:
                        self.to_visit.append((link, depth + 1))

    def fetch_links(self, url):
        try:
            response = requests.get(url)
            response.raise_for_status()
            soup = BeautifulSoup(response.text, 'html.parser')
            links = [a.get('href') for a in soup.find_all('a', href=True)]
            return self.filter_links(links, url)
        except requests.RequestException as e:
            print(f"Failed to fetch {url}: {e}")
            return []

    def filter_links(self, links, base_url):
        # Normalize and filter valid links
        valid_links = []
        for link in links:
```

```
            if link.startswith('http'):
                valid_links.append(link)
            elif link.startswith('/'):
                valid_links.append(base_url + link)
        return valid_links

# Example usage:
crawler = WebCrawler(start_url='<https://example.com>', max_depth=2)
crawler.crawl()
```

The explanation is as follows:

- **WebCrawler class:**
  - **start_url:** The URL where the crawler begins.
  - **max_depth:** How deep the crawler should go.
  - **visited:** A set to track visited URLs.
  - **to_visit:** A queue of URLs to visit, initialized with the starting URL and a depth of 0.
- **crawl() method:**
  - Uses a BFS approach to crawl web pages up to the `max_depth`. For each page, it extracts the hyperlinks, filters them, and adds them to the queue if they have not been visited.
- **fetch_links() method:**
  - Fetches the HTML content of a page using the requests library.
  - Parses the page with BeautifulSoup and extracts all the hyperlinks (`<a>` tags).
- **filter_links() method:** Filters and normalizes the extracted links, ensuring they are valid URLs.

Approach 2: Multithreaded web crawler

To make the crawler more efficient, you can use multithreading to crawl multiple pages concurrently. This is particularly useful when crawling large websites, as it reduces the waiting time between network requests.

Code example: Multithreaded web crawler:

```
import requests
from bs4 import BeautifulSoup
from collections import deque
import threading
```

```
class MultithreadedWebCrawler:
    def __init__(self, start_url, max_depth, num_threads):
        self.start_url = start_url
        self.max_depth = max_depth
        self.visited = set()
        self.to_visit = deque([(start_url, 0)])
        self.num_threads = num_threads
        self.lock = threading.Lock()

    def crawl(self):
        threads = []
        for _ in range(self.num_threads):
            thread = threading.Thread(target=self.worker)
            threads.append(thread)
            thread.start()

        for thread in threads:
            thread.join()

    def worker(self):
        while True:
            with self.lock:
                if not self.to_visit:
                    break
                url, depth = self.to_visit.popleft()

            if depth <= self.max_depth and url not in self.visited:
                self.visited.add(url)
                print(f"Crawling: {url}, Depth: {depth}")
                links = self.fetch_links(url)
                with self.lock:
                    for link in links:
                        if link not in self.visited:
                            self.to_visit.append((link, depth + 1))

    def fetch_links(self, url):
        try:
            response = requests.get(url)
            response.raise_for_status()
            soup = BeautifulSoup(response.text, 'html.parser')
            links = [a.get('href') for a in soup.find_all('a', href=True)]
            return self.filter_links(links, url)
        except requests.RequestException as e:
```

```
            print(f"Failed to fetch {url}: {e}")
            return []

    def filter_links(self, links, base_url):
        valid_links = []
        for link in links:
            if link.startswith('http'):
                valid_links.append(link)
            elif link.startswith('/'):
                valid_links.append(base_url + link)
        return valid_links

# Example usage:
crawler = MultithreadedWebCrawler(start_url='<https://example.com>', max_
depth=2, num_threads=4)
crawler.crawl()
```

The explanation is as follows:

- **MultithreadedWebCrawler class:**
    - Similar to the first version, but uses multiple threads to crawl concurrently.
    - The **worker()** method is run by each thread, fetching and processing pages concurrently.
- **Concurrency handling:** A **lock** is used to synchronize access to shared resources like the **to_visit** queue and the visited set, ensuring thread safety.

Approach 3: Distributed web crawler

In large-scale systems, web crawlers are often distributed across multiple machines to cover large portions of the web. Implementing a distributed crawler involves breaking down the workload and using a central system (like a message queue) to assign tasks to different machines.

This level of complexity goes beyond basic interviews but demonstrates your understanding of large-scale systems.

The edge cases to consider are as follows:

- **Dead links**: Pages that return 404 or other error codes.
- **Duplicate links**: Ensure that the crawler does not revisit the same page multiple times.
- **Infinite loops**: Some websites have circular links. Ensure the crawler does not get stuck in an infinite loop.
- **Rate limiting**: Many websites limit the number of requests you can make in a short time. Your crawler should respect such limits to avoid being blocked.

The key takeaways for interviews are as follows

- **Focus on efficiency:** Be ready to explain how your crawler minimizes redundant work by avoiding revisiting the same pages.
- **Scalability:** Discuss how to scale the crawler, either by adding threads (multithreading) or distributing the load across multiple machines.
- **Edge case handling:** Always mention how your solution handles dead links, circular links, and rate-limiting mechanisms.

Problem 98: Design a simple key-value store

Problem statement: Design a simple key-value store where you can store data in the form of a key (similar to a name or identifier) and a corresponding value (the data associated with the key). The store should support the following operations:

- **Put(key, value)**: Insert or update a key with the given value.
- **Get(key)**: Retrieve the value associated with the given key.
- **Delete(key)**: Remove the key-value pair from the store.
- **Keys()**: Return all the keys in the store.

Understanding the problem: A key-value store is one of the simplest forms of databases, often called a NoSQL database. The store holds a collection of key-value pairs, where each key is unique and maps to a value. Key-value stores are highly efficient for fast retrieval and updates, and they are widely used in applications like caching, session storage, and configuration management.

For this challenge, we will implement an in-memory key-value store using Python's built-in data structures.

The basic operations are as follows:

- **Put**: Insert or update a key-value pair.
- **Get**: Retrieve a value by its key.
- **Delete**: Remove a key-value pair.
- **Keys**: Return a list of all keys currently stored.

The step-by-step explanation is as follows:

1. **Using a dictionary for efficient storage:** Python's **dictionary** (or **dict**) data structure is perfect for implementing a key-value store because it offers:

   a. *O(1)* average time complexity for insertion, lookup, and deletion.

   b. A clean and simple API for managing key-value pairs.

2. **Defining the interface:** We will define a class **KeyValueStore** to encapsulate the key-value store functionality. The class will have methods to perform the operations (put, get, delete, and keys).

Code example: Basic key-value store:

```
class KeyValueStore:
    def __init__(self):
        # Initialize an empty dictionary to store key-value pairs
        self.store = {}

    def put(self, key, value):
        """Insert or update a key-value pair."""
        self.store[key] = value
        print(f"Key '{key}' added/updated with value: {value}")

    def get(self, key):
        """Retrieve the value associated with the key."""
        if key in self.store:
            return self.store[key]
        else:
            print(f"Key '{key}' not found.")
            return None

    def delete(self, key):
        """Remove a key-value pair."""
        if key in self.store:
            del self.store[key]
            print(f"Key '{key}' deleted.")
        else:
            print(f"Key '{key}' not found.")

    def keys(self):
        """Return all keys in the store."""
        return list(self.store.keys())

# Example usage:
kv_store = KeyValueStore()
kv_store.put("name", "Alice")
kv_store.put("age", 30)
print(kv_store.get("name"))  # Output: Alice
kv_store.delete("age")
print(kv_store.keys())  # Output: ['name']
```

The explanation is as follows:

- **Initialization**: The **KeyValueStore** class uses a dictionary (**self.store**) to store key-value pairs.

- **put() method**: Adds or updates a key with a given value. If the key already exists, its value is updated.
- **get() method**: Retrieves the value for the specified key. If the key does not exist, it returns None and prints a message.
- **delete() method**: Removes a key-value pair from the store if the key exists.
- **keys() method**: Returns a list of all keys currently in the store.

Approach 2: Adding expiration times (TTL)

A common extension to key-value stores is the addition of expiration times (**Time To Live** (**TTL**)). In this approach, keys automatically expire and are removed after a certain amount of time.

The explanation is as follows:

We can modify our **KeyValueStore** class to support TTL by storing not only the value but also the expiration time for each key. We will periodically check and remove expired keys.

Code example: Key-value store with expiration time:

```
import time

class KeyValueStoreWithTTL:
    def __init__(self):
        self.store = {}

    def put(self, key, value, ttl=None):
        """Insert a key-value pair with an optional time-to-live (TTL)."""
        expiry_time = time.time() + ttl if ttl else None
        self.store[key] = (value, expiry_time)
        print(f"Key '{key}' added/updated with value: {value}, TTL: {ttl}s")

    def get(self, key):
        """Retrieve the value associated with the key, considering TTL."""
        if key in self.store:
            value, expiry_time = self.store[key]
            if expiry_time and time.time() > expiry_time:
                print(f"Key '{key}' has expired.")
                self.delete(key)
                return None
            return value
        else:
            print(f"Key '{key}' not found.")
            return None
```

```
    def delete(self, key):
        """Remove a key-value pair."""
        if key in self.store:
            del self.store[key]
            print(f"Key '{key}' deleted.")
        else:
            print(f"Key '{key}' not found.")

    def keys(self):
        """Return all keys in the store."""
        return [key for key in self.store if not self._is_expired(key)]

    def _is_expired(self, key):
        """Helper method to check if a key has expired."""
        if key in self.store:
            _, expiry_time = self.store[key]
            return expiry_time and time.time() > expiry_time
        return False

# Example usage:
kv_store_ttl = KeyValueStoreWithTTL()
kv_store_ttl.put("session", "abc123", ttl=5)  # Expires in 5 seconds
time.sleep(6)
print(kv_store_ttl.get("session"))  # Output: Key 'session' has expired.
```

The explanation is as follows:

- **put() method**: Adds a key-value pair with an optional TTL. If no TTL is provided, the key does not expire.
- **get() method**: Retrieves the value if it has not expired. If the key has expired, it is automatically deleted, and the method returns None.
- **_is_expired() helper**: Checks whether a key has expired based on the current time.

The edge cases to consider are as follows:

- **Duplicate keys**: The `put` method handles duplicate keys by updating the existing value.
- **Expired keys**: Ensure that expired keys are removed correctly when accessed.
- **Large dataset**: For a large dataset, you could extend this implementation to handle persistent storage using a database.

The advanced features for interviews are as follows:

- **Persistence:** Discuss how to make the key-value store persistent (e.g., by writing data to disk or using a database like Redis).

- **Scaling:** Discuss how to distribute the key-value store across multiple servers to handle large-scale data (e.g., consistent hashing for distributed storage).

The key takeaways for interviews are as follows:

- **Efficiency:** The basic implementation uses a Python dictionary, which offers *O(1)* time complexity for key lookups, insertions, and deletions.
- **Edge cases:** Be ready to discuss handling duplicate keys, expired keys, and edge cases like large datasets or memory management.
- **Scalability:** In a system design interview, mention how you would scale this solution by distributing the data or adding persistence layers.

Problem 99: Design a search autocomplete system

Problem statement: Design a search autocomplete system that provides suggestions as the user types in a query. The system should return the top relevant search terms based on what the user has entered so far. Consider implementing the following features:

- **Input(query)**: Accept a string input from the user.
- **Autocomplete()**: Return the top N suggestions for the current query.
- **Update(search_term)**: Add a new search term to the database of suggestions.

Understanding the problem: Search autocomplete is a feature we use every day, whether typing in Google's search bar or looking for products on an e-commerce platform. This challenge involves designing a system that provides real-time suggestions based on partial input.

At its core, autocomplete takes in an incomplete string (or "prefix") and suggests possible completions based on past searches or a pre-defined dictionary of terms. The key challenges are efficiency and relevance; suggestions must be provided quickly as the user types, and they should be ranked by relevance or popularity.

The key components are as follows:

- **Efficient lookup**: The system needs to quickly retrieve possible completions based on the user's input.
- **Ranking by relevance**: Suggestions should be sorted by relevance or popularity.
- **Scalability**: The system must handle large datasets and many users typing simultaneously.
- **Data structures**: Trie (prefix tree), hash maps, or databases can be used to store search terms and their frequencies.

The step-by-step explanation is as follows:

1. **Using a trie (prefix tree) for efficient search:** A trie (pronounced "try") is a tree-like data structure commonly used for search autocomplete. Each node in the Trie represents a letter, and paths from the root to the leaf nodes represent complete words. This allows efficient lookups of all words that start with a given prefix.
2. **Data storage and ranking:** In addition to storing search terms, we also need to rank them based on popularity or frequency of past searches. Each node in the trie can store:
    a. **IsWord**: A Boolean indicating whether the node represents the end of a valid word.
    b. **Frequency**: The **`insert()`** method is invoked whenever a user submits a search term, so each call increments that term's frequency counter. In production, you might separate dictionary loading from user-search logging, but we merge them here to keep the example short.
3. **System design considerations:**
    a. **Input handling**: The system should update suggestions as the user types (character by character).
    b. **Update mechanism**: When new search terms are added or old ones are updated, the system must incorporate these changes in real-time.
    c. **Scalability**: As the number of search terms grows, the system must scale to handle thousands or millions of terms efficiently.

Code example

Implementing a search autocomplete system using a trie:

```
class TrieNode:
    def __init__(self):
        # Initialize child nodes as an empty dictionary and other attributes
        self.children = {}
        self.is_word = False
        self.frequency = 0

class SearchAutocompleteSystem:
    def __init__(self):
        # Root of the Trie
        self.root = TrieNode()

    def insert(self, word, frequency=1):
        """Insert a word into the Trie with an optional frequency count."""
        node = self.root
```

```
        for char in word:
            if char not in node.children:
                node.children[char] = TrieNode()
            node = node.children[char]
        node.is_word = True
        node.frequency += frequency
        print(f"Inserted word '{word}' with frequency {node.frequency}")

    def search_prefix(self, prefix):
        """Return the node where the prefix ends."""
        node = self.root
        for char in prefix:
            if char not in node.children:
                return None
            node = node.children[char]
        return node

    def autocomplete(self, prefix, top_n=5):
        """Return the top N autocomplete suggestions for the given prefix."""
        node = self.search_prefix(prefix)
        if not node:
            return []

        # Perform DFS to find all words starting with the prefix
        results = []
        self._dfs(node, prefix, results)

        # Sort the results by frequency in descending order and return the top
N
        results.sort(key=lambda x: (-x[1], x[0]))  # Sort by frequency
(highest first)
        return [word for word, freq in results[:top_n]]

    def _dfs(self, node, prefix, results):
        """Perform a depth-first search to collect all words starting with the
given prefix."""
        if node.is_word:
            results.append((prefix, node.frequency))

        for char, child_node in node.children.items():
            self._dfs(child_node, prefix + char, results)

# Example usage
autocomplete_system = SearchAutocompleteSystem()
autocomplete_system.insert("apple", 3)
```

```
autocomplete_system.insert("app", 5)
autocomplete_system.insert("apricot", 2)
autocomplete_system.insert("banana", 4)

# Autocomplete for prefix 'ap'
print(autocomplete_system.autocomplete("ap", top_n=3))  # Output: ['app',
'apple', 'apricot']
```

The explanation is as follows:

- **TrieNode class**: Each node has a dictionary of child nodes, a Boolean to indicate if it forms a complete word, and a frequency counter.
- **insert() method**: Inserts a word into the trie. If the word already exists, it increases its frequency.
- **search_prefix() method**: Finds the node corresponding to the last character of the given prefix.
- **autocomplete() method**: Collects all words starting with the given prefix and sorts them by frequency.
- **_dfs() method**: Performs a depth-first search to gather all words from a given node in the trie.

Approach: Using a hash map for simpler search

If the dataset is smaller and does not require complex prefix searching, a hash map (dictionary) can be used to store search terms and their frequencies. This approach sacrifices some efficiency but simplifies the implementation.

Code example: Autocomplete using hash map:

```
class SearchAutocompleteHashMap:
    def __init__(self):
        self.search_terms = {}

    def insert(self, term, frequency=1):
        """
        Insert a term into the Trie or increment its search-frequency.
        In this simplified demo we call insert() every time a user
        actually searches for the term, so each call bumps the term's
        frequency counter by `frequency` (default 1).
        """
        if term in self.search_terms:
            self.search_terms[term] += frequency
        else:
            self.search_terms[term] = frequency
```

```
    def autocomplete(self, prefix, top_n=5):
        """Return the top N suggestions for the given prefix."""
        # Filter search terms that start with the prefix
        results = [(term, freq) for term, freq in self.search_terms.items() if
term.startswith(prefix)]

        # Sort by frequency and return the top N
        results.sort(key=lambda x: (-x[1], x[0]))
        return [term for term, freq in results[:top_n]]

# Example usage
autocomplete_hashmap = SearchAutocompleteHashMap()
autocomplete_hashmap.insert("apple", 3)
autocomplete_hashmap.insert("app", 5)
autocomplete_hashmap.insert("apricot", 2)
autocomplete_hashmap.insert("banana", 4)

# Autocomplete for prefix 'ap'
print(autocomplete_hashmap.autocomplete("ap", top_n=3))  # Output: ['app',
'apple', 'apricot']
```

The explanation is as follows:

- **search_terms dictionary**: Stores the search terms as keys and their frequencies as values.
- **insert() method**: Inserts a search term into the dictionary or updates its frequency if it already exists.
- **autocomplete() method**: Filters the dictionary for terms starting with the prefix and returns the top N sorted by frequency.

The system design considerations are as follows:

- **Backend architecture:**
    - o **Database**: For large-scale systems, the key-value store or search index can be stored in a database like *Redis* (for in-memory caching) or *Elasticsearch* (for more advanced search capabilities).
    - o **Data updates**: Regularly update the frequency of search terms based on user input. This could be achieved via batch updates or real-time syncing.
- **Handling large-scale data:**
    - o **Sharding**: For large datasets, shard the trie or hash map across multiple servers based on the first character or a hash of the prefix.
    - o **Caching**: Use in-memory caching (e.g., Redis) to store frequently accessed queries for fast retrieval.

- **Concurrency and latency:**
  - Optimize for low-latency lookups, especially when handling many users typing simultaneously.
  - Use asynchronous processing or message queues (e.g., RabbitMQ, Kafka) to handle high volumes of incoming search terms.
- **Ranking and relevance:**
  - **Popularity-based ranking**: Prioritize suggestions based on the frequency of past searches.
  - **Contextual relevance**: For more advanced systems, consider using machine learning models to rank results based on user preferences, location, or past search behavior.

The edge cases to consider are as follows:

- **Empty query**: What happens if the user provides an empty query? Return a list of popular search terms by default.
- **Case sensitivity**: Ensure the system is case-insensitive when searching for terms.
- **Misspellings and typo handling**: Consider adding support for fuzzy matching or typo correction, especially if handling user input in real-time.

The key takeaways for interviews are as follows:

- **Efficient data structures**: Use a trie for fast lookups, or a hash map for simpler implementations.
- **Scalability**: Be prepared to discuss how the system can handle millions of search terms and thousands of concurrent users.
- **Relevance ranking**: Make sure to mention how search results are ranked by frequency or relevance.

Problem 100: Implement a disjoint set (union-find)

Problem statement: Design and implement a data structure called a **disjoint set** (also known as **union-find**) that supports two primary operations:

- **Find(x)**: Determine which set *x* belongs to. If *x* and *y* are in the same set, this function will return the same identifier for both.
- **Union(x, y)**: Merge the sets containing *x* and *y* into a single set.

The union-find data structure is commonly used to solve problems involving dynamic connectivity, such as determining whether two nodes in a graph are connected. This structure is also crucial for implementing algorithms like *Kruskal's Minimum Spanning Tree Algorithm* and for problems involving groups, connected components, and clusters.

Understanding the problem: The disjoint set or union-find is a data structure that tracks a partition of a set into disjoint subsets. The idea is that you have a collection of items, and you want to efficiently manage groups of these items, merge groups, and check if two items belong to the same group.

The key operations are as follows:

- **Find(x)**: Determines the "representative" or "parent" of the set that contains *x*. This helps to identify which set *x* belongs to.
- **Union(x, y)**: Merges the sets containing *x* and *y* into a single set. The two sets are joined under a single representative.

The step-by-step explanation is as follows:

1. **Data structure setup:** The disjoint set data structure typically uses two arrays:
   a. **Parent array**: Stores the "parent" of each element. Initially, every element is its own parent (self-loop), meaning each element is its own set.
   b. **Rank array**: Keeps track of the "rank" or "height" of each set (used to optimize the union operation). The rank helps to minimize tree height, making future operations faster.
2. **Find operation with path compression:** To make the **find** operation more efficient, we use **path compression**, which flattens the structure of the tree by making every node in the path point directly to the root. This ensures that subsequent find operations are faster.
3. **Union operation with union by rank:** The **union** operation merges two sets. To keep the tree flat, we use **union by rank**, where the tree with the smaller rank is merged under the tree with the larger rank. If both trees have the same rank, one is arbitrarily chosen, and its rank is incremented by 1.

Code example: Implementing disjoint set (union-find):

```
class DisjointSet:
    def __init__(self, n):
        # Initialize parent and rank arrays for n elements
        self.parent = [i for i in range(n)]  # Each element is its own parent
initially
        self.rank = [1] * n  # Rank is initialized to 1 for all sets

    def find(self, x):
        """Find the representative of the set that x belongs to, with path
compression."""
        if self.parent[x] != x:
```

```
            # Recursively find the parent and apply path compression
            self.parent[x] = self.find(self.parent[x])
        return self.parent[x]

    def union(self, x, y):
        """Union the sets containing x and y using union by rank."""
        root_x = self.find(x)
        root_y = self.find(y)

        if root_x != root_y:
            # Union by rank: attach smaller rank tree under the larger rank
tree
            if self.rank[root_x] > self.rank[root_y]:
                self.parent[root_y] = root_x
            elif self.rank[root_x] < self.rank[root_y]:
                self.parent[root_x] = root_y
            else:
                # If ranks are equal, arbitrarily choose one root and
increment its rank
                self.parent[root_y] = root_x
                self.rank[root_x] += 1
        else:
            print(f"{x} and {y} are already in the same set")

# Example usage
ds = DisjointSet(5)
ds.union(0, 1)
ds.union(1, 2)
ds.union(3, 4)
print(ds.find(0))  # Output: 0 (root of set {0, 1, 2})
print(ds.find(4))  # Output: 3 (root of set {3, 4})
print(ds.find(2))  # Output: 0 (root of set {0, 1, 2})
```

The explanation is as follows:

- **find() method**: This method finds the representative (or "root") of the set that contains x. It applies path compression, meaning that once the representative is found, it rewires all nodes along the path to point directly to the root.

- **union() method**: This merges two sets containing x and y. Union by rank ensures that the tree remains balanced, so subsequent operations are efficient.

- **Rank array**: The rank array tracks the depth of each tree. When merging two trees, the tree with the lower rank is merged under the tree with the higher rank to keep the tree shallow.

Approach: Without path compression or rank optimization

If you want a simpler version without path compression or union by rank, the implementation can look like this:

```
class SimpleDisjointSet:
    def __init__(self, n):
        self.parent = [i for i in range(n)]

    def find(self, x):
        """Find the root of the set containing x."""
        while self.parent[x] != x:
            x = self.parent[x]
        return x

    def union(self, x, y):
        """Union the sets containing x and y."""
        root_x = self.find(x)
        root_y = self.find(y)
        if root_x != root_y:
            self.parent[root_y] = root_x

# Example usage
ds = SimpleDisjointSet(5)
ds.union(0, 1)
ds.union(1, 2)
ds.union(3, 4)
print(ds.find(0))  # Output: 0
print(ds.find(4))  # Output: 3
print(ds.find(2))  # Output: 0
```

The explanation is as follows:

- **find() method**: This method finds the root of the set containing x by following parent pointers until it reaches the root.
- **union() method**: This simply connects two sets by making one set's root the parent of the other, without considering tree height or optimizing future operations.

This approach is simple, but it becomes inefficient for larger datasets because the tree can become skewed and tall, leading to longer paths in the `find()` operation.

The time and space complexity are explained as follows:

- **Time complexity:**
  - The find operation, with path compression, has an amortized time complexity of $O(\alpha(n))$, where α is the inverse *Ackermann* function, which grows extremely slowly. In practice, this is nearly constant time.

  - The union operation, using union by rank, also takes $O(\alpha(n))$ time.
- **Space complexity:** Both the **parent** and **rank** arrays require $O(n)$ space, where n is the number of elements.

How to think about this problem:

- **Clarify the use case**: Ask whether the union-find structure will need to handle large-scale problems, such as connected components in a graph or clusters. The size and frequency of the operations will determine whether optimizations like path compression and union by rank are necessary.
- **Discuss optimizations**: Always mention the optimizations you are using (such as path compression and union by rank). This shows that you understand how to improve both time and space complexity.
- **Handle edge cases**: Edge cases can include:
  - Repeated unions of the same sets (which should not affect the result).
  - Operations on elements not yet in any set (clarify the input constraints).
  - The use of negative or non-integer values (ensure you have clearly defined the input).

The edge cases to consider are as follows:

- **Same element union**: What happens if you try to union two elements that are already in the same set? The implementation should efficiently handle this.
  - `ds.union(1, 1)` → Should do nothing.
- **Single-element set**: What happens when an element is alone in its own set? The **`find()`** function should return the element itself as the representative.
  - `ds.find(3)` → Should return 3 if no union has been performed.

The key takeaways for interviews are as follows:

- **Optimizations matter**: Always explain how path compression and union by rank optimize the solution. These optimizations ensure that the disjoint set data structure is efficient, even for large-scale problems.
- **Scalability**: Be prepared to discuss how this data structure can handle millions of elements and operations, especially in problems related to connectivity and clustering.
- **Clarity in thought**: When explaining your approach, ensure that the interviewer understands how the union and find operations work, particularly in edge cases and large inputs.

Appendix

Congratulations on reaching the end of this book. You have embarked on an incredible journey, tackling some of the most common and advanced coding challenges asked by top companies during technical interviews. By working through this book, you have sharpened your Python programming skills, deepened your problem-solving abilities, and built the confidence needed to approach any coding interview.

What you have achieved

Throughout this book, you have learned to:

- **Master the fundamentals**: From reversing strings and manipulating data structures to optimizing algorithms, you have gained hands-on experience in solving Python coding challenges.
- **Tackle advanced problems**: You have looked into complex areas like recursion, dynamic programming, and graph algorithms, preparing you for high-level interview questions.
- **Optimize your solutions**: You have learned not just how to solve problems, but how to write efficient and scalable code, discussing time and space complexity at every step.
- **Think like a programmer**: With each challenge, you have honed your ability to break down problems, think critically, and devise solutions that can scale, all while explaining your thought process clearly and effectively.

Moving forward

Now that you have completed this book, it is time to keep up the momentum! The coding interview world is ever-changing, and the more you practice, the sharper your skills will become. Continue to explore new coding challenges on online platforms, participate in mock interviews, and challenge yourself with real-world projects.

Remember, coding interviews are as much about demonstrating your thought process and problem-solving skills as they are about finding the right answer. The techniques you have learned in this book, from clarifying problem statements to optimizing solutions and handling edge cases, will serve you well in any technical interview or coding competition.

Keep learning, keep growing

The journey does not stop here. Python is a versatile language that can take you far beyond just interviews. Whether you are interested in web development, data science, machine learning, or building large-scale systems, your foundation in Python is the stepping stone to endless possibilities.

Explore new libraries, contribute to open-source projects, and never stop learning. The skills you have acquired here are just the beginning of your growth as a software developer and problem solver.

Final tip

Stay curious, stay persistent, and most importantly, enjoy the process of learning and coding. Interviews can be challenging, but with the right preparation and mindset, you can approach any technical question with confidence. You have put in the hard work, and now it is time to show the world what you can do.

Good luck with your interviews, and remember, coding is not just about landing a job; it is about solving problems, building great things, and continuously learning along the way.

Thank you for taking this journey with *Python Interview Preparation: 100 Coding Challenges and Solutions*. Wishing you success and fulfillment in your career and beyond!

Index

B

C

D

F

N

P

Q

R

S

T

www.ingramcontent.com/pod-product-compliance
Lightning Source LLC
Chambersburg PA
CBHW061740210326
41599CB00034B/6740

* 9 7 8 9 3 6 5 8 9 7 9 3 7 *